1947

WHEN ALL HELL BROKE LOOSE

IN BASEBALL

By Red Barber

1947—WHEN ALL HELL BROKE LOOSE IN BASEBALL

THE BROADCASTERS

SHOW ME THE WAY TO GO HOME

WALK IN THE SPIRIT

RHUBARB IN THE CATBIRD SEAT—with Robert Creamer

THE RHUBARB PATCH—Pictures by Barney Stein

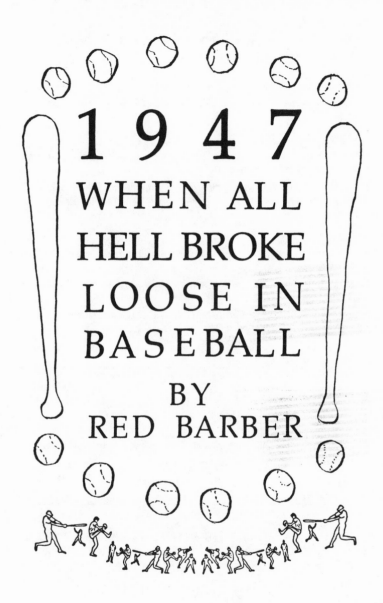

1947
WHEN ALL HELL BROKE LOOSE IN BASEBALL
BY
RED BARBER

A DA CAPO PAPERBACK

Grateful acknowledgment is made to the following for permission to reprint their copyrighted material:

Excerpts reprinted with permission from the book *Baseball Confidential* by Arthur Mann, copyright 1952. Published by David McKay Co., Inc.

Excerpts reprinted with permission of *The Sporting News*, St. Louis, Missouri.

Excerpts from the following article are reprinted courtesy of *Sports Illustrated* from the April 26, 1971 issue, copyright © 1971 by Time, Inc.: "How I Jumped from Clean Politics into Dirty Baseball" by A. B. (Happy) Chandler with John Underwood.

Excerpts from the following article are reprinted courtesy of *Sports Illustrated* from the May 3, 1971 issue, copyright © 1971 by Time, Inc.: "Gunned Down By The Heavies" by A. B. (Happy) Chandler with John Underwood.

Excerpts from *I Never Had It Made*, by Jackie Robinson with Alfred Duckett. Copyright © 1972 by Jackie Robinson and Alfred Duckett. Reprinted by permission.

Excerpts from *The Lords of Baseball*, by Harold Parrott. Copyright © 1976 by Harold Parrott. Reprinted by permission.

Excerpts from *Nice Guys Finish Last*, by Leo Durocher. Copyright © 1975 by Leo Durocher. Reprinted by permission.

DESIGN BY RAYMOND DAVIDSON

Library of Congress Cataloging in Publication Data

Barber, Red, 1908–
   1947, when all hell broke loose in baseball.

   (A Da Capo paperback)
   Reprint. Originally published: Garden City, N.Y.: Doubleday, 1982.
   Includes index.
   1. Baseball—United States—History. I. Title.
CV863.A1B37   1984   796.357'0973   83-26246
ISBN 0-306-80212-0

This Da Capo Press paperback edition of *1947, When All Hell Broke Loose in Baseball* is an unabridged republication of the first edition published in New York in 1982. It is reprinted by arrangement with Doubleday & Co., Inc.

Copyright © 1982 by Walter Red Barber

Published by Da Capo Press, Inc.
A Subsidiary of Plenum Publishing Corporation
233 Spring Street, New York, N.Y. 10013

All Rights Reserved

Manufactured in the United States of America

Dedicated
to
Baseball Wives
Who have the hardest jobs
Staying home . . . holding families together
Waiting, hoping, sometimes doubting but believing
in their husbands
No publicity . . . little appreciation
I don't know what the men in this book would have
done the trying season of 1947 without:
Jane Rickey
Rachel Robinson
Jean MacPhail
Mildred Chandler
Laraine Durocher
Elizabeth Harris
Mary Shotton
Hazel Weiss
Josephine Parrott
Dodger/Yankee wives
Lylah Barber

CONTENTS

PREFACE

This is not just a book on baseball, although there is much baseball in it. This is about Joe DiMaggio, Joe Page, Frank Shea, Bill Bevens, Phil Rizzuto, Bucky Harris and other New York Yankees. This is about Pee Wee Reese, Dixie Walker, Hugh Casey, Pete Reiser, Harry Lavagetto and Burt Shotton of the Brooklyn Dodgers. However, these colorful performers were not the only stars of the dramatic 1947 season. Not at all.

There was great excitement about the 1947 pennant races: the Dodgers often played before turn-away crowds, and even vast Yankee Stadium overflowed. When the Yankees and the Dodgers clashed in the World Series this excitement increased until twice it exploded. There has not been another season like it.

This is a book about Branch Rickey and Larry MacPhail, two of the most important and brilliant men in baseball's history, who between them brought baseball into the twentieth century. One man started working for the other, they developed a close friendship, then after seventeen years neither baseball nor New York City itself was big enough to hold them both.

This is about the second Commissioner of Baseball, Happy Chandler, and his unwitting involvement with Dodger manager Leo Durocher—which cost Durocher his job for a year, and began costing Chandler his commissionership.

This, too, is about the high-water mark of radio in sports, and the almost unnoticed beginnings of television.

Above all else, this is a book about Jackie Robinson, the first black man in the big leagues, put there by one white man,

Branch Rickey, against the strong opposition of baseball, even against the advice and wishes of his own family.

I had the microphone at Brooklyn when Robinson came. It was the hottest microphone any announcer ever had to face.

Baseball has not been the same since 1947. Baseball that year became a force, not only in sports but also in the overall history of this country.

This is not a history book. It is a book about strong, vital, and at times violent men, who used baseball as a stage. Then again, it is American history.

THE SCORE

The most important fact the sports announcer can broadcast is the score. The audience cannot understand the status of the game without knowledge of the score. All strategy is based on whether a game is even, a team is behind, or is ahead.

As for the score on this book: it was fortunate I was retired and had a full year to work on it. When I first talked to Ken McCormick at Doubleday the idea seemed not only exciting but also fairly simple. As I began the work I kept discovering I needed more and more specific data.

Here in Tallahassee I have a good friend, Harold Goldstein, who is Dean of the School of Library Science at Florida State University. He had told me the library had complete sets of the New York *Times*—and other newspapers—on microfilm. He took me to meet Joe Evans, who is in charge of micro-materials. Between them I was made welcome, shown where to find what I needed, shown how to operate the equipment, and turned loose. Turned loose, in this case, meant about three months of reading the daily stories for the season of 1947 on both the Dodgers and the Yankees. Day labor, but necessary.

There was one catch to my using the FSU library: parking. Harold got me a permit from the campus police, but I couldn't find a place open. If I couldn't park for the weeks and months I needed, I couldn't use the valuable data waiting for me. There is a Travelodge motel a short block from the library. Motels have parking space in the mornings, but this one had been having serious problems with students and professors who had no business to park there. I had no choice: I told Jim Ebeling, the owner-manager, my problem. He was interested that I was doing a baseball book. He confessed to being from Chicago and a Cub fan. I consoled him for rooting for a team that hadn't won a pennant since 1945, talked of the times I had broadcast from Wrigley Field, and so it was that a Cub fan became very pivotal in this book.

I remembered that John Underwood had done several articles on Happy Chandler for *Sports Illustrated*. That was as easy as writing a letter to Robert Creamer. Bob has been with *Sports Illustrated* since its beginning, and in 1966 he and I did *Rhubarb in the Catbird Seat* for Ken McCormick. Creamer sent photocopies.

The Sporting News, I recalled, had massive coverage of the Chandler-Durocher explosion. One letter to C. C. Johnson Spink took care of that. Johnson and I go back to when he was starting on the family paper under his dad, J. G. Taylor Spink.

I wanted to be certain of the ratio of black players to white, and Joe Reichler of Baseball, Dick Maxwell of the NFL, and Matt Winick of the NBA were promptly helpful.

When I succeeded Ted Husing as Director of Sports at the Columbia Broadcasting System in 1946 I began a friendship with Harry Feeney, who as Director, Press Information, is still at CBS-TV. Harry supplied various New York broadcast pieces of information—this was a great help for me operating in Tallahassee.

Finally, Ken McCormick decided he himself would edit the book and contribute his more than forty years of Doubleday experience.

All of which proves what my dad used to tell me. "Son," he would say, "the best thing a man can have is a good friend." Plus a good wife. It goes without saying: without an understanding wife, who is also a crack editor, a man isn't going to spend a year, working largely at home, writing a book.

1947

WHEN ALL HELL BROKE LOOSE

IN BASEBALL

BOOK ONE

BRANCH RICKEY, LARRY MACPHAIL
AND LEO DUROCHER

Larry MacPhail walked into Branch Rickey's office in St. Louis late in 1930. He came by appointment. From the first meeting their conflict was inevitable. Of course it could not be seen that day in St. Louis—it wasn't visible for years—but it was a gathering storm that would shake baseball to its foundations in 1947.

This is a good time to write this book. Many of the principals involved can't write it. They are dead. I have passed the estate the psalmist described as "three score and ten." Not that I now feel a hastening of time so much as that the view is clearer looking back some fifty years. The past is an open book if one will but read it. Baseball has a bitter saying, "The second guess is never wrong." The Monday morning quarterback never calls a bad football game. Hindsight has 20-20 vision.

Branch Rickey devoted most of his eighty-four years to baseball: at Ohio Wesleyan . . . professional player . . . college coach . . . manager of two big-league teams . . . front office boss at St. Louis, Brooklyn, Pittsburgh . . . builder of championship teams . . . acknowledged as baseball's shrewdest judge of players . . . astute trader . . . creator of the farm system . . . the man who broke the color line with Jackie Robinson . . . at his death adviser to August Busch, president of the St. Louis Cardinals . . . and, the man who brought Larry MacPhail into baseball.

MacPhail was in organized baseball a span of only seventeen years, and was actively in the game only thirteen of those years —two seasons at Columbus, Ohio, three at Cincinnati, five at

Brooklyn and three with the Yankees. It is remarkable what he achieved in his brief career as a baseball executive.

Both men are in the Hall of Fame. Otherwise the Hall would be a mockery.

I have no idea what my life would have been without these two men. When MacPhail walked into Rickey's office in 1930 my fate was being formed without their—or my—knowledge. About the time MacPhail made Rickey a proposition in St. Louis, I was being offered a part-time student announcer's job on the University of Florida's radio station, WRUF in Gainesville.

Inasmuch as Rickey had been in professional baseball since 1903 when he caught 41 games for LeMars, in the old Iowa-South Dakota League, let me start with a sketch of him. He spent two years catching at Dallas. In 1906 he was in the American League with the St. Louis Browns. He was traded to the New York Yankees and was with them the season of 1907. He made it to the big leagues the hard way—he refused to be in the ball park on Sunday, baseball's biggest day.

After the year with the Browns, and on the strength of going to New York, he and his hometown sweetheart, Jane Moulton, were married. The big leagues, the Big Town, and newly married—the future seemed rosy.

Rickey looked exactly as you'd expect a catcher to look. He was stocky, thick-chested, heavy hands, and his legs were slightly bent. I knew he spent money on his clothes, but he always looked as if he had slept in them. MacPhail paid money for his clothes and looked it, as if he'd just stepped out of the store. Rickey would be at the office, get a call from a farm club, go straight to the airport and keep on going—he'd phone the bellman in his hotel to buy him a new shirt and discard the shirt he had on, repeating this as many days as the trip demanded. MacPhail, like Durocher, always traveled with many changes of apparel, with after-shave and cologne.

After the 1907 season Rickey faced a crisis. As the season went on he knew something was wrong. His batting fell off drastically. He didn't have his usual strength and spark . . . tuberculosis. He was sentenced to Saranac Lake, New York. The treatment then was complete rest. He was there a year. One year married, his playing career ended, and months and months flat on his back to think about it.

He made the decision to study law. He went to Michigan and while getting his law degree coached the baseball team. One of the players he had was George Sisler. Another was Charley Thomas.

He hung out his shingle somewhere in Montana. There weren't many people or clients and after sitting in an empty law office he went back to baseball. He became manager of the St. Louis Browns in 1913, then became also general manager. He moved to the Cardinals in 1917 in charge of the front office. He also began managing the Redbirds in 1919 and continued both responsibilities until June 1, 1925, when Sam Breadon fired him as manager in favor of Rogers Hornsby.

Breadon was a hard-nosed businessman with a cold eye on the cash register. He was in the automobile business in St. Louis, had the Pierce-Arrow Agency and joined a group who took over the down-and-out Cardinals. Breadon put up $2,000. Dividends didn't start coming in and members of the syndicate started dropping out. Breadon bought their stock, and by 1922 had 67 percent and was in control. He later owned more than 80 percent. He became Rickey's boss.

Breadon decided Rickey couldn't ride two horses at the same time. He didn't think Rickey could run the office and supervise the extensive farm system that he had created, and also be the field manager of the ball club. Further, Breadon wasn't too pleased with Rickey's way of running the team. He thought Rogers Hornsby would be a better man for the job.

Hornsby and Rickey were not buddy-buddy. Breadon didn't talk the matter over with Rickey. He told Rickey he was to be executive vice-president and general manager of the Cardinals, and that as of now, June 1, 1925, Hornsby would be the field manager. Period.

Tuberculosis. Saranac Lake. Montana. St. Louis. Sam Breadon. Branch Wesley Rickey, full-time executive. One of the very best in all of baseball.

The next year Rogers Hornsby led the players Rickey had assembled to a smashing triumph over the New York Yankees in the World Series of 1926. The highlight came in the seventh game when in the seventh inning, with two men out, the Yankees got the bases loaded. The Cardinals were leading 3–2. Tony Lazzeri was the next Yankee batter. Hornsby summoned veteran Grover Cleveland Alexander from the bullpen. Old Alex had pitched the day before and had won. It was his second Series victory, and as was his custom, he celebrated. He thought his pitching was done. He had had a considerable night. He had earned it.

But here it was: the entire year's work hanging on a dynamite-packed situation at Yankee Stadium. The Cardinals had never been in a World Series before. It was old stuff for the mighty Yankees of Miller Huggins, Babe Ruth and company.

Alexander was thirty-nine, had always been a superb pitcher under pressure, and had tremendous control. A base on balls now would tie the game and probably start a rout.

So, Hornsby waved for Alexander, and met the pitcher briefly. Hornsby looked at Alex's eyes. Then he handed him the ball.

Alex threw a called strike. Lazzeri hit the next pitch into the left-field stands, but foul by a few feet. Almost a grand slam home run. I have heard it was foul by about a yard. Alexander threw ball one. Then the old man with the effortless motion unleashed a curve. Lazzeri swung and struck out, one of the most famous strikeouts in history.

A lot of people think that was all Alexander did that day. He stayed in and pitched the last two innings. The only man to get on against him was Babe Ruth, with two out in the last of the ninth. Alex walked The Babe and thus put him on ice at first base, which was the smart way to handle Ruth, who could have tied the game with one swing. Ruth then surprised everyone. He ended it by trying to steal second base. The Cardinals were world champions for the first time.

That World Series triumph by the Cardinals was also the climax of a revolution Rickey had set in motion. Baseball was never going to be the same thereafter. Rickey had won a World Series with his brains and not with money.

When Rickey took over the Cardinals they didn't even have the money to go to a training camp in Florida. They stayed home. John McGraw, the legendary manager of the New York Giants, had money. When McGraw needed a player he bought him. Rickey couldn't compete with McGraw's money or with the money other established National League teams could command.

The New York Yankees came to greatness because Col. Jake Ruppert, guided by the astute Ed Barrow, bought great players, such as Babe Ruth, Waite Hoyt, Herb Pennock and Red Ruffing. Rickey had neither money nor established players with whom to trade.

But Rickey could think. He never got in a situation he didn't think his way out of. He also had the courage and the patience to execute his thinking.

So, here he was at St. Louis, the doormat of the National League. Other teams with money had splendid players. McGraw always bought the finished product; he wouldn't wait for a player to develop.

Rickey thought, "This country must be full of fine young ballplayers who would love a chance to play professional baseball. . . . I'll hire scouts and have them search for young, raw, talented players who need to be trained and taught and polished. . . . I'll have some tryout camps around the country and have these young men come to them to see how good they are. . . . I'll make arrangements with various minor-league teams to play these boys. . . . My managers will be first of all teachers. . . . It will take years for these boys to develop, to work their way up through the minor leagues—but when they do, as long as it takes, I'll have them. I'll keep the best ones and I'll trade or sell the surplus. . . . I'll have in effect a farm system."

It was Rickey's farm system that won the 1926 World Series. From then on the St. Louis Cardinals were one of the dominant teams in both big leagues. Rickey made baseball change. The Yankees under Ed Barrow and George Weiss soon created a farm system that produced stars as efficiently as did Rickey's. When MacPhail took over at Cincinnati in 1934, one of his first efforts to revive a moribund ball club was to found a farm system. MacPhail's farm system was the foundation for the Cincinnati pennants of 1939 and 1940, and the 1940 Reds won the World Series. MacPhail created a sound farm system at Brooklyn, which Rickey built upon when he came to Ebbets Field.

I don't think MacPhail and Rickey had met before their appointment in late 1930. Both at different times had attended the University of Michigan, both had gotten degrees in law. Rickey was nine years older. Neither followed law as a profession.

Leland Stanford MacPhail in World War I served in the field artillery with distinction. He became a captain. He and six other officers tried to kidnap Kaiser Wilhelm II. They came close to succeeding but had to settle for an ashtray on the kaiser's desk, which MacPhail grabbed and kept on his desk the rest of his life. Every time I was in his office I saw it.

After the war MacPhail got the job of restoring health to a sick department store in Nashville, Tennessee. He was a genius in troubled situations. From Nashville he went to Columbus, Ohio. He did some law work, took over an ailing automobile agency, got into real estate, and into the promotion, financing and construction of the local Medical Science Building. The new building didn't go well, so he needed something else.

The Depression was in full blast. Sidney Weil, an automobile dealer in Cincinnati who owned the Reds, also owned the baseball team in Columbus. Weil needed money and had to sell the Columbus franchise. When MacPhail heard about this, he telephoned Rickey in St. Louis and set up a meeting.

It didn't take long. MacPhail said he could buy the Columbus team for $100,000—franchise, players and ball park—lock, stock, and barrel. He would front for the Cardinals, and it would be their ball club outright. In return he wanted $10,000 or a contract to operate the team. Rickey signed him as president of the Columbus team, starting with the coming 1931 season.

There is a folk saying in the Talmud that goes this way: "from the forest itself came the handle of the ax that laid it low." Or, as my dad used to tell me, "Son, be careful who you do a favor for." Or, as William Saroyan told my wife Lylah at dinner one night, describing Armenian humor, "A priest was being beaten to death by a robber . . . just before the priest died he said, 'My son, why are you killing me? I never did you a favor.'"

MacPhail got Rickey to buy the Columbus ball club, and then began working for him. The ball park was painted, new life was breathed into the franchise, Rickey fed MacPhail fine young players, the radio reports sold the team, and MacPhail's promotions were vibrant. I don't know exactly what went wrong. MacPhail was explosive, especially when he was drinking. He was impulsive and he was a free spender. Anyhow, Rickey suddenly fired him in 1933, and replaced him with George Trautman. Rickey wrote down four reasons for the firing, and they were put into the records of the ball club. I guess they're still there.

This was a bitter parting for both men. Rickey had grown very fond of the flaming redhead who had so many ideas and so much energy and wasn't afraid of anything. MacPhail had worshiped at the feet of the master, the great man of baseball. MacPhail drank. Rickey never took a drop in his life. MacPhail was often profane. Rickey's strongest expletive was "Judas Priest." Sunday was just another day for MacPhail. Rickey promised his mother when he went into professional baseball that he'd never go in a ball park on Sunday—and he didn't, except for one Sunday at Ebbets Field for a War Bond sale during World War II, and he left before the game began. MacPhail got into fights; Rickey didn't, although one afternoon he started for Rogers Hornsby and had to be restrained in the dugout. MacPhail was abrupt in his speech. Rickey was a master of the language and a nationally known speaker. He was a spellbinder.

Both, as I have reason to know, were men of great charm. I found both of them men of their word. They were strong, creative, determined, courageous, dramatic and finally, when the crunch came in 1947, absolutely unforgiving.

MacPhail was out of baseball before the 1933 season ended. He soon petitioned Rickey for another chance. His brother Herman asked Rickey to give him another chance. L. W. St. John, the athletic director at powerful Ohio State, put in a good word for MacPhail. So did many others.

Sidney Weil's financial troubles had made the purchase of the Columbus ball club possible by Rickey. After the 1933 season ended, Weil was forced to give up the Cincinnati Reds. He had to turn the Reds over to the Central Trust Company. The bank wanted to get out from under as fast as possible and offered Rickey the job of bailing out the Reds, on his own terms. Rickey said no—he had the Cardinals as the new dominant team in the National League . . . he'd had the Cardinals in the World Series in 1926, 1928, 1930, 1931, and he could see that his Gas House Gang of 1934 would be a formidable force. Also he had established a most comfortable home in St. Louis for Mrs. Rickey, their five daughters and one son. Rickey was a wonderful family man. Wonderful.

"But," said Rickey to the bank, "I've got just the fellow for you. Larry MacPhail. He's available. He'll turn the ball club around for you. He had some trouble at Columbus but that's over with. He's your man."

The first major achievement of MacPhail at Cincinnati was to sell Powel Crosley, Jr., majority stock in the Reds. This bailed the bank out, and made Crosley the new president of the ball club. Crosley owned radio stations WLW and WSAI, plus his manufacturing company for radio sets and refrigerators. WLW was then the most powerful radio station in the world—500,000 watts, experimental license—and was making money faster than the U.S. Treasury could print it.

MacPhail couldn't know it, or care if he did, but when he got Crosley to buy control of the Reds, he changed my life. I started announcing on WRUF, the University of Florida radio station at Gainesville, in 1930. It was a daylight station, educational (which meant no commercials), with all salaries frozen by the state legislature. I began at WRUF as a part-time student announcer at 35 cents an hour. I finally got to $135 a month and that was as far as I was going to go. The Depression was on.

For the three summers of '31, '32, and '33, I rode buses at night to save hotel bills, went into barbershops for a bath, shave and fresh linen, and auditioned for the announcing staffs of WBT in Charlotte, WSB in Atlanta, WHAS in Louisville, all the stations and networks at Chicago, and always, always WLW in Cincinnati. WLW was the big station, the one we heard in Florida. WLW in those days had a talent staff as large as a network, and often fed programs to NBC. I auditioned three times at WLW. Everywhere the same, sad story. "Sorry, but we are laying off people."

The chief announcer at WLW was Chet Thomas. Crosley said that as long as he now had a ball club and two radio stations, he might just as well broadcast some games on his smaller station, WSAI. Then he asked if anybody on the announcing staff did baseball. Nobody did. So Thomas said, "Remember that boy from Florida—the one in the white linen suit—who did so well on the last audition? He says he does baseball." Crosley said to send for him.

The morning of March 4, 1934, I got a wire from Thomas asking, "WILL YOU COME CINCINNATI . . . DO REDS GAMES . . . $25 A WEEK . . . ANSWER SOONEST."

Soonest for me was right now. Just like that, out of the blue, I was on my way—the big leagues, Cincinnati Reds, WLW-WSAI . . . get my foot in the door. My dad was furious. He said, "Have I raised a dumb son? You're going North where it's more expensive to live, you're going for less money than you're getting in Gainesville, you are having to leave your wife behind. Why?"

"Dad," I said, "it's my chance." He said no more.

Thomas wired back for me to go to Tampa where the Reds were in spring training, look up Scotty Rustum, stay one week, then report to the Crosley studios in Cincinnati for routine announcing assignments until the team got home.

I'd never seen a big-league player, much less a big-league team. I'd never even broadcast a professional minor-league game. Anyhow, I was on the bus for Tampa the next day. When I got to the fairgrounds where the Reds were working out I kept asking for Mr. Scotty Rustum, just the way the telegram spelled the name. Finally a neatly dressed young man looked at the wire, and said, "I'm Scotty Reston . . . you must be looking for me."

That was the fellow who became James B. Reston of the New York *Times*. MacPhail had seen him play golf for the University of Illinois and hired him to do publicity for the Reds. Scotty soon joined the Associated Press in New York, was sent to London, and there switched to the *Times*. We've had a long friendship.

The first time I saw MacPhail was later, in March, when he called a press conference in Cincinnati to announce his season ticket plan—first in the majors—and I sat in the back of the room. He didn't know me from Adam's off ox.

MacPhail was warmly appreciative of Rickey for the job at Cincinnati. They kept in close touch. For example, one afternoon the second-string catcher broke his hand, and after the game I came by the offices just as MacPhail said to the telephone operator, "Get me Rickey . . . I need a catcher."

MacPhail was at Cincinnati three years. He turned the ball club around, and he began turning the rest of baseball around. His relationship with Rickey at St. Louis was smooth and fruitful.

MacPhail took charge of a drab, last-place ball club. His Reds lost Opening Day 1934, his first year and also my first, at Cincinnati, and never came out of the cellar all that long season. That summer—and summers in Cincinnati are always hot and humid —a record was set that still stands: for ten days and nights the temperature stayed above 100 degrees. What with the weather and the makeup of the team, you couldn't give away a pass to the ball park.

MacPhail, however, never let up. He flew the team in 1934 for a series in Chicago, the first time a major-league club had flown during the season. He began seeking permission from the National League to install lights, and with the help of Commissioner Landis he got the go-ahead and began making plans for the installation. The first night game was Friday evening May 24, 1935. President Franklin D. Roosevelt, in the White House, pressed a button and Crosley Field was flooded with the first lights in the big leagues.

MacPhail laid the foundations for a Cincinnati farm system. He had radio going full time. He painted the ball park and put new uniforms on the ushers. He hired Charlie Dressen in August 1934 to manage the Reds, and Dressen livened things up. Then on the night of September 24, 1935, there were two notable fights.

MacPhail threw a lavish dinner that evening in Cincinnati for the writers, club officials, radio people and their wives. It was at the Netherlands Plaza Hotel. Beautifully catered and served. Lylah and I had never been to such a dinner. Cocktails and wine and cordials. MacPhail arranged for a radio set to be installed in order that we might hear the Max Baer-Joe Louis fight from Yankee Stadium. Louis finished Baer in the fourth round.

After the dinner, according to police testimony, MacPhail got into an argument with a strange man in the hotel. Detectives John Oman and William Sweeney separated the two. Later the detectives discovered MacPhail on the eleventh floor with an empty ginger ale bottle in his hand. He said, "I'm waiting for that son of a bitch to come out." The detectives took MacPhail to an elevator in an effort to get him out of the hotel. Inside the elevator MacPhail struck Oman in the mouth, cutting it. Oman hit MacPhail several times and knocked him down.

At 3 A.M. MacPhail called the police department and said that two detectives had "just beaten the life out of me" at the Netherlands Plaza Hotel. The next day MacPhail, with a cut lip, black eye and cut face, denied to the Cincinnati *Post* that he had been in a fight with anybody, claiming that he had just been injured.

The two fights made the front page of both Cincinnati's afternoon papers the next day. I heard that Mr. Crosley was deeply upset, as was his lawyer, Charles Sawyer. Cincinnati then was a small, very conservative town. Rickey pleaded for MacPhail. Crosley relented.

I don't know what happened between MacPhail and Crosley after the season of 1937, MacPhail's third and last year at Cincinnati. There was little written or said when MacPhail left. I certainly never asked either of them why. It was abrupt. Painful. Suddenly MacPhail was back in Michigan working in his father's banking business.

Crosley turned to Rickey, and Rickey nominated Warren Giles to run the Reds. Rickey said later he felt an obligation to Crosley about MacPhail, and in Giles he gave Crosley the best baseball man he had in the St. Louis organization. Giles had been running the Rochester, New York, team. He was a superb general manager at Cincinnati. His teams won the pennants in 1939 and 1940, and in '40 defeated Detroit in a 7-game World Series. When Ford Frick became Commissioner of Baseball, Giles became president of the National League.

It was inevitable that Giles would hate MacPhail and vice versa. Every time Giles looked up in Cincinnati somebody said,

"MacPhail started that." Giles traded for Bucky Walters, brought in Ival Goodman, quietly and skillfully built the Reds into contention. One of Giles's first moves was to fire Charlie Dressen and bring in Bill McKechnie from Boston. Under McKechnie the Reds matured and, led by pitchers Paul Derringer and Bucky Walters, the Reds won the pennants in '39 and '40. Walters and Derringer each won 2 games against Detroit in the World Series of 1940. But Giles was never completely free of the MacPhail shadow.

MacPhail got back into the National League in 1938 after being out of baseball one year. He took over the Brooklyn Dodgers. He and Giles were now head-to-head competitors. The more Cincinnati improved, the more MacPhail resented it. Giles had replaced him and now was reaping the harvest that he, MacPhail, felt should have been his. Giles, however, had the final word—as a member of the Veteran's Committee he kept MacPhail out of the Hall of Fame for many years.

About Brooklyn: Charley Ebbets started to build Ebbets Field for his Dodgers in 1912 and ran out of money. The McKeever brothers, Steve and Ed, lent Ebbets the money in return for exactly half interest in the ball club. The 50-50 ownership wasn't too serious a problem as long as Ebbets lived. Ebbets ran the team with Wilbert "Uncle Robbie" Robinson as his manager. Ebbets died in 1926, and this house divided against itself became increasingly a problem to everyone concerned.

One set of heirs would order, the other set would cancel. The even division of the Ebbets-McKeever heirs meant that the ball club suffered under divided authority. Casey Stengel, for example, was hired as a manager by one faction and then paid for a year by the other not to manage. The Brooklyn Trust Company, headed by George V. McLaughlin, had lent considerable money to the ball club and wanted to get the money back. The situation was acute. The franchise itself was endangered.

Dearie Mulvey was the daughter of Steve McKeever, and she owned 25 percent, which was unencumbered. Her husband Jim was a motion-picture executive with a hard business head. Jim talked to Ford Frick, president of the National League. Both agreed that something decisive had to be done. So did McLaughlin at the bank. Mulvey approached Branch Rickey at St. Louis.

Mulvey offered Rickey the job of running the Dodgers, on his own terms, with the possibility of buying into the club. This was in December 1937, during the winter baseball meetings held that year at Chicago. Rickey was staying at the Stevens Hotel, Mulvey at the Blackstone. The meeting took place in Mulvey's hotel. Rickey thought about it, realized he didn't wish to leave St. Louis, and thanked Mulvey. Then he said:

"Jim, I think I have the man for you. He's available . . . he hasn't had a drink for a year, just as he promised me . . . he's Larry MacPhail. Let me call him in Michigan and get back to you."

Rickey telephoned MacPhail and advised him to be in Chicago that night for an important meeting the next morning. At that meeting with Mulvey, Rickey, and MacPhail was Ford Frick. Rickey strongly recommended MacPhail. However, MacPhail first demanded that he have full authority—no more 50-50 stalemates—so that he, MacPhail, would run the Dodgers. The deal was struck. MacPhail came to Brooklyn for the season of 1938. Things were never the same again.

The MacPhail formula was put into swift execution: Ebbets Field was painted and repaired, new rest rooms were installed, especially for women, ushers were put into fresh, colorful uniforms and instructed to be courteous, especially to women, and George V. McLaughlin, president of the Brooklyn Trust Company, found out firsthand with whom he was now dealing. Before the 1938 season even began, MacPhail knew that the Dodgers needed a first baseman who could hit. Also, he knew that Dolph Camilli at Philadelphia could be purchased for $50,000—Gerry Nugent, who owned the Phillies, always needed money. MacPhail walked into McLaughlin's office and said, "George, I need $50,000 to buy Camilli . . . put it on the tab."

The word was action. MacPhail went back to McLaughlin for still more money for park improvements, and then for a lighting system. MacPhail was lucky—when the lights went on at Brooklyn, with the old park jammed to the rafters, Vander Meer pitched his record-breaking second straight no-hitter. MacPhail had three teams: one coming, one playing, and one leaving. With one hand he started a farm system and with the other he picked over the boneyards of the other teams. Two of the players he got for almost nothing in 1939 were Dixie Walker and Whitlow Wyatt—MacPhail had become almost as shrewd a judge of players as his tutor, Branch Rickey. Almost.

MacPhail was a master of showmanship. In his first year at Brooklyn he badly needed a promotional explosion. Babe Ruth was out of baseball. Nobody wanted him. MacPhail hired him to be a coach. The ball park was filled to see The Babe wearing a Dodger uniform for the first time, and it roared at his every swing when he took batting practice. MacPhail kept things at Ebbets Field popping like a string of Chinese firecrackers. Action.

The first radio station to begin a regular schedule of broadcasts was KDKA in Pittsburgh, in 1920. It was owned by Westinghouse. It became instantly famous for its reports of the Harding–Cox presidential election. On the afternoon of August 5, 1921, something else happened at KDKA that began changing my life in a mighty but then unknown fashion. One of the Westinghouse plant foremen, Harold Arlen, set up crude broadcasting equipment inside the foul screen, behind home plate, at Forbes Field. The Phillies were playing the Pirates. Arlen announced the first ball game on radio. The real dramatic impact of radio on baseball and on the public was when Graham McNamee broadcast the World Series of 1923. The first full season of regular play-by-play coverage was done by Hal Totten in Chicago in 1924. Other Chicago stations began doing baseball largely because William Wrigley, Sr., from the start believed in the positive values of radio coverage, and he welcomed all the local stations to Wrigley Field.

Most of the other baseball owners and executives were deathly afraid of radio. They cried, "Why give people something for nothing? They'll stop coming to the ball parks and paying admission—especially on cloudy, threatening days."

At the winter meetings following the 1933 season, the owners voted whether or not to ban all broadcasts from all parks. Wrigley led the forces for radio. The vote was close. But for Wrigley, radio would then have been banned by baseball. The final decision was to leave it to each club to do as it wished. The three New York teams—Giants, Yankees and Dodgers—immediately entered into an agreement that prohibited any and all radio reports of any of their home games for five years. The three New York teams would not allow a station anywhere in the country even to re-create a game from Western Union reports. It was an absolute ban in New York. Five years—1934 through 1938.

So it was that Vander Meer's second straight no-hitter in 1938 was not broadcast. The first news of his achievement came to the radio stations on a bulletin from the Associated Press. That bulletin, when it was put on the air, was like a bomb exploding in Cincinnati. The beer gardens stayed open the rest of the night. My phone never stopped ringing. The things people celebrate!

MacPhail had the press keeping a twenty-four-hour watch on him and on the Dodgers. He had the fans pouring into the park. He decided early in 1938 that Burleigh Grimes, a holdover manager, was not the manager he wanted in 1939. He decided something else: he decided that he would not renew the radio-ban agreement with the two New York clubs. He was going to broadcast all his games starting in 1939.

The main sponsor of baseball then was General Mills, makers of Wheaties. Cliff Samuelson was the principal executive of General Mills who arranged the radio rights with the various teams, and then made the deals with various radio stations. Wheaties had just about everything in baseball but New York. Samuelson wanted this market of some sixteen million people in the metropolitan area the way he wanted his next breath. He knew he had no hope with either the Yankees or the Giants. But he knew he had a chance with MacPhail. As the orator said at Montgomery, Alabama, when Jefferson Davis was introduced as the first president of the Confederacy, "The man and the hour are met."

MacPhail said, "I want three things: $70,000 for the rights for one year, any 50,000-watt radio station in New York City, and Barber from Cincinnati." Wouldn't I have loved to have known that! But Samuelson was no virgin in negotiations. He told MacPhail it was a deal, but it must be kept secret that I was part of the package—that if I knew about my inclusion, I would hold up poor old General Mills for all the Wheaties in Minnesota. MacPhail agreed. I was led a merry corporate chase. I was told that maybe there would be broadcasts in New York City next year . . . that maybe I could get one of the jobs but dozens of fellows wanted them . . . that I was under consideration because they liked me very much . . . and that money was tight. The New York assignment was talked about almost to the exclusion of the Brooklyn one, which was all right with me. The Giants and the Yankees then were the big teams in New York. I just wanted to catch on in New York. Anywhere. Let me in.

In December I was brought to New York and signed a contract with General Mills to broadcast baseball in New York City wherever General Mills assigned me in 1939. I went to New York on the train and Bill Terry was also riding it. He then was manager, and general manager, for the Giants. He said he wanted me to broadcast at the Polo Grounds, and was going to take it up the next day with Horace Stoneham, the owner. That's how tightly kept was MacPhail's third stipulation . . . when my assignment came, it was for Brooklyn.

Bill Corum wrote in his column in the New York *Journal-American,* which went to all the Hearst newspapers, that I got $25,000 my first year at Brooklyn. Other papers used that figure. Corum even wrote I had told him so. I never told anybody what I came for, except my wife. It was $8,000. Samuelson and MacPhail had a falling-out after 1940, the second year of the broadcasts. Only then did MacPhail tell me what he had been forced to do. He did say then that he was very sorry.

The Brooklyn pot began boiling more furiously in 1939. Leo Durocher, the veteran shortstop (traded to Brooklyn by Rickey at St. Louis after the 1937 season) was selected by MacPhail to manage the Dodgers. Leo and Larry at Ebbets Field. Sound and fury. The fans and the press ate it up. The players came alive.

The impact of the radio broadcasts in 1939, so they told me, was tremendous. Out of the five-year silence of no ball games on radio, suddenly here it was—turn the switch and live excitement came pouring from the loudspeaker. The ball games buried the afternoon soap operas.

MacPhail was smart—brilliant is a better word. In 1939 he had his spring exhibition games in Florida broadcast. He had continuity—the Dodgers on the air every day, home or away—and he had a 50,000-watt station, WOR, that covered the area. The

Giants and Yankees were half and half—whichever team was at home would be on the air. No continuity. Both New York teams felt it was below their proud status to have exhibition games on the air in New York. They waited for the 1939 regular season. The Dodgers thus got a five-week jump on the huge audience that was hungry and thirsty to hear baseball. The New York broadcasts didn't catch up with the one at Brooklyn until MacPhail broke away from the Giants and put Mel Allen on the road with the Yankees in 1946. Then it became a question of which broadcast—the Dodgers or the Yankees. The Giants fell out of it.

Keep Durocher in mind. Rickey traded for Leo—got him from Sidney Weil in Cincinnati, May 7, 1933—and Leo cemented the Gas House Gang together with his brilliant play at shortstop. When MacPhail came to Brooklyn in 1938 Leo was there, sent by Rickey from St. Louis after the 1937 season. MacPhail gave Durocher his first job as manager in 1939. When Rickey came to Brooklyn in 1943, there was Durocher as the holdover manager. Try to untangle Durocher from either Rickey or MacPhail and it's no story.

MacPhail was at Brooklyn only five years. His short time there was marked by almost unbelievable accomplishments: cleaned-up park, lights for night games, exciting players, radio, first tele-vision (in 1939) of a big-league game, Durocher as manager, a pennant in 1941 which took the entire country by storm, and a bitter defeat to Rickey's Cardinals in 1942. Then MacPhail went into the Army. Some accounts say the directors of the Dodgers and the bank had cooled on his expensive operation. But there was no question of his deep patriotism and his eagerness to ac-cept an Army commission as lieutenant colonel. As I look back, I don't think MacPhail was capable of sustaining his interest with any one ball club too long. His forte was taking a broken ma-chine and getting it running again; once it was smooth and purr-ing, he turned to something else. MacPhail sought the quiet in the center of the hurricane.

So . . . Rickey hired and then fired MacPhail at Columbus. Then a year later Rickey got MacPhail the job at Cincinnati. I was broadcasting the Reds the three years MacPhail was there, and I know his relationship then with Rickey was on the constructive side. MacPhail often turned to Rickey for players, and for advice. Next, a year after being out at Cincinnati, MacPhail was recommended by Rickey for the Brooklyn job. All still remained well between the two men. In fact, on the night of the afternoon the Dodgers clinched the 1941 pennant in Boston, Rickey and MacPhail were standing together on the platform at the 125th Street station in New York.

The Dodgers won at Boston and eliminated the Cardinals for the 1941 pennant. The ball club got aboard their special train for New York. There was champagne everywhere. All the free iced champagne the winners could drink, shower each other with, and in general celebrate the first Brooklyn pennant in twenty-one long, dry years. Only the team had the train. Manager Leo Durocher knew there'd be a big welcome at Grand Central. Leo also began to hear reports that most of his players were planning to get off the train when it made its regular stop at 125th Street, and thus avoid the waiting crowd. Durocher ordered the conductor not to stop at 125th Street. He wanted the fans to have their turn at bat.

Leo couldn't know it. Nobody could have forecast it, but the fans in Brooklyn had swarmed into Manhattan. It became the largest welcome in the history of Grand Central. The main floor was packed solid with wild-eyed Dodger fans. When I signed off the game that afternoon I had broadcast the arrival time of the train.

MacPhail had built well at Columbus and was dismissed a few months before that team won the pennant. He had built again at Cincinnati but wasn't around when the Reds began winning. He had put in four years building at Brooklyn, and he wasn't going to miss any of this triumph. Eleven years, counting the two in exile, MacPhail had waited for a winner. He took a taxi for 125th Street in order to come into Grand Central with Durocher, Whitlow Wyatt, Dixie Walker, Joe Medwick, Dolph Camilli, Pee Wee Reese, Billy Herman, Pete Reiser, Freddie Fitzsimmons, Kirby Higbe, Mickey Owen, Hugh Casey, Curt Davis, Harry Lavagetto and the rest of the triumphant Dodgers. The borough had waited and suffered and hungered for twenty-one years. MacPhail had produced. He wanted to be there when the band struck up.

The conductor remonstrated with Durocher. Trains into Grand Central always stopped at 125th Street. But as many an umpire could have told the conductor, Leo was not called The Lip for nothing. Then, too, this was a special train for the Dodgers. Durocher won, hands down. What chance would a poor hard-working train conductor have with Durocher?

Branch Rickey had been in New York on business and was catching a train to St. Louis. The two men met on the platform. A photographer who happened to be there snapped a picture of them embracing as Rickey congratulated MacPhail although Rickey's team had been edged out of the chance to play the Yankees in the World Series.

Here came the Dodgers Special. MacPhail prepared to board the train and be a part of the roaring welcome ten minutes later in Grand Central. The only roar MacPhail heard that night was that of the train as it swept by without even slowing down. There in Rickey's presence MacPhail got his humiliation.

MacPhail took a taxi to the New Yorker Hotel where he was living, as was Durocher. When Durocher walked into his room the phone was ringing. It was MacPhail. Leo expected to receive congratulations. Instead MacPhail fired him. Win the pennant in the afternoon at Boston and as soon as you reach New York you get fired. They say the path of true love never runs smooth. Certainly the relationship between Larry MacPhail and Leo Durocher never stayed on an even plane. Nor did that between Rickey and Durocher either.

Durocher stayed fired all night. The next morning Leo went to MacPhail's office and was rehired. Leo will tell you MacPhail fired him a hundred times. But when Rickey took over late in 1942 after MacPhail had gone into the Army, Durocher was still the Brooklyn manager.

As I look back, the cooling of MacPhail toward Rickey began in the early afternoon of June 18, 1940, when Joe Medwick lay in the dirt at home plate in Ebbets Field, felled by a pitch from Bob Bowman, of Rickey's St. Louis Cardinals.

When Durocher played shortstop for the Cardinals, Medwick was the left fielder. Medwick was a holy terror at bat. Medwick simply hit any pitch he swung at. Yogi Berra, a boy then in St. Louis, was so inspired by Medwick that he followed his example of hitting pitches that were high, low, inside or outside. Those two—Medwick and Berra—were the best bad-ball hitters in history. Each of them decided they'd hit the next pitch, and that was that. Veteran pitchers with pinpoint control often told me the way to pitch both Medwick and Berra was not to try to fool them—just throw the ball over the plate and hope for the best.

As soon as MacPhail gave Durocher the managing job at Brooklyn in 1939, Leo started dreaming of getting Medwick. MacPhail soon caught the fire. Stanley Frank once wrote an article for the *Saturday Evening Post* on MacPhail and titled the piece "As Subtle As a Punch in the Nose."

MacPhail went right to work. He started talking to Rickey about Medwick in 1939. Rickey said nothing doing, Medwick was too valuable; Joe always hit well above .300 (in 1937 he hit .374 with 154 runs batted in and 31 home runs) and Rickey just couldn't think of trading him.

Medwick was completely self-centered. He wanted his base hits. It came out after the season of 1939 that many of Joe's teammates resented his selfishness. Joe had gotten into fights with his fellow players. Dizzy Dean said, "The trouble with that Medwick is, he don't talk none, he just hits you." Joe once went after both Dizzy and his brother Paul with a bat.

Durocher wanted Medwick with a passion. As I remember, both Leo and MacPhail felt in spring training of 1940 that if they could get Medwick the Dodgers might win that pennant.

Rickey changed his mind. He could do without Joe Medwick. He now had other ballplayers. Further, Rickey had a clause in his contract that provided that he get a percentage of any cash he got for a player he traded or sold. He knew he had a willing buyer in MacPhail. He knew Durocher thirsted. Also in his farm system he had a kid named Musial. He telephoned MacPhail that a deal for Medwick could be considered. MacPhail was on the next plane to St. Louis.

The deal was announced on June 12, 1940: Medwick with veteran pitcher Curt Davis to Brooklyn, in return for pitchers Carl Doyle and Sam Nahem, players Ernie Koy and Bert Haas, and $125,000.

Durocher later won a pennant at Brooklyn, won two with the Giants at the Polo Grounds including a World Series, had Bobby

Thomson hit that play-off home run in 1951 against Ralph Branca, managed Willie Mays, and in 1934 was shortstop for the Gas House Gang, but I doubt that Leo was ever as deliriously happy as when he knew he had Joe Medwick as his ballplayer at Brooklyn. No one ever accused Leo of being a holy man, but when MacPhail called him about the deal Leo just might have walked on water. Joe Medwick with that big bat! And not a bad fielder either.

Medwick reported promptly to Leo and took a room at the New Yorker Hotel where Leo stayed. The sixth day Medwick was a Dodger, the St. Louis Cardinals were to open a series at Ebbets Field. The Cardinals also stayed at the New Yorker. The morning of the first game Durocher and Medwick got on an elevator. A few floors later several of the Cardinals got on, including right-handed pitcher Bowman, who was to start the game that afternoon. There were some rough words between Medwick and his former teammates and Bowman said something to the effect, "We'll fix you this afternoon," or, "We'll get you this afternoon." A threat. Durocher had a punctured eardrum that kept him from being drafted in the war, but nobody ever said Leo couldn't hear. He heard, and he told MacPhail before the game.

In the last of the first inning Medwick came to bat for the first time against his old ball club. He and pitcher Bowman faced each other. Medwick with his slightly open stance dug in firmly at the plate, his bat drawn back on the ready. Bowman delivered and the ball struck Medwick squarely on the left side of his head, right at the temple. He fell flat. Unconscious.

MacPhail roared through the stands, into the Dodger dugout and across the field toward the Cardinals' bench. He was raging. He challenged the entire St. Louis ball club. He had to be physically restrained. I never saw a man in such a rage. He didn't know where he was or what he was doing. Medwick beaned. And a threat made that morning by the pitcher.

MacPhail threatened to call in Miles McDonald, the Brooklyn District Attorney. It certainly would have been very serious had Medwick died. Anyhow, Medwick was never the tiger again at the plate. He didn't dig in again as he had. His power was gone.

Rickey wasn't at Ebbets Field. He was in St. Louis or someplace. MacPhail never suggested Rickey had anything to do with it. But as I know MacPhail, with his fantastic memory, down deep inside, this beaning of Joe Medwick changed for all time his feelings about Branch Rickey. Rickey had won. Mac-Phail had lost, and lost heavily. Bitterly. Taste of wormwood.

It is doubtful the Dodgers even with a completely healthy Medwick could have beaten Cincinnati for the 1940 pennant. The Reds had a smoothly functioning team with Ernie Lombardi catching and hitting, Frank McCormick at first who also hit, and two superb pitchers, Paul Derringer and Bucky Walters. Derringer won 20 and Walters won 22. The Reds took the pennant by 12 games over the Dodgers.

MacPhail put the winning touches on the 1941 Dodgers. He got the catcher he needed, Mickey Owen, from Rickey before the season began. He got pitcher Kirby Higbe from Philadelphia. Then, shortly after the race started in '41 MacPhail made a deal with the Chicago Cubs for second baseman Billy Herman. Whitlow Wyatt was an unbeatable pitcher in the clutch games, winning all told 22. Pee Wee Reese matured enough at shortstop to replace Durocher.

MacPhail had built the Dodgers in 1941 thinking he had to battle Cincinnati for the pennant. But the Cardinals provided the challenge. Rickey had replaced Medwick in left field and at the plate with Stan Musial. The Dodgers had to beat the Cardinals 2 out of 3 in St. Louis with a week to go. The game that turned the tide was when Whitlow Wyatt outpitched Mort Cooper 1–0. The Dodgers edged the Cards by 2½ games. Mac-Phail finally had his pennant, and had it over Rickey.

The Yankees won the first World Series game behind Red Ruffing 3–2. The next day Whitlow Wyatt beat Spud Chandler 3–2. All was back in balance. In game three Fred Fitzsimmons and Marius Russo were locked in a scoreless duel. Russo came to bat for the Yankees in the eighth inning and hit a savage line drive that broke Fitzsimmons' kneecap. The Yankees defeated relief pitcher Hugh Casey. MacPhail couldn't know, but as he watched Fitzsimmons being helped off the field, that was the turning point.

Game four: Casey relieved again and in the top of the ninth the Dodgers led 4–3. With two out and nobody on base Tommy

Henrich swung and missed a third strike. The game was Brooklyn's, 4–3, and the Series was even at 2 games apiece. But catcher Mickey Owen was unable to hold the wicked curve that fanned Henrich. Henrich reached first. DiMaggio singled, Keller doubled, and after a walk, Gordon doubled. The Yankees scored four runs and won it 7–4.

After the game, in the pressroom, I saw MacPhail weep openly. Then he went to the dressing room to try to comfort Mickey Owen. The Yankees finished it off routinely the next day in game five.

1942 was the last year for MacPhail at Brooklyn, and it was also the final season for Rickey at St. Louis. Rickey had built a young team at St. Louis. Terry Moore in center field was the old man on the club at thirty. He was flanked by two kids, Stan Musial in left and Enos "Country" Slaughter in right. MacPhail's veteran Dodgers got off winging. The Cardinals under manager Billy Southworth found themselves in midsummer. But the Dodgers had a 10½-game lead in mid-August.

MacPhail knew there was trouble between some of his players. He knew the Dodgers played card games for high stakes. Medwick became a point of dissension as he was again accused of being interested only in his hits, and Durocher was always defending him. Just before the Dodgers left for a 4-game series at St. Louis, and with a 7½-game lead and five weeks to go, MacPhail acted. He went to the clubhouse and told the entire ball club he was dissatisfied with it, and if they were not careful they were going to lose the pennant. Dixie Walker answered MacPhail and offered to bet him $200 right then that the Dodgers would win it. MacPhail turned and walked out. But he had warned them. Further, he warned Durocher not to let Medwick curdle the cream.

In the final series at St. Louis the young Redbirds of Branch Rickey won 3 of the 4 games. From then on the Dodgers played well but the Cardinals played better. With two weeks to go the Cardinals stormed into Ebbets Field and swept the final 2 games between the two clubs. This sent St. Louis for the first time into first place. In the stretch Cooper beat Wyatt twice in 1-run squeakers. The Dodgers won their last 8 games. So did the

Cardinals. Brooklyn totaled 104 wins, St. Louis 106. Rickey's young Redbirds then humbled the Yankees in 5 games in the World Series.

MacPhail left for the Army. His last Brooklyn team had won 104 games, yet still lost to Rickey's last St. Louis team. The organization Rickey left at St. Louis won three of the next four pennants. The Dodgers didn't win again until 1947 after they had been rebuilt by Rickey.

I think MacPhail left his heart and his pride in Brooklyn. Certainly he left Leo Durocher with whom he had lived and died for five years, four of them as his manager. This is important to remember.

John McGraw, Ed Barrow, George Weiss and Branch Rickey were four builders of dynasties. McGraw was the first National League manager to dominate his league. McGraw ran the New York Giants and won ten pennants. The Giants had money, McGraw was impatient and used money to buy the "finished" ballplayer he either needed or wanted. He sneered at Rickey's farm system. McGraw wouldn't wait.

Barrow was an old-line baseball man. He discovered Honus Wagner. He was the two-fisted field manager at Boston when Babe Ruth came to the major leagues. Once Barrow threatened to lock the clubhouse door and physically handle Ruth; Babe wisely cooled down. Barrow was a rugged man with an uncanny ability to grade the worth of a ballplayer. Rickey often told me, "Ed Barrow is the best judge of a ballplayer I know . . . he can grade them as closely as they grade the cadets at West Point—to a decimal point." When Col. Jake Ruppert got control of the Yankees he hired Barrow to be his general manager. It was Barrow who knew which Boston players to get, and under Barrow, Yankee Stadium was built and the Yankees became the winningest team in all baseball. Not only pennants but world championships.

Unlike McGraw, Barrow could change, and he could also wait. Barrow saw the value of Rickey's farm system when the Cardinals defeated the Yankees in the World Series of 1926. Barrow selected George Weiss of New Haven, Connecticut, to start building a farm system for the Yankees. Weiss created a superb minor-league organization, but Barrow was sitting on top of it all. After Barrow and MacPhail were gone, Rickey told me, "Weiss inherited great riches . . . he is surfeited with wealth . . . every time I see the Yankees, I see the hand of Ed Barrow." Weiss was the general manager who hired Casey Stengel and had five straight world championships and five other pennants in twelve years.

Rickey had become the great builder of teams in the National League. He was acknowledged the master judge of young players as well as of the polished professional. He knew when to trade a veteran just before the veteran began fading. Teams traded with Rickey at their peril. He was the master. One of his prize pupils was MacPhail.

Sam Breadon, however, owned the Cardinals. Breadon was a tough-minded fellow, and as time went by Breadon learned enough from Rickey to decide that he, Sam Breadon, could run the organization. Rickey got a percentage of the sales of all players. Rickey got the credit for the Cardinals' successes. Basically, it was two strong men in too-cramped quarters. The one who owned the team was going to stay. Rickey's contract ended after the Cardinals defeated the Yankees in the 1942 World Series.

The timing was exquisite. MacPhail went into the Army. Rickey, who had turned down offers at Cincinnati for 1934 and at Brooklyn for 1938—and I suspect many others—was now available. He had no contract at St. Louis. He had to make a move. He had to save his pride and he had to find a suitable position where his superb skills could continue to work. Baseball was Rickey's professional life.

Jim Mulvey had long been an admirer of Rickey, as had Ford Frick, National League president. Mulvey had offered Rickey the Brooklyn post five years before. Now, speaking for the other Brooklyn club owners, he offered Rickey the job MacPhail had just left. Rickey warned Mulvey that with the war on, with the Dodgers loaded with overage players, with such Dodgers as Reese, Reiser and Casey in military service, nothing dramatic could be expected. All was spelled out and understood. Rickey came to Brooklyn. He retained the right to receive a percentage from player sales.

Rickey was a lifelong teetotaler; MacPhail had operated a

generous bar in the pressroom. The first question the New York writers asked was, "Will Rickey close MacPhail's saloon?" Rickey didn't.

Ford Frick, as league president, was sick and tired of Durocher getting into violent arguments with his umpires. Further, under Durocher, the Dodgers had acquired a reputation all over the league of their pitchers throwing at opposing hitters. Durocher, who loudly justified every action he ever took, claimed his pitchers were only knocking down hitters in self-defense, that the other teams were picking on the Dodgers. MacPhail had heatedly backed up Durocher and his pitchers, and had publicly blasted Frick. Frick devoutly hoped Rickey would put restraints on Durocher.

Even more serious, both Frick and Mulvey knew the Dodgers under Durocher had been a wide-open ball club for all kinds of gambling: card games, dice, horses, anything. After the veteran left-hander Larry French joined the Dodgers he said, "This is the gamblingest ball club I ever saw . . . give any one of several players the right odds and he will bet you that your right ear falls off next Thursday."

Bookmakers had free access to the Dodger clubhouse, especially Memphis Engelberg, a racehorse handicapper and bookmaker. Memphis was a longtime friend of coach Charlie Dressen, and Dressen was a longtime horse player. Memphis was constantly besieged by the players for tips, and he handled action for them. Clubhouse doors could be shut at times to newspapermen but never to Memphis, or George Raft or Danny Kaye or anybody else from Broadway or Hollywood. Durocher played cards with his players, and liked a hot tip on a horse. Leo gambled and therefore was in no position to stop gambling on the ball club. This was all well known. MacPhail knew it and didn't care, apparently. He let Durocher have his clubhouse.

Baseball had paid a heavy price about gambling and gamblers. During the 1919 World Series eight Chicago White Sox players were accused of being influenced by gamblers to throw certain selected games against Cincinnati. It took a while for the story to break, but when the American public learned about it the entire nation was aroused. The country was shocked.

Preachers delivered sermons on how baseball had betrayed the people who believed in it. The White Sox became the Black Sox.

Baseball had been run by a three-man commission—the two league presidents and an owner. This commission had little power and no real ability to supervise. Baseball just ran along its accustomed way. Everybody took everything for granted. The good old boys were not disturbed.

Then the Black Sox lightning struck and baseball abruptly realized that its main asset was public confidence in its integrity. A completely frightened industry turned to Federal Judge Kennesaw Mountain Landis and asked him to become Commissioner. The Judge in 1920 made the owners accept his terms: absolute authority with power to do anything he deemed in the best interests of baseball. He was soon called a czar. He was. This had a strong bearing on his successor, Happy Chandler.

When Commissioner Landis took office he immediately suspended all eight White Sox players for "life," and that included Shoeless Joe Jackson, one of the bright stars of the game. While Landis was in office he suspended for life fourteen players for gambling implications.

Under the Judge, gambling in all forms was frowned upon. In fact, in 1943 Judge Landis barred an owner from baseball. William Cox bought the Phillies from Gerry Nugent—had them about a year—and made small bets on his own team to win. Landis ordered him to sell his stock, get out, and stay out. That's when the Carpenter family bought the Phillies.

While Landis lived, no person who owned a racehorse or a race track could get into baseball. Betting was baseball's number one enemy.

Rickey was determined to stop gambling on the Dodgers. He did. He lectured Durocher publicly. He delayed signing Leo as manager while he laid down the law on gambling and pointed out its pitfalls. He made certain Leo got the message and was properly repentant. In addition, Rickey called in Charlie Dressen, complimented him on his baseball abilities, then fired him for betting on horses.

Dressen took it like a man. He promised Rickey he would not make another bet. Rickey said he couldn't do it, that he was addicted. Dressen asked if he could come back if he proved he had stopped all betting. Rickey said yes. Dressen proved it and Rickey rehired him.

The writers? Most of them gave Rickey a bad press for scolding Durocher and firing Dressen. The writers loved the free-wheeling MacPhail, the abrasive, rambunctious, colorful Durocher, and the hail-fellow-well-met Dressen. Rickey was painted as a do-gooder, a holier-than-thou, a hypocrite, a stuffed shirt who never drank, gambled or used profanity. Rickey was also presented to the public as a penny pincher.

One of the most irritating traits to many writers was Rickey's superb use of the English language. Rickey said things some of them didn't understand. It was impossible to pin him down when he didn't wish to be. He used words as an art of misdirection. I've heard some writers after a lengthy press conference ask each other, "What did he say?"

Rickey took over late in 1942, just in time to reap the whirlwind of World War II. Reese, Lavagetto, Casey, Herman, Rizzo, French, Higbe—player after player went into the armed forces. Dolph Camilli aged, and when Rickey tried to trade him Camilli quit. Arky Vaughan stayed on his farm for the duration.

Rickey's first Brooklyn team in 1943 won 23 fewer games than MacPhail's team the year before. It was worse in 1944. Then the Dodgers limped in seventh with only 63 wins against 91 losses. One of the complaints voiced loudly in Brooklyn was, "Rickey ruint the Dodgers."

Rickey made an early decision. He told the board of directors that he knew the United States would win the war, that he wanted to sign every young player of promise even if they went into the armed forces the next day, so that when the war was ended and the players returned, then he, Rickey, would have most of them. Other clubs retrenched, cut down on their scouting staffs, and played it conservatively. But Rickey signed young men, played them if he could, told them good-bye and waited for them to return.

Baseball struggled to endure for the duration. It got so that anybody who could breathe could play. Old men and kids. The St. Louis Browns used Pete Gray a season and a half; Gray was one-armed. Rickey used Tommy Brown, a sixteen-year-old short-stop. Cincinnati pitched Joe Nuxhall when he was fifteen.

Every so often manager Leo Durocher would bark, "Tell Rickey to back up the truck and unload another batch of kids."

While it seemed that the worst was happening at Brooklyn, Rickey laid the foundations for another dynasty. In 1945 the team was third and for the rest of Rickey's years at Brooklyn his Dodgers were always near or right at the top. Rickey completely rebuilt the franchise MacPhail had left. His foresight and his patience were remarkable. His judgment of players, especially youngsters, was never sharper. It all fell down around him when he came, but he put it together again and in much stronger depth.

When Rickey came to Brooklyn Leo Durocher was the hold-over manager from the MacPhail era. Rickey and Durocher were not strangers to each other. Not at all.

Rickey's Cardinals defeated Connie Mack's Philadelphia Athletics in the 1931 World Series. At shortstop for the Cardinals was Charley Gelbert. Gelbert was fast, a splendid fielder, good hitter, had excellent habits on and off the field, and was a money player. He was a star. After the 1932 season Gelbert was hunting and somehow his shotgun went off and severely damaged one of his legs. His career was over. He played later as utility but he was never again the same Charley Gelbert. Rickey had to get a shortstop in 1933 who could take over right now.

Sidney Weil at Cincinnati comes into the picture again. Weil had shortstop Leo Durocher. Weil—an automobile dealer—was in severe financial trouble. 1933—the Depression. Weil needed money and he needed players. Rickey got Durocher from Weil—but one of the players he had to send to Cincinnati in the deal was Paul Derringer.

Rickey hadn't met Durocher but he knew about him. He knew that Leo had been brought up by the Yankees in 1928, had gotten into a near fight with Babe Ruth, had the reputation of being fast-talking and brash, high-living and free-spending. He had high-style clothes, and also he owed everybody. He knew that Durocher had been waived by the Yankees to the Reds in 1930 immediately after he cursed general manager Ed Barrow in a contract dispute. Weil had told Rickey that Durocher was deeply in debt.

More than anything else, Rickey knew Durocher could play shortstop. Further, Rickey had a fascination for the shining ones; otherwise how explain his repeated and continued involvements with both Durocher and MacPhail.

It began May 11, 1933, at the Alamac Hotel in New York, where the Cardinals were staying for a series at Brooklyn. Rickey was in bed with a heavy cold. After Sidney Weil told Durocher of the deal, Leo went to beard the lion in his den. Leo walked into Rickey's room belligerent, resentful and loud. He left somewhat later in a most sober frame of mind. And quiet.

Leo balked at first when Weil told him of his trade to St. Louis. Weil then promised that Leo would get a thousand dollars if he agreed, and that Rickey would pay it. Leo, always in desperate need of cash, hurried to Rickey's hotel. A thousand dollars cash money!

Rickey quietly, calmly and leaving no doubts about the situation informed his new twenty-six-year-old shortstop that yes, he would receive $1,000 above his Cincinnati contract, but that Weil would pay it, not Rickey . . . that Leo would not get any more money than $50 a week to live on . . . that he'd have to get by on that amount . . . that the rest of his salary would be prorated among his debtors, and that this arrangement would continue until Leo's debts were paid . . . that Leo was not to sign a check—in fact, he was not to have a checking account— he was not to charge anything.

Rickey didn't know whether this austere program of practical poverty for the freewheeling Durocher would break his spirit or not. He did know Durocher couldn't play shortstop while creditors were threatening him or suing him and he was getting deeper and deeper into debt. When a man gets into serious financial straits, sooner or later ugly trouble occurs. In one of Burl Ives's folk songs is the line, "A troubled mind sure knows no rest."

Leo was a realist. He knew $50 a week was better than nothing. He knew his only hope was playing shortstop and playing it as well as he could. He knew it would take a World Series to bail him out. He knew this was his last chance.

Leo went to work at St. Louis. He had the quickest hands of any shortstop I ever saw, or maybe that anyone ever saw. His arm wasn't a rifle—his throws always had an arc in them—but he got to the ball so quickly, and he got rid of it so rapidly, it was like the work of a magician. He grabbed the ball and the ball was on its way.

For St. Louis, Frank Frisch was the manager and the second baseman. Frisch had been playing ball for the Giants and the Cardinals fifteen years when Durocher was teamed with him in the infield. The legs were now giving the Old Flash trouble. Leo made it easy for Frisch. They made a remarkable combination. Leo cemented the infield of Rip Collins at first, Frisch at second, himself at short, and Pepper Martin at third.

The next season, 1934, Dizzy and Paul Dean won 49 games between them—Dizzy 30 and Paul 19. Paul also delivered a no-hitter in the second game of a doubleheader at Brooklyn after Dizzy had pitched a one-hitter in the first game. Dizzy was bitter afterward, claiming Paul should have told him he was going to throw a no-hitter, because then, said Dizzy, he'd have thrown one too, for a double no-hitter. Dizzy might just have done it. . . .

Durocher played superbly. In 1934 the Cardinals became known as the Gas House Gang. The Dodgers beat Bill Terry's Giants the last two days of the season, while the Cardinals swept the Reds 3 straight and squeaked into the World Series against Mickey Cochrane's Detroit Tigers. Durocher had a great Series, and the Cardinals won in 7 games.

Leo got $5,389.57 as the winning player's share. He was suddenly home-free from his debts. Also, he had met Grace Dozier, a charming, mature, experienced businesswoman. They married. Grace held the reins from then on. It took some doing but she kept Leo solvent after Rickey had forced him to even the board.

Rickey was beaming. He had gotten his shortstop, and while he hadn't reformed him completely he had gotten him back on an even keel. You've heard about the ninety and nine sheep? Rickey was the living example of the man who knew one sheep was missing, left the ninety and nine and searched until he found the missing one. Rickey, to my personal knowledge, not only read and knew the Bible, he practiced it.

Dizzy Dean, another wild one, had married and his wife, Pat, was taking care of his money.

There is no record today of why manager Frisch later on said what he did to Rickey. Frisch said, "Branch, do me a favor . . . get rid of him . . . it's him or me." October 4, 1937, Rickey traded Durocher to Brooklyn. Leo was there when MacPhail came to Ebbets Field, and then when Rickey came.

Who knows what would have happened if Frisch hadn't made his sudden and determined demand? Frisch went to his death never saying why. He didn't tell Rickey and he didn't tell Durocher. The best guess is that Frank, unable to play actively any longer, feeling insecure in his job as manager, felt that Leo had just the touch to replace him. Perhaps Frisch saw before Rickey and MacPhail did that Leo would be a manager.

Rickey talked to Grace and said, "Brooklyn is not as bad as it is painted . . . just don't let Leo paint it too often. They always have manager trouble. Don't be surprised if he becomes a manager . . . he has the drive to do it."

Branch Rickey, the master at building baseball teams, the creator of the farm system, the astute appraiser of ability, had recognized talent in MacPhail and in Durocher. He had to discipline each of them, but he was the living example of the forgiving father of the Prodigal Son. MacPhail and Durocher both had charm and talent. I expect the Prodigal Son had a certain irresistible spark about him, too. Talent is precious, and when you add devastating personal charm to it, it is addictive.

Rickey moved to Brooklyn for 1943. In spring training during the war when the Dodgers were training at both Bear Mountain Inn and at West Point, New York, Leo got to going into New York City to be on radio shows with Milton Berle, Jack Benny and people like that. Rickey wanted Leo one night for an important meeting, and was told Leo was in a radio studio in Manhattan. Rickey exploded. The next morning he told Durocher, "Leo, make an election of profession." Leo replied, "Branch, Milton Berle just lost."

If you worked for MacPhail or for Rickey, as long as you worked for them, they could haul you over the coals but nobody else had better try it. They stood behind you.

Both said to me repeatedly, "You in your booth are closer to your work than any other person . . . you do it." Tom Meany, then writing for the New York *World-Telegram,* told me, "One night in a game against St. Louis, MacPhail was standing at the bar listening to the broadcast. Hymie Green was the veteran bartender. A Cardinal runner at first tried to go to third on a hit and you said he was out at third. Then the ball rolled out of the third baseman's glove, the umpire changed his call, and you said he was now safe. Green said, 'That Barber don't know the difference between safe and out.' MacPhail said, 'You tend bar and let Barber broadcast.' Green said, 'You can't talk like that to me.' MacPhail said, 'Take off your apron, get your check . . . I won't have to talk to you like that . . . you're through.' Green was gone."

One time Durocher was critical of my philosophy of broadcasting as compared to that in Chicago where the announcers were rabid Cubs rooters rather than reporters. The Chicago fellows would say such things as, "I don't care who wins this game today . . . as long as it's the Cubs." Leo thought that would be just fine for the Brooklyn broadcast. Just fine. He told me so.

Leo and I had always worked together very well. This suggestion troubled me enough to repeat to Rickey what Leo said. Branch never hesitated. He said, "If you start doing what Leo wants you to do, he'll get you in more trouble than the Commissioner and I together can get you out of." Mr. Rickey certainly knew what he was talking about.

The only time I saw Durocher backed down was by Tim Cohane, a writer for the *World-Telegram.* It was in July 1943. The war was on, Rickey was in charge, and Durocher got mad at a pitch Bobo Newsom delivered that got past catcher Bobby Bragan. Durocher told Hugh Casey, on leave from the service, in reporter Cohane's presence, that to his mind Newsom was trying to "show up" Bragan by throwing a spitter when Bragan had called for a fast ball.

Cohane not only wrote it but he also told the other writers about the statement. They all wrote it. I was sitting in Leo's office during batting practice the next day—it was a Friday— when Arky Vaughan stepped in the door unannounced. He was furious. He yelled, "I just heard what is in the papers about what you said about Newsom . . . if that's so . . . here is my uniform." Dixie Walker yelled from outside the door, "If that boy takes off his uniform then you've got mine, too." Suddenly the entire ball club was in rebellion. Leo said he didn't say it, and wanted to know where Cohane was.

Cohane had the day off, and was at home in nearby Westchester County. Leo got him on the phone and complained that he, Cohane, had gotten his ball club in an uproar over something he hadn't said. Cohane coldly said, "I don't come to a ball park on Saturday . . . but I'll be there tomorrow." Then Tim telephoned Rickey and demanded a meeting with Durocher in the clubhouse before the entire squad. Rickey tried to persuade Cohane not to do it. Tim was adamant. Tim said Durocher had called him a liar.

The showdown was held. The angry players deserted batting practice to be there. The writers were there. Durocher sat on a trunk, his arms folded, kicking his heels against the side of the trunk. Cohane stood before Leo and cross-examined him thoroughly. Cohane by his questions made Durocher admit everything Cohane had written. Everything.

Newsom then took over and asked Leo why he had said what he did to Casey before Cohane, and then had told him and the players he had not said it. Leo had no answer. It appeared he had lost control of his team. Some writers even wrote that Leo would have to go.

But Rickey stood solidly behind his manager and hoped that Leo could regain command. Instead of Durocher it was Newsom who went, traded by Rickey to the Browns. Leo was soon back in the driver's seat, but damage had been done. It was Rickey who put down the rebellion.

K. M. LANDIS AND L. S. MACPHAIL

One of the truly great men of baseball died November 25, 1944.
The nation was too concerned with World War II to pay much
attention to his death. Also he had ordered that there be no funeral and no viewing of his remains. He went quietly.

He was the first Commissioner of Baseball, Federal Judge
K. M. Landis. His father had lost a leg at Kennesaw Mountain,
Georgia, in the Civil War, and he named his son for that bloody
battleground.

Landis was appointed to the federal bench by President
Theodore Roosevelt, and received national fame in 1907 when
he fined Standard Oil $29,240,000 in a freight-rebate case. The
Supreme Court later nullified the fine, but by then Landis had a
strong reputation as a decisive man who wasn't afraid of even a
major corporation.

In 1915 Landis came to the attention of the baseball owners
when the Federal League, in an attempt to start a third major
league, sued the two established leagues, the National and the
American, for conspiracy, restraint of trade and violation of anti-
trust laws. The case came before Landis, and what he did was
sit on it until the warring leagues made their own settlement.
This suited the established leagues. They remembered Landis
favorably.

As said before, eight Chicago White Sox players were accused
of being involved with gamblers to throw certain 1919 World
Series games against Cincinnati. When this story broke early in
1920 the entire country was outraged. The integrity of baseball
was shaken. The owners needed, and quickly, a strong man with

impeccable credentials to take command. The country's belief in the honesty of the game had to be restored. They turned to Landis.

Landis drove a hard bargain. He was secure on the federal bench, which he liked. To give it up to become Commissioner, he demanded complete authority. Anything that he decided was "detrimental to baseball" was just that—there was to be no appeal from any of his rulings. He was to be a czar. He was. He ran baseball from 1920 until his death in 1944. His first action was to banish for life the eight "Black" Sox. The public breathed easier.

Babe Ruth joined the New York Yankees in 1920 and hit an almost unbelievable total of 54 home runs. Ruth stirred up an interest baseball had never had. Landis gave back integrity, Ruth added excitement. Baseball boomed. Good times soon followed the end of World War I.

It is important to sketch something of Judge Landis. I got to know him quite well, and my first nine World Series broadcasts, beginning in 1935, were under his commissionership. He gave me a philosophy that carried me through the years. Without that philosophy I could not have broadcast when Jackie Robinson came to Ebbets Field in 1947.

Before the first game of the 1935 World Series, Chicago at Detroit, Landis held a meeting of all the radio people concerned. Three networks then carried the broadcasts: NBC, CBS and, for the first time, Mutual. Executives, commentators, and play-by-play men crowded into the Commissioner's suite. In brief, this is what he said:

"Gentlemen, I'm too old to try to tell experts how to do their business. You men are the best in your business or you wouldn't be here. However, this afternoon two teams will be on the field, and for this year, they are the best in their business. Report what the players do. They don't need your help in telling them how to play. Report."

The Judge was slender, with a white head of hair which he shook to emphasize his points. He had thin, aristocratic features. He was a commanding, impressive, colorful figure. The room was completely quiet.

"This afternoon," the Judge continued, using a cigarette as a pointer, "there will be two managers in the park. You probably won't see much of them because they'll be in their dugouts. But for this year they are the best in their business. They don't need your help. Don't try to manage for them. Your job is to report what they do, what decisions they make. You are to have no opinions on their decisions. Just report them."

Now the Judge got down to the heart of the matter.

"There is an announcer who is not here this morning, and all of you know who he is and the reason why he is not here. [Ted Husing, who had criticized some umpiring decisions in a previous World Series.]

"This afternoon there will be four umpires. You'll recognize them by the blue suits they'll have on. For this year, they are the best in their business. They certainly don't need or want your help or advice. They are perfectly able to make their own decisions. You report their rulings. Don't have any opinions on what they rule, ball or strike, safe or out. You haven't the training and you haven't the proper perspective. Report their decisions. Report the reactions of the players or the managers but have no opinions. Report.

"You are to report everything in the game, everything in the ball park that you can see. You are to report everything, but leave your opinions in the hotel. By reporting everything, I mean this: suppose a player gets a mouthful of chewing tobacco and walks over to my rail box and spits it in my face. Report from where the player started, report how many steps he took, report how close he got to me, report the accuracy of his delivery, report the amount of chewing tobacco on my face—if your eyes are that good—and report the reaction of the Commissioner, if he has one. But have no opinions. Report."

Nobody said a word. All eyes were on the Judge.

"Gentlemen," he continued, "I want you to know the full force of the Commissioner's office will see to it that this afternoon no player, no manager, and certainly no umpire will leave the field and come up to your booth and disturb you in your work. Report this World Series to millions of people who can't see it for themselves. Report.

"Gentlemen . . . good day."

Judge Landis kept his office and his home in Chicago. Both

leagues had teams there, the Cubs in the National League and the White Sox in the American. So he was on top of the major-league picture. He didn't hold press conferences. He announced his decisions. The writers didn't take liberties with Landis. He was available, but once he said on the telephone what was on his mind, he would suddenly say "Good-bye." And that was that. Judge Landis awed people. He had an air of authority. He wasn't a small-talk man. His personal letters would often be one sentence long.

Landis didn't bother much with New York. Some of the New York writers early in his commissionership said if he'd come to New York they'd give him a special dinner. He agreed, and that was the beginning of the New York Baseball Writers Annual Dinner, which is baseball's most prestigious.

Landis hated the farm systems and he freed many players, especially from Rickey's St. Louis Cardinals and the Detroit Tigers. One of the Cardinals Landis made a free agent was a kid named Pete Reiser. Rickey tipped off MacPhail, and Reiser was signed for $500, or less.

The ballplayers believed that Landis was their friend, that they could take their troubles with the owners to him and get help. He was a fair man.

But he could get mad. In March of 1940 baseball decided it would hold a benefit game during spring training on behalf of Finnish War Relief, directed by former President Herbert Hoover. The game was to be played in Tampa where the Cincinnati Reds trained. I was across Tampa Bay with the Dodgers in Clearwater. Judge Landis for years stayed every spring at the swank Belleview Biltmore in Clearwater.

The Mutual Broadcasting System was going to do the game coast to coast. Inasmuch as I was already there, I was given the assignment to announce it. Ticket sales were going very well to see National League stars against American League stars. The crowd finally came to 13,180 with $22,000 raised for the fund.

Judge Landis called me one day and asked would I drive over to Tampa, see Tom Swope of the Cincinnati *Post*, and make the arrangements for broadcasting space. Swope was a churlish, rude fellow who despised radio and all the people in it. When I was broadcasting in Cincinnati he used to sit in the nearby press section and growl about radio, and sometimes his words were quite profane.

I drove over, told Swope what I was sent to do, and he said in effect that there was no room in the press area for me and an engineer with his equipment . . . that he had assigned all working space, and to hell with it . . . that he didn't care if the game was broadcast or not.

I drove back and when I got to the hotel the Judge was coming in from his afternoon golf game. He must have done pretty well. He was smiling, and he said, "All set in Tampa?" Well, he had told me in Detroit in 1935 to "report," so I reported. The Judge said, "Tom Swope said that?" I said, "Yes, sir."

The next morning after breakfast Judge Landis said, "Would you do me one more favor? Will you drive back to Tampa and see what Mr. Swope has to say now?"

You hate to see a man grovel, but that was what Mr. Swope did. He asked if I wanted the entire press section. I said I only wanted room for two men and equipment—three seats of space. He wanted to know exactly where I wanted those three seats, and he insisted on it being five seats to be certain we were not going to be crowded.

The Judge said, "What did Mr. Tom Swope say this time?" I just grinned, and he smiled back.

Landis kept the club owners afraid of him. Should things get tight between them, he'd threaten to tear up his contract and resign. That would bring the owners to scratch.

Judge Kennesaw Mountain Landis ruled baseball with an iron hand—owners, players, radio—for twenty-five years. He wasn't perfect. Many of his decisions were questioned, and today one wonders about some of them, especially when he allowed Bob Feller to remain with the Cleveland Indians. One couldn't be certain which way he would rule. But he would rule, and that would be that.

The death of Judge Landis set in motion the election of Senator A. B. Happy Chandler. Without Chandler as Commissioner this might not be a book. However, if Charlie Gelbert had not shot himself accidentally in the leg, had not Sidney Weil gone broke in Cincinnati, had not Branch Rickey traded for Leo Durocher, had not Rickey three times been instrumental in placing Larry MacPhail in baseball, et cetera, this would not be a book.

The death of Col. Jake Ruppert in 1939 made it possible for MacPhail to get back into baseball after his tour in the U.S. Army as a lieutenant colonel. Ruppert and Col. Tillinghast l'Hommedieu Huston in 1915 were friends who wanted to buy a ball club—preferably the New York Giants, then the toast of the town, led by John J. McGraw. When they approached McGraw about buying into the Giants, McGraw said there was no chance, but that they could get the Yankees, and cheap. World War I raged in Europe. The times were uncertain. The Yankees were the new American League team, and had been in town only since 1903. They had never won, and for the preceding four years had been down in the second division. The two men who owned them needed cash and wanted out. McGraw knew about this because the Yankees were tenants of the Giants, playing at the Polo Grounds when the Giants were on the road.

The two colonels bought the Yankees on January 11, 1915, for $460,000. The team had no star. Colonel Huston soon went overseas in the Army, leaving Ruppert to run the ball club. In 1918 he made his first master stroke: he hired Miller Huggins as manager. Then in 1920 Ruppert struck oil. Harry Frazee owned the Boston Red Sox and had among other players the young Babe Ruth. Frazee had some Broadway shows go sour—he was always more interested in staging shows than in running his ball club—and Ruppert gave Frazee $100,000 in cash plus a personal loan of $350,000 for Ruth.

Edward Grant Barrow was the Red Sox manager from 1918 to 1920. Under Barrow, Ruth was switched from a superb left-handed pitcher who played every fourth day to an outfielder who played, and batted, every day. Ruth in 1920, his first year with the Yankees, hit 54 home runs. The next year he hit 59. Ruth and the Yankees began taking the play away from McGraw and his Giants, and right in their own Polo Grounds.

Again Ruppert struck pay dirt—he hired Barrow after the 1920 season to become the general manager of the Yankees. Barrow, who knew firsthand the playing personnel of the Red Sox, promptly traded for Harry Harper, Mike McNally, Waite Hoyt and Wally Schang. In 1923 Barrow got Herb Pennock from Boston. Miller Huggins was the manager, and with the stars Barrow had gotten from Boston the Yankees won the pennant in 1921, again in 1922, and again in 1923. The Yankees became the dominant team in all baseball, and Boston has never forgiven Harry Frazee.

Colonel Ruppert was a tremendous fan of his ball club. He wanted a team so great it would win every game of the season. He made some important decisions until he hired Ed Barrow to make them for him. Branch Rickey always claimed Barrow was the master builder of winning teams. Barrow ran the Yankees with an iron hand.

Ruppert later bought out Huston and became sole owner. He got into the habit of going into the Yankee clubhouse after games. Barrow told him not to do that anymore, that the clubhouse belonged to the players and to the manager. Ruppert never went back again. The Yankee team under Barrow was a tight ship.

McGraw of the Giants was getting deeply disturbed. His tenants, the Yankees, were drawing the crowds and taking the spotlight. McGraw ordered the Yankees to vacate the Polo Grounds. He thought they'd have to go out to Queens where they'd "wither on the vine." Babe Ruth alone, hitting home runs in the Polo Grounds, was enough to give McGraw nightmares.

But right across the Harlem River was a piece of land just right. Ruppert put up the money, Huston supervised the construction, and Yankee Stadium was built in twelve months. It opened April 18, 1923. The rest is history.

Colonel Ruppert died in 1939. He was a bachelor. His estate was left mainly to two nieces. Barrow was made president of the Yankees and continued running the ball club. Joe McCarthy then was the highly successful manager. George Weiss had been brought in to run the farm system. Under Barrow the Yankees won fourteen pennants, ten World Series, and in five of those Series didn't lose a game. A steamroller.

Late in 1944 it became known that the Ruppert estate wanted to sell the team. MacPhail was in the Army but his hearing was perfectly sound. He talked to a few people, trying to form a syndicate with himself as headman, but wasn't making progress until he talked with Dan Topping. Topping was in the Marines, but he was soon to be mustered out. Further, when MacPhail had been running Ebbets Field, Topping had the then National Football League Brooklyn Dodgers and was MacPhail's tenant. They got along well at Brooklyn.

Topping was born wealthy. Topping knew Del E. Webb, who had made a fortune in the construction business, and Webb had been a minor-league ballplayer. Topping and Webb had the cash, MacPhail had the know-how and credit. The three of them bought the Yankees on January 1, 1945, for $2,811,835, with MacPhail as president and general manager. Barrow, then seventy-seven, was "elevated" to chairman of the board.

There was no room for both MacPhail and Barrow. The old man sort of sat around for two years and then quit. Weiss had to work under MacPhail, take orders and keep a low profile, or quit. There was no warmth in the MacPhail-Weiss relationship. Manager Joe McCarthy and MacPhail tolerated each other until May 1946, when McCarthy quit and went to his home outside Buffalo. Bill Dickey got a shot at the job, didn't last long, and Johnny Neun finished out the season. Bucky Harris was named manager for 1947.

MacPhail made a daring move after the 1946 season: he traded second baseman Joe Gordon to Cleveland for right-handed pitcher Allie Reynolds. Gordon was a darling of the New York writers. The trade shook up New York. But Reynolds became the Chief, and then the Super Chief of winning teams later. MacPhail was never afraid. By 1947 he had both hands on the Yankees.

Here they were—Branch Rickey in Brooklyn at Ebbets Field, Larry MacPhail in the Bronx at Yankee Stadium. They were now in the same town, in the same market, competing for the radio and television audience, for money; both fighting for space in the same newspapers, needing strong promotions, and building ball clubs. Rickey was content to stay in his own area, but MacPhail never was to be fenced in; further, he still regarded Ebbets Field as his personal property. Some have said MacPhail was jealous. I don't know about that, but I know he felt that now, by all the gods that be, he was going to show Branch Rickey how to operate a big-league ball club. The challenges came from MacPhail.

Larry MacPhail was, as I look back and try to assess him, an actual Dr. Jekyll and Mr. Hyde. He could be as thoughtful, generous, and forgiving as any man who ever lived. He certainly had creative genius. Then he could suddenly go into a rage that was fearsome to be around. I never let my guard down in any conversation I had with him. I wasn't involved, but I had seen some of his rages. In Havana, Cuba, in the spring of 1941, when he had the Dodgers training there for a few weeks, I found out firsthand.

An exhibition game was called off at noon because of rain. MacPhail was in an expansive mood. He invited the press to the bar for drinks. He and I were at the same table with a couple of writers. The drinks came and were disposed of. MacPhail was most agreeable. He turned to me and asked:

"You've been around this ball club since Dixie Walker came . . . do you think the Dodgers can win the pennant with Walker playing center field?"

I was flattered to have him ask my opinion. I was relaxed. I knew the Dodgers didn't have anybody else at the moment for center field, so I said:

"Sure—why not?"

His face reddened, his neck swelled, and he started roaring. He berated my evaluation of Walker, he said I should know damned well Walker was no center fielder, that he couldn't throw, etc. I was struck dumb. As soon as I could I walked out of the room. Too late I remembered that Walker had been a stubborn holdout, which had enraged MacPhail. Never again did I stay around him one minute after I saw him take the first drink—from then on I was already late for an appointment. Very late.

I have heard Scotty Reston say that MacPhail was the only man he had ever known of whom he was physically afraid when he got into a rage.

MacPhail's anger was of two types. He could explode, and usually after an eruption he would be apologetic. He would even cry in an effort to make amends. He and Red Patterson of the *Herald Tribune* got into an actual fight in which Patterson hit him, and years later MacPhail hired Patterson to be his publicity man with the Yankees.

Then again, MacPhail could carry down deep inside a smoldering anger like a fire buried in a coal bin in a ship. His relentless anger for Rickey never ended, not even with Rickey's death. I think MacPhail never forgot, way down inside, that Rickey had fired him in Columbus, Ohio, in 1933. Rickey's good offices for him at Cincinnati and again at Brooklyn didn't eliminate that hidden burning. And as I said, I'm sure that seeing Joe Medwick, on his sixth day as MacPhail's player, lying unconscious on the ground at home plate, felled by Rickey's pitcher, added to the subconscious storm.

I didn't see MacPhail after he left Brooklyn to go into the Army. But I'm certain he brooded over Rickey's being brought into Brooklyn to take over what he, MacPhail, had operated for five colorful years. I don't know what transpired late in the season of 1942 between MacPhail, the board of directors of the Dodgers, and the Brooklyn Trust Company. There were stories MacPhail was considered too expensive and too expansive. I don't know, except he left to take a commission as lieutenant colonel. When Rickey was hired, the door was shut behind MacPhail at Ebbets Field. He couldn't return.

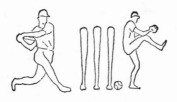

BRANCH RICKEY AND JACKIE ROBINSON

Do you remember where you were, and how you reacted, when
you heard the news of Pearl Harbor? I was sitting in the upper
stands, right under the football press box, at the Polo Grounds.
The then NFL Dodgers were playing the New York Giants. The
Giants had already won the eastern title and would go to
Chicago two weeks later to face the Bears in the national championship game. I had the assignment to broadcast in Chicago
and was scouting the Giants, one of the few times I got to see a
team play before I had to announce it.

The section I was sitting in was reserved for guests of the Giants and for the wives of the players and writers. During the
half Lou Effrat of the New York *Times* left the press box, came
down to where we were sitting, and said, "Pearl Harbor has
been bombed by the Japanese." I didn't hesitate. I got up,
walked out of the Polo Grounds, got in my car and turned on
the radio, which by now was filled with nothing but accounts
coming in from Hawaii.

A few days later I read about the people in Honolulu, the civilians who stood in long lines waiting to give blood to those
who were wounded in the attack and surely needed it. I thought
to myself, this is wonderful of the civilians to give their blood,
but the war is going to put our military in distant places, far
from any civilians . . . and what then?

Pearl Harbor touched each of us, changed everyone's life. Its
impact on baseball wasn't drastic immediately, but began a continuing series of changes. The big-league teams went to spring
training as usual in 1942. Judge Landis didn't restrict the train-

ing camps to the North to save transportation until the following spring. The Dodgers trained at Havana, Cuba—MacPhail had pulled out of Clearwater, Florida, or Clearwater had cooled off on MacPhail, or both.

Opening Day, Ebbets Field, 1942. I always got to the broadcasting booth at least a half hour before the game began. This gave me ample time to write the lineups in the scorebook, to check the commercials, and in general to be in command of what I was assigned to do. A person can't be composed on the air unless completely composed at air time.

There was a knock on the door of the booth. A man I'd never seen before said he was Walter Ripperger, a volunteer for the Red Cross blood donor program in Brooklyn. He was ill at ease. He had something more to say and he found it difficult to express it. He went on, by fits and starts, to say the blood donor program was new, that it wasn't well known, that the Red Cross was having trouble getting people to come in and donate blood. Further, he said, most people thought giving a pint of blood was a major operation of sorts and they were afraid; they'd seen too many motion pictures of blood transfusions.

I suppose I'm a slow learner. I stood there listening to Ripperger and wondered what all this had to do with me. This was Opening Day and I was busy.

"All of Brooklyn," the man then said, "will be listening to you this afternoon. Everybody will be listening. Will you tell them about the blood donor center? Tell them something about it? Something of the needs? Say that people aren't coming in to give blood for the armed forces?"

Until that afternoon it was an unwritten law not to say "blood" on the air. It was felt that listeners would be upset—radio was such an intimate force, coming into people's homes at various times, such as when a meal was being served. Speaking of "blood" on the air was taboo.

But Pearl Harbor came to my mind. I remembered the lines of civilian blood donors in Hawaii. The war was mortal. I took Ripperger to see MacPhail, who I knew was in the press club room. "Larry," I said, "this is Walter Ripperger from the Brooklyn blood donor center. He has something to talk to you about."

Ripperger told his story. MacPhail never hesitated. "Hell," he said, "there's a war on."

That was all I needed. The blood donor center gave me their phone number and the schedule of donors needed for the next day. I announced it. Nothing happened except people called in and made appointments. This continued all through the war. We are often afraid of shadows.

This got me into Red Cross work. For the campaigns of 1943-44 and 1944-45 I was fund-raising chairman of Brooklyn, and for 1944-45 also for the entire City of New York. I asked Rickey to head public relations both years in Brooklyn and, busy as he was, he did. And did it well.

Late in March 1945 he and I had attended a lengthy Red Cross meeting in Brooklyn Borough President John Cashmore's office. When you deal with volunteers, most meetings are drawn out. If a volunteer can't talk, what does a volunteer get out of it?

. We went into Joe's Restaurant for something to eat. The place was empty. The lunch hour was over. Rickey led the way to a table in a back corner. There was no one near us. We gave our orders and were left alone. He obviously had something on his mind. He took a hard roll and began breaking it into small pieces as he talked.

"I'm going to tell you something only the board of directors of the Brooklyn ball club and my family know. You will tell your wife, of course, but no one else."

Rickey was a wonderful teller of a tale. He had the voice, the timing, the language, and he always enjoyed building to a dramatic conclusion. He didn't telegraph his punch line.

"In my third year as a student at Ohio Wesleyan University I was also the baseball coach. In the spring 1904, I took my squad down to South Bend, Indiana, for a series with Notre Dame. We were staying at the Oliver Hotel.

"One by one the players came to the desk and signed the register. My catcher, Charley Thomas, the only Negro on the squad, started to register. He was a fine young man, fine family, good student and my best player. As Charley picked up the pen the clerk jerked the register back and said in a loud voice, 'We do not register Negroes here.' I said, 'You don't understand . . . this is the Ohio Wesleyan University baseball team . . . this young man is our catcher . . . we are the guests of the University of Notre Dame.'

"The clerk said, 'I don't care who you are . . . We do not register Negroes at this hotel.' I said, 'Suppose he doesn't register . . . can he sleep in the other bed in my room?' The clerk grudgingly agreed. I handed Charley the key to my room, told him to go there and wait for me . . . that I'd be up just as soon as I got the rest of the team settled."

Rickey had heavy, expressive eyebrows. His hands were gnarled, as you would expect those of a former catcher to be. He broke another roll, raised his eyebrows, and went on.

"When I opened the door I saw Charley. He was sitting on the edge of a chair. He was crying. He was pulling at his hands as though he would tear the very skin off.

"'It's my skin, Mr. Rickey . . . it's my skin! If I could just pull it off I'd be like everybody else . . . It's my skin, Mr. Rickey.'

"That was forty-one years ago," Rickey continued. "And for these forty-one years I have heard that fine young man crying, 'It's my skin, Mr. Rickey . . . If I could just pull it off . . . It's my skin.'

"Now I'm going to do something about it. Mrs. Rickey and my family tell me that I'm too old at sixty-four and that my health is not up to it. They say that I've gone through enough in baseball and from the newspapers. That every hand in baseball will be against me. But I'm going to do it."

He looked me straight in the eyes, fixing my attention.

"I'm going to bring a Negro to the Brooklyn Dodgers."

He didn't ask me to respond. He broke the roll again, dabbed some butter on it, put the broken piece in his mouth. He had told me.

Red Cross was forgotten. He was the president and general manager of the Brooklyn Dodgers. I was the principal announcer with a considerable standing in the area. I was born in Columbus, Mississippi. When I was ten the family moved to Sanford, in central Florida. It was a small town. I saw black men tarred and feathered by the Ku Klux Klan and forced to walk the streets. I had grown up in a completely segregated world and had gone to the University of Florida. In the words of the song in *South Pacific*, "I had been carefully taught."

Organized baseball has its own legal structure, separate from the law of the land. Baseball did not want or intend to have Negroes in it. It was a white man's game except for an occasional Indian or a Cuban. Whenever some writer would press Commissioner Landis as to when a Negro would be allowed to play in organized ball—and rest assured that in the Negro leagues there were many wonderful black players fully capable of playing in the big leagues—the Judge would say, "There is nothing in the laws of baseball that prevents a Negro from playing in it." And he would change the subject or walk away, or both.

All the men in baseball understood the code. A code is harder to break than an actual law. A law is impersonal. Often a man breaks a law, is clever enough to get away with it, and people think he is a smart fellow. But when you break an unwritten law, a code of conduct, you are damned, castigated, banished from the club, so to speak. You are a renegade, a scoundrel, an ingrate, a pariah.

The life and work of an announcer with a ball club is extremely personal, close, intimate. It is on a first-name basis. You travel together, eat together, mix together in the clubhouse, dugout, behind the batting cage, at microphones. Baseball starts the end of February and ends in October. It is a long season. Day after day, night after night. It is a hard season for a small group of men thrown together as defeats occur, as games are won, and as it gets hot or cold or when it rains.

As I sat there, I knew several basic facts: I was white, I was Southern, I was troubled, and above all else I knew that if Mr. Rickey said he was going to bring a Negro to the Brooklyn Dodgers, then by all that was holy he was going to do just that. He went on.

"I've put a team in the Negro leagues called the Brooklyn Brown Dodgers. They will play at Ebbets Field when the regular Dodgers are on the road. I've got my best scouts—Clyde Sukeforth, George Sisler, Wid Mathews, Andy High—combing the Negro leagues, studying the players in the Caribbean league, searching for the best Negro players. They think they are scouting for the Brown Dodgers. They don't know that what they are really searching for is the first black player I can put on the white Dodgers.

"I don't know who he is or where he is. All their reports funnel to me at my office. I study them, narrow them down. I'm doing that now. When the time is ripe for a decision on the one man, I'll make it.

"As I said, I don't know who he is or where he is, but," and he said very slowly, very intently, very positively, "he is coming."

I was on the scene when it was announced that Rickey had signed Jackie Robinson—to be technically correct, had ordered Robinson to go to Montreal, to be actually signed by that farm club. The Dodgers then owned Montreal, so it was merely a matter of how Rickey wanted it done. This meant that Robinson wasn't signed by a big-league team until a year later. In any case, the color line in organized baseball was broken on October 23, 1945, in Montreal.

I was well aware of the storm of criticism that was immediately leveled at Rickey. Judge W. G. Bramham, the commissioner of the minor leagues, accused Rickey "of the carpetbagger stripe of the white race who, under the guise of helping, is in truth using the Negro for their own self-interest, to retard the race." Judge Bramham then warned Father Divine to be alert or there soon would be a Rickey Temple built in Harlem.

Alvin Gardner, president of the Texas League, stated, "I'm positive you'll never see any Negro player on any of the teams in organized baseball in the South as long as the Jim Crow laws are in force."

Rogers Hornsby warned, "Ballplayers on the road live close together. It won't work." Dixie Walker, a Dodgers star, said, "As long as he isn't with the Dodgers, I'm not worried." Bob Feller of the Cleveland Indians, who had played against Robinson in exhibition games, said flatly, "He's tied up in the shoulders . . . he couldn't hit an inside pitch to save his neck . . . if he were a white man I doubt they would even consider him as big-league material." Jimmy Powers, sports editor of the New York *Daily News*, wrote, "He won't make the grade in the big leagues, next year or the next." Powers went on to evaluate Robinson as a thousand-to-one shot.

Red Smith in his New York *Herald Tribune* column was encouraging. So was Dan Parker, sports editor of the New York *Daily Mirror*. Smith and Parker were in the small minority.

Branch Rickey, Jr., in charge of the farm system for the Dodgers, was in Montreal for the actual signing of Robinson. Branch, Jr., spoke for his father as well as for himself. The storm of protest was expected.

"My father and Mr. Racine [president of the Montreal club] are not inviting trouble," young Branch said, "but they won't avoid it if it comes. Jack Robinson is a fine type of young man, intelligent and college-bred, and I think he can make it, too."

Then he got down to the fundamentals.

"Some players, especially from the South," he said, "would steer away from a club with Negro players on its roster. Some of them who are with us now may even quit, but they'll be back in baseball after they work a year or two in a cotton mill."

Branch Rickey had been coming to his decision to break the color line for many years. He had not only set his mind on the decision but he had also ordered his mind to evaluate every step of the way. Yes, Rickey would walk through a 10-foot brick wall, but he would do it with his eyes wide open, dislodging every brick in its proper turn.

Rickey knew his fellow big-league owners would be against him. He knew he would have adverse reaction from every side, from his players, even from his friends. His immediate family had asked him not to take this drastic action. More than anything else, he knew he must not fail with his first Negro player. He must select the one Negro who could do it. Who not only could do it, but would do it.

When Rickey made his decision in principle, he first got the approval of the directors of the Dodgers. They were under orders of absolute silence, as were his family, and after my meeting with him in March 1945, so were Lylah and I. He could not hope to locate the player he sought if there was publicity about it. Publicity would create such controversy that the project would have to be abandoned.

Rickey diverted all attention from his purpose as he had told me he would, by announcing he was about to form a Negro team called the Brooklyn Brown Dodgers, and would even form a new Negro league, and hoped that in the distant years ahead this new Negro league would ultimately be merged into organized baseball. That did it. Nobody paid any further attention to Rickey and Negro baseball.

Rickey's scouts, searching for Negro players, were making written reports on their skills and sending them as usual to Rickey's office at 215 Montague Street, Brooklyn, New York. These scouts were unaware of what they were searching for as they studied players in the established Negro leagues, in Mexico, in Cuba, in Puerto Rico. Rickey's artful cover was never blown. He selected Robinson under the inquisitive noses of the New York press.

Wendell Smith of the Pittsburgh *Courier,* a Negro writer of much ability who had often talked with Rickey and other baseball men about bringing Negro players into the big leagues, told Rickey about the abilities of Jackie Robinson of the Kansas City Monarchs. Rickey had Wid Mathews evaluate Jackie. The report was good. George Sisler was then assigned to Robinson. Another good report. Finally, Clyde Sukeforth was ordered to scout the player. Another sound report. Robinson had outstanding qualities as a ballplayer. But this wasn't nearly enough.

Rickey had thought it through. He knew the first Negro had to be able to succeed not only on the field but off the field—and also in matters over and above hitting, catching and throwing a baseball. Could this first black man hold his temper at the insults, taunts, curses, indignities that would be inevitable? Rickey accepted the judgment of his scouts as to the physical ability of Robinson. His spiritual depth Rickey himself would have to judge.

Before Rickey laid eyes on Robinson he knew much about him. He knew from Mathews, Sisler and Sukeforth that Jackie could play baseball. He began to know more from reports from two other sources: UCLA and the U.S. Army. These reports caused Rickey to do still more thinking.

Robinson at UCLA had been an outstanding athlete—football, basketball, track, and, least of all, baseball. All through his col-

lege years (Robinson lacked a few hours' credit for graduation)
Robinson demanded equality. He would not be demeaned because of his race. He was to be treated equally. At UCLA he
was more than able to make his stand stick. Had he been white,
the report Rickey got would have said Robinson was "extremely
competitive." As it was the report indicated he was "a racial agi-
tator."

This report told Rickey that Robinson was strong of spirit, as
Rickey knew the first black player would have to be. A black
man who was an Uncle Tom couldn't do it. A black man who
was bowing and scraping and saying "Yas suh, boss" couldn't do
it. But could such a strong-spirited man control himself in the
serious struggle of breaking the color line?

The reports of Robinson in the Army were more disturbing.
Robinson discovered in 1943 that the Army then was Jim Crow.
He fought against being segregated, and when he became a
second lieutenant—after officer candidate school—and had command of black soldiers, he fought for them. He was soon embroiled with various white officers, some from the South. Jackie
was first sent to Fort Riley, Kansas, and then to Fort Hood,
Texas. He refused to move to the back of a Texas bus, and this
incident led to a court martial. (In his book *I Never Had It
Made,* Jackie details this over a dozen pages.)

Jackie was cleared in the court martial but he was now a
marked man. He was not "competitive," he was "an uppity
nigger." And to put the Army chain of command in full rage,
Jackie had had enough of the Army by then and wrote the Adju-
tant General himself, bypassing all the brass he was expected to
go through. He told his story so well he was given an honorable
discharge.

It was now up to Rickey. He alone must make the judgment.
He alone must do the testing of the man Robinson. Would he be
the man? Rickey sent Clyde Sukeforth to Chicago, where the
Kansas City Monarchs were playing, with orders to bring Robinson to Brooklyn for a personal interview.

It happened that Robinson had a bad shoulder and wouldn't
be playing for a week, so he was free to come to Brooklyn with
Sukeforth. But Robinson wasn't too eager to go East to meet
Rickey. All that Sukeforth could say to Jackie was, "Mr. Rickey

wants to see you . . . you know he is thinking about a new team, the Brooklyn Brown Dodgers."

That's all Sukeforth knew to tell him. Jackie had had a sour experience with people in the big leagues. Early in 1945 Wendell Smith had arranged for the Boston Red Sox to give three Negro players—Sam Jethroe, Marvin Williams and Jackie—a "tryout" at Fenway Park. The Red Sox were forced into this by a threat from a politician to get a bill passed banning Sunday ball games in Boston unless Negroes were given a chance. The Red Sox let the three hit, run and field, had them fill out cards of application, and then never contacted the three again. They'd had their "chance."

Sukeforth insisted that Mr. Rickey really wanted to see Jackie Robinson. Jackie went with Sukeforth on the train to New York. Sukeforth went to a hotel in Brooklyn, Jackie to the Theresa Hotel in Harlem. When it was time for Jackie to go to Brooklyn he told some friends to wait for him, that he was going to see how much Branch Rickey would pay him to play for the Brown Dodgers, and that it wouldn't take long. It took longer than anyone except Rickey expected.

Sukeforth introduced Robinson to Rickey. The rest of the meeting was between the two principals. Rickey had prepared for this meeting all the years since he found Charley Thomas in South Bend, Indiana, crying and pulling at his hands, saying, "It's my skin, Mr. Rickey . . . it's my skin! If I could just pull it off I'd be like everybody else . . ." Rickey had even placed a book in a desk drawer with a passage marked. In case.

I know about this meeting from both Rickey and Robinson in person, and from their books. This meeting was when the color line was broken, not when Robinson was signed at Montreal, not when he was put on the Brooklyn roster, not when he began playing for the Dodgers. This was it. Robinson walked into Rickey's office with two spiritual strikes against him—UCLA and the U.S. Army—yet with the vital third strike unspent. Robinson came to the meeting aggressive, suspicious, almost hostile—Larry MacPhail would have been embroiled with Robinson in a very few minutes.

Rickey broke the ice with a question. "Do you have a girl?" Jackie was taken by surprise. What sort of a question was this?

He didn't know then that Rickey always asked this of young players he first talked to. Rickey well knew the temptations of ballplayers on the road. He believed in married men. He wanted all his players to be married and settled down.

Rickey got Jackie to tell him about Rachel, his girl in California . . . of their plans to get married . . . their hopes. (Rachel, the girl he did marry.)

This pleased Rickey. Then he said:

"When we get through today you may want to call her because there are times when a man needs a woman by his side." Then he said, "The truth is, you are not a candidate for the Brooklyn Brown Dodgers. I've sent for you because I'm interested in you as a candidate for the Brooklyn National League club. I think you can play in the major leagues. How do you feel about it?"

Before Jackie could frame a reply, Rickey demanded, "Do you think you can play for Montreal?"

Jackie answered, "Yes."

The stage lost an actor of consummate skill and range when Rickey cast his lot with baseball. He had the commanding presence—rugged face . . . heavy, mobile eyebrows that responded to his change of mood . . . dark, penetrating eyes. He used an unlighted cigar as an actor would a stage prop. He knew when to run a gnarled hand through his still-thick hair. His voice was strong, resonant, and flexible as though it came from a pipe organ. He could whisper, he could expel intensity with his words, and he could reach a vocal crescendo of dramatic power. He had complete command of the language. He didn't talk like anybody you'd ever talked with. He was a formidable man, a strong man, an intelligent man. And he knew it.

He had put Robinson at ease, then had shaken him. He had Robinson's complete attention. It was as though the overture had been played. Now the curtain was rising on the stark drama of two powerful men who had to work out their roles against each other, against an ominous future of trouble, resistance and uncertainty.

Rickey went to work. He had to probe, test, assay. Maybe Robinson was not the man spiritually to undertake this assignment. He had to feel his way step by step. He had to evaluate

Robinson's every reaction. Was this the man morally? Could this man handle not only himself but his people, his race? Could this man endure, day after day, night after night? If he succeeded at first, could he handle the adulation of the black people who'd be wildly excited? Could he take the abuse certain to come, abuse of words, abuse of actions not only from opposing players but from his own teammates? Rickey had to dig deeply into Robinson. He had to decide. He had to have a man who would not fail.

"I know you're a good ballplayer," Rickey said in a deadly serious voice. "My scouts have told me this. What I don't know is whether you have the guts."

Robinson almost came out of his chair. Rickey had, in effect, implied that he was a coward. All his life Jackie had fought for what he thought he should, and no one had called him a coward, no one, and gotten away with it. Rickey told me later that Robinson was the most competitive man he'd known since Ty Cobb—instantly violent by natural disposition, immediately ready to counterattack, relishing physical involvement and capable of dealing physically with anyone he encountered. Before Jackie could react, Rickey said:

"Have you got the guts to play the game no matter what happens?"

Let me set down here what Robinson said about the next few minutes. He wrote it in his final book. It made a lasting impression.

"He had me transfixed as he spoke. I could feel his sincerity, and I began to get a sense of how much this major step meant to him. Because of his nature, and his passion for justice, he had to do what he was doing. He continued. The rumbling voice, the theatrical gestures, were gone. He was speaking from a deep, quiet strength.

"'So there's more than just playing,' he said. 'I wish it meant only hits, runs and errors—only the things they put in the box score. Because you know—yes, you would know, Robinson—that a baseball box score is a democratic thing. It doesn't tell how big you are, what church you attend, what color you are, or how your father voted in the last election. It just tells what kind of baseball player you were on that particular day.'

"I interrupted. 'But it's the box score that really counts—that and that alone, isn't it?'

"'It's all that ought to count,' he replied. 'But it isn't. Maybe one of these days it *will* be all that counts. That is one of the reasons I've got you here, Robinson. If you're a good enough man, we can make this a start in the right direction. But let me tell you, it's going to take an awful lot of courage.'"

As Robinson said in his book, Rickey now had him transfixed. If ever a man knew baseball—as player, manager, general manager, club president—it was Rickey. He knew this land and the people who lived in it. He had no illusions. He was intelligent, and intelligently vocal. He got on his feet, moved out from behind his desk.

The meeting, according to Rickey in his book *The American Diamond*, lasted three hours. Most of the time was spent as Rickey took Robinson through every situation that would confront him if he tried to be the first black player. Rickey took him into Jim Crow dining cars, segregated hotels and restaurants, living apart from the team in St. Louis and all over the South . . . what his wife would hear in the stands . . . what he would hear on the field.

Rickey took Robinson into the batter's box where he would have his head thrown at. Rickey, who never used profanity, came close to Robinson's face and spit out at him every curse and obscenity he would hear. He said, "Suppose a player comes down from first base—you are the shortstop—the player slides, spikes high, and cuts you on the leg. As you feel the blood running down your leg, the white player laughs in your face, and sneers, 'How do you like that, nigger boy?'"

Robinson said, "Mr. Rickey, are you looking for a Negro who is afraid to fight back?"

"Robinson," he almost exploded when he answered, "I'm looking for a ballplayer with guts enough *not* to fight back!"

Rickey had made his decision. This was the man, *if*. He reached into the desk drawer where he had placed the book, and opened it to the passage he had carefully marked. The book was *The Life of Christ* by Giovanni Papini. The chapter was on nonresistance. Before Rickey began reading, he said:

"There is only one way you can be the first Negro to break the color line. Only one way. You can't retaliate. You can't answer a blow with a blow. You can't echo a curse with a curse."

Then, his voice low, strong, intense, he read slowly:

"'Ye have heard that it hath been said, An eye for an eye, and a tooth for a tooth: But I say unto you, That ye resist not evil: But whosoever shall smite thee on the right cheek, turn to him the other also. . . .' For an infinite number of believers this principle of not resisting evil has been the unendurable and unacceptable scandal of Christianity. There are three answers which men can make to violence: revenge, flight, turning the other cheek. The first is the barbarous principle of retaliation. . . . Flight is no better than retaliation . . . the man who takes flight invites pursuit . . . his weakness becomes the accomplice of the ferocity of others. . . . Turning the other cheek means not receiving the second blow. It means cutting the chain of inevitable wrongs at the first link. Your adversary is ready for anything but this. . . . Every man has an obscure respect for courage in others, especially if it is moral courage, the rarest and most difficult sort of bravery. . . . It makes the very brute understand that this man is more than a man. . . . Man is a fighting animal, but with no resistance offered, the pleasure disappears; there is no zest left. . . . And yet the results of nonresistance, even if they are not always perfect, are certainly superior to those of resistance or flight. . . . To answer blows with blows, evil deeds with evil deeds, is to meet the attacker on his own ground, to proclaim oneself as low as he. . . . Only he who has conquered himself can conquer his enemies."

Rickey laid the book upon his desk. He looked into Robinson's eyes. This is what he said:

"Can you do it? You will have to promise me that for your first three years in baseball, you will turn your other cheek. I know you are naturally combative. But for three years . . . three years . . . you will have to do it the only way it can be done. Three years. Can you do it?"

Robinson looked straight back into Rickey's eyes. He answered softly.

"Mr. Rickey," he said, "I've got to do it."

I've heard Rickey say, "For three years—that was the agreement—this man was to turn the other cheek. He did, day after day, until he had no other to turn. They were both beat off. . . . No one knows the trials and tribulations of Robinson during those three years. Jackie's wife, Rachel, knows most about them. She was Jackie's tower to lean on and constant guidepost, too. She was a great help. The first contribution of Jackie Robinson, so well known to Rachel and a few others, that qualified him for greatness was the self-imposed restraint in order to preserve and advance healthy race relations under terrifically trying circumstances. . . . Negro Americans should feel and show only quiet gratitude for the load this fellow citizen carried for their sake."

I was the announcer at Brooklyn when Jackie came in 1947. I stayed until 1954 when I went over to Yankee Stadium. In those seven years I saw a lot of Jackie. We talked together easily and often. We traveled together. We had meals together. He told me repeatedly, "This guy said this . . . this fellow did that . . . and I almost felt like laughing, because that is exactly how Mr. Rickey said it would be. I haven't experienced a thing Mr. Rickey didn't tell me I would."

BEFORE THE MIRROR

Make no mistake, when Rickey told me in March 1945, at Joe's Restaurant in Brooklyn, that he was going to—not thinking of doing, not doing it perhaps or if the pieces came together—but that he was going to bring a Negro player to the Brooklyn Dodgers, it gave me serious trouble. Jackie Robinson's coming to the Dodgers didn't bother me at all. By the time Jackie was selected by Rickey later that year I had found personal peace. I hadn't found it so much as that I had heard a voice from the grave.

When Rickey bound me to secrecy, except for my wife, and said he was going to break the color line as soon as he found the right black player, I was stunned. I had been born in Mississippi, raised in central Florida, was white and had been taught a strict code of relationships with Negro people. I went home, told Lylah, and blurted, "I'm going to quit." I didn't think I could have the close, intimate associations I had to have with ball-players if one of them—or more than one—was going to be black. I had made no response to Rickey at Joe's. I had gone to the subway, gotten off at Grand Central Station, caught a commuting train for Scarsdale, and walked into the house.

When I said I was going to quit, Lylah, being a very wise woman, said, "You don't have to quit tonight. You can do that tomorrow. . . . Let's have a martini."

I began thinking. There is a force on this earth called economic determinism. That force whispered to me that at Brooklyn I had the best sports announcing job not only in the country, but in the world. I had it. I not only had it, I had helped create it. If I threw it away, what would I do?

I didn't quit. I didn't say anything about it to either Rickey or Lylah. I started looking into myself. I had time. Rickey had given me time. There was no hurry, but I knew I had to come to a decision of what to think and what to do.

I made myself realize that I had had no choice in the parents I was born to, no choice in the place of my birth or the time of it. I was born white just as a Negro was born black. I had been given a fortunate set of circumstances, none of which I had done anything to merit, and therefore I had best be careful about being puffed up over my color. Chance, sheer chance.

Then I began to ask myself who I was and what my work was. I wasn't Branch Rickey; his problems and decisions weren't mine. I wasn't a sociologist—I wasn't a racist—I wasn't a player on the team who would use the clubhouse with a black player, play alongside him, travel with him. I wasn't the manager—I wasn't a fan—I wasn't any of these people, and I didn't have any of their problems. And I certainly wasn't the black player, whoever he would be when Rickey decided he was the one. Who then was I? What was my work? How would I handle what was coming?

There is a sentence in The Book of Common Prayer, ". . . and hast opened the eyes of the mind to behold things invisible and unseen." In my situation it was more an opening of the ears of the mind. I heard a voice from a grave in Indiana. I heard a voice that had been silent on earth for over a year. I heard the voice of that white-haired, slender man with the sharp features, standing in the room in Detroit before the first game of the 1935 World Series. I heard Judge Landis say:

"You are not to manage . . . you are not to play . . . you are not to umpire . . . you are to report. Report everything you can see, but leave your opinions in your hotel room. Report."

Peace, when it comes, is blessed. I heard that word, "Report" and peace came. I knew who I was and what I was to do and how I was to do it.

I knew millions were listening to my Southern voice. I knew they were listening for what I said as well as for what I didn't say. But it was easy. There was no trouble. I got no complaints. I reported what Robinson did as a ballplayer. That was all there was to it. I reported him as I would any other player. That was all the public wanted, all Rickey wanted and all Robinson wanted. Robinson did the ballplaying. I discussed this with my associate announcer, Connie Desmond. Connie and I reported. So did Ernie Harwell, and then Vin Scully when they joined us.

Rickey—and Lylah—gave me time to think. Landis spoke to me again.

Happy Chandler

It was as inevitable as a Greek tragedy.

Judge Landis died November 25, 1944. There were then sixteen major-league teams. The owners began informally discussing various men to succeed Landis. The war was soon to be over, the owners were in no hurry, there was nothing of a major nature to be decided, and the owners, I suspect, enjoyed their tight little club that permitted them their behind-the-scenes maneuvering. Among the men most prominently mentioned were Thomas E. Dewey, James J. Farley, J. Edgar Hoover, Ford C. Frick and Albert B. Chandler.

I don't believe any formal records exist about who was pushing whom for baseball's second Commissioner. MacPhail got into the action as soon as 1945 began when he, Topping and Webb got the Yankees. Anything that MacPhail went into, he wanted to win. He wanted his way.

The owners didn't know who they wanted but they knew one thing: they were never again going to have a Commissioner with the absolute power that Landis had demanded, gotten and retained for a quarter of a century. The owners were now free. The czar was dead.

I would think Tom Dewey was never a serious consideration for two reasons: one, he didn't project to the public as a warm personality, and second, Dewey would have demanded more authority than the owners were now willing to give. Baseball was in no trouble; in fact, it was ready to enter a boom period as soon as the war could be tidied up. I never heard that J. Edgar Hoover even entertained the idea of leaving the FBI, and he too would have been a man of too much strength.

Jim Farley or Ford Frick would have been ideal as Commissioner. Farley had played first base as a young man at Haverstraw, New York, just up the Hudson River. Farley had for years been a staunch Yankee fan with a box on the first-base side. He was often at Yankee Stadium. He knew all the sportswriters and they knew him. Farley was the political force behind F.D.R. in his first election, and was made postmaster general. Farley knew the game, knew how to get along with men of all persuasions, knew the pulse of the public. He had an impressive appearance. He would have given dignity and ability to the office, and would have made no mistakes.

A major-league meeting was set for April 1945, to elect the new Commissioner. I'm certain there is no record anywhere of what transpired. However, Arthur Mann was then assistant to Rickey, and Harold Parrott was road secretary for the Dodgers. Both told me—and they must have gotten their information from Rickey, who was in the meeting—that "someone" (apparently Rickey didn't name him) read a terribly damaging report on Farley. When he was challenged to prove it, he wilted, took it back, disclaimed it—but the damage had been fatal to Farley's chances.

There never was any secrecy about the next two names. Rickey had openly been a supporter of Ford Frick, longtime president of the National League. Frick knew baseball, got along with the owners he dealt with, had public charm and smoothness, had been a sportswriter and radio announcer, and rocked no boats. Frick had developed the idea for the Hall of Fame at Cooperstown. He would have been just the man to transfer baseball from the Landis iron rule into the era of the owners taking back power. (Frick in 1951 succeeded Chandler, to keep the record straight.)

But Frick, despite his well-nigh perfect credentials, had a serious stumbling block: Larry MacPhail. MacPhail and Frick had differed hotly over the repeated rhubarbs Leo Durocher had had with Frick's umpires. Frick warned Leo many times—sometimes fined him—and always got back a blast from MacPhail. Durocher's pitchers were accused of throwing at opposing batters. Frick warned Leo about this, threatening fines, and MacPhail told the press that Leo was to continue doing what he thought his pitchers should do, and to do so no matter what Frick said. MacPhail coupled Frick with all the people against Durocher and the Dodgers. Further, Frick was Rickey's man, and this was MacPhail's first joust with Rickey since MacPhail returned to baseball.

MacPhail's smoldering anger at Frick didn't cool during the war years he was away. I don't know when or where MacPhail met Chandler—maybe when MacPhail was stationed in Washington and Chandler was a U.S. Senator from Kentucky. Anyhow, MacPhail led the opposition to Frick. MacPhail was a formidable opponent. Finally MacPhail persuaded the owners, by now tired of the whole thing, to vote for Chandler. There has never been any doubt but that MacPhail was the key to Chandler's election.

This has a decided bearing on the events of 1947.

Branch Rickey, Larry MacPhail, Judge Landis, Ford Frick are dead. A. B. "Happy" Chandler is very much alive in his home town of Versailles, Kentucky. He is an easy man to talk to, and when you talk with him, he'll tell you exactly how he sees it. He always "let it all hang out," which the New York writers just didn't understand after the cold reserve of Landis. Even the nickname "Happy" somehow upset the eastern writers. The baseball writers in New York never liked Chandler from the moment they met him. Some of the owners soon felt the same way.

Albert Benjamin Chandler had to scramble all the way. When he was four his mother left his dad. His father raised him, and the two survived as his dad did a series of odd jobs in Corydon, Kentucky, where Chandler was born. Chandler went to Transylvania College, where he worked his way through school. He did the same for a while at Harvard, and then at the University of Kentucky, where he got his law degree in 1924.

He was an all-around athlete. At Transylvania he pitched, and is proud to this day of beating the University of Tennessee 10–4. He still has the game ball in his study. He pitched professionally for a year at Grafton, North Dakota, in the Red River Valley

League, and won 12 out of 13 games. He did some umpiring in the minor leagues.

Chandler knew baseball and beyond question loved it. He loved the players and he loved the umpires. He knew how it was down below. He got to know "Uncle" Charley Moran when Moran was football coach at Centre College of Kentucky—the team that once upset mighty Harvard. Moran went on to umpire in the National League for twenty-two years. Much of Moran rubbed off on Chandler.

Chandler got into politics when he became lieutenant governor of Kentucky in 1931. He went on to the governorship in 1935. He resigned this post to become a U.S. Senator in 1939. He was in the Senate when the baseball owners elected him to follow Landis. However, before he would resign his Senate seat he required the owners to sign a document pledging themselves "to loyally support the Commissioner" even when they believed him mistaken, and not to criticize him or each other.

That document was like a lot of treaties between nations—not worth the paper it was written on.

Chandler had a broad Southern speech pattern. He had a wide smile with flashing white teeth, really beautiful teeth. If he'd waited for television he could have made a fortune selling toothpaste. He got the name "Happy" because he smiled constantly and looked happy. The name fit him. I was about the only one around him who didn't call him "Happy"—I called him either Senator or Commissioner.

Chandler was immediately ridiculed by the New York writers because he often said, "Ah love baseball"—that was the way he talked. I didn't need an interpreter to understand him; I had pretty much the same Southern background he had. Also, I remembered that MacPhail had been criticized by the New York writers when he brought me to broadcast at Brooklyn in 1939—they said, even before I got to a microphone, that I was Southern and my accent would never get by in Brooklyn or in New York. H. Allen Smith wrote in one of his books that I was a famous man in baseball because I "further polluted the most polluted speech in the world—Brooklynese."

Chandler was blessed with a clear, rich tenor. He loved to sing but when, as the new Commissioner of Baseball, he sang

"My Old Kentucky Home" for the New York writers, it was as though a grave act of desecration had been done.

Chandler took the commissionership seriously. He expected to run things the way Landis had; in that he meant to run the game for the fans, for the players, for the umpires and then for the owners. He told the owners this after he took office, and they didn't exactly like it. It was Chandler who supported the players' pension fund with the bulk of World Series television receipts, which many owners resented. Chandler fought for better pay for the umpires, and even tried to bring all the umpires under his control instead of having National League umpires and American League umpires, with their different loyalties and differences in making certain decisions. The two league presidents hit the ceiling. (In professional football, all the officials are controlled by the NFL Commissioner, and always have been.)

Chandler didn't want players covered up more than the rules permitted. He didn't want high school boys signed before their graduations. He fined a few clubs, and he made free agents of some players, and in so doing he made fresh enemies, especially Del Webb of the Yankees and Lou Perini of the then Boston Braves.

Chandler went to work as hard as he knew how to be Commissioner of Baseball. He took the job seriously. But his outgoing personality, speech, action and laughter didn't sit well in New York. Then too, I thought then and I still think that Chandler made a serious mistake in establishing the office of Commissioner in Cincinnati, some hundred miles from his home in Versailles, Kentucky.

Cincinnati was the smallest town in the big leagues. It was a National League town. No American League teams went there, and thus no American League writers. In the minds of the baseball world, Chandler was immediately isolated from half of the big leagues. By having his office in Cincinnati, he was isolated from New York City with its three teams, big buildings and the metropolitan press. Landis had had both leagues in Chicago, a major city in its own right, and his distance from the New York press added to the remoteness he intended to have and did have all his years in office.

When Chandler came to New York for a World Series it was

almost as though a stranger had arrived and was taking over. Ford Frick, the National League president who had been passed over in favor of Chandler, had his office in Rockefeller Center, and every day had luncheon at Toots Shor's. Frick always had the front table on the left as you entered. It was in effect "his" table and he was always available for talk, stories, food and drink. Chandler was absent.

I have wondered what might have been had Chandler set up shop in New York and been frequently in the places where the writers and broadcasters and well-known people were. Chandler had a wonderfully warm personality when you understood it. Would his being around Toots Shor's have gotten Toots on his side? Would he have charmed the writers, and would they have found him a constant source of stories? As I know the writers, had Chandler been around them some would have remained critics, like, say, Jimmy Powers, who made a campaign of calling Branch Rickey El Cheapo. Other writers would have taken Chandler's side merely to have something to write about. Writers love to write against other writers. Material is hard to come by, day by day.

But Chandler gave the New York writers little opportunity to know him, to be around him, or to hear from him his side of it. Maybe it wouldn't have changed a thing had he been in New York instead of Cincinnati, but I wonder. When you look back, do things change or do they grind themselves out until nothing is left to be ground?

As I said, Chandler is alive. He gave a most penetrating insight into his mistake in taking the commissionership in the first place, and in his early relations with the New York press, in an article in *Sports Illustrated* April 26, 1971, written by John Underwood. Let me excerpt some of it:

"Under normal circumstances a politician who engages in a contest he cannot win is no politician and deserves what fate leaves him. In the spring of 1945 I accepted the high commissionership of major league baseball. Two factors contributed to this lack of sanity: 1) I thought of the position as nonpolitical and myself as a qualified candidate, more qualified, in fact, than the man who preceded me (later I was to include, especially, those who succeeded me); and 2) it paid $50,000 a year to start.

I was making $10,000 as a United States Senator from Kentucky and losing the battle then common to Senators who tried to maintain separate residences in Washington and their home state."

This is how he began his interview with Underwood. Later in the article Chandler is most perceptive about his beginnings in New York, the comparison between himself and Judge Landis, and the breaking of the color line:

". . . Jackie Robinson came into baseball in 1947 as the first black major-leaguer in modern times. Many of the owners didn't want the change.

"I wasn't asked for a decision, so I never gave one. The dissenters had to think they were on firm ground because Judge Landis had been in office 24 years and never lifted a finger for black players. He always said, 'The owners have the right to hire whom they please.'

"Obviously Branch Rickey, part owner and general manager of the Brooklyn Dodgers, thought so, too. He came to see me at my home in Versailles. . . . He may already have made up his mind. He said, 'I can't bring Robinson in unless you back me.'

" 'Can Robinson play baseball?' I asked.

" 'No question about that.'

" 'Is he a major-leaguer?'

" 'Yes, sir.'

" 'Then bring him on.' The die was cast, and baseball changed forever and for the good.

"Rickey said, 'Well, how shall we treat him?'

" 'Just like any other player. No better or no worse.' "

After a few paragraphs about Robinson as a player, and about his disposition, and a run-in Robinson had with World Series umpire Cal Hubbard over a called strike, Chandler said:

"I do not mean this account of the integration of baseball as a criticism of Judge Landis for not having ordered it before. The owners simply didn't want it, and Landis washed his hands. If he did nothing to help the Negro, it could be argued that neither did he do much to assure high school coaches that their kids would not be raided or to improve the sorry conditions the umpires worked under in those days or help to introduce a pension or raise the players' salaries. Judge Landis was, nevertheless, good for baseball at a critical time in its existence and stands almost unchallenged as the most respected executive in the history of the game. The fact that he was mostly a myth does not alter that."

No matter how hard the owners looked in early 1945, they could not have found a man for Commissioner who was more different from Landis than was Happy Chandler: background, appearance, disposition, lifestyle, speech patterns. Landis liked a drink of whiskey and smoked cigarettes incessantly. Chandler drank milk and didn't smoke. As I think about it, Chandler shook up baseball just about the way Jimmy Carter did Washington. From the start of both Chandler's and Carter's terms in office it was an adversary relationship with the press. The speech that was indigenous to Kentucky and to Georgia was foreign in the North.

Chandler was constantly being compared with Landis. He was goaded into the major decision he made in the Durocher case, I think, because it was said over and over that Chandler wasn't tough enough—certainly not as tough as the old Judge would have been.

In the *Sports Illustrated* article, April 1971, Chandler went on to add it up as he saw it, looking back over some twenty-five years. He told John Underwood:

"I knew Landis well. He was always very friendly to me, and he wasn't a naturally friendly fellow. After the Black Sox scandal of 1919 he was hired to look mean, and he played the part. He didn't go to many ball games, but when he did cameramen always caught him in the same posture, his fist under his chin, his white hair ruffled and flying, his face a deep scowl. I don't know what he saw at a game because I'm not sure that he knew much about it. He might have been sitting there just puzzling.

"Landis was once a federal judge in Chicago and had a reputation for taking on the big shots. In every respect he was what he did not find others to be—an honest man—and I think he did the best he could to shore up confidence in the game. But picture him and imagine me, a man named 'Happy,' succeeding him. Happy does not frown. He smiles. He does not try to look mean. He laughs. Worse, not long after he became Commissioner, it was discovered that Albert Benjamin (Happy)

Chandler sang. This happened at a banquet in my honor in Newark, N.J. I spoke of my beloved Kentucky, the good fishing, the barefoot days at school, my career as a minor-league ballplayer and as an umpire in the old Blue Grass League, and of my family and my home. Then, on an impulse, I said I would wind up the dinner with a song. I have always loved to sing, and I have sung on the campaign trails, often accompanied by the beautiful soprano Mrs. Mildred Chandler. My choice that night was 'My Old Kentucky Home.'

"Can you see the effect of that on the assembled New York writers that night in 1945—the Red Smiths and Arthur Daleys and Dan Parkers, that sharp-eyed group? It was immediately evident that I was a Southern country fellow, and New York writers look down their noses at Southern country fellows. New York writers know, of course, that milk comes from wagons and that anything west of the Alleghenies is Indian territory and that only a clown would sing at his inauguration. Can you imagine Judge Landis doing such a thing?

"They never let me forget it. They called me 'Sappy' and 'Playboy,' and when I said I loved baseball they saw fit to ridicule that, too, and when I had to chasten some of their heroes, people like Del Webb and Leo Durocher, they never failed to take their side. But I don't embarrass easily. If you are sober and diligent and forthright, there is no reason to be embarrassed. The record will show that the reflection was on them. And I know—now—that they just didn't understand country boys."

Chandler gave the New York press grist for their mills over and above singing and spouting what they called "platitudes." There was the matter in 1942 of a swimming pool built at his home in Versailles by a Louisville contractor, and Chandler was supposed not to have paid for it. The Truman Committee did an investigation because the pool was supposedly in return for favors done in securing war contracts. Chandler told the Committee the pool "was a gift built in the name of friendship and accepted in the same spirit." The writers, especially Dan Parker, sports editor of the New York *Daily Mirror,* never let the pool story run dry.

Too, Chandler was vigorous in keeping gambling out of baseball. He knew that was of tremendous importance. Rickey at

Brooklyn had stopped gambling of all kinds on the Dodgers, and forbidden gamblers the clubhouse. However, without thinking too deeply Chandler and his wife attended the Kentucky Derby. The Derby is the pride of Kentucky. Chandler as governor had annually presented the winning trophy. But when the picture of Baseball Commissioner Chandler and his wife at the Derby hit the papers, the writers were off and running again. There is betting at Churchill Downs.

There is quite a parallel between Happy Chandler and Jimmy Carter. Both are good men. Both meant well. But the men and the jobs and the times didn't blend. The tide began changing in 1982 for Jimmy Carter, bringing him more appreciation. For Happy Chandler it was also a very good year—the Veterans' Committee elected him to the Hall of Fame at Cooperstown to take his proud position with Judge Landis, Branch Rickey, Larry MacPhail, Ford Frick and the other great men in baseball.

A STORM IS COMING FROM
THE BRONX

MacPhail was back in baseball by the beginning of 1945. He was president and part owner of the Yankees. He had his first skirmish with Branch Rickey over the election of Happy Chandler. Rickey had favored Ford Frick.

Shortly after Chandler became Commissioner, MacPhail gave him an afternoon press party in New York. I recall visiting briefly with Chandler, and I recall, too, that he was asked to sing, and did. His voice was good, Stephen Foster wrote beautiful words and music, but the writers sort of stood around. The song was not wildly received.

Then MacPhail took me aside and said, "I want to see you in my office as soon as possible. It is important."

"Larry," I told him, "I don't know when I can get there. My dad is dying down in North Carolina and every day the Dodgers don't play I go to see him."

Dad died the twenty-eighth of June, and shortly thereafter I went to see MacPhail in the Fifth Avenue offices of the Yankees. I didn't know then but this was another shot MacPhail fired at Rickey.

MacPhail was in his shirt sleeves. He always wore expensive clothes and wore them well. He lighted a cigarette.

"Now," he said, "here's why I wanted to see you: I'm offering you $100,000 for the next three years to broadcast the Yankee games. That's $100,000 guaranteed by me. I'll worry about selling the games to sponsors. But sponsors or not, it's $100,000 firm.

"Before you say anything," MacPhail went on, "I have told Horace Stoneham (New York Giants) that next year I will not share the broadcast with him . . . that I am going to have my own broadcast, home and away. And starting next year all the Yankee games will be broadcast live, no matter where they are played—no more Western Union re-creations. The announcers will travel with the team." (Another MacPhail first.)

"Larry," I said, "thank you very much. This is some offer, but I'm under contract to do the Dodgers the rest of the year. I can't give you an answer now. I've got to tell Rickey of your offer."

"I expected you to say that. Of course," he said, "you should tell Rickey. Go tell him."

And he paused, then said, "I'm not overly fond of Rickey, but I'll say this—once he makes up his mind, he'll walk through a ten-foot brick wall."

When MacPhail said, "I'm not overly fond of Rickey" I heard it and I have remembered it. When a man offers you what he offered me you remember every word he said. Or you should. But that day I didn't realize what MacPhail was really saying. I had no idea the dead aim he was taking at Rickey, or how hot were the inner, smoldering coals.

Let me explain something: until MacPhail offered me the Yankee job, to my knowledge no announcer had been under contract to a baseball club. We all worked for radio stations or for sponsors. When I went to Cincinnati I did not work for MacPhail. I was on the staff of the Crosley Radio Corporation. When I wasn't doing a baseball game I was doing studio programs or football or special news events. During the winters I had a regular announce shift—sometimes I got up at 4:30 in the morning to sign WLW on. Then again, I might draw the night shift and get home around 2 A.M. I didn't work for the ball club although Crosley owned the team.

MacPhail had stipulated that I come to Brooklyn in 1939, but when I came I was under contract to Knox Reeves, the advertising agency for Wheaties. Two years later Wheaties dropped out and Old Gold cigarettes came in. I went under contract first to J. Walter Thompson and then to Lennen and Mitchell, advertising agencies for Old Gold. I wasn't under contract or obligated in any way to the Dodgers.

MacPhail was again breaking new ground.

When I walked out of MacPhail's office I was so elated I could have stepped on eggs and not broken any of them. I was almost floating. A guaranteed $100,000 for three years. Yankee Stadium, the American League, no more Western Union re-creations but traveling with the team and doing the games as I saw them played.

Also—and this was the biggest reason for my elation; something MacPhail didn't know about, something Rickey didn't know about—Ray Vir Din of the Lennen and Mitchell agency had told me that I could not expect to make any more money doing the games for Old Gold cigarettes; that I was at my peak and this came from Bert Kent, the president of Lorillard. I was thirty-seven and I wasn't willing to have a lid placed on my advancement. MacPhail had shown me a new land with new rewards.

I went first to Vir Din because he held my contract. I told him of the offer by MacPhail. Vir Din coldly told me that what he had already said about my not getting any more money stood. I went next to see Bert Kent and told him of the offer; he reminded me that he had already notified me I was getting all I was ever going to get from him, and that was firm. As a courtesy I then went to Rickey.

I told Rickey of MacPhail's offer and his expectancy that I would tell him of it. I told him of Vir Din's reaction and that of Kent. I told him I felt the Yankee job was too good in every way not to take it. Further, I told him I had come to see him not to involve him, but as a personal courtesy. I said that now that I had notified the advertising agency, the sponsor and now him, I had touched all the proper bases.

Rickey listened without saying a word. He let me finish.

"Walter," he said as he laid aside the cigar he had been chewing, "I completely understand your position. I well understand that this offer from MacPhail at the Yankees would be irresistible to you. You worked with MacPhail in Cincinnati, and he brought you here. The two of you have worked well together, and there is no reason you would not work well in Yankee Stadium.

"Ray Vir Din and Bert Kent have been hard on you, harder

than they should have been. You have gone as far with them as you can. You have handled yourself openly, honestly and with dignity.

"I know you have not come to me in a effort to negotiate anything. I know when a man walks through the door if he comes hunting a bargain. You have not. I must leave in a few minutes for the airport for an important meeting which has been scheduled for a considerable time." He came straight to the point.

"When I was at St. Louis the contract of the announcer rested with the sponsor. It has been the same here. The Brooklyn club has been in the position of accepting whoever the sponsor delivered. That has been most satisfactory in your case. But now that you are preparing to leave, it becomes the proper business of both the Brooklyn baseball club and myself to secure the announcer of our choice. I won't try to mince words. You are most valuable and important here.

"I must go to the airport. Does the friendship that lies between us, does the work you have done here in Brooklyn, civic as well as announcing the games, does any of that mean enough for you to keep an open mind on your decision for three days, until I can return and make you a counteroffer? Will you delay your answer to MacPhail until I can see you Monday morning?"

I said I would do the best I could to keep an open mind. But when I got home and told Lylah, we celebrated. I was going to Yankee Stadium.

Over the weekend the Dodgers were playing at Ebbets Field. As I walked the streets from the subway station to the ball park, as I went into the park, I felt the warm friendship of Brooklyn. I remembered the reaction of the Brooklyn people who made their appointments to give blood to the Red Cross. The broadcasting booth was familiar and it was mine. I had built something alive and vigorous. I was the first play-by-play announcer in Brooklyn. True, MacPhail had brought me, but when it was time to turn the microphones on, I had done it. Brooklyn had responded happily, almost overwhelmingly.

Still, when I entered Rickey's office Monday morning I was going to the Yankees.

He was ready. He repeated again what a wonderful offer

MacPhail had made me. He restated my value to him, to the ball club and to the community. He went to some lengths to assure me the offer he was about to make came freely and in respect to my value, and not just because of MacPhail's offer.

"Walter," he said, "I make you an offer on behalf of the Brooklyn baseball club of $105,000 for three years. You will no longer have to deal with Ray Vir Din or with Bert Kent or with any advertising agency or any sponsor. Your contract and your dealings will be with me, and with me alone."

Rickey had now made it possible for me to simply choose which job I wanted: to stay and continue building at Brooklyn, or to start a new job with a new team in a new league, and, at Yankee Stadium, to compete with what I had built at Brooklyn. I got along with MacPhail but I had come to a rich personal relationship with Rickey. (Years later I dedicated one of my books, *Walk in the Spirit*, to both Rickey and my father.)

I was deeply troubled, however, that Rickey's offer might be because MacPhail's offer had put him on the spot, that in time he might regret having had to make such an offer. Sometimes in our needs a completely unplanned, unprepared, unrehearsed response breaks through.

"Branch," I began, "down in North Carolina recently—in fact, the day before my dad was to be buried—the kinfolks and friends from all around gathered at my aunt's house. There were so many there they had to stand in the yard. They didn't come to mourn, they just gathered like a clan, to sort of strengthen everybody. They just visited.

"One fellow said to another, 'Jim, what did you ever do with that piece of land you had down on the South Carolina line?' And Jim said, 'I found me a willing buyer.'"

Rickey got up from behind his desk, walked around to me, stuck out his hand and said, "I'm a willing buyer."

That settled it. When I told MacPhail I was staying in Brooklyn, that I deeply appreciated his offer, he grinned and replied, "My offer didn't hurt you, did it?" I said, "No, sir."

Then MacPhail stopped grinning. "I told you I'm going to travel my broadcasts beginning next season. Now that you've decided to stay in Brooklyn I don't know who'll be the announcer —but it won't be one of the fellows doing the games now. [Mel

Allen came out of the Army and was hired.] But I'm telling you, starting next year you won't have the broadcasting monopoly you've had at Brooklyn."

There was a behind-the-scenes struggle between Rickey and MacPhail in 1945 over Negro players. At an owners' meeting there was a secret vote taken, and it was 15 to 1 against bringing in black players. Rickey cast the sole vote in favor. The owners didn't want the color line broken. However, a policy committee was formed, with MacPhail as chairman to "study" the Negro question. The other members were Tom Yawkey of the Red Sox, Phil Wrigley of the Cubs and Sam Breadon of the Cardinals. Two from each league. But not Rickey.

Rickey had not confided in any of his fellow executives that he had made up his mind, that he was using the Brooklyn Brown Dodgers as a cover, and that he was getting excellent reports on Jackie Robinson. When, late in 1945, Rickey signed Robinson for the farm team at Montreal, meaning that he had brought a black player into the framework of organized baseball and that Robinson would begin the 1946 season with Montreal, MacPhail bellowed.

MacPhail claimed that Rickey had "jumped the gun" . . . that "baseball had planned to take 'an orderly course' and had established a study, or policy, committee" . . . that "Rickey had 'raped' the Negro leagues."

Think it over. MacPhail was a trail blazer. He flew a big-league team for the first time during a pennant race, he introduced night baseball, he pioneered radio and television. Was it that he was thinking about being first with a black player? And Rickey had trumped his secret ace?

For a while 1946 went along without open warfare between MacPhail and Rickey. Many Dodgers were coming back from the armed forces and an exciting team was being put together, one which tied the Cardinals for the pennant and lost to the Redbirds in the play-off.

Jackie Robinson was tearing up the International League—he won the batting championship with a sizzling mark of .349, was a holy terror on the bases, scored 113 runs, was the most valuable player in the league, and after Montreal had won the pen-

nant and the play-offs in the International League, Jackie led the
Royals to a victory over Louisville in the Little World Series of
the American Association. Jackie started at Montreal in high
gear in the first game, and was never headed.

Montreal's opening game was at Jersey City. Rickey didn't
cross the Hudson River to see it. He knew his being there would
add to the pressure on Robinson and also create a strong press
diversion. He knew Jackie had enough on his mind without
Rickey's presence in the stands with newspapermen and photographers buzzing around. Also, the Dodgers had a game of their
own that same afternoon at Ebbets Field.

Rickey gave a small dinner party at Leone's Restaurant on
West Forty-eighth Street after the game. Lylah and I were included. Just as we were walking into Leone's, one of Rickey's
lesser-known assistants, who had been sent quietly to Jersey City
to observe what went on, came rushing up. He was excited. His
eyes were almost rolling.

"Mr. Rickey," he burst out, "Mr. Rickey . . . Jackie Robinson—" and here the man had to stop to get back his breath. "Mr.
Rickey, Jackie came up in the third inning with two men on and
hit a home run!"

Rickey was pleased. "He did?"

"Yes he did, Mr. Rickey," the man said. "And, Mr. Rickey, he
got three singles and he stole two bases!"

Rickey thanked his man and we continued into Leone's. I
remember Rickey took my elbow, squeezed it and said, "That's a
pretty good way to break into organized baseball."

It was a happy dinner party.

THUNDER AND LIGHTNING

Question: Did MacPhail want Durocher as his manager for the Yankees in 1947?

Fact: MacPhail hired Durocher's two top coaches, Charlie Dressen and Red Corriden. Dressen was Leo's right hand. Corriden was a good first-base coach, but was easily replaceable. Dressen was a sharp-eyed, cunning, extremely valuable third-base coach. Dressen was the fellow who stood at third and got the signs from Durocher in the dugout for the next play, and then relayed them to the players. They, Leo and Charlie, had signs nobody could detect. Leo needed Charlie. Leo had gone to Rickey to get Charlie a hefty raise for 1947, and Charlie had agreed orally with Rickey to sign a contract for 1947. But when MacPhail called, Dressen went to him. Broke his word.

Facts: Joe McCarthy had been the Yankees' manager since 1931. He had been very successful, winning eight Yankee pennants and seven World Series. He was Ed Barrow's man. Once before a World Series game, I was talking to Bill Dickey, then the star Yankee catcher. We were standing outside the batting cage. I asked Dickey why the Yankees were so successful, and he said, "That man," and pointed to McCarthy, who was sitting in the dugout. McCarthy ran his ball club and was not interfered with by Barrow. Joe was a proud man, accustomed to authority. It was merely a matter of time before he and MacPhail would part. McCarthy quit May 24, 1946. Bill Dickey, a Yankee hero, was back with the team after two years in the Navy, and was closing out his playing career. MacPhail named Dickey as manager. Bill quit September 12. Johnny Neun was a coach, and

MacPhail gave him the job. Neun said at the end of the season that he had had it—after only three weeks.

Fact: MacPhail needed a manager. Needed him badly. This was an element in the explosion at Havana, Cuba, in March 1947.

When you look back some thirty-five years you see how things began, things that at the time seemed of little importance but that led, just as surely as a stream runs downhill, to drastic repercussions: 1945 saw MacPhail, Dan Topping and Del Webb buy the Yankees . . . 1945 also saw Rickey, Walter O'Malley and John L. Smith buy 75 percent of the Dodgers.

Walter O'Malley came into the Dodger picture in 1943 as the lawyer for the club. He was already involved in various business enterprises and was a protégé, so to speak, of George V. McLaughlin, the strong man of the Brooklyn Trust Company.

John L. Smith was the president of Charles Pfizer Company. He was a chemist and did much pioneering work with penicillin.

Each of the three partners had 25 percent of the ball club. They had an agreement that if one of the partners wanted to sell his stock he had to give the other partners the opportunity to purchase it at the same terms. This meant that Rickey, O'Malley and Smith ran the Dodgers without consulting Jim Mulvey, whose wife, Dearie, owned the other fourth. Mulvey, who had brought in first MacPhail, then Rickey, was now out in the cold.

So it went: Rickey was president and the baseball brains, but O'Malley and Smith soon began operating in tandem. O'Malley coveted control, and when Smith died shortly after the 1947 war between Rickey and MacPhail ended, O'Malley became legal adviser for Mrs. Smith. O'Malley now controlled 50 percent of the stock. He began a drive to change Rickey's status, title, contract and earnings. O'Malley wanted Rickey on a straight salary—no bonuses, no percentages from sales of players.

When Rickey, O'Malley and Smith each bought their one-quarter interest in the Dodgers, the figure I heard they each paid was $350,000. O'Malley wanted that figure used for tax purposes in settling Smith's estate, and then he planned to buy the Smith stock from the estate for the same amount—$350,000.

Rickey's contract ran out in October 1950. As that season wore down, the mortal struggle between O'Malley and Rickey was devastating. O'Malley thought he had Rickey trapped, that he would take control of the Dodgers and then force Rickey to work for him on his, O'Malley's, terms. Rickey told me this himself, and at one time was in utter despair. He told me O'Malley was the most devious man he had ever known. Rickey was in financial straits, having put his life insurance in hock to buy his quarter share.

O'Malley was certain nobody in his or her right mind would think of buying Rickey's quarter interest when he, O'Malley, had control of 50 percent and Dearie Mulvey had the other quarter.

Rickey in his painful dilemma turned to his friend and fraternity brother John Galbreath, who owned the Pittsburgh Pirates. Galbreath took Rickey to William Zeckendorf, for many years a big-time wheeler-dealer in Manhattan real estate. Zeckendorf was intrigued with the situation and made Rickey an offer of $1,050,000 for his quarter. The $50,000 was to go to Zeckendorf for his time and trouble should O'Malley meet the million dollars Rickey now demanded.

O'Malley was furious but had no choice but to pay Rickey a million dollars and let him walk away scot free. In fact, Rickey went to Pittsburgh to take over the running of Galbreath's Pirates. What made O'Malley angrier than anything else was having to pay Zeckendorf the $50,000. Also, this placed a million-dollar price tag on the Smith quarter, which O'Malley had to pay Mrs. Smith.

This is how Walter O'Malley got control of the Dodgers. The reason I have gone into this is that O'Malley no sooner got into partnership of the ball club than he started planning to get full control. Harold Parrott, the road secretary of the Dodgers, who continued working for O'Malley after Walter moved the Dodgers to Los Angeles, pointed out step by step in his book *The Lords of Baseball* how O'Malley did little, if anything, to help Rickey, Durocher, or Jackie Robinson, but played it cozy and waited for time and events.

The first evidence of O'Malley and Smith moving against Rickey and Durocher came in August 1946. MacPhail needed a manager for the Yankees in 1947. There was speculation by various writers that MacPhail wanted Durocher. Together they had been a smashing success during MacPhail's five years at Brooklyn.

Before continuing with the MacPhail-Durocher-Rickey involvements, let me state that I now begin moving into areas where I was not present, had no right to be present, or for other reasons simply wasn't around. No one person could keep up with MacPhail and Durocher and Rickey.

I was not privy to the crosscurrents about contracts or the amounts of money involved in them. That was not my business. Actually, I tried to stay away from talking about things that were not in my broadcasting area. As soon as a game ended, I went home. I kept away from much trouble by avoiding the press club bar after the games, especially when MacPhail was in charge. And let me say, many of my best broadcasts were those nobody knows anything about—they were broadcasts of things I did not broadcast.

Harold Parrott was in and out of Rickey's office, and confidence, constantly. He traveled with the team. He knew things nobody else knew or could know. Harold was a baseball writer for the Brooklyn *Eagle* when Rickey hired him. Further, and this is important to our story, Harold ghosted a daily column in the *Eagle* for Durocher—"Durocher Says." When the explosions came in March and April 1947, Parrott and "Durocher Says" were deeply involved.

Harold talked to me several times about writing a book. I advised him to only if he would let it all hang out. In *The Lords of Baseball*, which was published in 1976, he did.

Arthur Mann was hired by Rickey to be his executive assistant. Arthur was a veteran baseball writer who had done many articles and books. He was a trained writer, and as the war with MacPhail developed, Arthur was fully aware of the worth of his material and kept careful notes and dates. Writers are like squirrels. Mann wrote *Baseball Confidential: The Secret History of the War among Chandler, Durocher, MacPhail and Rickey* in 1951 when his material was still fresh.

Leo Durocher in 1975 did a book with writer Ed Linn. Leo talked (that's his specialty) into Linn's tape recorder. The book is *Nice Guys Finish Last*. Jackie Robinson, with writer Alfred Duckett in 1972, just before Jackie died, did *I Never Had It Made*. J. G. Taylor Spink, then alive and publisher of *The Sporting News*, wrote in 1947 *Judge Landis and 25 Years of Baseball*. The *Sporting News* also has numerous standard record books. In 1945 the late Frank Graham wrote *The Brooklyn Dodgers*. Also along the way I did five books when events and memories were fresher.

My dad used to tell me that one of the important things in life was to have good friends. Robert Creamer, articles editor of *Sports Illustrated*, sent me photocopies of the two articles Happy Chandler did for the magazine with John Underwood. C. C. Johnson Spink, retired chairman of the board of *The Sporting News*, sent me copies of the coverage his paper did on Chandler's suspension of Durocher. Harold Goldstein, a friend and neighbor, is Dean of the School of Library Science at Florida State University. He made microfilm copies of the New York *Times* and the *Herald Tribune* for 1947 available. Florida State University has complete sets.

MacPhail didn't write a book. About 1968 he approached me about my doing his life story. We were both living on Key Biscayne, Florida. I didn't think that was exactly down my alley, and as it shortly turned out, it wasn't.

Rickey did one book, *The American Diamond*, with writer Robert Riger, but Rickey didn't get into any of the matters covered in this book—except, of course, about Jackie Robinson.

Much material is at hand. I have thought for a long time that 1947 was one of the most pivotal, vital and dramatic years in baseball—if not the most.

Question: Did MacPhail want Durocher as his 1947 manager?

To establish an orderly sequence, let me begin with a story from Havana, Cuba, by Joe Trimble in the New York *Daily News* March 15, 1947, which takes the Durocher-MacPhail Yankee managerial question back seven months. Trimble was the regular Yankee writer assigned by the *News*. He was always accurate:

"I could have had Durocher if I wanted him," MacPhail explained today, "and two of the Brooklyn owners know that. Both

John Smith and Walter O'Malley were present at the New York
Athletic Club one day last August when the matter of Durocher
managing the Yankees came up. O'Malley told me then that I
was free to deal with Durocher if I wanted him. At this time
permission was given in confidence and Smith backed it up. But
in the light of recent statements by Rickey and Durocher that I
tampered with Leo and Dressen, Smith and O'Malley have given
me permission to reveal their consent to any dealing I care to
have with Durocher."

To my knowledge neither O'Malley nor Smith ever denied
MacPhail's statement as quoted by Trimble. This shows plainly
that in August 1946 both O'Malley and Smith were not fond of
Durocher and certainly were not working in harmony with
Rickey. To locate the beginning of the split between Rickey and
O'Malley, this is a most likely starting point. It also explains
somewhat O'Malley's passive role during the troubles of
Durocher with Westbrook Pegler, Father Vincent Powell of the
Catholic Youth Organization, the judge in Los Angeles who
presided over the divorce of Laraine Day, George Raft, Mac-
Phail, and Commissioner Chandler.

Now in sequence: In September 1946 Durocher's right-hand
man, coach Charlie Dressen, went to Leo and asked him to try
to get him a raise from Rickey. Leo went straight to Rickey, and
Rickey agreed to see Dressen promptly and do the best he
could. On the morning of September 16 Dressen orally accepted
terms to coach the Dodgers in 1947 and 1948 for $15,000 a
season—a hefty raise. Dressen asked to be released should an
opportunity to manage another big-league team come along.
Rickey not only agreed, but while Dressen was in his office
Rickey telephoned Pittsburgh to see if that job was still open.
The Pirates answered by saying they had just hired Billy Herman as their new manager. Dressen seemed completely pleased
and left. The contract was to be signed later.

John Corriden, another coach for Durocher, had not discussed
with Leo or Rickey his contract for 1947. There seemed to be
nothing about Corriden's status that required earlier attention
than the usual routine of contract renewals.

When Durocher appealed to Rickey on behalf of his number
one coach, Dressen, Rickey asked Leo what about himself for

1947. Leo replied that he was satisfied with his contract, and that it was okay for the next year. Rickey thought that settled that.

The Dodgers and the St. Louis Cardinals ended the 1946 season in a tie and went into a play-off for the pennant, which St. Louis won. Before the first play-off game several reporters questioned Durocher on the rumors he might be offered, or might be interested in, the Yankee job. When a reporter asked would Leo see MacPhail, Leo said:

"Of course I'll see him. He's a friend of mine. Why shouldn't I see him?"

Arthur Mann states that shortly after the 1946 season ended, Rickey told both Mann and Harold Parrott, "MacPhail is after Durocher. There is no alternative . . . I must sign him promptly."

Rickey then telephoned Durocher, who was staying at the home of George Raft, and Leo was ordered to be at the offices of John W. Bricker, in Columbus, Ohio, at two-thirty the next afternoon. Rickey filled in the figures and Durocher signed the contract without looking at the amount he would be paid. Rickey asked Leo why he didn't read the figures and Leo said, "If it's good enough for you, it's good enough for me." Rickey then said, "It's for $50,000 . . . you'll be the highest-paid manager in history."

On October 25 the newspapers said, "Charlie Dressen resigned from the Dodgers yesterday and will join the Yankees." Rickey replied, "I not only did not accept his resignation, I am not going to accept." MacPhail said Dressen "asked" him for a job and that he "would hire any of my old organization."

MacPhail signed Dressen the next day. Rickey wondered out loud if this meant Dressen would be the new Yankee manager in accordance to the oral understanding Rickey had with Dressen about a managing opportunity. MacPhail blasted back that "Rickey isn't naming Yankee managers yet."

Rickey tried repeatedly to contact Johnny Corriden at his home in Indianapolis. Corriden wasn't answering. Rickey concluded that Corriden was switching to MacPhail, which Corriden soon did. But Corriden had made no commitment and his going to the Yankees was not a story.

On November 6, Bucky Harris was announced as the new Yankee manager. At the press conference MacPhail said:

"Durocher contacted me. That is, he sent word to me that he would like to manage the club. I did not tell Leo he could have the job. I did not think he would be the logical man for it."

In mid-November 1946 at a luncheon at Los Angeles, Durocher told the guests:

"About a month before the season ended, Larry MacPhail called me at my apartment in New York and asked to see me. I went over and he offered me the Yankee job. I told him I had a verbal agreement with Mr. Rickey and couldn't take it. That was the last I heard of it."

Durocher in his book *Nice Guys Finish Last* says, in reference to the storm that broke over his head:

". . . it was Larry MacPhail, a man who wished me no harm, who started the juggernaut rolling. MacPhail, having come home from the wars, had, as always, landed on his feet as co-owner and president of the New York Yankees. For reasons of his own, probably nothing more than publicity, he decided it would be nice to get a little feud going with his old friend and benefactor Branch Rickey. To get things started, he hired Charlie Dressen away from us—something I couldn't really object to. Charlie had managed for MacPhail at Cincinnati and coached for him at Brooklyn. Larry MacPhail was Dressen's Big Man, the same way that Branch Rickey was mine. For good measure, he then hired away my other coach, Red Corriden, who had also worked for him in both Cincinnati and Brooklyn.

"The one thing he still didn't have was a manager. In Larry's one year with the Yankees, three managers had quit on him. Joe McCarthy, the most successful manager in baseball, had taken all he wanted of MacPhail after the first month. Bill Dickey, an old Yankee hero who had been hired to appease their fans, had quit with a few weeks left, and Johnny Neun, who had been one of McCarthy's coaches for years, had let it be known after about a week that he knew now what McCarthy and Dickey had been talking about and, by God, he didn't have to take that from anybody either. If it was possible for Larry MacPhail to be embarrassed, a highly debatable point, he was in a highly embarrassing position, and he rose to the occasion nicely by making noises all through the winter that he was negotiating with me. I kept needling him back by saying, in one way or another, that yes, Larry had tried to hire me but I wasn't interested in anything except managing the good old Brooklyn Dodgers. It was a lot of fun and kept us in the papers during the off season. When Larry finally got around to signing Bucky Harris he kept it going by saying that he hadn't been trying to sign me after all, he had only been helping me get a better contract out of Rickey."

Branch Rickey had Durocher come to Brooklyn for the announcement of the signing of Leo's 1947 contract. It was Monday, November 25. Several reporters asked Durocher about the rumors he might have gone to the Yankees.

"I want to manage the Dodgers till the day I die," Leo began. "In answer to a recent statement by Larry MacPhail that I sought the Yankee job: the fact is MacPhail called me before the season was over last year [1946], made an appointment with me and made me an offer, larger than my new Brooklyn contract, to manage the Yankees. He telephoned me three times at George Raft's house, where I don't live anymore. You can check it through his long-distance calls. But I wouldn't accept. He must have wanted me badly, because he said he would not announce the name of his new manager until I had completed my deal with Branch Rickey."

According to Arthur Mann's book, MacPhail called a press conference the next day to deny he had offered Durocher the Yankee job, and Mann noted that no writers thought enough of the story to quote MacPhail directly.

Rickey thought MacPhail had tampered with his manager. He knew he had with his coach Dressen. But Rickey wasn't interested in calling any of this to the attention of Commissioner

Chandler for several reasons: one, he had Durocher signed; two, Dressen wasn't worth trying to bring back against his will; three, stirring up Chandler would be increased publicity which would have been just what MacPhail wanted. But Rickey did wonder, where was Chandler? Certainly some of this, played up as it was in the press, must have reached his attention.

Certainly had Chandler located the Commissioner's office in New York instead of Cincinnati, he would have been obliged to take a position, and to make certain rulings. The New York press would have been on his doorstep daily. However, had that happened there would not have been the Havana rhubarb—or this book.

Rickey had pressing and mounting problems with Durocher even though he had him signed. Why would Rickey over many years go to such extremes for Durocher? He appreciated his quick decisions, his courage, his willingness to do anything to win, his baseball savvy, his personal charm, his handling of his players, his fan appeal—and Rickey knew that Durocher would support him without question with Jackie Robinson. Leo would play anybody who or anything that could help him win a ball game. Rickey knew Durocher would fight for Robinson, and Rickey knew he would need everybody and everything when Robinson took the field at Brooklyn. The rest of the league would be against the black man. Leo relished such a fight.

I think we need to understand more of Branch Rickey's complex personality in order to explain his relationship with Leo Durocher. Rickey never took a drink of alcohol in his life. He didn't use profanity. When he was serious about going into professional baseball as a catcher, his mother, a deeply religious person, was upset. Rickey promised her he would not go into a ball park on Sunday. He kept his word.

It was a severe handicap to be a professional player and not play on the big day of the week. When Christy Mathewson first pitched for the Giants, he would not appear at the park on Sunday. However, Mathewson changed after a few years. Rickey's catching career ended when he developed tuberculosis and had to spend a year at Saranac Lake, New York.

Rickey was a sincerely religious man and often spoke from

pulpits. He read and knew and practiced the Bible. He loved the Methodist hymns he had been brought up with, and he liked to sing them. He talked about Jesus as easily and as naturally as he would have talked about one of his ballplayers. I remember one evening when he, Mrs. Rickey, Lylah and I were having dinner, he got to talking about Jesus, and he said something that made Christ more human and alive to me than anything I had heard before. He said, "Would that I knew the turbulence of his adolescence, and the questionings of his young manhood." Until Rickey said that, it hadn't occurred to me that of course Jesus went through His teens and into His adulthood just as each one of us has had to do.

Rickey had only one wife and no one ever suggested that he even looked at another woman. He was a strong family man with five daughters and a son. Pretty dull, strait laced fellow? Not at all. He was one of the most interesting men I was ever around.

Rickey was most tolerant. He understood that men would fail. He accepted as a fact of life that a man would have problems. Baseball once was full of men to whom Rickey had given second, third, even fourth chances. Billy Southworth had lost his way because of alcohol. Rickey worked with him, stayed with him, gave him a second chance to manage at St. Louis after Southworth went on the wagon. Southworth became a splendid manager, winning three straight pennants in St. Louis and another at Boston. Billy lost his way again after his only son was killed in a plane that crashed into the water at La Guardia Airport, and his body was never found. Billy was crushed.

It was a drunk who nailed down the 1926 World Series for the Cardinals over the Yankees. It was old Pete Alexander who came out of the bullpen to strike out Tony Lazzeri with the bases full in the seventh inning of the final game. Rickey had picked up Alexander on waivers in June of that year after the Chicago Cubs had given up on the troubled veteran.

Roy Campanella, the Hall of Fame catcher, once told me about Rickey's tolerance and understanding of other men. When Roy was catching for the Dodgers—Rickey brought him into the big leagues as the first black catcher—he opened a liquor store in Harlem. He didn't talk much about it, and he had people running the store for him. I was curious why Roy had the liquor store.

"Remember in the winter of 1950," Roy began, "my hot water heater exploded and scalded my face? I got blisters on my eyes. I was blind. The doctors put patches over my eyes. For days I couldn't see anything, and I didn't know if I would be able to see again when they took off the patches. I had my wife and three children. Baseball was all I knew, and I might never be able to play again. I prayed to the Good Lord. I said to Him, 'Lord, how am I going to support my family if I can't see?' And, 'Lord, if you let me see again after this . . . give me enough sense to find something to do besides play ball.'

"When I got out of the hospital I could see, and I had come up with the idea of getting myself a liquor store. I went straight to Mr. Rickey, who was running the team. I wanted him to give me an advance on my salary. Mr. Rickey didn't drink, he never took a drink in his whole life, and he said right off, 'Roy, why not a sporting goods store?' And I said to him, 'Mr. Rickey, I can't survive the competition of a sporting goods store. In a package store there are always the same number of bottles of liquor in every case, and the liquor won't go bad waiting to be sold. Mr. Rickey, being a Negro without much education, there ain't many businesses open to me.'

"And I said to him—he was just watching me, listening to me —'Mr. Rickey, you won't ever have any trouble with me about that liquor store; you'll see me play every day; you won't see nothin' wrong.' And Mr. Rickey said I was right to think about my family, and he started helping to get me a store. Then he sold out his interest to Walter O'Malley, and Mr. O'Malley finished helping me."

Rickey knew and accepted realistically that no man was perfect. He looked for talent and when he found it he gave the owner of it every chance to redeem it. Rickey never quit on a man until the man quit on himself. As long as a man battled, Rickey fought alongside him.

Rickey had his own strict personal rules which he never tried to impose upon anyone else. He was a man of abiding toleration. He was interested in what made men tick, and in why they sometimes failed to do as well as their talents indicated they should. He studied his players carefully.

For example: if a player began to play badly, below his abilities, Rickey talked to the manager. What's wrong with the man? If the manager couldn't provide the right answer, Rickey sent for the trainer. Players and trainers get very cozy when the player is on the table being massaged. Private affairs are often discussed in the trainer's room. But should the trainer be unable to tell Rickey the trouble with the slumping player, then Rickey sent for the player's wife. He would point out to the wife that they, she and Rickey, had a joint interest in the player and in his performance . . . that they both had an economic interest . . . that something was wrong with the player . . . that it behooved them both to get to the bottom of it, no matter what it was— money, sex, shaky marriage, alcohol, infidelity, fear, illness. Rickey would find out what was the matter, and then do whatever was indicated to straighten out the trouble. He worked to help his people. He went to enormous efforts. Many times he welcomed home the Prodigal Son.

Let's take Leo Durocher. Rickey watched over, labored over, hoped for, even prayed for Leo from early in the season of 1933 until 1938 when he sold him to Brooklyn. Then when Rickey came to Brooklyn after the season ended in 1942, there was Durocher waiting for him as the manager of the Dodgers. This lasted until midseason 1948 when Rickey sold Horace Stoneham the idea that Leo should come to the Giants to replace Mel Ott as manager.

The greatest fear in baseball is of gamblers and of gambling. Under Durocher the 1942 Dodgers had a wide-open clubhouse. Coach Charlie Dressen played the horses and often had his close friend Memphis Engelberg, a known handicapper, in the clubhouse. All sorts and conditions of men came and went. The players gambled and Leo gambled with them. The Dodgers took the train for their last trip to St. Louis, where they lost the series and ultimately the pennant, and the night was a wild one with gambling all over the train. Many, including Rickey felt that that train night was fatal.

The first matter of importance to Rickey, when he took the job at Brooklyn following the 1942 World Series, was to stop all gambling. He made it plain to Durocher that gambling in the clubhouse, and on the ball club, was over. Leo agreed and was as good as his word. Dressen was fired. Memphis Engelberg was not to be allowed in the clubhouse, nor was anyone of his ilk. Durocher pleaded for Dressen but Rickey was firm. Later he hired Dressen back.

Leo always had a fondness for show-business people both in New York and in Hollywood. His great friend was George Raft, actor and gambler, and it was in Raft's house that Leo spent his winters. When the Dodgers won the 1941 pennant, Leo wanted Raft to have four seats in his, the manager's, box. Commissioner Landis hit the ceiling and said Raft could not have those seats. Leo got mad. Leo and Landis were getting into a serious argument when MacPhail took Leo outside and made him accept four seats from MacPhail's allocation.

In March of 1944 the Dodgers were in spring training at Bear Mountain, New York, using the field house at West Point. Leo was with the ball club, but he had his New York City apartment. George Raft came to town for a ten-day visit and borrowed Leo's apartment. Leo happily gave Raft the key.

Six months later a fellow, a sucker for gambling, hollered copper. He claimed that he had been clipped for $12,000 in Durocher's apartment in a dice game staged by Raft. Nobody claimed Leo was there, and the sucker finally admitted Raft was not in the dice game himself but was playing gin rummy. Anyhow, this made headlines and stories—Leo Durocher's apartment, George Raft, and gambling.

Yet, when the season ended, Durocher went to Hollywood and again to Raft's house for the winter. The two men remained inseparable.

Westbrook Pegler got into the picture in November of 1946. He telephoned Rickey at home one night and demanded to know when Rickey was going to get rid of Durocher. He said that Durocher was a moral delinquent who would bring baseball crashing down, and that he, Pegler, was going to do a series of columns on Durocher. Rickey argued Durocher's case and challenged Pegler's right to judge any man's chance for rehabilitation or how long the chance should last.

Pegler ended his call by asking why, if Durocher was so solid a citizen, was he still living with George Raft?

Rickey had signed Durocher to manage the Dodgers for 1947 for some $50,000, but had not released the signing because of all the turbulence with MacPhail, plus the Pegler situation. Rickey wanted Leo to manage the Dodgers in 1947 for every reason, especially because of the supportive strength Leo would give Jackie Robinson. What to do?

Rickey dispatched his assistant, Arthur Mann, on a secret trip to Cincinnati to ask Commissioner Chandler to help. No one, certainly not Leo, was to know. Chandler agreed to see Mann, and agreed that Mann's visit would remain confidential.

Mann's visit is no longer classified information, and hasn't been for years. Durocher refers to it in his book. Mann wrote about it at great length in 1951 in his book *Baseball Confidential*. What I will write here about that pivotal mission is from Mann himself. He should know. Also, let me say, looking back over the years, had Rickey not sent Mann to get Chandler into the Durocher problem, the events of March 1947 might not have happened. One never knows, when one starts an action, what may follow. Stir up a breeze, it may become a wind and finally a hurricane.

Chandler did not know what Mann wanted. Mann explained that Rickey needed help in getting Durocher to realize that his friends could become his unwitting enemies, and that Rickey felt Leo might be more impressed if the Commissioner himself warned him . . . "that Durocher must sever connections with all kinds of people regarded as undesirables by baseball—gangsters, known gamblers, companions of known gamblers and racketeers." There was the controversy that followed the use of Durocher's apartment by George Raft for a dice game. "Judge Landis advised Durocher to steer clear of Raft . . . Durocher is a guest of Raft right now, living under his roof . . . Rickey wants Leo to move, and he believes your hand will help."

Mann went on to explain there was nothing basically wrong with Durocher, but Rickey felt Leo needed help in this situation and was worthy of help.

Commissioner Chandler willingly got into the action, an action that finally brought both Durocher and Chandler much travail, pain and sorrow. Chandler put in a call for Leo at Raft's home, and was told Leo was at the NBC studios rehearsing for a spot on the Jack Benny Show. Chandler called NBC and was told, "Mr. Durocher is in rehearsal and cannot be disturbed."

"Tell him," Chandler said, "Commissioner Chandler is calling —that'll disturb him—and tell him to get to the phone now."

Leo came right on. Chandler ordered Leo to meet him on a certain golf course at Oakland five days later, Friday morning November 22. Leo demurred because he had to go to Texas on pressing personal business. Chandler replied, "You'll be there, boy—Oakland . . . Friday morning . . . eleven o'clock. I know you won't disappoint me. Now go back to your rehearsal and give a good show tonight."

Leo was on time at the Claremont Country Club, which is in Berkeley, not Oakland. Word had gotten out and the press was on hand. Chandler and Leo walked away from everyone and, according to Durocher's book, walked three holes of the golf course in a misty, drizzling rain.

Leo also noted that Chandler and everyone else in sports was and had to be concerned then about gambling, that a point-shaving fix in basketball had been uncovered, that five minor-league baseball players had been discovered fixing games and had been given lifetime suspensions, that bribes and rumors of bribes were being exposed in boxing, that U.S. Attorney-General Tom Clark had appealed to the sportswriters to help clean up sports, and that Chandler was being assailed by the writers as a do-nothing Commissioner.

From here on the story moved in an inevitable direction. The pieces, one by one, kept coming together forcing Rickey, Mac-Phail, Durocher and Chandler into an arena where finally blood had to be shed.

Chandler, when he was certain he and Durocher were out of anyone's hearing, pulled a list of names from his pocket and began telling Leo there were certain men to stay away from. Leo was all ears. He knew this was serious. He knew he was signed to manage the Dodgers in 1947, and he certainly didn't want to blow that. And he knew something else that he would soon drop on Chandler.

Chandler read from his list the names of Joe Adonis and

Bugsy Siegel, two mobsters Leo had merely nodded to once or twice. Leo readily agreed to avoid all contact with them. Chandler read the names of Memphis Engelberg and Connie Immerman. Leo knew Memphis well and liked him and had always found him honest. Immerman went back many years to when he was running the Cotton Club in New York; now he was running a gambling casino in Havana, Cuba. Leo agreed to stay away from both of them.

Then Chandler lowered the boom. Leo was to move out of George Raft's house. Leo said he'd get his things and move out as soon as he could return to Los Angeles. He said, "I'll stay clear of all those guys you've mentioned . . . they'll call me a louse, but I'll do it."

Chandler assured Durocher that if he did that, all was in order and everything was fine.

Then Leo told Chandler he was planning to marry actress Laraine Day. Chandler asked when, and Leo said as soon as she gets a divorce.

From then on Durocher was in the headlines almost daily. First, the United Press had a story that same day that Commissioner Chandler had called Durocher on the carpet. The New York *Journal-American* ran a similar story the next day.

Ray Hendricks, Laraine's husband, accused Leo of breaking up his home. Hendricks named Leo as corespondent. Leo's lawyers quickly proved that Leo and Laraine had never been alone at any time, but the damaging publicity mill was rolling. The fact was that Laraine and Hendricks's marriage had come apart long before she and Leo met by chance in an airport.

Laraine filed for divorce and got an interlocutory decree that was to become final in a year. The judge was George Dockweiler, who pointed out that she and Leo were not to marry in California for a year. However, legally they were free to marry in any of the other states. They decided to go to Juarez, for a Mexican divorce for Laraine and to get married in El Paso, Texas. They were careful not to live together in California.

Laraine's lawyer warned her that Judge Dockweiler might not be very happy about her marriage to Leo, so Leo called the judge and asked for an appointment, hoping to explain matters and cool the temperature.

Sure enough, Judge Dockweiler was angry. He told Leo on the phone that as far as he, Judge Dockweiler, was concerned the marriage was illegal and that he was going to see that it was annulled . . . that if Leo and Laraine lived under the same roof in California it would be adultery. Finally an appointment was granted for the next day.

The judge alerted the press. There was a crush of writers and photographers as Leo and Laraine arrived outside the judge's chambers. Leo told the judge he and Laraine had no intention of living together in California, that they had separate residences, and that he would soon be gone for spring training and then gone for the baseball season, and when the year was up, if the judge wished, they would get married again in California.

Judge Dockweiler seemed to get madder and madder. He repeated his opinion that Leo and Laraine were committing adultery. Then Leo got testy and began working on the judge as though he were just another umpire.

"Your honor," barked Leo, "would you be making such a fuss about this if our names were Sarah Zilch and Joe Blow?"

The judge replied, "No, I wouldn't." He went on to explain that he couldn't watch everybody but that he could make an example of Leo and Laraine.

Now Leo was steaming, and accused the judge of condoning adultery by other people but not by himself and Laraine, and further, that what the judge was really interested in was publicity for himself.

Then the judge complained that Leo and Laraine had made the court look bad, and what they should do was to get the Mexican divorce set aside . . . and if they did that they could go ahead and live together . . . that that part of it wouldn't concern him.

Leo was now burning. He said, "Let me tell you something, your honor. This is my wife you are talking about. I am married to this girl. You can do any goddam thing you want but I am going to stay married to her." And they left.

Leo then spoke to the press, and said the judge was "a pious, Bible-reading hypocrite."

Judge Dockweiler replied in kind in the press. He threatened to set aside the divorce decree on grounds of "collusion, bad faith and fraud." Judge Dockweiler was removed from the case by a three-man panel of judges for possible bias. Another judge ruled there were no grounds for setting Laraine's divorce aside. She and Leo were remarried a year later in California.

Mixed with these doings in California was Leo's trip to New York for the formal announcement of his contract to manage the Dodgers in 1947, which reopened the MacPhail crossfire about Leo wanting or not wanting the Yankee job. Then in mid-December came the Westbrook Pegler attack. Pegler disinterred the George Raft dice game in 1944 in Durocher's apartment, called Leo "a moral delinquent" and tried to link Raft to gangsters Ownie Madden and Bugsy Siegel. Pegler did his best—or worst—on Durocher.

The timing could not have been better for the gathering storm. That same mid-December the story exploded that two New York football Giants, Frank Filchock and Merle Hapes, were somehow involved with a gambling fix for the NFL championship game. I broadcast that game and I remember the pall that hung over it after the news broke earlier that morning. Also, at this time it was confirmed that five minor-league baseball players in the Evangeline League were crooked.

Commissioner Chandler was now assailed by various writers who took their cue from Pegler. Chandler was asked what he was going to do about the gambling element in baseball . . . and, what was he going to do about Durocher? Chandler pointed out that the Raft dice game had taken place when Landis was Commissioner, that he had talked with Durocher for two hours in Oakland and found everything in order with Durocher, and that if any writer had any evidence of gambling in baseball he should come forth with it and present it to the Commissioner for action.

The pot was boiling. The news from California about Leo and Laraine, the threats by Judge Dockweiler, and the impertinent reactions by Leo to the judge created an undertow that was gathering strength. Rickey began getting letters demanding that he dismiss Durocher. Many Roman Catholics were unhappy about Leo's having had two divorces and getting involved with Laraine's divorce. The director of the Brooklyn Catholic Youth Organization was a young priest named Vincent J. Powell. His organization had some 50,000 kids in it, and they had been eager participants in the Dodgers' Knothole Club, a civic promotion that brought youngsters free to Ebbets Field.

Father Powell made his views known—he disapproved of Durocher as the manager of the Dodgers, and threatened to remove the CYO from the Knothole Club. After several fruitless meetings with Father Powell, Rickey, a Protestant, turned the priest over to his partner, Walter O'Malley, a prominent Catholic.

Back to O'Malley and his intentions about Durocher, Rickey and Robinson. In August 1946 O'Malley and the other partner, John Smith, without telling Rickey had told MacPhail he could approach Durocher for the job of manager at Yankee Stadium if MacPhail so wished.

Harold Parrott, former writer for the Brooklyn *Eagle*, was then traveling secretary for the Dodgers and privy to the inner office currents and crosscurrents. Parrott, a Catholic, has this to say in his book *The Lords of Baseball:*

"All the anti-Durocher noise had been started by a mildly eccentric Catholic priest who screamed at regular intervals in the newspapers and pulpits around town that Lippy's 'immoral private life' was a bad example to the youth of Brooklyn.

"Leo had just married divorcée Laraine Day against a judge's explicit orders. Father Vincent Powell announced that he was withdrawing the Catholic Youth Organization's 'support' of the Dodgers.

"'Support' was hardly the word. The CYO received four hundred thousand free passes for their youngsters each season, and this meant that it would turn down these Annie Oakleys.

"Rickey, a thoughtfully religious man, was deeply hurt by the Catholic's public spanking of Durocher. During several long meetings with the Reverend Powell, the old psalm-singer had me sit in as a kind of Catholic interpreter or spokesman for the Dodgers. In these debates the Mahatma [Rickey] badly outpointed the priest at every turn. He kept asking if the Catholics, like most other churches, weren't still dispensing mercy and forgiveness. And wouldn't it be better to use the colorful Durocher's appeal to youngsters, which was considerable, instead of blackening the man's character?

". . . the priest remained unmoved. All he wanted was Durocher's scalp.

"O'Malley, the original Smiling Irishman when it came to blarney, carried a large prayerbook in the Catholic Church. He was respected by the clergy and was in all ways a powerful Catholic who could have stopped all this anti-Durocher nonsense had he wanted to. His best pal was Judge Henry Ughetta, head of the Sons of Italy and a Knight of St. Gregory, which meant his connections went all the way to Rome. One word from them both and the Reverend Powell, as well as Monsignor Edward Lodge Curran, another anti-Leo scold, would have piped down, and so would their Catholic Youth Organization.

"But O'Malley never gave the word.

"Rickey had reason to wonder who had put the churchmen up to this. The Catholics never boycotted Hitler or Mussolini the way they went after Leo.

"Yes, there was indeed dirty work at the crossroads, the Old Man [Rickey] reflected.

"Obviously, O'Malley enjoyed seeing Durocher revolving on the red-hot rotisserie, because Leo was Branch Rickey's favorite reclamation project, and that meant the Old Man would collect some of the critics' heat."

On March 1, the first day of spring training, the blow fell. Rickey had failed to soften Father Powell, and O'Malley apparently hadn't really tried. Chandler was provided additional ammunition he hadn't asked for but couldn't avoid. Durocher's fate for 1947 was sealed March 1, although it wasn't apparent to anyone—unless it was to O'Malley.

It was in all the papers March 1, 1947. Father Powell published the letter of resignation . . . the Brooklyn CYO was withdrawing from the Dodgers' Knothole Club. Further, the priest stated that "he [Durocher] is undermining the moral training of Brooklyn's Roman Catholic youth and the CYO could not continue to have our youngsters officially associated with a man who represents to them an example in complete contradiction to our moral teachings."

Father Powell's statement continued:

"Mr. Durocher has finally climaxed a long series of events both off and on the baseball diamond. This has convinced us

that the effect of his example will be a powerful force for undermining the moral and spiritual training of our young boys. These
events have been publicized to an extent where all young men
are fully aware of them."

There was now nothing more Rickey could do about the CYO
except to attend to his busy schedule and let time bring what it
would. Rickey had sent the Dodgers, as well as the Montreal
farm team, to train in Havana, Cuba. Too many Southern states
and cities had laws that prevented Jackie Robinson, a black
man, from playing games with white teammates. Robinson was
still on the Montreal roster. Rickey hoped enough of the white
Dodgers would see the value of Robinson as a player and ask
that he be placed on the Brooklyn roster. This hope never happened. In fact, it took an enraged Durocher first, and an angry
Rickey second, to put down an insurrection by some of the
white Dodgers about the coming of a black man to the team.

All the players were back from the armed forces. The player
wealth Rickey now possessed had to be sorted, observed, graded
and assigned to different clubs in the farm system. The Dodgers
had to be carefully put together. Where would Robinson play?
Second base, where he was at Montreal in 1946? It was manager
Durocher's problem to begin grading the players on the big
team.

THE STORM BREAKS

For the spring of 1947 Rickey had leased most of the naval air training station at Pensacola, Florida, as a minor-league training camp for some two hundred players for the lower classification teams in the farm system. Rickey was everywhere: all day at Pensacola observing young players, then in meetings much of the night in staff discussions of them and their abilities. The Dodgers had a private plane, and suddenly Rickey would fly to Havana. The Dodgers also had games scheduled in Venezuela with the Yankees, plus a twelve-day stint in the Panama Canal Zone against Montreal and Robinson.

Durocher kept his word to Commissioner Chandler. He lived the life of a hermit at Havana. Laraine was in California working on a motion picture. Leo went to the ball park, directed the workout, returned to the Nacional Hotel where the Dodgers were quartered, and had his meals in his room. When he saw a gambler, he fled. Memphis Engelberg was there, as was Connie Immerman, who was running the gambling casino. Leo avoided them. He kept his pledge to Chandler without a single variation. Also Leo kept his word to Rickey about gambling by the Dodgers themselves. He stopped all gambling on the ball club.

Harold Parrott was a staunch Durocher man. They were quite close and in constant contact with each other, as their two positions required. By now Parrott was ghostwriting a column for Leo in the *Eagle* called "Durocher Says." One of the columns incensed MacPhail.

The Dodgers and the Yankees were scheduled to play 3 games in Venezuela. First, Durocher and a half dozen of his players almost went off a mountain road when their car skidded. A Dodger pitcher, Eddie Chandler, had been pitching in Venezuela several weeks, and the local promoter threatened to put Chandler in jail if he didn't stay in Venezuela another week or so. Leo refused and would play only 1 of the 3 games scheduled, which made MacPhail sore. The Yankees under their new manager, Bucky Harris, and the Dodgers then flew to Havana for games Saturday and Sunday afternoon.

On March 3, dated Caracas, Venezuela, this was in "Durocher Says" in the Brooklyn *Eagle,* as written by Parrott under Leo's name:

"This is a declaration of war . . . I want to beat the Yankees because of MacPhail and Dressen. . . . He [MacPhail] tried to drive a wedge between myself and all these things I hold dear. When MacPhail found I couldn't be induced to manage his Yankees, he resolved to knock me and make life as hard as possible for me. . . . Dressen was very close to me for years and he cannot deny that he had agreed to Brooklyn terms for two more years.

"Dressen's only out as far as his Brooklyn contract was concerned was that he could sign to manage a major-league club elsewhere.

"Has MacPhail promised Charlie this? What does this mean to Bucky Harris? Be sure I will ask these questions when we meet in Caracas tomorrow."

The bomb was ready to explode.

The Yankees had won the only game played in Venezuela 17–6. The Dodgers bounced back in the Saturday game at Havana with a 1–0 win before a crowd of some 10,000. But when Branch Rickey walked into the lobby of the Nacional Hotel after the game, instead of beaming over the results of the afternoon, he was angry. Herb Goren of the New York *Sun* and Arch Murray of the *Post* were standing in the lobby on the alert for any story they could find. Goren asked Rickey what was the matter.

"Did you see those two men out there today?" Rickey said. "Those gamblers—sitting in MacPhail's box?"

Rickey fumed at some length. He named the two men as

Memphis Engelberg and Connie Immerman. He said that if he saw them at Ebbets Field he'd have them thrown out of the park. He said he had been worried all winter about gamblers and gambling . . . that Commissioner Chandler had warned Durocher, and that Durocher had stayed strictly away from any possible undesirables. Rickey was indignant and asked what would happen to Durocher if those two gamblers had been seated in the Brooklyn club box behind the Dodger dugout. When Goren asked if his remarks were on the record, Rickey said they certainly were.

New York had some nine newspapers then. Each paper had a writer traveling with the Yankees with another writer assigned to the Dodgers. Also there were several columnists at Havana drawn by the 2 games between the interborough rivals, headed by the two dominant men, MacPhail and Rickey. There were photographers. If it had been planned there couldn't have been more intense coverage.

Goren and Murray alerted the press corps about Rickey's explosion. Goren was also filing for the Associated Press, and he advised his colleagues what he was sending back to the United States.

The Sunday game drew another large crowd. The weather was ideal. Would Engelberg and Immerman again have their same box seats alongside MacPhail? They did. There is a picture showing the scene. The New York *Daily News* featured it.

Once the two known gamblers were seated behind the Yankee dugout the writers descended upon Durocher. Dick Young of the *Daily News* first called Durocher's attention to Engelberg and Immerman, and Leo immediately repeated what Rickey had said the day before: what would happen to him if the two gamblers had been seated in the Brooklyn club box?

Leo had been taking a beating from all sides for months. He had been plastered all over the papers for this and for that, with the CYO as a bitter finale. Leo had been staying to himself. He had been a hermit at Havana. He was understandably upset. Young quoted Leo as saying, "Are there two sets of rules, one applying to managers and one applying to club owners? Where does MacPhail come off, flaunting his company with known gamblers right in the players' faces? If I ever said 'Hello' to one of those guys, I'd be called before Commissioner Chandler and probably barred."

MacPhail was always a most formidable opponent. He went into rages and didn't count the cost of any actions that followed. He was a lawyer and knew the legal loopholes. He had great strength. And he had a devastating one-two retaliation when assailed. First, he denied. Second, he attacked with such force that he didn't remain on the defense. MacPhail was almost impossible to corner and contain.

Dick Young, after getting his story from Durocher, went straight to MacPhail and told him what Durocher had said.

MacPhail attacked. He was quoted as saying, "In the first place, it is none of Durocher's business who I have in my box. In the second place, if Durocher was quoted correctly, he is a liar. I understand that in the box next to me were two gentlemen later identified as alleged gamblers. I had nothing to do with their being there. And you can quote me as saying it is none of Durocher's business."

A few minutes later MacPhail was quoted by Arthur Daley of the New York *Times* as saying, "Leo's got a persecution complex."

The Yankees flew back to St. Petersburg, the Dodgers and their farm club, Montreal (with Jackie Robinson), flew to the Panama Canal Zone, and Rickey got into the Dodgers' plane and flew to Pensacola.

Things were quiet for a few days, deceptively quiet. But if you thought peace and quiet would last very long, then you didn't know MacPhail. And you didn't know the New York writers.

At the recent annual New York Baseball Writers' Dinner, February 2, Ford Frick, president of the National League, gave a strong speech warning all baseball men to steer clear of gamblers and other known undesirables. The writers were doubly alert to any story involving gamblers in a baseball park.

Rickey plunged into his evaluation of players at Pensacola. When he was content that matters there were running smoothly, he decided to fly in the private plane to see how the Dodgers and the Montreal Royals were doing in their games in Panama.

The trip would be via Miami for clearance papers. It was March 15.

The Dodgers' plane was ready to take off from Pensacola. Rickey got aboard but was asked to answer a long-distance call. Arthur Mann, Rickey's special assistant, got off the plane to see what the call was about. It was from Walter Mulbry, assistant to Commissioner Chandler.

Mulbry said, "Tell Mr. Rickey it looks as though MacPhail is serious about the charges."

"What charges?" Mann asked.

"Conduct detrimental to baseball," Mulbry replied. "We have the charges here at the Sarasota Terrace Hotel. It's in the Commissioner's hands. It's official."

Mann protested. "We're just leaving for Panama. We're due in Miami to catch an evening plane."

Mulbry said, "I guess you better stop off here . . . we'll have a car at the Bradenton airport in about two hours."

Mann reboarded, sat down, strapped himself in, and when Rickey said something about the bother of having to stop in Miami, Mann dropped the news. "The next stop," Mann told Rickey, "will be Sarasota. We're stopping there to see the Commissioner."

It happened that the Rickeys had old friends then in Sarasota, former U.S. Senator George Williams and his wife. While Rickey conferred with Chandler, Mrs. Rickey visited with the Williamses. Mann met with Mulbry and copied MacPhail's charges:

"I am attaching a summary of quotations attributed to Branch Rickey and a summary of statements appearing in the articles signed by Durocher.

"These articles, appearing in the Brooklyn *Eagle*, are allegedly written and/or publication-authorized by officials of the Brooklyn Baseball Club. Either the president of the Brooklyn Club made the statements attributed to him or he has been misquoted.

"In any event, the charges are either true or false. If true, they should properly have been communicated to the Commissioner of Baseball. If false, their utterance and/or publication constitutes slander and libel and represents, in our opinion, conduct detrimental to baseball.

"For these reasons the New York Club requests the Commissioner to call a hearing to determine responsibility for the statements and then whether they are true or not.

"When these matters have been determined, the New York Club takes it for granted, in view of the publicity which has followed these charges, that the Commissioner will make his findings public. Mr. Will Harridge, president of the American League, joins me in making this request."

It was official. MacPhail had thrown the fat into the fire. His aim was to embarrass Branch Rickey. MacPhail had acted out of anger and without considering what might be the final upshot. As I knew MacPhail, had he had the slightest idea whom he would severely hurt, damage and cripple, he would not have brought this action. MacPhail often fought with Durocher when Leo was his manager, but he admired Leo, liked Leo, and as Leo himself said in his book, certainly wished Leo no harm.

MacPhail was, of course, well aware that Chandler was under a strong obligation to him. It was MacPhail who beat down Rickey's nomination of Ford Frick for the vacant commissionership and led the behind-the-scenes maneuvering that got Senator Chandler elected.

It is my opinion that MacPhail wanted a hearing before Chandler, and an apology from Rickey. MacPhail had an obsession: to win any contest he got into, no matter how small. However, once MacPhail officially put this rhubarb into Chandler's hands, Chandler felt the time and the opportunity had come for him to be a decisive Commissioner.

Chandler held two hearings—one at Sarasota, the second at St. Petersburg. The only full account I know of of these two hearings is in Arthur Mann's book. The press was not allowed in, and Chandler called in different people one at a time, and after each was questioned he was told to leave the room and to say nothing of what had gone on. Rickey himself was not at the first hearing. MacPhail was at both with one of his partners, Dan Topping only at the first. Walter O'Malley was at both. Senator Williams was at the first. Mann, as Rickey's special assistant, was at both, heard it all, and as a professional newspaperman wrote it down for Rickey's use as well as for the book Mann later produced.

Charlie Dressen, Red Corriden, Arthur Patterson, Durocher himself, Harold Parrott were only in the hearings when they themselves were in the witness chair. Then they were silenced. Chandler made his own rules as he went, and as you add up various things he said and the way he conducted his hearings, apparently his mind was set, no matter what was said or not said. When Chandler did make his judgment public it created a nationwide storm of press coverage that was almost unbelievable.

Chandler set Monday March 24 for the first hearing. Rickey and Durocher, both in Panama, were ordered to attend.

Rickey was determined to bring Jackie Robinson to the 1947 Dodgers, now that Robinson had shown he was an excellent player. Rickey kept waiting, hoping some of the white Dodgers would ask that Robinson be put on the team to help win the National League pennant. Instead of asking for Robinson, some of the white Dodgers started a movement to demand that the black man not be put on the team.

Now you'll see one strong reason Rickey wanted Durocher as his manager. Harold Parrott as traveling secretary was aware of what happened at Panama. He put it down in his book. Durocher detailed it even more strongly in his book. Here is what happened, according to Durocher, and let me say Durocher has an almost infallible memory. In fact, any successful manager must have a mind that recalls events as quickly and as accurately as a computer. I asked Joe McCarthy when he was managing the all-conquering Yankees what was the secret of managing, and he told me two things—"memory and patience," and "who to keep and who to get rid of."

Now that baseball has drastically changed in its contracts with the players, McCarthy's second dictum is more difficult to enforce. Ball clubs now are tied up with long-term, big-money player contracts and often find themselves unable to deal or dispose of players because of no-trade agreements. However, the "memory and patience" still holds true. A manager must remember what all opposing players can and can't do, just as he must know his own players' strengths and weaknesses.

One time, after an afternoon game at St. Louis, the Dodgers

got on a train for Chicago. Several of the writers broke into a heated argument about a situation in the middle of the game. The writers had their scorebooks in which they had put down all the basic plays. Still they had different opinions about what had happened. Durocher came into the club car and sat down. The writers appealed to him, and he gave his version of the play in question. A writer who had a differing opinion challenged Leo's memory.

Leo was angered. He roared, "All right, fellows—look at your scorebooks . . . you don't think I don't remember that one play? . . . I'm now going to give you every single play in the whole damn game." And he did, without a mistake. His memory was never challenged again to my knowledge. Managers have complete recall, and I stress this to have you believe that what Durocher says in his book is just what he did and what he said in Panama. It was pivotal.

Pages 203–6, *Nice Guys Finish Last* by Leo Durocher with Ed Linn:

"My part in the signing of Jackie Robinson was zero. I read about it in the paper like everybody else. I never even saw him play until he came to spring training in Havana, the year after he had led the International League in hitting. And even then, Rickey kept Jackie with the minor league squad, attached to the Montreal roster, through the entire training period. Mr. Rickey had some kind of pipe dream that as soon as the players recognized how much Jackie could help us, they were going to demand that he be brought up.

"What happened was exactly the opposite. Early in the spring we went to Panama for a weekend series against a squad of Caribbean All-Stars. The Montreal club, including Robinson and three other Negro players —Roy Campanella, Don Newcombe and Roy Partlow —came to Panama too. The Dodgers stayed at the U. S. Army barracks at Fort Gulick. The Montreal players had their own quarters on the other side of the Isthmus.

"We had been there about a week when one of my

coaches, Clyde Sukeforth, reported he was picking up talk that the players, led by Dixie Walker and Eddie Stanky, were getting up a petition to warn us that they would never play with Robinson.

"I had seen Robinson in a couple of the Montreal exhibition games, and that was all it took to convince me that I wanted him. He was still playing second base with Montreal—he wasn't handed a first baseman's mitt until the season was about to start—and you could see how he could move in the field and could run the bases. But most of all, you could see he was a really good hitter. And that nothing in the world scared him.

"Since Mr. Rickey was due to join us in a couple of days, I decided to hold off and let him handle it. I was not completely convinced, understand, that the story was true. What did the damn fools think they were going to do—strike? To check it out, I spent the day testing some of the players. I'd turn the conversation around to Jackie Robinson and say, 'Doesn't bother me any . . .' or 'If this kid can play ball, boy, I want him on the ball club. . . .' The reactions, though somewhat guarded, were far from encouraging. The rumors were true, all right.

"As I lay in bed that night, unable to sleep, I suddenly asked myself why I was being so cute about it. Hell, I was getting as bad as Rickey. The thing to do, I could see, was to nip it in the bud, step on them hard before they had taken the irretrievable step of signing the petition and presenting it to anybody. Once the battle lines were drawn, it was going to become a very messy situation. And while they couldn't possibly win, the club couldn't possibly come out of it without being ripped apart, either. I made up my mind right there that there was going to be no petition. Not if I had anything to say about it.

"I jumped right out of bed, woke up my coaches and instructed them to round up all the players and bring them downstairs. Still in my pajamas, I scouted around for a meeting place and stumbled across the perfect place. A huge, empty kitchen right behind the mess hall.

"In came the players, some in pajamas, some in their underwear, some buckling their trousers. They sat on the chopping blocks and on the counters; they leaned sleepily against the refrigerator and the stoves.

"I said: 'I hear some of you fellows don't want to play with Robinson and that you have a petition drawn up that you are going to sign. Well, boys, you know what you can do with that petition. You can wipe your ass with it. Mr. Rickey is on his way down here and all you have to do is tell him about it. I'm sure he'll be happy to make other arrangements for you.

"'I hear Dixie Walker is going to send Mr. Rickey a letter asking to be traded. Just hand him the letter, Dixie, and you're gone. GONE! If this fellow is good enough to play on this ball club—and from what I've seen and heard, he is—he is going to play on this ball club and he is going to play for me.'

"I said, 'I'm the manager of this ball club, and I'm interested in one thing. Winning. I'll play an elephant if he can do the job, and to make room for him I'll send my own brother home. So make up your mind to it. This fellow is a real great ballplayer. He's going to win pennants for us. He's going to put money in your pockets and money in mine. And here's something else to think about when you put your head back on the pillow. From everything I hear he's only the first. ONLY THE FIRST, BOYS. There's many more coming right behind him and they have the talent and they gonna come to play. These fellows are hungry. They're good athletes and there's nowhere else they can make this kind of money. They're going to come, boys, and they're going to come scratching and diving. Unless you fellows look out and wake up, they're going to run you right out of the ball park. So,' I said, 'I don't want to see your petition and I don't want to hear anything more about it. The meeting is over; go back to bed.'

"That was that. I still couldn't tell you whether they

ever got to the point of actually drawing the petition up. Mr. Rickey got in the next morning, called the key players into his room individually, and laid down the law. I don't think I ever saw him that mad. Mr. Rickey was not only adamant about the question of any petition, he was equally adamant that they say not a word to the newspapermen. Since there weren't that many newspapermen in Panama with us, and they had all been comfortably asleep at the time of the meeting, the story of the aborted strike never got out—a minor miracle in itself.

"It ended right there. The one player who didn't back off completely was Dixie Walker, who did send his letter to Mr. Rickey. I was told that a trade for him was in the works with Pittsburgh, but then Mr. Rickey reverted to type. He couldn't make the deal he wanted—Dixie, after all, was thirty-six—and so he called it off. It wasn't until the next year that Dixie was sent to the Pirates.

"I wasn't with the Dodgers during Jackie's first season. I was suspended the day before he was brought up. But I have been told by several of the players that when Jackie joined the team, Eddie Stanky, always a stand-up guy, walked up to him and said, 'I want you to know something. You're on this ball club and as far as I'm concerned that makes you one of twenty-five players on my team. But before I play with you I want you to know how I feel about it. I want you to know I don't like it. I want you to know I don't like you.'

"'All right,' Jackie said, 'that's the way I'd rather have it. Right out in the open.'

"By the time I came back the following season, Eddie was Jackie's greatest booster. By then, of course, the club had won a pennant. They knew him as a person and they appreciated him as a ballplayer. And they knew he had put money in their pockets."

I have included Durocher's recital because it is the only complete record of that decisive meeting in Panama when Durocher alone turned aside the almost fatal petition threat. This was Durocher in action, the Durocher Rickey knew and counted on. This was the Durocher Rickey needed to pilot Robinson not only through the National League but also through the crosscurrents of the Dodgers themselves. This, too, was Durocher obeying Chandler's orders without a false step.

MacPhail was trying to out-bully Rickey. MacPhail thought that at long last, for real or fancied wrongs, he could feed his ego by bringing down in public the great Branch Rickey. Who, after all, was Branch Rickey?

Commissioner Chandler wasn't thinking about Rickey. His benefactor, MacPhail, had put a shining sword in his hands, an instrument that, like Excalibur, would show him to be another Landis.

The swift rush of events the next several weeks was confusing. As each new development sprang up, it had to be faced for what it appeared to be. The Dodgers, whose spring training quarters were in Havana, were in Panama. Main office communications were uncertain between Brooklyn, Panama, and Havana. On the other hand, the Yankees were entrenched at St. Petersburg, always in easy contact with the New York office and constantly surrounded by the press corps.

Durocher was called away from Panama suddenly. His Los Angeles attorneys needed him for examination relative to Judge Dockweiler's show-cause order involving Laraine Day's California divorce decree. This meant more adverse publicity for Durocher in the area the Brooklyn CYO had made sensitive.

When I went to Cincinnati in 1934 the veteran baseball writer for the Cincinnati *Enquirer* was Jack Ryder. A few years later when Ryder died he was succeeded by Lou Smith. Smith soon became a crack newspaperman, accurate and very aware of what was going on. I never found anything unsound in Smith's work. I say this to point up what Smith wrote in his paper several days before the trial at Sarasota was to begin, March 24, 1947.

Smith interviewed Chandler on a Tampa golf course and quoted the Commissioner as saying:

"Somebody may wind up getting kicked out of baseball. I'm

taking off my kid gloves and I intend to make things tough for the baseball people who won't toe the line and whose conduct I consider detrimental to baseball."

Later, Chandler refused to admit that he had said this. Smith insisted that the Commissioner had, and plenty more which he, Smith, had not published.

March 22, 1947, was Saturday. Ford Frick, president of the National League, of which Brooklyn was one of eight members, flew into Havana. He was to confer with Rickey the next day. Sunday was cleared by Rickey to work with Frick, to examine whatever defense the Dodgers thought necessary to answer the rather unclear charges by MacPhail, to have Walter O'Malley, himself a lawyer, pull everything together, and in general to prepare to fly to Sarasota on Monday for the afternoon hearing before Chandler.

Saturday night Mrs. Rickey was informed that her older brother, Frank Moulton, had died in Lucasville, Ohio. She got ready to fly to Lucasville early Sunday, and Rickey was certainly not going to let her take that sad trip without him. Rickey sent word immediately to Chandler and asked for a brief postponement of the hearing, inasmuch as he could not attend for evident reasons. Chandler sent word back that the hearing would go on as scheduled. The Rickeys by then had gone to Ohio.

Sunday morning, as the Rickeys were packing to leave, Frick had a lengthy breakfast with O'Malley. Frick never had his meeting with Rickey. What Frick and O'Malley discussed will never be known—both are dead—but it is interesting to note that Frick did not attend Chandler's hearing the next day. He sent word that he didn't wish to attend. That was all.

Will Harridge, veteran president of the American League, was not there. Although MacPhail had stated to Chandler that Harridge joined him in his protest, Harridge made it plain that he did not join MacPhail in any complaint against the Dodgers.

Commissioner Chandler sat at a table with his assistant, Walter Mulbry, and a public stenographer using a pad and pencil. There was a centrally placed witness chair. MacPhail was joined by one of his partners, Dan Topping. For the Dodgers there were O'Malley, Arthur Mann as Rickey's personal representative, Branch Rickey, Jr., as assistant general manager, and Rickey's longtime friend, former Senator Williams acting as Rickey's personal attorney. This was all. The press was barred. The hearings would not be open despite Rickey's request that they be.

My authority for the accounts of the hearings is Arthur Mann in his book. As a trained newspaperman, he took full notes.

The first witness was Ted McGrew, a genial veteran scout who had worked for both MacPhail and Rickey. Apparently Chandler expected McGrew to recall that back in 1943, during the war, Rickey had told all his coaches and scouts that if they could find a better job they were free to take it. His testimony was meaningless. As McGrew was excused, he was warned not to say anything to anyone about what went on. All witnesses were so silenced.

John Corriden, recently hired as a coach by MacPhail from Rickey, was next. He said he had been treated fairly by Rickey, but decided to take the MacPhail offer. That was all.

Next came Augie Galan, who played under Durocher but was now with the Cincinnati Reds. Chandler asked Galan to testify about the Dodgers' gambling, and especially that Durocher gambled with them and won their money. Galan would not say Durocher took advantage of any of his players. In fact, Galan began to defend Durocher, and was thanked and excused.

The fourth witness was the first who had any connection with the Havana incident that resulted in MacPhail's charges. He was Harold Parrott, the traveling secretary who had ghost-written the "Durocher Says" column that angered MacPhail. Parrott admitted his authorship, and the Commissioner told him to decide whether to return to full-time newspaper work or be a full-time baseball man. Parrott said he would be a baseball man, was warned strongly not to repeat anything of the hearing, and was excused. He never wrote another column for Durocher.

Chuck Dressen was brought in. Dressen had broken his word to Rickey about terms of employment at Brooklyn and had jumped to MacPhail. Dressen was curt. MacPhail stirred uneasily. Had Chandler gone deeper, a charge of tampering might be brought against MacPhail. But the Commissioner didn't get to the bottom of it.

For some reason, perhaps because O'Malley didn't want the hearing to become a dog-eat-dog affair, O'Malley made his only participation. He asked for and was granted permission to examine Dressen, and then merely assured Dressen that the Dodgers knew him to be a sound coach, a good fellow, and that Dressen should remember the Dodgers hadn't demanded this hearing—the Dodgers were defendants and were not trying to prosecute anyone. O'Malley then had Dressen sketch the fact he was fired by Rickey, then rehired by Rickey, and that Memphis Engelberg was Dressen's friend. Then O'Malley sat down and never got up again all afternoon.

Arthur Mann writes in his book:

"It was impossible for any of us three at the Dodger table to overlook the fact that O'Malley had not yet found it necessary to cross-examine or check statements or turn the questioning into a sharper scrutiny of information. It was also impossible to overlook the fact that no witness thus far had injured the Dodgers."

Now came the star witness, Leo Durocher. MacPhail produced a copy of the "Durocher Says" column written in Caracas by Parrott. Durocher took responsibility for the entire column, although it was doubtful he ever saw it—he trusted Parrott completely.

"'It seemed just another rhubarb,' Leo explained. 'We went on like that, Mr. MacPhail and I, for years. Why, he fired me many times after such arguments and hired me back. But we always laughed it off.

"'If I've said anything in that article to hurt Larry's feelings,' Leo went on, 'I'm sorry, and I apologize.'

"MacPhail got up and took Leo's hand. 'That's good enough for me,' MacPhail said, and sat back down."

Chandler switched the subject from the MacPhail charges to gambling in the Dodger clubhouse. He asked Leo, did he gamble for high stakes with one or with any of his players? This was a complete surprise as this had nothing whatsoever to do with MacPhail's charges. Chandler had tried to get such information from Galan but failed. Now he questioned Durocher himself.

Leo admitted he gambled for high stakes with only one player, a pitcher, Kirby Higbe. Then Leo explained that he never kept any of Higbe's money but gave it back to him as a "bonus" for pitching a good game . . . that this was a way of keeping Higbe from going into debt, keeping him solvent and stimulating his pitching efforts.

Chandler then asked Durocher about his statements to the press before the Sunday March 9 game at Havana concerning gamblers in MacPhail's box. Leo admitted he had said plenty, but hadn't seen what the writers sent back to the United States, and was unable to recall verbatim what he had said.

However, Leo started reminding Chandler of their meeting in Oakland back on November 22 when Chandler warned him to stay away from undesirables and gamblers, and Leo reminded Chandler that one man named by him was Memphis Engelberg, one of the two sitting behind the Yankee dugout.

Let me quote from Mann's book:

"Poor Leo did not get very far in his protestations at this point, because the Commissioner nodded and assured Leo that he did remember, with such vocal emphasis that Leo was obliged to cease reminding him of the important meeting, and the nature of their November conversation.

"This was not only the crux of the hearing, it was the fulcrum of the entire situation. Durocher's attempts to link his protestations in the Havana ball park to the warning given him by the Commissioner in Oakland on November 22, 1946, at the request of the Brooklyn Baseball Club were definitely sidetracked."

Then, while Durocher was still in the witness chair, Chandler asked MacPhail, "Colonel MacPhail, did Durocher ask you for the job managing the Yankees?" According to Mann, MacPhail never said yes or no. Further, Durocher was not asked if MacPhail ever offered him the job, as Leo had stated publicly many times. Again, the issue of tampering by MacPhail was evaded.

Durocher was excused, with the warning to remain absolutely silent about the hearing.

There seemed to be nothing more to be done. Chandler then asked MacPhail if there was anything else to be covered. MacPhail replied that he was not satisfied by the hearing . . . that he had not had any reply to his demands and that the results of the hearing had fallen far short of his expectations.

When Chandler asked MacPhail what he wanted him to do, MacPhail replied that he wanted some kind of statement—admission, denial or apology—from Rickey.

No one was empowered to speak for Rickey. Chandler then said the next hearing, with Rickey present, would be in St. Petersburg Friday March 28.

Mann noted that the heart of the matter—were the two known gamblers guests of MacPhail in the Yankees' box?—had not been touched upon. As the hearing began to break up, Mann laid before the Commissioner and Mulbry, his assistant, the picture that ran in the *Daily News* March 15 showing Engelberg and Immerman as occupants of the Yankee box with MacPhail in close proximity, and a deposition from the management of the Havana ball park that the tickets for the Yankee box had been turned over to the Yankees for both games March 8 and 9. Both Chandler and Mulbry acknowledged Mann's material.

On the morning of March 28 Rickey flew from Ohio to Miami in the Dodgers' plane. O'Malley and Mann flew to Miami from Havana. Mann had written a full report of the first hearing at Sarasota which Rickey read en route to St. Petersburg.

The second hearing began with Chandler, Mulbry, MacPhail, Rickey, O'Malley and Mann. Rickey explained his absence from the Sarasota hearing and then repeated in principle his remarks about undesirables being in the Yankees' club box. Yes, he had said plenty in Havana, Rickey stated, and he felt he was entitled to do so.

Chandler then sent for Arthur Patterson, traveling secretary of the Yankees, who handled tickets for the team. Patterson was evasive about the tickets Engelberg and Immerman had for the 2 games because, he said, he handled so many he didn't remember. Patterson was on the spot in front of his boss, MacPhail. All he would say was, "I can't recall."

Patterson was excused. Chandler then asked everyone present to leave the room except Rickey, O'Malley and Mann. Even the public stenographer left.

Here is what Mann wrote, and here is the key to it all:

"When the door had closed, Chandler arose and came over to the Brooklyn Dodger table.

"The three of us were seated. We looked up into his glistening, sunburned face as he leaned over and said, 'How much would it hurt you folks to have your fellow out of baseball?'

"The scene and reactions that followed defy description. It was the first inkling we had that Durocher might be punished at all . . . Rickey was completely torn asunder by emotion . . . he emitted a gasp of tortured amazement . . . 'Happy,' he said, 'what on earth is the matter with you?'"

Then Chandler took a letter from his inside coat pocket, explained it was from a "big man" in Washington, a man too important to be ignored, who wrote that Durocher should be expelled from baseball. Chandler then told the Dodger trio that he was just sounding them out.

As Rickey started to leave, MacPhail walked in the door, and quickly pulled him into the bathroom. MacPhail asked Rickey, "Are you interested in Nick Etten?" Etten was a first baseman MacPhail was trying to dispose of. MacPhail by now had had his fun with the two hearings. He moved on to something else. "Are you interested in Nick Etten?" Rickey wasn't. He had other things on his mind.

MacPhail remained in St. Petersburg for a few days, then returned to New York. He was pleased with the way his new manager, Bucky Harris, was handling the ball club and the writers. The writers, in fact, were delighted with Harris. In contrast to the reserved Joe McCarthy, Harris was easily approached, answered all questions, sat around, had drinks and shot the bull. Harris was always good for a story. Yet he was a shrewd judge of ballplayers. His experience went back to 1924, when as the twenty-eight-year-old second baseman of the Washington Senators he was made manager. He led the Senators to a world championship his first season. The "Boy Manager."

Harris had managed twice at Washington, once at Detroit and briefly at Philadelphia in the National League. His years as a major-league manager totaled a full score. In 1945 he took over managing the Buffalo club in the International League, and the next year was its general manager. MacPhail brought him to the Yankees to be a special assistant, and when he needed a manager for 1947, after the rumors surrounding Durocher and Dressen had been blown away, there on hand was Harris.

In October of 1946, the season before, MacPhail had shocked many of the New York writers by trading one of their favorites, second baseman Joe Gordon, to Cleveland for right-handed pitcher Allie Reynolds. Reynolds in four years with the Indians had won 51 games against 47 losses. In 1945, his best year, he was 18–12, then in 1946 he dropped off to 11–15. MacPhail's deal didn't look good to most of the press. MacPhail told me once that Bill Corum said he was of a mind not to speak to him again —but he did after Reynolds got going at the Stadium. This was the notable change MacPhail—on his own—made for 1947, and it was pivotal. That season Reynolds won 19 against 8, had some saves in relief, and won a game in the World Series.

However, Reynolds was one of the question marks for Mac-Phail and Harris as spring training wound down. Another was the Big Man, Joe DiMaggio. DiMag had a sore left heel. The Yankee team physician was Dr. Mal Stevens, orthopedic surgeon and former football coach at Yale and NYU. Dr. Stevens spent most of his time with DiMaggio, but Joe was slow to heal. When the team broke camp, Joe and Dr. Stevens remained in St. Petersburg for specialized exercises. Both MacPhail and Harris believed Snuffy Stirnweiss would fill Gordon's spot at second base, which Snuffy did. Rizzuto had matured at shortstop, and Billy Johnson, a veteran, had third base nailed down. And George McQuinn, a fine fielder, was at first, which settled the infield.

Harris had another problem, which was of a very pleasant nature. This problem was Yogi Berra. Yogi came out of the armed forces in midseason of 1946 and was sent to Newark, one of the two top teams in the Yankees' farm system. He caught, played the outfield, and hit .314 with power. The Yankees brought him up for the final 7 games of the season. Berra caught. Most important, he hit .364 with 2 home runs.

Harris didn't know where to play him. Yogi was a crude defensive man, but as Harris said, "The way he swings that stick, he's going to play somewhere." Yogi shuttled between catching and outfielding, but by the end of the season had the catching job pretty much to himself. In baseball, the name is power: hit hard and you play somewhere, throw hard and you pitch. A classic case was Rudy York with Detroit. In the period 1937–39 the Tigers tried York in the outfield, behind the bat, at third and at first. Rudy belted the ball but could play only first base. However, the Tigers had Hank Greenberg, a premier first baseman and power hitter. Hank was asked, for the sake of the team, would he move to left field? He did, one of the few generous things I know that happened in baseball, which is an extremely selfish enterprise.

Peace hovered over the Yankee camp. DiMaggio and Dr. Stevens kept close company. Reynolds was impressive. The Yankees left St. Pete, April 3, and played Atlanta on the fifth, their first game in four days. They won 3–1. Spud Chandler did most of the pitching, and was sharp. The next day the Yankees clubbed Atlanta 14–1 with Reynolds throwing bullets. All Yogi did with the bat was belt 2 home runs, a double and 2 singles. The next day at Norfolk the Yankees won 19–5 and Berra added a home run, a double and a single. He was "swinging that stick."

While the Yankees were having a picnic at Norfolk it was announced in Detroit that Babe Ruth had signed with the Ford Motor Company to be a consultant in American Legion Junior Baseball, in which Ford was very interested. Ruth was well into his final illness but his picture and the story made news.

The Yankees had one more stop before getting home to the Stadium. They defeated Baltimore 7–3, and made it to New York the evening of April 8. It rained out the work scheduled for the next day.

The highlight baseball story on April 8 came from Sheffield, Alabama. The New York Giants were barnstorming home with the Cleveland Indians. In their game that afternoon young Whitey Lockman, fleet as a startled deer, slid into second base and broke his leg. Manager Mel Ott was crushed. Lockman was to be out of action for at least three months.

The Dodgers remained at Havana, Cuba, until almost the last minute. Rickey stayed with the club. The Dodgers continued their games with Montreal, and one day Robinson would play second, the next day he would be at first. Rickey and Durocher wanted Robinson to work at first, but Montreal manager Clay Hopper kept saying he had to find out who would play first base for him once Robinson was put on the Dodgers.

The big relief pitcher, Hugh Casey, on April 4 was hit on his pitching arm by a line drive belted by George Shuba, but was expected to be out only a short time. On the fifth Bruce Edwards, in sliding back to first base, bowled Robinson over and shook him up. Jack had to leave the game and was to be out of uniform an indefinite time. On the last day at Havana, April 6, Pete Reiser, who had hurt his collarbone in the armed forces, started throwing hard again.

The Dodgers played 2 games en route to Brooklyn. They beat the St. Louis Browns 12–4 at Miami, but Pee Wee Reese sprained his ankle. Durocher groaned. Reese was the defensive sparkplug. (In the pennant drive in late 1941, Durocher had taken himself out of the lineup and given his old job to Reese.) The next day, the eighth, the Dodgers won at Charleston, South Carolina, 9–2.

That day New York *Times* columnist Arthur Daley wrote that it was an open question whether Rickey would keep Robinson at Brooklyn or send him back to Montreal.

The team headed for Ebbets Field for 2 games with Montreal and 3 with the Yankees. Then the curtain would rise.

Looking back, this is significant: On April 3 Bert Bell rendered a decision that may very well have influenced the decision Chandler would make six days later. Bell had been Commissioner of the National Football League fourteen months. He had succeeded Elmer Layden (former fullback of the Four Horsemen of Notre Dame) who hadn't been firm enough to suit some of the owners and writers. The question was, how much authority would Bell exert?

The sports world had been shocked and deeply shaken back on December 5, 1946, the Sunday of the NFL championship game at the Polo Grounds. It came out that morning that two of the Giants, Merle Hapes and Frank Filchock, had been offered bribes by gamblers to "fix" the game. They had taken about a week to inform the team of the offers. They had not reported the offers promptly. A heavy cloud of suspicion draped itself immediately over the Polo Grounds. I was one of the announcers of the game. I tried to get Commissioner Bell to come on my mike and say something but he refused. He was stunned.

Finally Bell made his move April 3. He suspended both players "indefinitely," which meant for life. This was the biggest scandal in sports since the "Black" Sox World Series in 1919. Bell reacted as had Landis, who barred for life all eight Chicago baseball players involved. Bell also announced that he had waited to make public his sentences at the request of the New York District Attorney, who asked for the delay until three key would-be fixers (not the players) could be sentenced.

Bell's decision made big, black headlines. All the writers, without dissent, applauded the new Commissioner for his strong action with its thorough cleansing of suspicion. It makes one wonder—Bell's decision with its immediate favorable reaction was April 3, six days before Chandler's decision. Did Chandler note the widespread approval that Bell received, or had Chandler made up his mind on his decision before April 3? Was Bell's decision, and its timing, the final nail in the lid of Durocher's coffin?

The Dodgers and the Yankees arrived without fanfare in New York the night of April 8, expecting routine work for the next few days against the beginning of another season.

All hell broke loose at the offices of the Dodgers Wednesday morning April 9, 1947. In Rickey's office there was an important meeting for the purpose of assigning various players to different teams in the farm system. One wall was covered by a blackboard with players' names on it. Rickey presided.

Durocher was there, as were his new coaches Clyde Suke-forth, Ray Blades and Jake Pitler. Harold Parrott was sitting in, along with Branch Rickey, Jr. Arthur Mann was on hand. Eight men sat before the blackboard.

I wasn't at the meeting, but I have heard about it many times from Mann, Parrott, Durocher and from Rickey himself. It was brutally dramatic.

Rickey had left word that no calls, except of dire emergency, were to disturb this meeting. The season was near. Players had to be assigned. Teams had to be fleshed out. All eyes were on the blackboard when the private phone on Rickey's desk rang.

Rickey picked up the phone and began listening. Once he said, "You can't do that!" He listened again, intently. He lighted his cigar as he listened. He ran a gnarled hand through his hair.

Then he put the phone down, and sat back in his swivel desk chair, staring at the ceiling.

"That was the Commissioner," Rickey finally said. He looked at the ceiling again.

"Harold," he said to Parrott, "you have been fined $500."

He paused.

"The Brooklyn Club has been fined $2,000."

He puffed at his cigar, looked upward a moment, and went on:

"The New York Club has been fined $2,000."

Another pause, another upward stare.

"Dressen has been suspended for thirty days."

An even longer pause. Another running of his hand through his hair.

"And, you Leo, have been suspended from baseball for a year."

Durocher said, "For what?"

Rickey replied, "I don't know."

Commissioner Chandler released his statement in Cincinnati just before he telephoned Rickey. Pat Robinson, a sportswriter for INS, was outside the room waiting to see Mann. Pat's boss called him on the phone with the news that the wire services reported Durocher was suspended, and that he, Pat, had better get busy right now. From then on it was bedlam. Phones rang until shortly all phone lines were jammed. Radio programs were interrupted with bulletins on Durocher's suspension. Headlines screamed the suspension. I can't recall a sports story so suddenly dominating all the media. It seemed, certainly in Brooklyn, as though there was no other topic of conversation. The borough was stunned. . . . Manager Leo Durocher suspended for a year!

The exhibition game for that afternoon was called off because of rain. This freed the newspapermen to redouble their coverage. Durocher's history was disinterred and worked over from his beginning days with the Yankees, his troubles with Babe Ruth and Ed Barrow, his banishment to Cincinnati, his rehabilitation at St. Louis under Rickey, his troubles with Cardinal manager Frank Frisch which led to his trade to Brooklyn, MacPhail making him manager and hiring and firing and hiring him, the Dodgers' 1941 pennant, the war years and Leo's preoccupation with going on radio shows during spring training, his constant rows with umpires, his connections with George Raft including the dice game in Leo's New York apartment, alleged hitting of John Christian under the stands, the Westbrook Pegler columns, the withdrawal of the Brooklyn CYO from Ebbets Field, Leo's three marriages and his rhubarb with Judge Dock-weiler over Laraine Day's divorce. It was a field day for the press.

The New York *Times* wasn't then, and never has been, in the habit of putting sports on its front page. When it does, the story has thrust. Durocher's suspension made it on page one the next day. Louis Effrat wrote it under the heading "Chandler Bars Durocher for 1947 Baseball Season." Effrat began with these two salient points: one, ". . . most drastic action ever taken against a major league pilot," and, two, "The outgrowth of a feud that has been seething between the Brooklyn and Yankee organizations since L. S. (Larry) MacPhail, former Dodger president, moved over to the Yankees in the rival American League, the ruling by Chandler brought a strange stillness to Brooklyn yesterday."

The sports section of the *Times* was dominated by the Durocher suspension. Among the various stories related to Durocher, Chandler, MacPhail and Rickey, there was the entire text of Chandler's decision.

Some reporters who traveled with the Dodgers and were well known to Leo tried to ask him questions as he left the Dodger offices. To each he said, "Don't ask me . . . don't ask me . . . I can't say anything." He left and wasn't seen until the next afternoon.

Leo went into immediate seclusion. Possessor of a quick mind, a bench jockey without peer, widely known as "The Lip" because of his abrasive and constant talk, participant in countless arguments with umpires, Leo was now unable to speak a word for himself. The final sentence of Commissioner Chandler's decision was: "All parties to this controversy are silenced from the time this order is issued." Chandler felt very strongly that the entire matter was a disgrace to baseball—MacPhail, Rickey, Parrott, Dressen, Durocher, everybody concerned—and he wanted it quieted down. Thus his "silencing." But with the suspension of Durocher for a year, fresh fuel was added to the already blazing fire, which now exploded.

However, Leo knew that of all the people involved, he must stay silent lest Chandler increase his suspension—perhaps suspend him for life.

The next day, Thursday April 10, was the last exhibition game for the Dodgers with Montreal. As the broadcaster, I was at Ebbets Field earlier than usual. Who knew what would happen next? The Dodgers as the home team took batting practice first, then left the field for the Montreal team. All the Dodgers went to the clubhouse. All the writers were in the clubhouse, waiting and watching should something take place. Coach Clyde Sukeforth was temporarily in charge.

The door swung open and in walked Durocher. He was dressed quietly, neatly, expensively. He had on a beautifully tailored dark blue suit, white shirt, dark tie, black shoes shined so you could have used them as mirrors. A white handkerchief was tucked in his coat pocket at just the right angle. His hat was dark. One of his brothers was with him. Just the two. He knew exactly when the team would be in the clubhouse and he timed his entrance perfectly.

"Fellows," he said softly as he looked at the writers, at me, at anyone else who wasn't wearing a uniform, "I want to talk to my players. Just my players." We left. I remember he used the pronoun "my" in reference to the players. "I want to talk to my players." They were still his for the next ten minutes.

I waited outside the clubhouse. The door opened again and Leo and his brother walked out, never hesitated or looked anywhere but straight ahead. They kept going, the two of them.

The players began coming out, headed for the dugout. I stopped Dixie Walker and asked him what went on inside the clubhouse with Leo.

"Red," Dixie began, "you know I've never liked the fellow. But I'll tell you this: he can get you to play better than you ever thought you could."

Dixie paused, then gave me a rundown.

"He waited till the door closed and the writers were out,"

Dixie said, "and began talking to us, very easy and quiet. No shouting or hollering like he can get. He never complained. He never said he got a bad deal. He never said anything about the Commissioner.

"He told us we were a good ball club . . . that we can beat the Cardinals for the pennant if we all bear down and work together . . . that wherever he was this summer he'd be pulling for us . . . that he had faith in us.

"Then," Dixie said, "he got even more serious. He said for us not to worry about who would be the new manager . . . that Mr. Rickey would get us the best one available . . . that no matter what happened, no matter what, not to worry but to trust Mr. Rickey . . . that Mr. Rickey would see to it we came out all right."

Eddie Stanky came along just as Dixie walked off. Eddie was always willing to talk. I asked him about Leo and the meeting in the closed clubhouse.

Stanky said practically the same things Walker had said. Then Eddie added:

"Red, the way the fellow went out, he's bound to come back."

I went up to the radio box to join forces with Connie Desmond. The two of us did the games. (Ernie Harwell didn't come to us until the next year, and when he left after the 1949 season Vin Scully became our third man.)

The game that afternoon with Montreal was in every way an exhibition. It had long been scheduled, people had paid to enter the park to see it, the players were getting final tune-ups for the impending pennant races. It would be Jackie Robinson's first game at Brooklyn, but all thoughts were on Durocher and his suspension.

Leo said, "Trust Mr. Rickey." Mr. Rickey woke everybody up later that afternoon, shook them out of any daydreams or speculations with this simple announcement handed out in the press box during the sixth inning:

> The Brooklyn Dodgers today purchased the contract of Jackie Roosevelt Robinson from the Montreal Royals. He will report immediately.
>
> Branch Rickey

That was it. That was when, where and how the color line in major-league baseball was broken. This made headlines although Durocher, Chandler, Rickey and MacPhail still made news. Durocher's suspension was completely unexpected. The announcement on Robinson had been expected all spring. It was just a matter of when Rickey would make it official that Jackie was to join the big ball club.

That same Thursday morning MacPhail held a press conference despite Chandler's edict of silence. MacPhail would be a most difficult man to silence. MacPhail stated he was completely surprised by Durocher's suspension. (He said later that the suspension was without grounds.) This morning, April 10, the day after Chandler dropped his bomb, MacPhail was angry. He and his Yankees had been fined $2,000, so Chandler must have thought him guilty of something. His coach Charlie Dressen had been suspended for thirty days, so more guilt of some sort was officially marked against MacPhail and the Yankees.

But as MacPhail told the press, "Under baseball law the Commissioner is prosecutor, judge and jury. There is no appeal from his decisions."

MacPhail got warmed up as his press conference continued. It was one of his traits that once he began talking on a subject that was in his craw, he would go on and on as his anger stimulated him. This ad-libbing, or talking at random, or "popping off," often got him into trouble. When he wrote his statements or letters he always was careful in his language.

He said that the Commissioner had no right to prohibit discussion of matters of interest to the press and to the public . . . that the Yankees would continue to provide such information to the press and public . . . that he was correct in his signing of Dressen as a coach and that he had a letter from Chandler himself and from league president Will Harridge saying so . . . that he saw no grounds for Durocher's suspension . . . that he had been, was still, and would continue to be Durocher's friend.

John Drebinger was the New York *Times* writer assigned. In his story, which just about sums up MacPhail and his position, Drebbie wrote:

"Only MacPhail still appeared in a loquacious mood, although he looked more like a man who, having scored a Pyrrhic victory, would gladly have seen the whole thing called off."

Nothing, however, could be recalled. What MacPhail had set in motion in his reaction to Rickey's and Durocher's accusations at Havana, plus Parrott's "Durocher Says" column, had now to run its course. Judge Landis had acted, Bert Bell had acted, and now Happy Chandler had acted. The eight players Landis suspended for life disappeared, as did the two football players banished by Bell. When Chandler acted it became "only the beginning" for many men, including Chandler himself.

At this point the era of good feeling between MacPhail and Chandler abruptly ended. MacPhail now turned his resentment and his anger toward the man he had largely made Commissioner. Time began running out on Chandler, April 9, 1947.

That evening Leo again came out of his seclusion. With Laraine he attended the annual Brooklyn Knothole Club Dinner to welcome home the Dodgers. The main ballroom of the St. George Hotel was packed by some thirteen to fourteen thousand Dodger fans. The players were on the dais—all but Robinson. I guess nobody thought to ask him. I was the master of ceremonies. Leo and Laraine made a stunning couple. The evening became a tribute to Durocher. It turned into a massive going-away celebration. Kirby Higbe spoke for the players when he said, "It is a hell of a decision."

When I introduced Leo all he said was, "Although I can't be with the team physically, I'll be dreaming of them in my heart." Then he and Laraine stood and waved. The house nearly came down with applause. Ford Frick was there. He hadn't cared to attend the hearings although one of his clubs and its manager were deeply involved. He said something about, "He who is without sin, let him cast the first stone." Rickey was not well and could not be there. Walter O'Malley spoke for the Dodgers and he said, "Leo, we aren't saying good-bye to you and Laraine. We say, we'll be seeing you soon."

Beneath the surface it was a most painful affair. That afternoon Leo had told his players good-bye. It was sinking in deeper to the Dodgers that they no longer had Leo as their manager, and also that they had no manager at all. They had certainly heard that Jackie Robinson had been put on the Brooklyn roster that afternoon and would report to the clubhouse tomorrow. The best grapevine in the world is in baseball. As they walked out of the St. George Hotel that evening the players walked into grave uncertainties.

Durocher and his wife went into graver uncertainties as they left for Leo's apartment in New York, and then for California and his exile. Leo was out of baseball for at least a year. He didn't know whether the Dodgers would pay him for the year he was gone, or whether they would take him back in the future. It was a black night in Brooklyn.

After Chandler had finished talking, Rickey put down the phone. Then he deliberately and dramatically—he never raised his voice; the epitome of raw drama is often achieved with understatement—relayed to the small group in his office the judgment of the Commissioner. Abruptly the meeting was over. Reporters began swarming like bees on a busted honey barrel on a hot afternoon.

Over and over Rickey explained to the insatiable press that the Dodgers would make no appeal . . . that the decision of the Commissioner was final. . . . No, of course not, he had no idea who the new manager would be . . . any one of his three coaches could do a creditable job with the team. . . . He would begin for now without a manager . . . coach Clyde Sukeforth would be temporarily in charge. To the questions of when would Durocher return, would he be rehired, would he be paid his salary, Rickey replied he had no answers then, and didn't know when he would have any answers. It was all too sudden.

Finally the room was cleared of the press. Finally some order began returning to the offices of the Dodgers. Rickey provided a sound medicine for his staff. He led them back to the work at hand. After all, the farm system teams had to be staffed. Various players had to be assigned. Discussions began in the inner circles about a manager. Joe McCarthy, highly successful manager of the Chicago Cubs and the New York Yankees—the Yankees especially—had quit MacPhail May 24, 1946, the year before.

Ed Barrow was telephoned and he assured Rickey that McCarthy would be ideal, and further, Barrow supplied Rickey with McCarthy's private phone number outside Buffalo, New York. Wouldn't that be something to bring McCarthy back to New York, across the river from MacPhail! McCarthy declined with thanks—he wasn't interested in a job this year. In the days that followed Bill McKechnie, Bill Terry, Burt Shotton, Rogers Hornsby were discussed. But only McCarthy was asked. My estimate is that McCarthy had had enough sound and fury with MacPhail, was enjoying his respite from the baseball wars and certainly wanted no part of the Brooklyn-Chandler-Durocher-Rickey, and above all, -Robinson rhubarb.

Rickey was often unfavorably compared to men of immediate action such as MacPhail and Durocher. MacPhail and Durocher made decisions on the spur of the moment, although MacPhail often planned his major moves. Often he didn't, as I'm certain he didn't about his charges filed with Chandler against Rickey and Durocher. Durocher for the only time in his life, when he had to do so, took his suspension with silent grace.

Neither Durocher nor MacPhail liked to have to wait on anything. Rickey could wait. He had enormous patience. He could wait for his ideas to mature and for his young players to grow and develop. Rickey had the strength of being quiet and looking into himself. He had learned that during the long year he spent at Saranac Lake getting over tuberculosis, knowing that when he left the sanitarium he had a young wife and no job.

But Rickey could and would act. I found that out when MacPhail offered me the Yankee broadcasting job. The Dodger players discovered in Panama, when the petition-plot against Jackie Robinson was brought to light by Durocher, that he could act and be fearfully angry at the same time.

Commissioner Chandler made his phone call the morning of April 9. Rickey acted. He disposed of the writers, then set his office staff back to work. He brought order and some calm to 215 Montague Street, although lightning bolts flashed throughout the day. He made up his mind about Robinson. In the sixth inning of the game with Montreal the next afternoon he announced to the press that Robinson was being put on the Dodgers. Rickey countered the whirlwind with action. He knew that the quietest place in a storm was at the very heart of it.

Rickey might well have been excused if he had turned off the phones, closed the doors, gone into seclusion, and read the Book of Job. However, he knew that book of troubles and plagues very well. Like Job, he was beset from every side, but while Job talked at great length, bewailed his bitter fate and did nothing, Rickey shook his head and went to work. He didn't speak about the hurt that MacPhail had become his adversary. He didn't cry out that his careful planning to assemble a team that could challenge the champion Cardinals was seriously upset. He didn't complain that his years of working with Durocher were now crushed. He didn't moan with disappointment that some Brooklyn players had almost rebelled against Jackie Robinson instead of asking for him to join the team. He didn't complain that in his most trying hour, when he was bringing the first black man into organized baseball, he was deprived of his manager. Say what you might about Durocher, he would have fought for Robinson every inch of the way, every inch.

Rickey was not a young man. He was sixty-six. For several years he had suffered from an inner-ear disturbance called Ménière's disease, a syndrome of recurring dizziness, nausea, vomiting and noises inside the ear. He would lose his balance at various times, sometimes on the street and have to ask strangers for help.

His wife and his children had advised him not to take on the "breaking of the color line." They had told him he was too old and not well enough. They had warned him that every hand in baseball would be against him. And it was so.

Just as MacPhail had told me he would, Rickey walked through a ten-foot brick wall. He brought order back into his office. He balanced his farm teams. He signed Robinson. He opened the 1947 season without a manager.

I was amazed at his stamina, his quiet determination, his utter belief that in good time all would be well. I saw to it that nothing about the broadcasts gave him more worry—and in those days the radio audience for the Brooklyn games was greater than the combined readership of all the New York papers.

It is difficult today, thirty-five years later, to appreciate the impact Chandler's suspension of Durocher made across the country. Today big-league managers come and go: Charley Finley hired and fired them, then George Steinbrenner outdid Finley. Led by Finley and followed by Steinbrenner, major-league owners have debased the lofty status of manager and stripped that position of much of the honor it once commanded.

Durocher wasn't even fired—he was suspended. Durocher had become, over the years, a national figure. Chandler was trying to become one, inheriting the commissionership held by a truly national and dominant figure, Judge Landis. Durocher's career had been marked by well-publicized highs and lows. Durocher was the manager of the Brooklyn Dodgers, and the Dodgers under Branch Rickey were making history with the first Negro ballplayer, Jackie Robinson.

Embroiled in the situation—in fact, he had initiated it—was the stormy, colorful, dynamic Larry MacPhail, new headman of the New York Yankees. Rickey had started MacPhail in baseball, then had gotten him top jobs at Cincinnati and Brooklyn. The pupil and the master were now at each other's throats. To round it out, Rickey now had the job at Brooklyn that MacPhail had held.

It was marvelous material for the writers. Irresistible. In this rich material they chose sides. It wasn't so much that the writers were assaying the suspension as that they were for Chandler or for Durocher. Certainly they were for or against Rickey and MacPhail. Some writers wanted no part of any of the men involved.

The Sporting News is a weekly. It had time, as it prepared its next edition in St. Louis, to gather samples from important writers from coast to coast. All in all, *The Sporting News* gave five full pages to the Chandler-Durocher story, and the reactions to it, in addition to various feature stories on Durocher.

A master playwright could not have created more human interest than this true-to-life drama. What made it explode in a red-hot climax was the surprise denouement of Chandler's deci-

sion. The press was waiting for the Commissioner to rule between MacPhail and Rickey. MacPhail had brought the case to
Chandler, demanding Rickey's blood. The battle was between
these two principals. Durocher had been a sinful man, but had
atoned, confessed, been absolved by Chandler, and had walked
the straight-and-narrow as Chandler had ordered. Instead of
MacPhail wounding Rickey, or Rickey repelling MacPhail's as-
sault, Durocher got suspended. Arthur Daley in the New York
Times wrote, "Leo Durocher is like the man who is hailed into a
traffic court for passing through a red light and then is sentenced to the electric chair. In this instance, the penalty does not
fit the crime and is much too severe." On the other side of the
coin, Jimmy Powers in the New York *Daily News* said,
"Chandler's decision was long overdue and too lenient. Landis
would have barred Durocher for life long ago."

J. G. Taylor Spink was running *The Sporting News,* and he
was obviously for Chandler and not for Durocher. On the first of
the five pages allotted to the story, a column by Joe Williams,
sports editor of the New York *World-Telegram,* was run, using
the entire length of the page, two columns wide. Williams was
scathingly against Durocher, Rickey, MacPhail and Dressen.
Williams was high in his praise of Chandler as a decisive man.
Then, in its lengthy editorial, *The Sporting News* didn't waste
time on the MacPhail-Rickey-Dressen involvement, but worked
on Durocher's past record and supported Chandler as a strong
Commissioner.

"Leo's suspension," *The Sporting News* said, "is a general
warning that the man running things is as severe a czar as the
late Judge Landis ever hoped to be . . . the sum total of all of
this for the game of baseball is a gorgeous benefice."

All told, *The Sporting News* carried comments by thirty-six
writers from around the sixteen major-league cities, as well as
from Los Angeles, New Orleans, San Francisco and Louisville.
The opinions varied from support for Chandler to criticism of
him for a too severe and unjustified penalty. Several writers accused Chandler of paying off his obligation to MacPhail for getting him the commissionership. Some writers said Chandler
acted only because he had been criticized for being a weak
Commissioner, and was thus provoked. Mike Gavin wrote in the

New York *Journal-American,* "Someone evidently made Chandler so mad that he just had to swing and when he did he struck the most vulnerable spot. The same punishment immediately following any of Durocher's old escapades probably would have been taken in stride. But to throw the book at him when he was laboring under the impression his sins were forgiven and was leading the life of a saint strikes a sour note."

Red Smith in the New York *Herald Tribune* said, "Chandler proved his courage by throwing the book at a couple of hired hands and tipping his hat to the insufferable mud-slingers who pay his salary."

The opinions were strongly divided. It depended on whom you talked to or what you read. As Danny Kaye sang in *Lady in the Dark,* "What a mess of a mishmash this is."

When the storm broke in Rickey's office Wednesday April 9, 1947, the weather kept in step. It rained out the game at Ebbets Field that afternoon. The next day Montreal, with Robinson playing first base, defeated the Dodgers 4–3 to end their spring work with the parent club. This was the first time Jackie had played since Bruce Edwards had accidentally knocked him down with a slide at first base on April 5 at Havana. It was also Jackie's first game at Ebbets Field.

Rickey's terse announcement Thursday that Robinson was being placed on the Brooklyn roster was in the sixth inning. It was the sports headline the next day, but the writers dutifully pointed out that Robinson wasn't a shining light in that day's historic game—he had gone hitless and had bunted a pop fly that began a double-play.

The Yankees came to Ebbets Field for intercity games Friday, Saturday and Sunday. The announcement that Robinson would be at first base for the Dodgers drew record crowds for spring exhibition games—a total of 79,441 for the 3 games in the bandbox ball park that seated some 32,000. The Dodgers won the first game 14–6 with 11 runs in the fifth inning. Robinson had no hits in his Brooklyn debut but looked quite professional at first base, a new position for him. He handled all his fifteen chances easily. He did bat in 3 runs with 2 long fly balls and an infield out.

The Yankees won the next 2 games. On Saturday Allie Reynolds, the big right-hander MacPhail had gotten from Cleveland for second baseman Joe Gordon, handcuffed the Dodgers for six innings. However, Jackie got a single off Reynolds (his first hit in Brooklyn) which drove in the only Brooklyn run as the Yankees took it 8–1. Robinson again played well at first. Yogi Berra belted a home run into Bedford Avenue, his first at Ebbets Field.

Sunday, April 13, the Yankees came up with 4 runs in the ninth inning to win 10–9. Then they rushed to Penn Station to catch a train for the special Opening Day, Monday at Washington, where President Harry Truman was scheduled to be the first-ball pitcher.

Pee Wee Reese, out a week with a sprained ankle, returned to short, which put the Dodgers at full strength.

The betting commissioners made the St. Louis Cardinals and the Boston Red Sox, who had been in the World Series the year before, favorites to repeat.

Also on this Sunday, April 13, Leo Durocher, unannounced, flew into Los Angeles to begin serving his sentence. To the stray reporters who happened to be at the airport, all Leo said was "No comment."

The Boston Braves were to open the season at Brooklyn on Tuesday. Coach Clyde Sukeforth was temporary manager. Under his direction the Dodgers won 2 games from the Braves: 5–3 and 12–6. The series was for 3 games but the second one, on Wednesday, was rained out. On Thursday in the fifth inning Jackie Robinson bunted toward third base—he had caught Bob Elliott playing deep—and beat it out easily for his first major-league hit. In his third game, the next one, at the Polo Grounds, he hit a home run into the left-field stands, plus a single.

So the Dodgers got their season started, winning their first 2 games at home against the Braves, then moving across the river to begin a series against the Giants at the Polo Grounds. But the Dodgers had no manager.

The three coaches—Sukeforth, Ray Blades, Jake Pitler—led by Sukeforth, went to Rickey and asked that Burt Shotton be brought in as manager. Shotton had been discussed, among others, the past few troubled days. My guess is that this is exactly what Rickey wanted, but he knew it would work better if the idea were presented by the coaching staff rather than have Shotton imposed on them. Shotton knew nothing of this. He was retired from baseball and living in Bartow, Florida. He enjoyed his days playing golf and fishing. He was sixty-three, white-haired and vigorous. Rickey had used him at the rookie camp at Pensacola for advice on certain young ballplayers. Shotton had favorably impressed everyone he came in contact with. However, for Shotton, Pensacola was just a change of pace. He had vowed when he quit coaching at Cleveland after the 1945 season that he would never put on another baseball uniform. He never did.

Rickey sent Shotton a telegram on the third day of the season, asking him to fly to New York for a conference, but to tell no one. Just that, fly to New York at once. Rickey met Shotton the next morning at La Guardia. Shotton got off the plane with only an overnight bag. He brought no change of clothes and was wearing his Florida-style two-toned shoes. He had told his wife, "Rick wants to see me about some players—I'll be right back."

Who was Burt Shotton—or Barney, as Rickey called him? Rickey knew who he was, pinned his hopes on him, and wasn't disappointed. I knew who he was to some degree, but the writers around New York, especially the younger ones, didn't know him—and never did like him, particularly Dick Young of the *Daily News* and Harold Rosenthal of the *Herald Tribune*.

When I went to the big leagues at Cincinnati in 1934, Shotton was one of manager Bob O'Farrell's coaches. Every time I asked Shotton for information he always said for me to talk to the manager. He was a strict chain-of-command operator.

Shotton had a biting, at times bitter way of saying things. When he was managing Columbus, Ohio, in 1937—in Rickey's farm system—Enos Slaughter reported as a rookie. Slaughter's uniform didn't fit well, sort of hung on him, his socks sagged and his shoes were split at the sides. Shotton took a glance and said, "You sure look like a country ballplayer." From then on he was Country Slaughter.

One afternoon Lou Effrat of the New York *Times* came into the Brooklyn dugout all excited. He went over to Shotton and said, "I just read where Candy Cummings invented the curve ball back in 1867."

Shotton looked at Effrat and said, quick as a flash, "I don't know who the fellow was who first came up with the curve ball . . . I don't know when or where. But whoever he was, when he did it he took all the joy out of baseball."

One morning in 1934 when the Reds were taking early batting practice (when a team is at home, and before the regulars take the field for their batting practice, the pitchers and the utility men who are not allowed to hit with the regulars come out and take turns batting and shagging) I was standing behind the batting cage. I was listening. I knew I was a green-pea announcer, and I knew the only way I was going to gain information was to hang around the players and listen to what they said. There came a lull. Larry Benton was on the mound, and he yelled to me to grab a bat and hit a few. I hesitated. Several of the other players urged me to get in the batter's box. Paul Derringer almost pushed me against the plate. Shotton was standing off to one side. He didn't say anything.

I got a bat. I had played baseball as a boy and in high school, but that was years gone by. Benton pumped and threw sort of sidearm—he was right-handed and I was batting right-handed. I pulled back from the pitch. Everybody laughed. Ballplayers are great kidders. Benton had his fun, throwing from byway of third base. Now he yelled, "Stand in there—I won't hit you."

I swung a few times and missed. Then I fouled one off. I had enough. I dropped the bat and walked back behind the batting cage. I was embarrassed. I hadn't hit one fair ball. I said to Shotton, "Burt, that's the first time I've had a bat in my hands in ten years." He didn't hesitate. "From what I saw," he snapped, "that ought to be enough for another ten."

Thanks to Shotton and to that brief experience, I never swung a bat or threw a ball or caught one in the next thirty-two years I was around ballplayers. I was perfectly content to be strictly a broadcaster.

Shotton was a genuine, case-hardened, thoroughly seasoned baseball man when Rickey wired him to catch the next plane to New York. He broke into pro ball in 1908, the year I was born, at Erie in the old Ohio-Penn League. He played minor-league ball for three years and came up to stay with the St. Louis Browns in 1911. He'd found out about the minor leagues with other stops at Steubenville, Omaha and Wheeling. He played seven seasons with the Browns, one at Washington, and went to the St. Louis Cardinals in 1919. He finished his active playing career with the Redbirds in 1922.

It's interesting to look back and observe the twisting of the threads of life. You meet a person today and years later that meeting proves to be pivotal. Or remove a person from your life as though he had never touched your destiny, and think what then might have been.

While Shotton was playing outfield for the Browns, Branch Rickey became manager. Rickey then moved to the Cardinals as manager. He didn't even have to change his clubhouse, as the Browns and the Cardinals shared Sportsman's Park. When Shotton came to the Cardinals, Rickey again was his manager. The two men liked each other, respected each other, and both were from small Ohio towns. Also, very important was Rickey's unbroken promise to his mother not to enter a ball park on Sunday. Shotton became Rickey's Sunday manager. That's how far back their association went.

Shotton won his manager's spurs with stints in the high minor leagues. He spent nine years at Syracuse, Rochester and Columbus. Seven of these years he managed clubs in Rickey's farm system. He got his big-league baptism as manager at Philadelphia. The Phillies then were owned by Gerry Nugent, who had to keep selling his best players to survive. Nevertheless Shotton lasted with the Phillies six years. He was fresh from Philadelphia when he coached one year, 1934, at Cincinnati.

Shotton later was a coach with the Cleveland Indians, 1942 through 1945. That's when he decided he'd had enough. He had saved his money. His habits were orderly. His needs were simple. He had his home in Bartow, Florida, and after the 1945 season at Cleveland, he said, and meant it, that he'd never put on a uniform again. Rickey had him do some easygoing scouting around southern Florida in 1946, and in the spring of 1947 had him at Pensacola. Once the two men met, back with the St. Louis Browns in 1913, their paths were never far apart. The threads of their lives twisted tighter and tighter until, to the complete and sudden surprise of both, Commissioner Chandler bound them again to each other, tied tighter than in any former association.

Rickey was at heart a dramatic actor, creating his roles as he played each scene. He was like a chess player who savored his future moves. He relished playing out a scene without tipping his hand. It wasn't that he played cat-and-mouse so much as that he got deep enjoyment out of his maneuvers, making the other fellow wait and wonder just what he was up to.

Shotton's plane got in early in the morning. Rickey hadn't said he would meet the plane, but he was there. Shotton wasn't surprised. Shotton wasn't surprised by anything Rickey did—he had known Rickey, or Rick as he called him, too long.

They went to breakfast in the airport restaurant. They talked of this and they talked of that. They were old friends. Rickey loved to talk. Shotton listened. Rickey didn't give a hint why he had wired Shotton to fly up. They finished breakfast and got into Rickey's car and started driving to Manhattan.

They drove all the way into mid-Manhattan and still Rickey said nothing about why he had sent for his old friend. They pulled up to the Union League Club on East Thirty-seventh Street. Rickey said he needed to get a haircut. Then he got out from behind the wheel.

"Burt"—maybe he said "Barney,"—"you know the way to the Polo Grounds. I want you to manage the Dodgers. Good luck."

I know this is how Rickey broke the news to Shotton and sent him to the Polo Grounds. Both Rickey and Shotton told me.

I know about Shotton's first day as the new manager of the Dodgers. I was sitting in the Brooklyn dugout when he walked in—sports jacket, light-colored pants, two-toned shoes, just what he would wear in Bartow, Florida. Sukeforth, Blades and Pitler knew he was coming but they had been ordered not to say a word about it to anybody—to no players, and certainly to no one in the media. They greeted him. He and I shook hands. It was too late to call a meeting in the clubhouse with his new players. The game was almost ready to start and the Dodgers were taking fielding practice. I had to get up to the broadcasting booth. Harold Parrott, the road secretary, was in the dugout.

Shotton said, "I'da been here sooner but I got going on the

wrong side of that Triple-Boro Bridge (the Triborough . . .) I was going the wrong way . . . I told the cop who I was and where I wanted to go and he turned me around and got me headed up here. . . . I haven't been in the Polo Grounds since I was coaching for Cincinnati in 1934."

I had to go. Time does not stand still even in such a surprising situation as Shotton dropping in, just like that, to manage the Brooklyn Dodgers. I had to be at the mike to sign on the broadcast. I was also the director of sports at CBS and had a fifteen-minute sports show at 5:45 across the board, Monday through Friday. As I left the dugout I said to Parrott, "Harold, I've got to have Shotton on my CBS show tonight." He nodded and said, "I'll have him there."

During the game I called my office at CBS and told them to cancel whoever had been scheduled because I'd have Shotton. I got down to CBS barely in time to shuffle some notes and go into the studio. Parrott brought Shotton in in a few minutes. We had no time to talk. We were on the air, as thoroughly unrehearsed an interview as ever went on a coast-to-coast network.

Shotton was in great good humor despite the fact the Giants had beaten "his" Dodgers in his debut as Brooklyn manager. He was beaming and readily answered every question I asked. After all, he had easy answers to make.

I got him to tell about the wire from Rickey, the breakfast meeting, the drive to the Union League Club, and Rickey's dropping the assignment on him. He told about going the wrong way on the Triborough Bridge.

I asked him if he was satisfied with the terms of his new contract to manage the Dodgers.

"I've never had a contract working for Rick," he said.

I asked him if he was satisfied with the money he would be paid.

"I'll be satisfied," he said, "I don't know what I'll get. Rick has always been fair with me."

I could hardly believe he didn't know how much he was going to get. He didn't, hadn't had time to bring it up, and wasn't in the slightest concerned. He expected no argument with Rickey about anything pertaining to his new status. He said a few more surprising things. It must have been quite a broadcast. The only time a man was made manager of a big-league team without knowing his salary or anything else, and having no signed contract.

"I don't even know where I'm going to stay tonight," Shotton concluded, "I haven't had time to call Mary (his wife) and tell her. I'm going to call her as soon as I can because she has to send me some clothes."

Shotton managed the Dodgers his first game wearing the clothes he had brought with him—the ones he had on when he stepped off the plane. That was his entire wardrobe. He wore the same clothes to the Polo Grounds the next day but once inside the park, instead of his sports jacket he put on a Dodger windbreaker. It was a short coat, Dodger blue with "Dodgers" in script on it. This was the jacket the pitchers wore in the bullpen. When a pitcher would be summoned from the bullpen he brought his jacket with him, and as he approached the mound he would hand the jacket to the bat boy who would take it carefully to the bench.

Shotton could have had a full-fledged Dodger uniform, but he had said when he quit coaching at Cleveland after the 1945 season that he'd never put on a uniform again. He didn't. However, the baseball rules are very specific about the matter of uniforms: a manager can wear street clothes if he wishes, but he must remain in his dugout. He cannot come on the field for any reason unless he is in complete uniform. Connie Mack in his half a hundred years as manager of the Philadelphia Athletics wore a suit, white shirt with high starched collar and tie. Mr. Mack never was seen during a game outside his dugout.

This meant that Mack and Shotton, unable to go to the mound to talk to the pitcher, or to go on the field for any reason, had to send a coach with instructions, or to find out if a player was hurt or tired or whatever. Mack was an institution at Philadelphia. Shotton was a surprise at Brooklyn. The Dodger fans were accustomed to seeing Durocher run out on the field to argue with umpires or discuss matters at the mound. The Dodger fans had become so accustomed to Durocher challenging umpires on close calls that they would start yelling "Leo . . . Leo" before Leo could even get out of the dugout.

Shotton was criticized by several writers for not wearing a

uniform and taking the field. The fans missed seeing their manager. However, I asked Pee Wee Reese once if he missed Shotton coming on the field at certain times. Reese said, "I know where he is . . . all of us know where he is . . . he is in the dugout in full charge. The fans may not see him but we see him. We know he is there."

BOOK TWO

THE CRUELEST MONTH

The Boston Red Sox and the St. Louis Cardinals won the pennants in 1946, and were again favored by the betting commissioners in 1947. The Red Sox had galloped to their pennant, winning by 12 games over Detroit. The Yankees had finished third, 17 games behind. Boston with Ted Williams appeared to be just as strong as the 1946 team that had won 104 games to dominate the league.

The Yankees had serious questions: What about the infield with Joe Gordon traded to Cleveland? Could Stirnweiss handle second base? Could thirty-six-year-old George McQuinn hold first base? What about the veteran third baseman Billy Johnson? Where would or could Yogi Berra play in order to "swing that stick"? Could Allie Reynolds pitch the "big games"? and, What about Joe DiMaggio and his painful heel?

Bucky Harris was the new manager of the Yankees, but he wasn't new to the league. Harris was easygoing, yet experienced, and knew his business. The writers looked forward to a good year as far as Harris went, but nobody was thinking the Yankees would overhaul Boston. The Red Sox made runs like bananas—in bunches.

Brooklyn was a different story any way you looked. In 1946 the Dodgers surprised even Rickey by jelling faster than expected and tying St. Louis for first place. This caused the first play-off in history, best of 3 games. Durocher won the toss of the coin to see where the first game would be played, with the next 1 or 2 to be played at the other park. Leo won the toss and said "St. Louis." He wanted games two, and three if needed, to be at Ebbets Field. The Cardinals won games one and two and went into the World Series against the Red Sox. Harry Brecheen, the Little Cat, the bowlegged left-hander with the wicked screwball, nailed down the play-off, and in the World Series he won 3 games as the decisive star for the Redbirds. Eddie Dyer, freshman manager of the Cards, didn't have to sweat out a maneuver—he just called for the Little Cat. Ted Williams, by the way, had a miserable Series getting only 4 singles in 7 games.

The difference for the 1947 Dodgers was one man, Jackie Robinson. Would Jackie hit major-league pitching? Would he be able to play first base, a brand-new position for him after playing short and second? Would Jackie's "breaking of the color line" break apart the Dodger team? Would Jackie's presence on the Dodgers put undue pressure on them from the rest of the league? The Dodgers didn't have Leo Durocher to manage them, to hold them in line, to support Robinson to the hilt, to lead the battle against the rest of the league. The smart money said St. Louis. One black man caused dark, ominous clouds to gather over Ebbets Field. They soon began gathering around other areas.

The actual weather in the East also threatened. The Yankees were scheduled to play the Senators in Washington on Monday April 14. This was 1947, when tradition had it that Washington, with the President of the United States on hand for the first ball, was always to open at home, just as Cincinnati, the first professional team, was also always to open at home, even if it meant playing on Monday when the leagues opened in full on Tuesday.

This Monday there were two nonpolitical matters for discussion at Washington: one, Who would win the game? and two, Which arm would President Truman use to toss out the first ball? The President was able to use either hand. Truman was ambidextrous, yes, but he wasn't ambivalent or ambiguous.

Some 30,000 fans were in Griffith Stadium, about all the old ball park could accommodate. It was raining. The President sat outside in his car. Joe DiMaggio had joined the Yankees, and though he couldn't play, he made the trip and put on his uniform.

One of the things we should be most grateful for in this land is that our politicians have no control over the weather. Despite the big crowd, the waiting President, the two ball clubs, DiMaggio himself, the fervent hopes of Clark Griffith (an old-line owner who made his living from his ball games), the rain continued. The President was driven back to the White House without giving the slightest hint whether he would have used his right or left hand. The Yankees went to the railroad station. They had their own Yankee Stadium Opening Day with the Athletics next afternoon.

According to reliable tradition it was Joe Jacobs, a fellow deep in the prizefight business, who first said "I shoulda stood in bed." Jacobs had been hauled up to Baker Field—most reluctantly—to see a Columbia University football game. It was cold, a biting wind blew down the Hudson River Valley, across the Spuyten Duyvil bridge, along the Harlem River, and without impediment (the press box was wide open) straight to where Jacobs huddled amid the suffering writers. Jacobs did not remain very long and was never seen again at a football game. He made his famous five-word lament as he departed.

Anyhow, the Yankees and Bucky Harris might have been justified if they had resorted to Jacobs's complaint. It rained them out in Washington on Monday, they did play at the Stadium on Tuesday, only to be soundly defeated by Connie Mack's Athletics 6–1, and then were rained out again Wednesday. Even MacPhail seemed to be losing his touch. Perhaps because he knew the weather was more than his match, MacPhail announced to the press, who needed something for a rainy-day story, that he was asking American League president Will Harridge to intercede with Commissioner Chandler to lift the suspensions of both Durocher and Dressen. (There is no record that Harridge ever involved himself.)

But, as Noah must have said, it can't rain all the time. On Thursday the Yankees entertained the Athletics less generously. Bill Bevens, with whom we'll have more to do later, pitched the Yankees to their first win under Bucky Harris. In his first start of 1947 Bevens went into the ninth inning with a 2–1 lead and protected it. (In his last start of the season, which was in Game

Four of the World Series, Bevens again had a 2–1 ninth-inning lead, and got two men out. He never got the third out, and he never pitched again in the big leagues.)

Things do right themselves. The Yankees took the train back to Washington for Friday and the delayed Opening Game. Somehow the schedule makers had foresight enough to leave Friday available for both teams. Griffith seized upon it avidly. President Truman warmed up both arms and with the eyes of 28,579 paid fans watching his every move, he threw out the first ball. He used his right hand. Then, to balance the books, he threw out a second ball left-handed.

The sun shone. Truman sat down. The big crowd cheered, and the Old Fox, as Clark Griffith was called for good reasons, beamed upon the benevolence that was his that sunny afternoon. That is, he beamed upon the spinning turnstiles. As the game went along, Griffith beamed less and less while his former boy manager, Bucky Harris, beamed more and more. MacPhail beamed the most. Allie Reynolds made his first start as a Yankee, scattered 8 hits, and won easily 7–0.

It might be of interest to historians, to say nothing of Yankee partisans, to note that Friday April 18, 1947, was a significant day for the destinies of the Yankees. Allie Reynolds from then on was a mighty man in the Bronx, starting or relieving, it made no difference. He was soon known as the Chief (he was part Indian) and in time became the Super Chief . . . free publicity for the Santa Fe Railroad.

Also, as another historical note (or for trivia), Bucky Harris on this day achieved a distinction no other manager was ever accorded, and now that Washington has no baseball team, no other manager is apt to. Truman was the fifth President to throw out the first Opening Day ball at Washington while Harris was manager of a team on the field—Warren G. Harding, Calvin Coolidge, Herbert Hoover and F.D.R. had all done the honors when Harris managed the Senators, before the Man from Independence threw out his two.

The Dodgers opened at Ebbets Field with a 5–3 win over the Boston Braves (who would become the Milwaukee Braves and then the Atlanta Braves). There were 26,623 of the faithful and the curious on hand to see Jackie Robinson in his first major-league game. Jackie had no hits but fielded first base as though he had never played any other position. The rain that fell in Yankee Stadium Wednesday fell just as steadily on Ebbets Field. Thursday the Dodgers whacked the Braves 12–6, and Robinson in the fifth inning got his first hit—a bunt single toward third. The ice was broken.

Friday the Dodgers went to the Polo Grounds. Friday, Burt Shotton walked into their dugout and took over, while the Giants took over on the playing field with 6 home runs. Mel Ott's fence-busters made off with the game 10–4. Almost unnoticed in Shotton's surprise appearance was Jackie Robinson's first home run, a shot into the left-field stands. Jackie also added a single. Shotton wore glasses. He saw both hits.

Joe Sheehan in the New York *Times* did a two-column piece the next morning on the new manager. He asked Shotton after that first game how much actual managing he had done. Shotton said he had "just watched, and would continue just watching. As soon as I think I know something about the club, and can help, I'll start to work. Until then I'll just watch."

Sheehan ended his piece with, "Now that he's back in the big league . . . he discovered yesterday it's a tough league." Shotton was well aware of that before Sheehan was born.

So the Yankees and the Dodgers got their seasons started. Both big leagues were under way. Durocher was in California, and by and large out of the news. However, the Cleveland baseball writers on the evening of Thursday April 17 gave a dinner to honor Bill Veeck, then president of the Indians. Commissioner Chandler was invited. He came.

Chandler must have been stung, indeed shaken, by the storm of comment after his suspension of Durocher. The dinner was attended by about five hundred persons, including many writers. Chandler knew he would be widely quoted, and in this setting he made the first major defense of what he had done.

"I have no obligations to anyone in baseball," he began, which of course meant MacPhail, "but only to baseball in general. I'm not afraid of anything now and will always take whatever actions I deem necessary. I intend doing this as long as I hold the Commissioner's post. I've had my share of catching the past couple of years, but if I can't take it, I shouldn't dish it out. I can do both. It's hard to hit major-league pitching at first but I'm catching on.

"We will always take vigorous action to drive out gambling in any form, and I assume full responsibility for personally kicking out all gamblers. All officials and players have been warned on this gambling issue, and they know what to expect."

Chandler then got into an area he was most sensitive to, the comparison between Judge K. M. Landis, his predecessor, and himself.

"Judge Landis was a magnificent character. I sometimes think today's sportswriters can commune with him because they always seem to know what he would have done. But I doubt it."

Chandler did not in this Cleveland appearance mention Durocher by name, but it was plain to whom he referred when he said:

". . . one writer tells me I should have given him a month; the next one says he deserved ninety-nine years. I'll still make my own decisions and I'll make them honestly."

The battle lines were drawn, and they would be defined even more sharply by the end of the month.

The weather in the East, and later in the West, plagued the start of the 1947 season. It was most uncertain and went hand in hand with the uncertainties of both Bucky Harris and the Yankees, and Burt Shotton and the Dodgers.

Harris had to reset his infield, which he did with McQuinn at first, Stirnweiss at second (replacing Gordon), Rizzuto at short and Johnson at third. Harris had to open the season without the Big Guy, DiMaggio, and with the veteran Charlie Keller in left slowing down. Tommy Henrich had an ailing wrist. Yogi Berra "swinging that stick" had to be fitted in somewhere, but until DiMaggio was ready the outfield could not be stabilized. The addition of Reynolds strengthened the pitching staff.

Shotton had a set infield *if* Robinson could make it both at first base and at bat. He had Stanky at second, Reese at short and a fine rookie third baseman, Spider Jorgensen. Bruce Edwards would catch—he had the year before when the Dodgers tied the Cardinals for the pennant and then lost the play-off. The outfield would settle down with Pete Reiser, Dixie Walker,

Carl Furillo and Gene Hermanski. The pitching was spotty, would remain so all season and all through the World Series.

The games in late April and early May were of interest, but the stories off the field, especially those relating to the Dodgers, were more demanding and of more interest. The introduction of Robinson wasn't going to go as smoothly as the first two series with the Braves and the Giants indicated. There were no negative incidents in those first 4 games.

The second game for the Dodgers at the Polo Grounds, the second game for Shotton, was Saturday afternoon. The old park was jammed to the rafters with 52,355 paid fans. They came to see Jackie Robinson. This should be noted, for wherever Jackie played, he drew large crowds. He became the biggest attraction in baseball since Babe Ruth. Robinson put serious money into the pockets of every National League owner. His abilities on the field, coupled with his gate appeal, persuaded the rest of the league to bring in black players too. Horace Stoneham of the Giants was most prompt to scout for and use black players, and as he watched this Saturday overflow crowd on April 19, the bottom line wasn't lost to him. Stoneham wasn't a wealthy man with other financial interests. He was strictly a baseball man who had to live from the revenues generated by his Giants. Robinson started putting hard fat on Horace that afternoon.

The Giants bashed a couple more home runs and made off with the game 4–2. Shotton had to swallow his second straight defeat. The Dodgers then moved to Boston for 2 games. For the opener, on Sunday, a banner crowd of some 35,000 was expected. Jackie was already a draw. But that game was snowed out as well as the Monday one. The team took the train to Ebbets Field, for 3 games with the Philadelphia Phillies, managed by Ben Chapman.

All had gone well the first 2 games at home, the next 2 at New York, and the two off-days in the hotel at Boston. No problems. The Dodgers hadn't warmed up to Jackie but they had accepted him as a member of the team. He was "let alone," shall we say, in the clubhouse. The Dodgers had pretty well settled down. Burt Shotton's strong hand was a settling-down influence. The Old Man said little, but had an air of complete authority. He looked straight at you through his steel-rimmed glasses. You didn't play games with Shotton, or if you did you found yourself in Canada the next day. That's what Duke Snider discovered.

Snider was a very promising, brash rookie. Shotton ordered him to bunt one night in a tight game. Snider didn't like it—he wanted to take some of his wild swings. He bunted at two pitches, but bunted so halfheartedly that he fouled off both pitches . . . then he had to swing, and struck out. As Snider came to the dugout he threw his bat and said, "What does that old so-and-so think he's doing, having a .300 hitter bunt?" Shotton said, "You'll find out tomorrow in Montreal." And Snider was sent to Montreal. He didn't stay there long, but when he returned, if that old so-and-so said "Bunt," Snider said "Yes, sir."

As the snow continued to fall in Boston, Rickey led a delegation to see Commissioner Chandler in his offices in Cincinnati. Rickey had with him Walter O'Malley, New York Supreme Court Justice Henry L. Ughetta—a member of the Dodgers' board of directors—and Arthur Mann.

Rickey spoke first, after the proper greetings had been expressed. He entered a formal appeal for a reconsideration of the Durocher sentence. He stressed the loss by the Brooklyn club of its manager and two of its coaches, and said he thought Durocher's cumulative conduct had not justified such a severe sentence.

Arthur Mann noted in his book that Chandler became redfaced and sat more stiffly. O'Malley spoke and went over the same grounds, and added his request for a new hearing. So did Justice Ughetta.

Then Chandler wondered if Mann had something to add. Mann asked Chandler if the Brooklyn club had the right to say as much in public as MacPhail had been saying. Chandler became angry and emphasized there would be *no talking* by anyone, and that he had already summoned MacPhail to appear before him in Cincinnati in a few days.

Chandler dismissed the four Brooklyn men, leaving no doubt that there would be no appeal from his decision on Durocher. The four departed for Brooklyn. The Phillies were to be at Ebbets Field the next afternoon. Shotton would be the Dodgers' manager.

Tuesday afternoon April 22, Ebbets Field. It was cold, 45 degrees at game time. But it was flaming hot in the dugouts and on the playing field. The bearbaiting had begun.

Ben Chapman, the manager of the Phillies, had been known as a hothead as a player with the Yankees, had had trouble with an umpire as a minor-league manager, was from Alabama, and came into Ebbets Field filled with racial venom. Chapman immediately began yelling insults at Robinson, then at the other Dodgers for playing with him. Some of Chapman's players joined their manager in verbal abuse. The truce on Robinson lasted only a week. It was completely shattered the three days the Phillies were at Brooklyn. Completely.

This was what Rickey had warned Robinson about, and had tried to prepare him for. Now, here it was.

Robinson was under a sentence of silence. He had promised Rickey that for three years he would not answer back, no matter what was said to him. He had promised, in effect, to "turn the other cheek." He kept his word his first year at Montreal. Now he was beginning his first year in the big leagues but his second year of "no retaliation." Rickey had told Robinson that this was the only way he, Robinson, could break the color line. The only way.

Much was written about the treatment Jackie got from Chapman and the Philadelphia bench jockeys. The writers, almost to a man, were incensed. The black press raged. I heard all about it as soon as I left the broadcasting booth and began talking with the Dodgers. The Dodgers talked freely to the press. They were angered.

I think it is best to quote from Robinson himself, from his book *I Never Had It Made*. Page 71:

> Early in the season, the Philadelphia Phillies came to Ebbets Field for a three-game series. . . . Starting to the plate in the first inning, I could scarcely believe my ears. Almost as if it had been synchronized by some master conductor, hate poured forth from the Phillies dugout.
>
> "Hey, nigger, why don't you go back to the cotton field where you belong?"

"They're waiting for you in the jungles, black boy!"

"Hey, snowflake, which one of those white boys' wives are you dating tonight?"

"We don't want you here, nigger."

"Go back to the bushes."

(Those insults and taunts were only samples of the torrent of abuse which poured from the Phillies dugout that April day. Let me add that Robinson edited and cleaned up much of the material he used in his book—what was yelled at him was rougher and dirtier.)

As Jackie continued:

I have to admit that this day, of all the unpleasant days in my life, brought me nearer to cracking up than I ever had been. Perhaps I should have been inured to this kind of garbage, but I was in New York City and unprepared to face the kind of barbarism from a northern team that I had come to associate with the Deep South. The abuse coming out of the Phillies dugout was being directed by the team's manager, Ben Chapman, a Southerner. I felt tortured and I tried just to play ball and ignore the insults. But it was really getting to me. What did the Phillies want from me? What, indeed, did Mr. Rickey expect of me? I was, after all, a human being. What was I doing here turning the other cheek as though I weren't a man? In college days I had had a reputation as a black man who never tolerated affronts to his dignity. I had defied prejudice in the Army. How could I have thought that barriers would fall, that, indeed, my talent could triumph over bigotry?

For one wild and rage-crazed minute I thought, "To hell with Mr. Rickey's 'noble experiment.' It's clear it won't succeed. I have made every effort to work hard, to get myself into shape. My best is not enough for them." I thought what a glorious, cleansing thing it would be to let go. To hell with the image of the patient black freak I was supposed to create. I could throw down my bat, stride over to that Phillies dugout, grab one of those white sons of bitches and smash his teeth in with my despised black fist. Then I could walk away from it all. But my son could tell his son someday what his daddy could have been if he hadn't been too much of a man.

Then, I thought of Mr. Rickey—how his family and friends had begged him not to fight for me and my people. I thought of all his predictions, which had come true. Mr. Rickey had come to a crossroads and made a lonely decision. I was at a crossroads. I would make mine. I would stay.

The haters had almost won that round. They had succeeded in getting me so upset that I was an easy out. As the game progressed, the Phillies continued with the abuse.

In the last of the eighth inning Robinson got on with a single. He stole second, and when the catcher's throw went into center field, he cruised over to third. Hermanski singled to score him. Inasmuch as Hal Gregg shut out the Phillies with 1 hit, that was it—the Dodgers won it 1-0. The run and the victory were Robinson's in more ways than one. The most eloquent answer to abuse, bench jockeying, and insults in baseball is a base hit. It has been said that a soft answer turneth away wrath—well, on a ball field a few base hits really turn it away and usually silence the other dugout. However, for the next 2 games the Phillies continued to pour it on Robinson, and even began yelling to the Dodgers such taunts as "Hey, you carpetbaggers, how's your little reconstruction period getting along?"

To quote Jackie again:

By the third day of our confrontation with the emissaries from the City of Brotherly Love, they had become so outrageous that Ed Stanky exploded. He started yelling at the Phillies.

"Listen, you yellow-bellied cowards," he cried out, "why don't you yell at somebody who can answer back?" It was then that I began to feel better. I remembered Mr. Rickey's prediction: that if I won the respect of the team and got them solidly behind me, there would be no question about the success of the experiment.

The reaction of the press was solidly against Chapman and the Phillies. Ford Frick, president of the National League, warned Bob Carpenter, owner of the Phillies. Commissioner Chandler sent word to Carpenter along with a stern warning against racial baiting. As a sample of the reactions of the writers, this is from Dan Parker, sports editor of the New York *Daily Mirror.*

> "Ben Chapman, who during his career with the Yankees was frequently involved in unpleasant incidents with fans who charged him with shouting anti-Semitic remarks at them from the ball field, seems to be up to his old trick of stirring up racial trouble. During the recent series between the Phils and the Dodgers, Chapman and three of his players poured a stream of abuse at Jackie Robinson. Jackie, with admirable restraint, ignored the guttersnipe language coming from the Phils dugout, thus stamping himself as the only gentleman among those involved in the incident."

The Philadelphia ball club became disturbed about the strong press and public reaction against Chapman. It hurriedly claimed that Chapman was not anti-Negro, that all he and his players were trying to do was find out if "the rookie could take it . . . that the Phils always tested new players roughly . . . that was baseball." It didn't wash. The Dodgers were due to come to Philadelphia in two weeks, May 9 to be exact. The Phillies put pressure on Rickey to persuade Robinson to pose for a picture shaking hands with Chapman. Rickey sent word to Jackie that it would be a good thing, gracious and generous on Robinson's part, and would go far to heal raw feelings. Robinson was of the opinion the Commissioner also wanted this done. Anyway, Jackie did it. He posed with Chapman, both in uniform. Jackie wrote later, "I have to admit that having my picture taken with that man was one of the most difficult things I had to make my-self do."

But before the Dodgers got to Philadelphia and the picture of Robinson and Chapman, the Dodgers swept the 3-game series with the Phils at Ebbets Field, and moved to within half a game of first-place Pittsburgh.

The Giants came to Ebbets Field for the weekend, and New York in general and Brooklyn in particular were ready for the fireworks. The height of baseball excitement was a Giant-Dodger ball game, whether it was played at the Polo Grounds or at Ebbets Field. Nothing in baseball ever equaled this inter-borough rivalry. When both teams moved to California, baseball lost something it has never regained and I doubt can ever be restored. This was the only time there were two teams in the same city that were in the same league. Further, Brooklyn always resented being put down at the expense of the New Yorkers, who were actually Manhattanites but usurped the New York mantle. I didn't know when I came to Brooklyn in 1939 that New York City comprised five boroughs—Manhattan (New York), Brooklyn, the Bronx, Queens and Staten Island. Brooklyn didn't have the skyscrapers Manhattan had, or the theaters, or the restaurants, or the rail stations. But Brooklyn had the Dodgers.

Brooklyn wasn't a borough until 1898 when the state legisla-ture passed a law forcing Brooklyn into New York City. The Brooklyn Bridge, the subways, the water system and other de-velopments made that necessary. However, there were many people in Brooklyn who lived and died resentful of being forced into New York City instead of being left alone as a separate city. But Brooklyn had its Dodgers, and when the Dodgers played the Giants it wasn't play—it was blood on the moon.

The rise of the modern Dodgers, starting in 1938 when Larry MacPhail took over, was a success story that was phenomenal. MacPhail started getting good, exciting ballplayers who starting winning. MacPhail broke the radio ban in 1939. Suddenly the Dodgers were moving up and were being broadcast on WOR, a 50,000-watt station—no station had a stronger signal, and I like to think I knew my business at the microphone. Brooklyn with its Dodgers and the broadcasts now was equal or better than the Giants. The Dodgers won the 1941 pennant and the entire country rooted for them.

The Giants were coming across the river for the first time in 1947. Added to the years of intense rivalry and strong personalities was Jackie Robinson.

Friday it rained. No game. Saturday the weather wasn't ideal but Ebbets Field was sold out. The paid attendance was 33,565. There wasn't even standing room. It was a great day for Brooklyn—the Dodgers beat the Giants 7–3 and moved into first place by half a game. Dixie Walker, probably the most popular player in Dodger history, got 4 hits. Little Vic Lombardi relieved the last seven innings and faced just twenty-two men in an airtight performance.

Sunday, again despite cold weather, the Dodgers outscrambled the Giants 9–8 in a wild and woolly struggle that had the 31,675 paid customers beside themselves. One of the people in a box seat alongside the Dodger dugout was Joe Louis. The heavyweight champion arrived in the fourth inning, and before sitting down stood and waved to Robinson. The crowd went wilder. When the Dodgers came in to bat, Jackie went over and he and Louis shook hands. Photographers sprang up around them like rain lilies after a cloudburst.

Earlier in the week Robinson had been brutally taunted by manager Chapman and some of his Phillies. Now with a full ball park roaring approval he shook hands with the great Joe Louis. This was a turning point.

And let it be noted that manager Mel Ott, a former Giant hero of genuine worth, and his players did not give Robinson a hard time in any way except when trying to get him out during the game. Sometimes they did, sometimes they didn't.

The tide was turning. It turned slowly, sometimes receded, but slowly, slowly it came in for Robinson on the field and for Rickey in his office. Rickey had warned Jackie of just what Chapman laid on him. Rickey's strength came to Robinson as he endured the Philadelphia series. And what was Rickey's reaction to Ben Chapman and his insulting taunts?

Rickey was to say later, after he had assayed pluses and minuses, "Chapman did more than anybody to unite the

Dodgers. When he poured out that string of unconscionable abuse, he solidified and unified thirty men, not one of whom was willing to sit by and see someone kick around a man who had his hands tied behind his back—Chapman made Jackie a real member of the Dodgers."

In contrast to the turbulence at Ebbets Field, the Yankees were getting some order out of uncertainty. The Big Guy, DiMaggio, pinch-hit against Washington on April 19, and though he grounded into a force play, he was back. The spirits of the team lifted. And when Joe started the first game of a doubleheader at Philadelphia the next day, the Yankees went on to win them both. Joe exploded a home run with two on. The crisp crash of his bat on the ball was the awaited signal from the bell cow.

The Yankees were idle April 21. At his estate-farm outside Buffalo their former manager, Joe McCarthy, marked his sixtieth birthday. McCarthy had led the Yankees to eight pennants and seven championships. He had quit MacPhail in late May the season before. Now he said he was through with baseball, he had a new life of flowers and birds and being home. Mrs. McCarthy said, "Joe is through with baseball forever." A week before his birthday McCarthy had turned down Rickey's offer to manage the Dodgers. The birds were around and the flowers would soon bloom. This was the first spring in forty years Joe had been home and not on the road with a ball club. (The summer must have gotten hot, dry and long. The birds must have migrated, or whatever birds do. The blooms certainly faded—they always do. McCarthy was back in business the next spring as manager of the Boston Red Sox. The Red Sox had Ted Williams, but didn't have either MacPhail or Robinson.)

Favored to repeat their pennant success, the Red Sox came into Yankee Stadium for 3 games at the same time the Phillies were at Brooklyn. (In the scheduling, the Yankees and the Giants were paired, so that when one team was home the other was traveling. Brooklyn was paired with Washington and could be at home when either the Yankees or Giants were in town.)

In the first game Ted Williams hit a home run for the Red Sox; so did Sam Mele and so did Rudy York, but they contrived to hit them with the bases empty. Charlie Keller slugged one for the Yankees with two on. Bevens again pitched a strong game for Bucky Harris, and the Yankees pulled it out 5–4.

In game two Allie Reynolds threw his second straight shutout for the Yankees, beating Williams, Mele, York and company 3–0. Reynolds gave up only 2 hits, singles by York. This got the Yankees into first place. Bucky Harris, MacPhail and a few others enjoyed their dinners.

However, as tangible notice that it would be a real race, a long summer and that into every life some rain must fall, Tex Hughson of the Red Sox allowed just 2 hits the next day, to beat Frank Shea 1–0, and cut the Yankees' first-place lead to half a game.

Rain got the Washington-at-New York game April 25, leaving ample room in the papers the next morning for the story that Commissioner Chandler had ordered MacPhail and his two partners, Dan Topping and Del Webb, to report to him in Cincinnati the next week. Chandler had told the Brooklyn delegation that this would happen, and here it came. Durocher was in California but the backlash of his suspension was very much alive and kicking back in the East.

It is doubtful New York City ever had as big a baseball day as Sunday April 27. The Dodgers were entertaining their mortal enemies the Giants before 31,675 fans.

Most of the entire country was tuned in to Yankee Stadium. Commissioner Chandler had declared it national Babe Ruth Day. There was local television, but local only. MacPhail, again pioneering, had sold the Yankee Stadium TV rights to Dumont the year before for $75,000. However, the number of TV receiving sets was limited. Radio carried the proceedings across the land. Ruth was ill, had been resting in the sun at Miami, had become associated with American Legion baseball, and this day was to salute The Babe. Ruth had cancer of the throat, as well as other places in his failing body.

MacPhail had ordered all stops pulled out in promoting Babe Ruth Day. His promotion man, Arthur "Red" Patterson, was one of the best in his business. Patterson had been carefully orchestrating Babe Ruth Day since spring training. Cardinal Spellman was to speak at the home plate ceremonies, as were Commissioner Chandler, American League president Will Harridge, National League president Ford Frick and many others. The ball park was dressed out in bunting and pennants and world championship flags. After all, no team could outfit its park with trophies nearly as well as the Yankees. The weather was good. The crowd was a tremendous 58,399 paid. Washington was the visiting team. There was no count of the invited guests who didn't pass through the regular turnstiles that provide the United States with its tax data. It was all-out, live national radio, it was front page in the papers the next day. The New York *Times* headline said, "58,399 Acclaim Babe Ruth in Rare Tribute at the Stadium."

Life moves in circles. Babe Ruth, fifty-three years old and with little more than another year of life remaining, stood at home plate in the splendid stadium he had helped create. Ruth, more than any other factor, had caused the building of Yankee Stadium. When Col. Jake Ruppert in January 1920 bought Ruth from Harry Frazee of the Boston Red Sox, and thus began building the Yankee juggernaut, the Yankees were tenants of the New York Giants at the Polo Grounds. The Giants until then had been *the* ball club in New York. Ruth began hitting home runs, the Yankees started winning, and suddenly John McGraw and the Giants were seriously challenged—and in their own ball park. Ruth smashed 54 home runs his first year as a Yankee, 1920, and the next year hit an astounding 59. The Yankees, led by The Babe, were becoming the talk of the town.

McGraw, never a peaceful or diplomatic man, demanded that the Yankees get out of the Polo Grounds. The Yankees were told that 1922 was their last year there. McGraw figured the Yankees couldn't find a place to build closer than Queens, out on Long Island. He thought he'd be rid of Ruth and the Yankees once and for all. McGraw's jealousy knew no bounds.

But Ruppert located a site just across the Harlem River from the Polo Grounds and in one year Yankee Stadium was built. Opening Day 1923, was opening day for Yankee Stadium, and a crowd of over 70,000 jammed and packed it. The Red Sox, the visitors . . . Howard Ehmke pitching for Boston . . . third inning . . . two Yankees on base—and Babe Ruth hit one ten rows back in right field. First home run in the Stadium. Of course Ruth would do it. He always rose to the heights. He was a star. He was Babe Ruth. Nobody like him before or since. Nobody.

Now another April afternoon—two dozen years and 516 home runs later. Another time standing at home plate at Yankee Stadium, often referred to as "the house that Ruth built." This time Ruth was wrapped in a warm camel's hair overcoat. Louis Effrat in his New York *Times* story the next day said he was "a sick man." After the notables had paid him tribute, here is how Ruth began, without notes:

"Thank you very much, ladies and gentlemen . . . you know how bad my voice sounds . . . well, it feels just as bad."

Then he went on briefly to salute the kids who played baseball, and to salute baseball as "the greatest game." He didn't stay in the windy park the entire game. He left early. His time was running out.

I remember when he died the next year—August 16, 1948. He was in Memorial Hospital. I was cater-cornered across in New York Hospital, getting over a massive hemorrhage from an ulcer. From my room I could see the knot of people who stood quietly and waited patiently on the sidewalk. Many people wanted any word about Ruth. I heard that the mail for him at the hospital was very heavy, pounds and bags of it. At the same time, in Boston, Ty Cobb was very ill, and I heard that nobody waited outside his hospital.

Babe Ruth Day was a natural bonanza for promotion. MacPhail and Patterson didn't blow it. They made it sing. Between them they could promote ice factories to Eskimos. MacPhail was a study in contradictions. When he was running the Dodgers, Patterson was writing baseball for the *Herald Tribune*. One afternoon at the press club bar at Ebbets Field the two of them got into a violent argument, which was not difficult to do with MacPhail at any time and especially when he was drinking. They were both redheads. Nothing would do but that they step into an adjacent room, shut the door and settle it. Patterson punched MacPhail in the belly and that was the fight. One of the first things MacPhail did when he returned from the Army and got control of the Yankees was hire Patterson from the *Trib*.

Circles? When I went to Yankee Stadium in 1954, Patterson was still public relations chief. One afternoon I did a pre-game TV show in the press box, with Patterson as the star guest. After the program he went to George Weiss's office, they got into a rhubarb, Patterson quit and went to work for Walter O'Malley at Brooklyn. He went West with the Dodgers, then moved on to Gene Autry and the California Angels.

Casey Stengel used to refer to pitchers as "a bunch of selfish men." Here it was, Babe Ruth Day. A full ball park. Washington versus New York. Sid Hudson certainly wished The Babe all the best—he had nothing but love for New York and its people, and I'm sure he was deeply moved by the home plate pre-game ceremonies. But Hudson was "a selfish man." He was a right-handed pitcher for Washington who survived only by winning a certain number of ball games regardless of when or where they were played. As soon as the formal salute to Ruth ended, Hudson took over. He was opposed by another selfish man, another right-hander, named Chandler. This was Spud Chandler, not the Commissioner, although Happy Chandler had pitched in college and for one year in minor-league ball.

Hudson proved to be either more selfish than Chandler or else he was determined to make it His Day. Hudson, late in the game, singled, moved to second, and scored on a single by Buddy Lewis. This was it. Hudson and the Senators won it 1–0.

Commissioner Chandler, who summoned MacPhail to Cincinnati for a hearing four days later, was on hand. He was a speaker at home plate. MacPhail was certainly there but was not among the dignitaries at the plate. Whether the two men had anything to say to each other that day, or whether they even came into contact with each other is unknown. Chandler had sent for MacPhail and his two partners for Wednesday. MacPhail had an appointment of note for that day and both Topping and Webb were out of the country, so MacPhail was booked for Chandler's office Thursday May 1.

The Yankees, clinging to first place, left for St. Louis after an open day Monday. True to the MacPhail custom, the team flew. It rained out the first game with the Browns, and I guess Joe Medwick repeated the old saying about it never rains but it pours. Medwick, a free agent trying for a job, was given his outright release by the Yankees. He had not played in a game for them. (He caught on again with the Cardinals but his days were running out.) The Medwick who was the center of the big trade to Brooklyn by MacPhail in 1940 was released by MacPhail seven years later without even one at bat.

April was closing out, but it still had a few kicks left before moving offstage. The Dodgers used Monday the 28th to visit West Point for an annual game with the Cadets. This was a courtesy that went back to World War II, when West Point helped the Dodgers in spring training by allowing them to use the field house. (The team stayed at the Bear Mountain Inn.) On Tuesday the Cubs came into Ebbets Field and the Dodgers exploded for 7 runs in the eighth inning to win 10-6 and extend their streak to 6 straight. Shotton was all smiles but was not taking anything for granted, not even the fact the Cardinals lost their sixth straight that same afternoon at the Polo Grounds. Stan Musial was in a dreadful slump. Shotton reminded his Dodgers that the Cardinals would still be the team to beat, and that Mr. Musial would wind up with his hits.

The Cubs, on the last day of the month, beat the Dodgers 3-1, broke their winning streak, and to make matters more serious, Jackie Robinson had now gone 0 for 20. When your bread and butter depends upon base hits and you go 0 for 20, you not only start talking to yourself, you start answering back—especially if you are the first black ballplayer in the big leagues.

On the last day of April the Browns, in St. Louis, beat the Yankees 15-5, and routed Allie Reynolds. This was the first time as a Yankee the Chief had even been scored on.

Before leaving his office for Cincinnati and his May 1 meeting with Chandler, MacPhail was quite defiant. To the press, in response to a question, he said:

"Why should I feel contrite? I don't even know what I should feel contrite about. All I know is that I received a telegram from Chandler telling me to come to Cincinnati. I assume I'm charged with insubordination.

"I repeat what I said last week in Newark: so far as any evidence developed in the Sarasota and St. Petersburg hearings is concerned, there was nothing to justify even a five-minute suspension for Durocher.

"Durocher's sentence marked the first time that a Baseball Commissioner had fined or suspended a man without stating in writing specific charges against him. Landis always put charges in writing and extended to the offender the right to appeal.

"Sooner or later baseball will have to redefine the powers of the Commissioner."

There it was, right out in the open from MacPhail. Subtle as a punch in the nose. There was no comment, reaction or response from Chandler. He waited for the next day. But the anger was smoldering inside MacPhail, and he would pass this anger on to his partners, Dan Topping and especially Del Webb. When Chandler's contract was to be renewed three years later, early in 1950, in a meeting of the owners held at St. Petersburg, Webb and Topping, joined by Fred Saigh of the Cardinals, led the movement that unseated Chandler as Commissioner.

So April 1947 ended. Baseball had never had such a month.

THE MERRY MONTH OF MAY

Reporters and photographers converged on Chandler's office Thursday morning May 1, 1947, like ships at sea hearing a distress radio call. The Commissioner had abruptly summoned MacPhail, who had made no secret that he disagreed with Chandler in his Durocher decision, which also penalized MacPhail. What was up? What would happen? MacPhail, who had been Chandler's strongest supporter for the highest office in baseball, was now being called on the carpet. Or was he? Further, this was Larry MacPhail, who had been general manager of the Reds for three years, and now was returning to create still more Cincinnati headlines.

Over a dozen reporters began their deathwatch outside the closed doors. The photographers remained at the ready. Nobody expected the meeting would last very long. Chandler would lower the boom on MacPhail, and that would be that. MacPhail would probably explode again when he came out, and that would add to the story. You know MacPhail. It might take a couple of sharp questions but before long he'd get his neck bowed and start spouting. MacPhail was always good for a story.

The press waited. An hour, two hours, three hours. Chandler canceled a golf date he had for that afternoon. Both men missed luncheon. After six hours and forty minutes MacPhail walked out. He managed a twisted half-smile.

"Gentlemen," he said, "I'm sorry I'll not be able to help you. If you want any information you must get it from this office."

He stepped into an elevator and departed. He was next seen

in a bar downstairs. He had at least won something this May Day. The AP said he had bet Dan Topping a thousand dollars earlier that he wouldn't take a drink before May first. He hadn't. He was now free to enjoy a drink on some of Topping's money. Then he went to the airport, flew back to New York, and to my knowledge has never said what went on those long hours behind closed doors with Chandler.

The reporters then tried to see Chandler, who remained unavailable. His assistant, Walter Mulbry, told them:

"There is no story—the Colonel and the Commissioner conferred for about six and a half hours—there was no lull in the conversation. The Commissioner will see no newspapermen or photographers and will answer no questions."

Jackie Robinson celebrated May Day at Ebbets Field. The Cubs were in and the day before had beaten the Dodgers, stopped their winning streak at 6 and blanked Jackie at the plate. His batting slump was o for 20. Earlier in the year Bob Feller, who had played against Robinson in some barnstorming games, gave his appraisal. Feller said for publication that Jackie wouldn't hit big-league pitching. There were many people who fervently hoped Feller was correct, many more people than stood up to be counted. Jackie was going upstream. A lonely trip.

Robinson wrote later that this first major-league slump worried him sick and put a serious doubt in his mind. He also wrote his appreciation that Shotton never wavered in his confidence in him, that the new manager left him in the batting order and said nothing to him. But Jackie knew that everyone was watching—Rickey, Shotton, his teammates, everyone.

Jackie hit a line drive to left his first at bat the first of May. It was good for a double. The slump and the questions were answered. There is no medicine in baseball as effective as a base hit. The Dodgers went on to win, and to hold first place.

It rained the next four days and the only action between the Dodgers and the Reds and the Pirates in that period was done in the front offices. Rickey sent pitchers Kirby Higbe (who modestly stated that he would win the pennant for Pittsburgh), Hank Behrman and Cal McLish, plus Gene Mauch and Dixie

Howell to the Pirates for utility outfielder Al Gionfriddo and cash, something over $125,000. The Pirates dealt hoping to become a pennant winner. Rickey had a surplus of players, had to reduce the size of his squad, and also, Rickey was never reluctant to replenish the bank balance. Neither was his partner, Walter O'Malley.

Two observations: Despite Higbe's prediction, the Pirates didn't win the pennant but finished seventh in an eight-team league, and Higbe didn't win quite as many games as he lost—he was 13–17. Rickey was the shrewdest trader around, and you took your chances when you dealt with him. Second, despite Rickey's ability to judge ballplayers, he had no crystal ball on his desk. What he got in Gionfriddo was the result of serendipity. The writers in reporting this transaction said Gionfriddo was expected to be sent to Montreal, that he was just a spare part. Well—he was some spare part for the Dodgers in October.

The St. Louis Cardinals came into Brooklyn for 3 games, Tuesday, Wednesday and Thursday, May 7–9. These are important dates. The defending world champions had lost 9 of their last 10 games. They were staggering. Stan Musial wasn't hitting his weight—he had hit the three preceding seasons .357, .347 and .365. The Cardinals had dropped into the cellar, although it was far too early to count them out of the race. Owner Sam Breadon arrived in New York. The papers said he had come to assure manager Eddie Dyer that his job was not in jeopardy. Also, Breadon got outfielder Ron Northey from the Phillies for Harry Walker and pitcher Fred Schmidt. Northey was no gazelle in the field or on the bases, but he could whack the ball.

To add to the St. Louis blues, Musial developed stomach pains and was flown to St. Louis for fear he had appendicitis.

The Dodgers managed to pull out the opening game 7–6 to the glee of the assembled faithful. Furillo tripled with the bases loaded, Reese hit his first home run, while Hugh Casey relieved and nailed it down. After all, the Cardinals were the Cardinals, and these two teams had battled tooth and toenail year by year since the Dodgers nipped the Redbirds for the 1941 pennant.

The story, however, wasn't all on the field. Leo Durocher showed up, sat behind the Dodgers dugout with Laraine, shook hands across the top of the dugout with Shotton as the flashbulbs exploded, and waved to the Dodgers. Leo said he had gotten a wire from Rickey telling him to fly in—for what, he, Leo, didn't know. All else he would talk about was his meeting with Chandler in Berkeley, California. Leo reminded the writers that Chandler then had put his arm around his shoulders and told him to walk the straight and narrow (which he had done), and further that Chandler had said, "Leo, I like you."

The next day Howard Pollet beat the Dodgers 2–1 with the help of a home run by the old war-horse Terry Moore. This set the stage for the first night game of the year at Brooklyn. The paid was 32,328—full house, screaming all the way. Another left-hander, the Little Cat, Harry Brecheen, who had won 3 games over Boston in the recent World Series, beat Brooklyn 5–1. While this left the Dodgers tied for first place, the Cardinals in eighth place were only 6 games back. And the Dodgers knew they'd have to cope with Musial when the two teams played again.

Baseball has the best grapevine in the world. Nothing is secret among ballplayers. The series with the Cardinals was exciting but the bomb was detonated by New York *Herald Tribune* sports editor Stanley Woodward the morning of May 9, just as the Cardinals were leaving town. Had this story been printed the day before, it would have been a dangerous event at Ebbets Field in that first night game of the season. There had been rumors among the players—the public was unaware of it—that some of the Cardinals were planning measures against Robinson. Woodward's story broke it wide open.

Woodward wrote that at least three of the Cardinals—all from the South—were going to get their fellow players to strike, and not take the field against the Dodgers when they came to St. Louis with Jackie Robinson. Further, the movement was to enlist other players on other teams to do the same. The idea was to force Robinson out of the league and out of baseball. Woodward stated that owner Breadon had learned of this, and that this was the real reason he had rushed to New York . . . that Breadon went to Ford Frick, president of the league, and between them they went to the Cardinal players. Neither Breadon nor Frick advised Commissioner Chandler of it, as they felt this was strictly a league problem, and therefore up to them to settle it.

Frick measured up. He minced no words. According to Woodward's story, Frick told Breadon to tell his belligerent ballplayers:

"If you do this you will be suspended from the league. You will find that the friends you think you have in the press box will not support you, that you will be outcasts. I do not care if half the league strikes. Those who do it will encounter quick retribution. All will be suspended and I don't care if it wrecks the National League for five years. This is the United States of America and one citizen has as much right to play as another.

"The National League will go down the line with Robinson no matter the consequences. You will find, if you go through with your intentions, that you have been guilty of complete madness."

This stand by Frick crushed the threatened strike of the Cardinal players against the black player. Any thoughts any players on other teams might have had about a strike went into thin air. Frick settled it, and at once. There was no mistaking his position. It was his finest hour in baseball both as president of the National League and later as Commissioner. In fact, I would say this show of strength and integrity and vision guaranteed that he would be the Commissioner to follow Chandler.

It was significant that Woodward also wrote in this same story:

"It is understood that Frick took this matter [manager Chapman's baiting of Robinson at Brooklyn] up with the Philadelphia management and that Chapman has been advised to keep his bench comments above the belt."

Today people take it for granted that black athletes will play when and where their talents permit—professional baseball, football, basketball, and in high schools and colleges. Today the bottom line is win—and you can't win today without some black players. Rickey and Robinson lived to see the full acceptance of black athletes, which was a benediction for them. They certainly fought hard enough for it.

When Rickey signed Robinson for 1946 there was not a black player in professional baseball, football or basketball. Not one. However, pro basketball was just getting started after World War II. It didn't hesitate.

One further note about Woodward's story: owner Sam Breadon of the Cardinals denied it but Frick confirmed the story. Woodward printed the denial and the confirmation the next day. Also on the next day, May 10, *Herald Tribune* columnist Red Smith wrote a scathing attack on the Cardinal players involved, called them misguided, and hoped they'd remember they were in the United States. Other columnists wrote in the same vein, without exception. Just as Frick had warned the dissidents, not a voice in a press box was raised in support of their plans to strike in order to return baseball to an all-white status.

The Dodgers were due in Philadelphia for the weekend. They went down on the train. Every player had his copy of the *Herald Tribune*. Woodward's story was thoroughly read. Robinson was increasingly a marked man. What must have been his thoughts as he read the story? Was anything said to him, and if so, by whom? The players had pretty well accepted him on the field—they had no choice. Rickey was firmly behind him and Shotton brooked no deviations. The Dodgers knew by now that if they wanted to stay on the team they had to play with Robinson. Rickey and Shotton meant business. But the other players had not accepted Robinson as a person. They left him strictly alone.

Shotton was for Robinson 100 percent. He valued Robinson as a player. Shotton was going to do all in his power to support Rickey in this, his most controversial project. But Shotton was not a man of easy speech. He used short sentences. Also, Shotton was the manager, and as manager he could not spend too much time with any one player—he had twenty-five men to think about. Managers, generals, key executives—leaders in any field must preserve a certain reserve, aloofness and privacy. Top leadership is a lonely life.

Probably Robinson sat with, or near, four men—the three coaches, Clyde Sukeforth (who had taken Jackie to see Rickey for their first meeting), Ray Blades and Jake Pitler—and the road secretary, Harold Parrott.

Parrott wrote his book *The Lords of Baseball* some thirty years after all the turbulence of early 1947; he was deeply involved with Rickey and with his planning and his thinking. Parrott confesses that at first he sided with Mrs. Rickey and the six Rickey children that Branch was too old to take on breaking the color line. But once the Old Man took it on, Parrott became all for it. Parrott was very sensitive to the Robinson problems and reported everything to Rickey.

A road secretary knows more about a ball club than anyone else. The road secretary makes out the rooming list for the hotels on road trips and has to go over and approve all charges, such as meal checks, and advance small sums to players on the road if they get short of money. The hotels report to the secretary all player indiscretions. Card games in rooms, women in rooms, drinking in rooms—all this data is routine material known by the secretary. The secretary is hand in glove with the manager and the trainer, and very close to the front office. The secretary is the mother hen of a ball club on the road. Parrott in his functions was an extension of Branch Rickey.

One of the most important duties of the road secretary is the checking of all turnstiles. The federal government for tax purposes demands to know the exact count of the paid attendance. The road secretary walks with the home team secretary, gate by gate, turnstile by turnstile. After each game the road secretary is given a check for the money due the visiting team.

The road secretary receives an agreed allotment of tickets for seats around the visiting dugout. He distributes these free tickets in response to the players' requests for their family, friends or guys they want to do a favor for, in return for a favor. Ballplayers are dealers. They are always looking for something for nothing. A pair of free seats for a game is valuable trading material. (This was what had Red Patterson, road secretary of the Yankees, in such an embarrassing and difficult position at the Chandler hearings, when Red had to say he didn't remember to whom he gave those box seats behind the Yankee dugout at Havana.)

Very likely Parrott spent some time with Robinson on the ninety-minute train ride to Philadelphia, yet Harold couldn't have spent all his time with Jackie. After all he had to settle accounts with the train conductor, be certain every player on the squad was on the train, confer with manager Shotton should Shotton want to know something. The details that beset a road secretary never end. But certainly Parrott sat awhile with Robinson.

Also, Parrott knew something Robinson didn't about this Philadelphia trip. In fact, he knew two things, and there was still a third thing Parrott himself didn't know.

Let him tell the Philadelphia story. Quoting from *The Lords of Baseball:*

> They [the owners] fought him [Rickey] tooth and nail! They really believed that the Negro would spoil their Grand Old Game, and they fought him under the table as well as openly. In fact, they voted fifteen to one against Rickey's Black Experiment in a secret meeting where the Old Man [Rickey] saw even the agenda and the ballots destroyed in a Watergate-type cover-up that was years ahead of its time. The lodge brothers insisted the meeting never happened; then, when I heard Rickey tell the whole story at Wilberforce University, they denied it again and again to press and radio.
>
> I remember the Old Man telling me to pick up an extension telephone in his Brooklyn Dodger office less than a week before we—Robinson and the other players to whom I acted as confessor, valet, and nursemaid as the team's traveling secretary—were to make our first trip to Philadelphia.
>
> We'd been looking forward to sleepy Philadelphia as a relief from the big-city pressure cooker that New York became when Robinson broke the color line . . . Robinson had never had any trouble when he played there before thousands of Negroes as the shortstop of the Kansas City Monarchs.
>
> Even the Benjamin Franklin Hotel, the second-rate house the Dodgers had used for years, didn't figure to be a problem. They'd had my rooming list, with the black man's name on it, for almost a month, and they hadn't called me to complain. . . .
>
> All these things were running through my mind as Rickey was motioning for me to pick up the extension phone. "Herb Pennock is calling from Philadelphia," he

whispered, holding a hand over his own mouthpiece. "I want you to hear this. . . ."

Pennock, known as the Squire of Kennett Square during his Yankee days as a southpaw pitching great, was now the suave, silver-thatched general manager of the Phillies, who were being revived by Bob Carpenter and the Du Pont millions.

". . . just can't bring the Nigger here with the rest of your team, Branch," I heard Pennock saying. "We're just not ready for that sort of thing yet. We won't be able to take the field against your Brooklyn team if that boy Robinson is in uniform."

"Very well, Herbert," replied the always-precise Rickey. "And if we must claim the game nine to nothing, we will do just that, I assure you."

(The score of a forfeited game is 9–0. In the early days of baseball when a forfeit situation first presented itself they didn't know what to make the score. Somebody suggested they make it the same as the first shutout game on record which, when looked up, was 9–0.)

The Dodgers got off the train. Parrott got them into taxicabs. A truck was waiting to take the baggage. The team moved to their home in Philadelphia, the Benjamin Franklin Hotel. The players got out of their cabs—the secretary would be billed for them. The baggage was unloaded.

Parrott wrote in his book:

When we arrived in Philadelphia, took cabs to the Franklin, I was bluntly told that there were no rooms for us. "And don't bring your team back here," the manager snapped, "while you have any Nigras with you!"

. . . I tried to call Carpenter and Pennock to see if they had any pull at the other hotels in town. No answer on either line, the Phillies' switchboard said. No, sorry, they couldn't be found anywhere.

I hired a truck to load the bags, got cabs to take the

players to the ball park where they could twiddle their thumbs for a few hours, and prepared to search for a hotel that would take in my homeless band. The thought crossed my mind that we might have to take the train back to New York after that night's game and become commuters for the rest of the series. . . .

. . . I very nearly didn't try the second hotel my cabbie took me to, because the fashionable Warwick looked too plush; but I brazened it out and asked anyway, mentioning our black problem boy. Delighted to have us, the manager told me. Of course the rates were almost twice those at the crummy Franklin, but any port in a storm, no matter how expensive. We stayed at the Warwick many seasons after that one. . . .

That night Pennock had the nerve to ask me if I had found a hotel.

Sometimes a person has to ask, "How much can I stand?" The day before the Dodgers made their first appearance in Philadelphia, Rickey announced that Robinson had received threatening letters—all unsigned, of course. These letters demanded that Jackie get out of baseball, and some said if he showed up at certain ball parks he'd be shot. Rickey turned the letters over to the police and to the FBI. A New York police captain called on Robinson at his residence to discuss the matter just before the Philadelphia series. . . . Such letters continued to come to Jackie over the next few years, and some were regarded by the FBI as serious threats.

Stanley Woodward's story in the *Herald Tribune* was reading matter on the train to Philadelphia. Then the refusal of the Benjamin Franklin Hotel to allow the Dodgers to stay there as long as Robinson was with the team was deeply embarrassing and humiliating for Jackie. His teammates said nothing to him, but they knew, and Jackie knew that they knew.

Then the Phillies won the night game, but at least the Dodgers got to play after the four straight days of rain that had washed out 2 games with the Reds and 2 more with the Pirates. Rickey cut down his squad again while fattening the bank balance by $50,000 by selling Howard Schultz to the Phillies. Schultz wasn't going to play first base with Robinson there.

All in all, this wasn't a too happy trip to the City of Brotherly Love. The Dodgers avoided a complete disaster by winning the Saturday afternoon game, but the bottom dropped out Sunday. The Phils took both ends of the doubleheader and dropped the Dodgers out of first place by 2 games. However, a record crowd of 40,952 paid to see the games. Robinson was a tremendous attraction.

Road secretary Parrott took a sizable check back to Brooklyn. There was more than enough money to pay the extra tariff at the Warwick, no matter if the players ordered double shrimp cocktails and extra-thick steaks. Which they did. Once Robinson was put on the Dodgers by Rickey, the Dodgers always drew heavily.

The check Parrott had in his briefcase was about the only cheerful thing that traveled to New York that evening of May 11, 1947. A doubleheader is a brutal day's work which exhausts and drains strength of body and spirit. Especially when you've lost both games. The players slowly walked into the clubhouse. Nobody said much to anybody. What was there to say? The Phillies had said it 7–3 and 5–4. The players showered, dressed and walked to the North Philadelphia station. There was no way to get dinner. The train had no diner and the ride to Penn Station was ninety minutes. Shotton sat alone, staring out the window into the black night. Then it was up to the players to go on to Brooklyn for something to eat, or to someplace around Penn Station.

There was a makeup game the next afternoon at Ebbets Field with the Braves. Monday afternoons are not ideal times to attract crowds, so the Dodgers had made this a Ladies' Day. Some 20,000 fans showed up. There would be no small crowds again for the Dodgers. After this game the team would start on its first western trip—to Cincinnati, Pittsburgh, Chicago and then St. Louis. The Bad Lands. The season was getting serious.

The Yankees flew to Chicago from St. Louis only to sit around a day because of cold weather mixed with rain. On Saturday May

2 the Yankees beat the White Sox 5–2 to hold first place; that day, too, Bob Feller delivered his second one-hitter of the young season against Boston. And Jet Pilot nipped Phalanx in the Kentucky Derby—he led from the starting gate and was never headed. However, the baseball races were not to be of that pattern. To demonstrate, the White Sox tumbled the Yankees out of the top spot by beating them twice on Sunday.

Detroit was next with more of the same treatment. The series began with a six-inning tie game, 2–2, called by rain. It rained the next day. About all the writers had to entertain their readers with was that manager Harris said the rookie, Yogi Berra, would catch Reynolds. Aaron Robinson was the first-string receiver, but he was having trouble with a bad back. This gave Harris the chance to see more of Berra, give Berra more needed work behind the plate, couple the raw rookie with an experienced pitcher, and above all let Mister Berra (as Casey Stengel was later to call him respectfully) "swing the stick."

Reynolds pitched the next day at Detroit, Berra caught, and Detroit won 3–2. Reynolds, Berra and company lost, but this was not to happen often. Now the weather really turned sour. The entire series at Cleveland, including a doubleheader, and an encounter with Bob Feller, was rained out. The Yankees had dropped 4 straight.

The last Yankee stop on this first major five-city swing was Boston with its friendly left-field wall, known in some quarters as the Green Monster. This was Joe DiMaggio's favorite place, next to his native San Francisco. Some of DiMag's biggest days were in Fenway Park, much to the shock of the sturdy New England fans. Joe was a dead pull hitter to left. Fenway Park was tailor-made for him, just as Yankee Stadium was against him with its vast distances in left, left center and center. Yankee Stadium with its short right-field porch was built for Babe Ruth. It would have been ideal for Ted Williams, a left-handed batter who pulled everything to right. Fenway Park had a deep right field.

Casey Stengel used to talk lovingly, admiringly and respectfully about DiMaggio and Williams and the two ball parks they played in at home. "They must be great men," the Old Professor would say, "because they succeed in ball parks that are backwards for them. Suppose," Casey would say, "suppose they were switched . . . suppose my man DiMaggio was to play half his games in Boston, and that Williams fellow was to have half a year pulling into right field at the Stadium. Just suppose . . ." and Stengel would start dreaming of the awful wreckage that would take place.

It almost happened. Larry MacPhail got to drinking one night with Tom Yawkey, who owned 100 percent of the Red Sox. MacPhail got to talking about an even-up swap of the two players—DiMaggio to Boston, Williams to New York. MacPhail recounted for Yawkey what DiMaggio had done by hitting balls against and over the Green Monster . . . how electric DiMaggio would be to the Italians in Boston . . . that Williams was having strained relations with the Boston writers . . . that DiMaggio got along splendidly with the press. MacPhail was a very persuasive man. The glasses clinked, the ice cooled the firewater and the evening wore on. Needless to relate, MacPhail didn't dwell upon what Ruth had done with the Stadium right field, and what he expected Ted Williams to do with it. Yawkey agreed to the trade—Williams for DiMaggio. They shook hands on the deal, had another drink, and both men went to bed.

MacPhail told me years later, "I thought it would have been a hell of a deal for both clubs." I was driving him to the Miami airport. We were both then living on Key Biscayne. This was the sort of a deal he wanted to make—an even trade of the two star players in the American League. MacPhail was never afraid when he made up his mind. "The next morning," MacPhail related, "Yawkey came to me and said that although he had given his word the night before on the deal . . . that he was a man of his word, but that after sleeping over it he just couldn't do it. He was canceling the deal—he had to keep Williams." MacPhail sighed as he remembered how close he had come to one of the most stunning, shocking trades in baseball.

It would have been a most sensational trade, ranking with the Hornsby-Frisch trade. Rogers Hornsby was traded to the Giants in 1926 shortly after he had led the St. Louis Cardinals to their first pennant and world championship for another star, Frank Frisch. Hornsby had hit over .400 three times for St. Louis—in 1924 his mark was .424—was a sound second baseman, and was the manager of the new champion Redbirds. Less than three months after Hornsby had achieved his tremendous triumph—that's when Grover Cleveland Alexander struck out Tony Lazzeri with 3 on in game seven—and was the toast of St. Louis, he was traded. Gone.

Hornsby was a blunt-speaking man who had said things about his owner, Sam Breadon, that Breadon wasn't about to take. Late in the pennant race of 1926, the Cardinals had an open date in New York. The players were bone-tired and badly needed a day of rest. But owner Breadon, always a man with an eye on the dollar, scheduled his Cardinals to play an exhibition in New England. Hornsby demanded the game be canceled in order to rest his weary ball club. Breadon wouldn't cancel. Hornsby then told Breadon in the public press to do with the exhibition game what Edward VIII is reputed to have told England to do with the crown jewels. Breadon couldn't physically execute Hornsby's demand, but he could and did order his general manager, Branch Rickey, to get rid of Hornsby. Think of it —Hornsby was the greatest right-handed batter baseball ever saw, manager of the just anointed world champions, and owner Breadon said to Rickey, "Hornsby must go."

Rickey had no personal love for Hornsby. Rickey had been the manager of the Cardinals himself from 1919 until June 1, 1925, when owner Breadon decided that Rickey should stay in the front office and Hornsby would be the manager. Rickey had also since 1917 been vice-president and business manager of the Redbirds. He had created the farm system, selecting players carefully, and had built the ball club with which Hornsby won the first St. Louis pennant and championship the next year.

Rickey was now on the hot seat. The fans of St. Louis were way up on cloud nine. They were ready to nominate Hornsby for canonization. Further, they knew that Branch Rickey was Trader Horn incarnate. Breaden sort of stayed in the shadows as far as the fan on the street went. Rickey knew that when he traded Hornsby—and Breadon had made it crystal clear Hornsby was to go—the outcry and the blame would fall largely on him. Rickey knew the fans would say that he got rid of the man who took over his, Rickey's, job as bench manager.

What player could he get for Hornsby? Anyway, who was

even close to Hornsby in value? Certainly there was no player who could hit like Hornsby.

There was one possibility: Frankie Frisch. A great second baseman for John McGraw and the Giants, Frisch was the sparkplug of four straight New York pennants, 1921–24. Frisch was a dangerous batter, a switch-hitter who always hit in the .330–.340 range. He was a money player and probably the fastest man in baseball. That's why they called him the Fordham Flash—for his speed, and the fact that he had jumped from the Fordham campus to the mighty Giants of McGraw.

McGraw had a nasty, vile tongue. He used it on opposing players, on umpires, on people in general, and on his own players. Somehow or other he seemed to single out Frisch for abuse, even after he had made Frisch his team captain.

"Red, it was terrible the things McGraw said to Frisch," Bill Terry told me, "simply terrible. Frank would answer back in kind. I don't know why the Old Man got on Frisch so much—maybe because he was a college ballplayer, maybe because Frank was a sassy fellow. McGraw would blame other players' errors on Frisch. And because Frisch was captain, when one of our pitchers made a bad pitch McGraw would yell and curse Frisch. They went at each other something terrible. Awful.

"We got to St. Louis for a series," Terry went on, "and it was hot as it always is in the summer in St. Louis. George Kelly and I had a suite in the Chase Hotel, and we got some beer. Frisch was there with us, and one or two others. Frank was burned up about McGraw getting on him, and we sympathized with him. We agreed with him.

"Then," said Terry, "I guess I was responsible for what happened. I never thought when I said it that Frank would do it. But I said to Frank, 'If I were you, Frank, I wouldn't take it any longer from McGraw—I'd get on the train and go back to New York.'

"The next day he did it. He went back to New York. Jumped the ball club. That's the maddest I ever saw McGraw."

Frisch rejoined the team a little later but he and McGraw were finished. Here were two brilliant stars, in their prime, and both had to go. The trade was announced December 20, 1926. The news of it spoiled many a fan's Christmas season. Rickey told me later that Frisch by his marvelous play for St. Louis "saved my life."

So MacPhail for one night had made one of baseball's biggest trades—Joe DiMaggio for Ted Williams. That was a trade just for sake of trading. Both players could go or stay. Yawkey saw to it they stayed.

May 10, 1947. The Yankees, with a 4-game losing streak, came into Boston for 3 single games. The Green Monster, Ted Williams—thanks to Yawkey—Joe Cronin and company waited. The Red Sox were trying to start the surge that had carried them to the pennant the year before.

Joe DiMaggio—still a Yankee, also thanks to Yawkey—felt that his injured, tender heel was well enough for a regulation baseball shoe. Just the sight of that nearby neighborly left-field wall was all the healing medicine DiMaggio needed. What would he have hit had he been a Red Sox? In the first game Joe had 2 hits and ran his consecutive string to 6. Mister Berra went 3 for 5, did the catching, and the Yankees won 9–6. This tied the two teams at a game out of first place. Bucky Harris enjoyed his dinner for the first time in a week.

He wasn't so hungry the next two evenings. The Red Sox belted Bill Bevens in the first inning, scored 6 times, and made off with the next game 8–7. The BoSox took the odd game 4–3 to send the Yankees limping home with 7 of 9 losses. However, Berra hit the first home run of the 358 he would belt in regular season play, plus a dozen more in World Series to make it 370.

Home cooking, Yankee Stadium and the St. Louis Browns got the Yankees turned around. They beat the Browns in a walkover 9–1. Reynolds pitched, Keller hit 2 home runs, and DiMaggio and Lindell each had one. It rained the next day, but the Red Sox won their eighth and ninth just to let the Yankees know there was a pennant race going on.

The first night game of the year at the Stadium was with Chicago, May 15. (MacPhail at Cincinnati in 1935 had installed the first lights in the big leagues, then in 1938 put in lights at Brooklyn—Vander Meer's second straight no-hit game—and had turned them on at the Stadium as soon as he got control of the

Yankees.) There were 44,325 paid and third-base coach Charlie Dressen returned to work, having served his thirty-day sentence. Before the game some of Dressen's friends said kind words and gave him a diamond ring. Commissioner Chandler was not there. He wasn't invited by either MacPhail or Dressen. However, the White Sox curdled the cream with an 8–2 win. Inasmuch as Boston won again not everybody in the Bronx slept well. In the Boston win over the Browns, Mr. Yawkey's favorite player, Ted Williams, hit a grand slam for his eighth home run of the young season.

Manager Harris, always calm and apparently unperturbed, had to get his ball club balanced and set. He knew this was by and large true of the other teams at this early stage of the race. The Yankee infield was McQuinn at first, Stirnweiss at second, Rizzuto at short and Johnson at third. Rizzuto and Stirnweiss were not hitting, but they would.

DiMaggio's heel was improving, which stabilized the team. Henrich was healthy now and available for either right field or first base. Charlie Keller was in left, with Lindell alternating. Aaron Robinson, Ralph Houk, a rookie, and Berra formed the catching staff, although it wasn't completely certain that Berra wouldn't be in the outfield from time to time. Robinson's back was troubling him—which gave Harris opportunities to use both Houk and Berra. Houk could catch but was a light hitter. Berra? He could "swing that stick."

The pitching one day looked solid, then again not. Harris and MacPhail counted heavily on their new man, Allie Reynolds, and as a surprise Joe Page was doing an impressive job coming in from the bullpen. MacPhail finally disposed of Nick Etten, a first baseman, by sending him to Newark.

The series with the White Sox called for a doubleheader on Saturday May 17. Then came Cleveland and Rapid Robert Feller, followed by Detroit and 4 games with Boston. There was big business on hand.

The White Sox doubleheader was a Yankee Junior Day. Some 12,000 yelling kids screamed and yelled all afternoon. All told the crowd totaled 66,666. DiMaggio hit a home run in the ninth inning of the first game to win that one 4–3, and the Yankees took the second game by the same score. The Browns beat the Red Sox as matters tightened.

The next day—Sunday—Mr. Feller was a little too much. He and the Indians beat their former teammate Allie Reynolds 5–3. Joe Gordon, playing against the Yankees for the first time since he was traded for Reynolds, got 2 walks and 3 hits out of 3 official at bats. The Indians won the next 2 games and swept the series. Bevens was beaten again, his third straight failure. The Yankees fell 4½ games back. Harris didn't have to read Longfellow to be reminded that life is real, life is earnest.

Wednesday was the second night game of the year at the Stadium. Detroit, in first place, came in and the Yankees turned around. Frank Shea shut out the Tigers. DiMaggio boomed a double with the bases loaded in the first inning that relaxed the paying crowd of 49,844. The final was 5–0. Shea was a bright spot. This was his fifth complete game, and he was just a rookie. Ralph Houk, also a rookie, got another look behind the plate. Harris was blending young players with veterans, searching for the combination.

One would have thought, after this satisfactory night at the Stadium, that all would be sunshine and bluebirds and peace with the world. One would have thought . . . with no MacPhail around.

The game with Detroit was rained out but MacPhail stirred things up—he announced he was fining DiMaggio a hundred dollars, and Keller, Aaron Robinson, Lindell, and two others lesser amounts because they had not cooperated on various Yankee promotions. In the standard players' contract is a clause that binds the players to assist the team in such matters as selected public appearances, talks, and public relations films.

Then, as if this weren't sufficient for the day, MacPhail got into the matter of the Yankees flying. He had pioneered air travel: in 1934, at Cincinnati, he had flown the Reds to and from Chicago for a series; the first time a big-league team had flown in the regular season. This year he had flown the Yankees on their first western swing, but several of the players had gone by train. There was a rumor that the players who took the train would have to pay their train fare.

MacPhail denied the rumor and said the players were free to elect the plane or the train. But he opened the subject of possible crosscurrents among the Yankees about flying. You had to believe MacPhail agreed with Robert Browning about "divine discontent."

There wasn't much time to chew over the MacPhail fining and flying episode. The Red Sox, breathing fire and fury, came in for 4 games—Friday through Monday night. The advance seat sale was heavy. There is no doubt that the Red Sox versus the Yankees, either in Boston or in New York, is the hottest rivalry in the American League. Yankee Stadium is almost in New England—leave the Bronx, pass through Westchester County, and you are in Connecticut. The Yankee broadcasts went over New England just as do those of the Red Sox. The Ted Williams-Joe DiMaggio battle of bats was enough to fill the park.

It was this series of 4 games that convinced a lot of people the 1947 Yankees were for real, that MacPhail had done well in his Reynolds-for-Gordon trade, and that Bucky Harris had the club that was to challenge the defending champion Red Sox—maybe beat them. It was this series that put a crimp in the Red Sox, plus planting a doubt in their minds.

The Yankees won all 4 games, moved into second place 3 games behind Detroit, and now had 8 wins out of the last 12 games. People poured into the Stadium. For the Monday night game the Stadium overflowed. A record crowd for a single game at the Stadium, 74,747, jammed in. Refunds had to be given to 1,140 who physically couldn't get into the park. Traffic was stalled for miles and for hours. By May 26 the Yankees had drawn, at home, 627,243 paid.

In the Red Sox series manager Harris saw what he wanted. Reynolds opened with his third shutout, beating Boston 9–0. The Chief was a most commanding figure on the mound when he had it, which was quite often. Spud Chandler followed suit the next day with a 2-hit shutout. Bevens in the Sunday game won easily, 17–2. Joe Page relieved to save and win game four 9–3. This strong performance by Page was all to the mustard for Harris. This now looked like a pitching staff.

The Yankees went to Washington, Philadelphia and Cleveland

to finish May. Reynolds lost at Washington, but the Yankees won the next 2. Shea got credit for the third game at Washington, his fifth victory, but Joe Page saved it. Berra caught Shea and hit his second home run. DiMaggio was on a hitting streak.

But Friday May 30 was a day to forget. The Athletics beat the Yankees a doubleheader, 1–0 and 4–0. Dick Fowler and Joe Coleman outdueled Spud Chandler and Bill Bevens. Chandler's 1–0 loss was tough, but that's the way it goes. A baseball season is a long time with aches and pains, ups and downs, and you never have a game won until you get into the clubhouse with it. The crowd at Philadelphia was another sellout, 30,261. The Yankees drew them.

It was a silent clubhouse. Two defeats in one day, not a run scored, and waiting the next day at Cleveland was one Mr. R. Feller.

Every day in baseball is a new day. Every ball game is different. The possible variations are beyond calculation. Feller didn't have his fine edge and the Yankees were delighted to find him still mortal, especially Charlie Keller who teed off on Bob for 2 home runs, his eleventh and twelfth. The score was 8–4. Karl Drews started but again Joe Page walked in and locked it up. It is worth noting this sentence in Jim Dawson's story of the game in the New York *Times:* "Page, who has developed into a capable relief hurler, came from the bullpen. . . ." DiMaggio extended his batting string through 14 games to end the merry month of May. It was merrier, certainly, than Bucky Harris and Larry MacPhail had hoped it would be.

Burt Shotton knew very little about the Brooklyn ball club when Branch Rickey suddenly made him its manager two days after the 1947 season opened, and just hours before the third game was to be played at the Polo Grounds. He hadn't been in the National League since 1934 when he was a coach at Cincinnati. His last years in the big leagues had been as coach at Cleveland in the American League.

However, Shotton was a thoroughly seasoned baseball man. He got into the business as a player in 1908 and was manager-coach through 1945. That's a total of thirty-seven years' hard experience. He had been a manager fifteen years—five with Philadelphia in the National League and ten with high minor-league teams in Rickey's far-flung farm system.

Shotton knew baseball, knew ballplayers, and he wasn't afraid to make decisions. By mid-May he knew all he needed to know about what he had and didn't have on the Dodgers. He knew he had a superb shortstop in Pee Wee Reese. Reese was so good that Shotton got to calling him "my ringer." (After I went to the Yankees in 1954, the veteran Bill Skiff, who along with Johnny Neun had scouted the Dodgers in their World Series meetings against the Yankees, told me he often warned Stengel and the players that Reese was the most dangerous of all the Brooklyn players—more dangerous than Robinson, Hodges, Furillo, Snider, or Campanella. Why the baseball writers haven't voted Pee Wee into the Hall of Fame I'll never know, unless it is that the writers go only by cold statistics rather than genuine value to a team—which I suppose they can't know, or won't take the trouble to find out.)

Shotton knew in short order he had a star in Jackie Robinson. He knew Robinson was an all-out competitor, that he would hit, would field, and would be such a menace on the bases that he would upset opposing pitchers and ball clubs. Rickey urged Shotton to encourage Robinson to run wild; Shotton needed no such urging. Robinson on base was always on his own. Robinson on base—on any base, first, second, third—was the most exciting player I've seen. When Robinson was on base every eye in the ball park was on him.

Stanky at second was a sound player, a solid competitor, and would get on base often, not only with hits but with walks. Spider Jorgensen was a rookie at third who was playing well. Shotton had an infield. That was the strongest part of his ball club: Robinson, Stanky, Reese and Jorgensen. Shotton was thankful for that department. His worries were elsewhere.

The outfield was constantly being reset, mainly because Pete Reiser was often hurt. When Reiser was well and in center field, the outfield was strong. It was fortunate that Rickey had been unable earlier in the year to make the trade for Dixie Walker he tried to make after the threatened rebellion at Panama. Walker was the anchor. He played well in right field and he hit .306 with 94 runs batted in. Dixie was in 148 games and steadied the outfield. As other outfielders, Shotton had the young Carl Furillo, and the younger Duke Snider, Gene Hermanski, and Al Gionfriddo. Gionfriddo didn't hit much but was the best fielder of all the outfielders. He had been a throw-in when Rickey made the deal with the Pirates for Higbe. Shotton valued Gionfriddo and, instead of letting him be sent to Montreal, kept him for special assignments. (It would have been a different World Series without him.)

Bruce Edwards was the first-string catcher. As a rookie the year before, he had done well. He had an arm scare but it proved to be just that, a scare. Edwards caught 130 games, hit .295, drove in 80 runs, handled pitchers well, and all in all turned in a splendid year's work. Bobby Bragan backed up Edwards, with a raw rookie, Gil Hodges, on hand.

So Shotton had a fine infield, good enough outfield, good catching, and strong reserves: Arky Vaughan, Cookie Lavagetto, Eddie Miksis, Stan Rojek and Tommy Brown.

What Shotton didn't have, and never had all season or in the World Series, was pitching. Except for relief pitcher Hugh Casey, Shotton didn't know what his pitching was going to be in mid-May. Ralph Branca was throwing bullets, but he was very young; Branca had won only 3 games the season before. Consider what Shotton's pitchers had done the year before: as noted, Branca had won 3 . . . Joe Hatten had been 14–11, Vic Lombardi was 13–10, and Casey in relief in 1946 was 11–5. The big winners in 1946—Hatten, Lombardi and Casey—had totaled 38 victories. The rest of the 1947 pitching staff had won in 1946 only 9 additional games—Branca 3 and Hal Gregg 6. Shotton had rookies Harry Taylor, Rex Barney, and Clyde King. When Rickey bought Dan Bankhead later in the season, Dan was the first black pitcher in the big leagues, and brought no record in organized ball with him. Kirby Higbe had won 17 for the Dodgers in 1946 but Rickey had dealt him to Pittsburgh early in '47. I don't know how often Rickey indulged himself in the luxury of a second guess, but as 1947 wore along he might have wished he hadn't dealt Higbe. Certainly Shotton could have used him. Hank Behrman was also in the Higbe–Pittsburgh deal, but was returned by the Pirates, and was useful. A game has nine or more innings—somebody has to pitch every inning. It takes bodies with throwing arms attached.

I have known two actual magicians—Blackstone, and Shotton. Blackstone was on the stage. Shotton, with what passed for a pitching staff in 1947, was in the Brooklyn dugout.

The Dodgers began their first western trip Tuesday May 13 at Cincinnati. The Reds had a sensational young pitcher, a treetop-tall sidearm right-hander named Ewell Blackwell, called the Buggy Whip. The Dodgers were going to face him Wednesday in the second game. After the opening game on Tuesday was over, Shotton might well have mumbled what Joe Jacobs said, "I shoulda stood in bed." It was a sandlot-looking affair. The Reds won it 7–5 with only 5 hits . . . Shotton used six pitchers, bases on balls flew in all directions, and some errors were thrown in for bad measure. The six pitchers were Harry Taylor, Clyde King, Rube Melton (soon to be released), Hal Gregg, Ed Chandler (soon to be farmed out) and Rex Barney.

Blackwell was as effective in the second game as the Dodgers had heard he might be. He delivered a 2–0 shutout. Jackie Robinson got a hit to extend his batting string to 11 straight. That was it.

To rub salt into the wounds at Cincinnati, Rickey sold outfielder Tom Tatum to the Reds the very day the Dodgers got to town. Tatum changed uniforms and delivered base hits in both games that beat Brooklyn. His single knocked in the winning runs in the first game, and he homered to give Blackwell all the margin he needed in game two. A ball club can have days like that.

At the same time, down in St. Louis, Eddie Dyer, the manager of the Cardinals, used his sweetest Texas drawl in talking to the New York writers traveling with the Giants. He assured the press there never was anything to the story about his little Redbirds starting a movement to strike against Jackie Robinson . . . nothing to it at all. Dyer's denial followed the denial made earlier by owner Sam Breadon. Why then, any denial or statement about this from manager Dyer to the Giants writers? Could it be because the Dodgers, with Robinson, were coming into St. Louis in exactly one week, and a little controversy somehow oils the turnstiles?

Thursday, Pittsburgh blasted the Dodgers. Ralph Kiner teed off for 2 home runs, and Billy Cox hit 1 and a triple. Robinson had a pair of hits but the Pirates won it 7–3. The Dodgers now led the second division, being down in fifth place.

Friday was a night game, and it promised to be a lulu. Kirby Higbe was to pitch for the Pirates, the first time against his old teammates. Young Ralph Branca drew the starting assignment for the Dodgers. Forbes Field was jumping. The old ball park strained to accommodate 34,814 paid. Matters were moving along smoothly until Pee Wee Reese came to bat in the fifth inning. Higbe's first pitch was right at Reese's head, and down went Pee Wee. This is what the boys in the trade call "the message." Pee Wee got up, dusted his uniform, and sent Higbe "a message." He hit the next pitch for a home run. There was a Dodger on base, and the Dodgers won 3–1. Pee Wee did it. It was a big win for Branca, who was becoming the bell cow. It was a big win for Shotton as he worked patiently to settle his ball club.

Branca's win looked even bigger the next day. Fritz Ostermueller, a veteran left-hander Rickey had sent to Pittsburgh, was a cat who came back. He shut out the Dodgers while Hank Greenberg belted a first-inning home run to get Fritz on his way. This made it 4 losses out of 5, which is not recommended as the way to get to first place in any league.

Early in the game Jackie Robinson and Greenberg accidentally collided on a close play at first base. Nothing was said at the time. Later Greenberg said to Jackie, "I should have asked you if you were hurt?" Jackie said, "No." Greenberg then said, "Stick in there . . . you're doing fine . . . keep your chin up." After the game Jackie said, "Class tells . . . it sticks out all over Mr. Greenberg."

The next day was Sunday, and they were waiting for Jackie and the Dodgers in Chicago. It was a record crowd at Wrigley Field—46,572 paid. There had been a bigger crowd but that was back when people were allowed to stand around the outfield. Nobody got on the field this day but the players. The Dodgers won it with 4 runs in the seventh. Robinson's hitting string was snapped after 14 games, but to ease matters the Cardinals dropped a doubleheader to the Phils.

The crowd the next day, despite its being Monday, was 21,875. People wanted to see Robinson. The Cubs eked it out 8–7. The Dodgers took the train to St. Louis for an announced sellout.

St. Louis was the tough town. If there was to be trouble for Robinson, it figured to be in St. Louis. As late as 1942 a Negro was not allowed to buy a seat in the grandstand at Sportsman's Park. Robinson knew in advance he would not be permitted to stay in the Chase Hotel with the rest of the team. He was to have a room in town with a Negro family. He would come and go to Sportsman's Park on his own, dress with the team, play the game, and depart by himself. He wouldn't be with the Dodgers off the field until the team got ready to leave St. Louis. St. Louis was strictly segregated, just as Rickey told Robinson it would be.

Stanley Woodward's story had killed the Cardinals' strike threat. But as the Dodgers rolled across the flatlands between Chicago and St. Louis, what lay in wait? The same players would be wearing Cardinal uniforms. Nothing untoward had occurred when St. Louis came to Brooklyn, but that was in Brooklyn. This was to be in St. Louis.

They wanted to see Jackie Robinson play ball in St. Louis. The 2-game series was to start at night. The seats were sold, but it rained. No chance. The next day the weather cleared and the game went ten innings before the Dodgers won it 4–3. Hugh Casey came in to hold the Cardinals and be the winning pitcher. Harry Brecheen lost it. For the Dodgers to beat the Cardinals— beat them at home, beat their ace, Brecheen—was powerful medicine. Musial was in the lineup too.

One of the first things Burt Shotton heard when he took over the managing of the Dodgers was how tough the Cardinals were, how hard they were to beat, especially in St. Louis. Shotton heard Cardinals this and Cardinals that. This was something Leo Durocher had left behind. Leo played for the Gas House Gang, came to Brooklyn from St. Louis, and when he began managing the Dodgers was in a constant struggle with the Cardinals. He and his Dodgers had to beat the Cardinals for the 1941 pennant, and they just barely did because that year Whitlow Wyatt was a truly great pitcher. Wyatt beat Mort Cooper 1–0 at St. Louis in the last game of the season between the two teams, which put the Dodgers in first place with a week to go. But the Cardinals had put a mark on Durocher—he was always looking ahead to when he had to play the Cardinals: when the Cardinals were coming to Brooklyn, when the Dodgers were going to St. Louis. The Cardinals had a hex on Leo, or so it seemed.

Shotton heard just so much about the Cardinals and he called a meeting. He told the Dodgers he didn't want to hear any more about the Cardinals than he did about the other ball clubs, that the Cardinals played under the same rules, they used only nine players at a time, they pulled their pants on one leg at a time, and for heaven's sake (he may not have said "heaven's") go out and play your own game. Shotton didn't give many lectures, but when he did they were right to the point. He stopped the Cardinal talk on the Dodgers for the time being. That ten-inning win in St. Louis buttressed what the Old Man had said.

Shotton, as you know, didn't wear a uniform, so after a game he didn't have to change clothes or shower. He would get a bottle of Coca-Cola and sit down on one of the team trunks. He'd sort of bang his heels into the side of the trunk, shake the Coke bottle around, take a sip, and watch what was going on. Once in a while he'd tell one of the players something, and after saying what he wanted to say, he'd often end up with, "I've got mine . . . all I'm trying to do is help you fellows get yours."

That old man was strong help. He took over a deeply divided, badly troubled ball club right after Jackie Robinson joined it. He quieted it down and he kept it quiet. He ran that ball club. He took the Cardinals off their bogus pedestal. He had the patience of Job with his young pitchers. No matter what happened today he remained the same strong figure. His mind was on tomorrow. He knew you won some and you lost some as did everybody else. He didn't get excited. He didn't get upset.

Once in a ball game several of the Dodgers got thrown at, and there were several plays on the bases in which the Dodgers got roughed up. It was the first game of an afternoon and night doubleheader. I figured Shotton would be steamed up about how his players got roughed up and knocked down. I saw him after the afternoon game, sitting on a trunk, shaking his Coke around, just sitting. I said, "Burt, I guess you'll send the team out tonight fighting mad after what happened this afternoon?" He just looked at me a minute, then he said calmly, "They ain't going to be mad tonight, or any other time. . . . I'm here to see they don't get mad. When a man gets mad he can't beat anybody doing anything. They are going out tonight and play their regular game and I expect them to win." They did.

I never forgot what Shotton said about a man can't beat anybody when he gets mad. He was right. When you get mad, you stop thinking. MacPhail made many of his mistakes when he got into his rages. Frank Lane was running the Cleveland Indians and had Roger Maris, a promising young player who could do it all. Something Maris did or said made Lane mad, and he traded Maris to Kansas City. The Yankees got Maris from the Athletics, and he went on to hit 61 home runs in 1961. Roy Hamey, assistant to George Weiss, told me the only reason Lane traded Maris was hatred, that he just got mad at him and wouldn't have him around anymore. Branch Rickey, George Weiss, Ed Barrow—men who built dynasties—didn't trade from anger. Always cold judgment—neither love nor hatred. They'd trade their own kinfolks. Clark Griffith, owner of the Washington Senators, in October 1934 traded Joe Cronin, his star shortstop, to Boston for Lyn Lary, a shortstop, and $250,000. A quarter of a million dollars in 1934 was a pile of hard money. Cronin, by the way, was not only Griffith's shortstop and manager, but also his son-in-law.

In that game at St. Louis which the Dodgers won in ten innings, Pete Reiser scored the winning run.

The umpire rules routinely on balls and strikes, fair and foul, and safe or out. However, in three situations in baseball the umpire is forbidden to rule unless he is "appealed" to for a decision. The "appeal" plays are: leaving a base too soon after the catch of a fly ball, not touching a base, and batting out of order. If an appeal is not made, the umpire can't render a judgment—it's as though it didn't happen.

This was a big game. You are serious when you start playing extra innings. Brecheen had been pitching his heart out for St. Louis all afternoon. Both teams knew that it would be between them for the pennant as the race ground on. Each Cardinal-

Dodger game meant something no matter what time in the schedule it was played. Or fought. The St. Louis-Brooklyn games were battles.

Joe Garagiola on NBC television is today the fountain of all wisdom and knowledge. Woe to the player who makes a "head" mistake. Joe at length explains how the play should have been made, and how much the oversight cost the erring player's team. The "dumb" play is meat and potatoes for Garagiola, and what he doesn't criticize, his partner Tony Kubek does.

As I said, Pete Reiser scored the winning run for the Dodgers in the top of the tenth inning. Roscoe McGowen, writing in the New York *Times* the next day, explained that Reiser scored in a headlong slide, for which he was famous, but in his slide missed the plate, got up and trotted to his dugout. McGowen then wrote, "catcher Joe Garagiola didn't observe" Reiser missing the plate. The umpire was forced to do nothing. Had Garagiola run after Reiser and tagged him, even sitting in the dugout, Reiser would have been out and they might have played long enough for St. Louis to win the game instead of Brooklyn. They certainly would have played longer than they did.

It is not my purpose to cover the 1947 pennant race in game-by-game detail. I have wanted, however, to bring out enough day-by-day developments to show how much the fortunes of ball clubs change overnight, what one or two players can mean to a squad of twenty-five, and the basic importance of all twenty-five players. Baseball is not just nine men. Certainly only nine men play at a time, but when you understand the length of the race you then appraise the depth of the squad. How good is the bench?

In that ten-inning game at St. Louis, Country Slaughter, always a hard-charging player, slid into Dodger second baseman Eddie Stanky and injured his wrist. At the same time, Dodger catcher Bruce Edwards had to leave the team and go to Johns Hopkins Hospital to have Dr. George Bennett examine his sore right arm, the one he threw with.

The mention of Dr. Bennett sets in motion a chain of events that go back to June 1940, when Joe Medwick, shortly after joining the Dodgers, was hit in the head by a pitch thrown by Cardinal hurler Bob Bowman. That one pitch changed Medwick's career—he was never the tiger at the plate again. That one pitch set in motion the sequence that led to all ballplayers wearing plastic batting helmets. And it brings MacPhail and Rickey into focus again.

Medwick was knocked unconscious, which made an impression on MacPhail in more ways than one. When the ball struck Medwick just above his left temple, all players wore cloth caps, and always had. MacPhail got in touch with Dr. George Bennett, noted bone surgeon at Johns Hopkins in Baltimore, discussed the need for some protection of such a vulnerable area of a batter's head, and asked Dr. Bennett to provide an answer. Dr. Bennett designed narrow, curved plastic shields that would fit inside the cloth caps. The caps, of course, had to be specially made to hold the shields. MacPhail ordered such caps and plastic shields for all the Dodgers. To the fans, if they noticed at all, the caps seemed as usual but somewhat larger. The players didn't want to appear to be so afraid of pitched balls that they wore protective headpieces at the plate. Macho.

Rickey watched this development. (He didn't miss anything—neither did MacPhail.) He left Brooklyn after the season of 1950, following his bitter struggle with Walter O'Malley, and went to Pittsburgh. One of the first things he did there was have a complete plastic cap made, a cap that at first glance looked like a regulation baseball cap, but covered the entire cap area of the head with plastic. Rickey made his Pittsburgh players wear the plastic headpieces at bat, on the bases, and in the field as well. It became full-time protection.

The plastic helmet caught on. Phil Rizzuto was the first American Leaguer to wear the helmet—he sent for one. He had been hit in the head and that once was enough for him. Finally it became mandatory in both big leagues that all batters wear the helmet. Ted Williams was the last one to wear it, but he did, and that was that. Some helmets now extend down and over the cheekbone.

This was the Dr. George Bennett that Bruce Edwards was sent to from St. Louis. Dr. Bennett, after meeting MacPhail, had become interested in ballplayers and their injuries. Many clubs began sending hurt players to him.

Stanky was to be out a week. The Dodgers limped home after

winning 3 of 8 games in the West. However, other teams weren't launching winning streaks. Back home for a night game with the Phillies, the faithful at Brooklyn turned out 33,136 strong, which packed Ebbets Field. The Dodgers won 5–4 in a wild scramble that required Shotton to use seventeen players, three of them pitchers—Branca, Barney and Casey. Casey again saved the game and got credit for the win. The Phils won the next day and the Dodgers took the odd game, which left them 1 game behind the first-place Giants. Jackie Robinson hit his second home run.

The action shifted straight to the Polo Grounds. It was a 3-game series, Tuesday, Wednesday and Thursday. Brooklyn won the first 2 behind Branca and Harry Taylor. The Giants salvaged the third one, and the two rivals were neck and neck for first place along with Chicago. The 3 games drew 104,314 paid. Edwards was back and played. Dr. Bennett had found nothing wrong and Shotton needed him. Edwards hit a home run.

Memorial Day at Boston was sad. The Braves took both ends of the holiday doubleheader from the Dodgers. Warren Spahn won his eighth of the young season, and Red Barrett, who was known to deliver a doozy at times, then threw a shutout. The Giants won their doubleheader with the Phils. Very sad.

Branca won the next day, a fine effort, 5–0. That was Branca's fifth win and fourth straight. He was holding the ball club up. Stanky returned to second base. The two days at Boston drew some 54,000. May ended with New York in first place, 1 game ahead of Chicago and 2 over both Brooklyn and Boston.

Robinson remained the story. People jammed the small Braves field to see him. They waited for his next at bat, his next dash on the bases, his next play in the field. On the other side of the coin, at Boston, Mort Cooper hit Jackie with a pitch for the second time in the young season. Jackie in 37 games had been hit by pitchers six times. But as he had promised Rickey, he said nothing, just took his base, licked his wounds . . . and went into his dances. Jackie could have given Bojangles Bill a lesson.

TWO GUYS NAMED JOE

The Yankees were in the West when June began. Detroit was in first place by 3½ games. MacPhail and manager Harris were conferring, according to the press, about their need for another starting pitcher, and perhaps for a catcher. They had two weeks, until the June 15 deadline, to make a trade. One Yankee name kept popping up, that of Johnny Lindell. He was referred to as Trade-Bait Lindell. Charlie Keller was doing so well in left field that Lindell seemed to be a spare part in the Yankee machine. Saturday, Keller banged 2 home runs as May ended, leading the Yankees to an 8–4 win over Cleveland and Bob Feller. Detroit still led by 3½, but Joe DiMaggio was in a batting streak.

Sunday June 1 was a doubleheader at Cleveland. The weather was threatening, yet 47,132 paid showed up. In the first game DiMaggio broke loose with 4 hits, 2 of them home runs—the second a grand slam. The Yankees stormed off with an 11–9 win. Joe Page relieved and saved it to get the win. The second game was postponed because of rain, mud and fog. Two guys named Joe—DiMaggio and Page—they were the two who gladdened Bucky Harris's heart that afternoon.

A doubleheader was scheduled for the next day but the bad weather got it, and the Yankees moved out of Cleveland for a head-to-head series with the first-place Tigers in Detroit.

Joe DiMaggio was always a money player. He did his best when the chips were down. He relished the extra money, excitement and fame that being in a World Series meant. Joe hadn't been in a Series since 1942 when the Cardinals upset the Yankees. New York won the next year and turned the tables on St. Louis, but DiMaggio by then was in the Army where he stayed for three seasons. Joe's first year back, 1946, wasn't a happy one for the ball club. Manager Joe McCarthy quit, Bill Dickey and Johnny Neun didn't fill the bill, and the Yankees finished third, 17 games behind the Red Sox and 5 behind Detroit.

After the dismal season of 1946 MacPhail called Joe in for a conference on Joe's 1947 contract. MacPhail told me later that he wanted a happy DiMaggio, and he didn't want any haggling over terms as had happened with Joe and Ed Barrow. MacPhail said the meeting with DiMaggio was very short . . . he told Joe, "Write on a piece of paper what you think you ought to get, and I'll write on a piece of paper what I think you should be paid. We'll turn the papers face down, then we'll turn the papers over and see what are the figures." MacPhail told me he made Joe turn first and then he turned. MacPhail said Joe was stunned because he had written down several thousand dollars less than MacPhail had. DiMaggio left MacPhail's office with a contract at MacPhail's figure, and he left a very happy, satisfied ballplayer.

The 4-game sweep at the Stadium in late May with the Red Sox took care of Boston for the time being. Now came this 4-game set of rich potential with the first-place Tigers. Young Shea blanked the Tigers in the opener on Tuesday. DiMaggio, healthy, happy and hitting, made it 16 straight with a bag of 4 hits. Joe now had 7 hits in a row. He was hot. He had hit safely in 26 of 28 games and surged to the top of the league in batting. Joe was making it happen.

Hitting streaks were not news for DiMaggio. He had set the record in 1941 when he electrified the country with his consecutive string of 56. When he was with San Francisco, before the Yankees bought him, he went 61 straight games with one or more hits in each.

In the Wednesday doubleheader DiMaggio was stopped in the first game, but began hitting again in the second. Detroit won the first, the Yankees took the second for a split, and Joe Page in relief was the winning pitcher. Two guys named Joe— one to hit, one to save.

In the fourth and getaway game, Spud Chandler didn't need any help. He shut out Detroit. Tommy Henrich hit 2 home runs and the Yankees took the series 3 out of 4. They cut Detroit's lead to just 1½ games. Nobody worried about it then, but in that fourth game at Detroit Charlie Keller had to leave in the fifth inning with a painful back. Lindell went to left field.

When the bad back forced Keller out of the game it marked a crossroads for both Keller and Lindell. Keller was a very strong man, so much so the Yankees called him King Kong. However, a back ailment floors all men, no matter how strong they may be otherwise. Keller's days as a regular were over. Lindell, given the chance to play regularly, began hitting at such a pace he was almost immediately removed from MacPhail's trading list. Lindell's opportunity came just when the Yankees were moving up. Rookie pitcher Frank Shea and new relief man Joe Page were both doing so well that trading pressures were eased. First-place Detroit went into a losing streak, and Boston didn't appear as formidable as the year before. MacPhail and Harris decided to go with what they had. When you have Joe DiMaggio, healthy and hitting, and Joe Page relieving as he did in 1947, you can make such a decision with profit.

Joe Page, and relief pitchers: Harris could not have won the 1947 pennant and the World Series without Page coming in from the bullpen to save one game after another. As the season went on, the writers covering the Yankees told me that when Harris would sit down to have a drink with them he would lift his glass and say, "Here's to Joe Page," or "Gentlemen, Joe Page."

I once asked Connie Mack about the origin of relief pitchers. I knew Mr. Mack had seen more baseball than any other man.

"I have always regretted," Mr. Mack began, "that it took me and the rest of us in baseball so long to learn the value of the pitcher who can pitch at top speed for a few innings, but can't pitch effectively the entire game. I had several men in my earlier years who got the other team out the first part of the game, then couldn't finish it. In the older days a pitcher was supposed to pitch the full game. We thought there was something wrong with a man who couldn't finish what he started. There was a false pride about pitching complete games. I know that I discarded men who couldn't last the distance, but who in today's baseball would have been wonderful relief men."

Mr. Mack looked back over his years in baseball, back to 1884 when he began as a player, back to 1901 when he started managing the Philadelphia Athletics (which he managed through 1950) and said:

"It was Marberry who was our first real relief specialist. Fred [Connie Mack always was formal—he referred to Marberry as Fred, not by his nickname of Firpo] was with the Washington club in 1924 when Stanley [Mack said Stanley, not Bucky] Harris was the new manager. Marberry could start and finish, and he was so strong he could also relieve. Harris needed somebody to finish games and he began calling on Marberry to relieve more and more. It was Harris who realized that Marberry had more value saving games than being in the four-day starting rotation.

"Then," Mr. Mack (I should call him Mr. Mack—his players did, even Ty Cobb did when Cobb finished his great career playing his last two seasons at Philadelphia) added, "the Yankees in 1927 had Wilcy Moore, the first out-and-out relief man Miller Huggins ever had."

I know that the deliberate development of relief pitchers didn't come until after World War II. In 1934, for example, when I got to Cincinnati Bill Terry of the New York Giants would call upon his star starting pitcher, Carl Hubbell, when he needed him to save a tight game. Frank Frisch of the St. Louis Cardinals did the same with Dizzy Dean. John McGraw never had a strictly relief specialist—he used to call on his great star, Christy Mathewson, to save games.

Hugh Casey was a "modern" relief star. His development of his specialty was not deliberate. Casey had been pitching in the minor leagues since 1932—had a brief trial with the Chicago Cubs in 1935—and MacPhail drafted him from Memphis in 1939. That was Leo Durocher's first year as manager of the Dodgers. Leo started Casey, then used him to relieve at times, but didn't put him in the bullpen exclusively until 1941.

The Dodgers clinched the 1941 pennant in an afternoon game at Boston. When their train got into Grand Central Station early that evening the welcome was almost unbelievable—biggest crowd Grand Central ever saw. WOR, which carried the games of the Dodgers that year, broadcast the arrival of the team.

When I got Durocher on the mike the first thing he said was, "We couldn't have won it without Casey!"

During the World War II years at Brooklyn, Durocher was the manager. I saw Leo operate. He operated the only way possible. He had to make do with what he had, with the players on hand, some of whom would soon be going into military service. Leo was no traditionalist. He broke the rules when it suited him, or when he had to. During the war Leo learned to use each player for what he could get from him, whether it was pitching a couple of innings, playing the outfield or pinch-hitting. He used multiple players, always trying to get any edge he could. I used to call it "managing in depth." When Casey Stengel came to the Yankees in 1949 and started moving his players around they called it "platooning."

The difference was that Stengel had good players to platoon, Durocher didn't. Leo was desperate. He would start a pitcher, bring in a man in the early innings (today they call early relief pitchers "middle-men"), bring in a left-hander to face a left-handed batter, then switch for a right-hander against a right-handed batter. In this process Durocher, and others, learned the value of fitting each player's abilities to a particular need.

When I got to the Yankees in 1954 I found that the Yankees had started training certain young pitchers in the minor leagues to be relief pitchers.

Jim Konstanty put relief pitching into full focus in 1950. He pitched the Phillies, the Whiz Kids, into the World Series. Jim relieved in 74 games, won 16, lost 7 and saved 22—that meant he was pivotal in 38 of the 91 victories of the club, over a third. Konstanty was voted Most Valuable Player in the National League. From then on relief pitching was "in." Today ball clubs have "long men" and "short men" in their bullpens. A winning team has a standout relief man. It used to be that a starting pitcher tried to finish. He gaited himself for the entire game. Today a starting pitcher is under orders to fire with everything he has on every pitch, and when he begins to lose his edge help comes from the bullpen. It's a different ball game today, and this development of always having fresh pitchers on the mound, bearing down on every pitch, has much to do with the lower batting averages of today as compared to before World War II.

Now about Joe Page. Joe's dad was an underground share-cropper. He mined coal in Cherry Valley, Pennsylvania. He had seven children and he didn't want his boy Joe going down in the mines. But Joe went down, there was nothing else to do. However, in his off-time Joe played semi-pro ball and was good at it, and his dad encouraged him to try professional baseball—anything to avoid being a coal miner.

Joe was a gift. (Everybody, every organization, even the Yankees can join in the chorus of "With a Little Bit of Luck.") First he tried to make it with a team in the Pittsburgh Pirates' farm system, was released, then caught on with a team in the same league that was in the Yankees' organization. This was in 1940. He wasn't scouted, he just showed up and asked for a chance. Butler, of the Yankees' farm team, liked him and signed him.

Joe made it up to Newark in 1942. He was 14–5 at Newark in 1943. He was big, 6'3" and 210, left-handed and hard-throwing. He began 1944 with the Yankees, won 5 of his first 6 starts, but hurt his shoulder. The Yankees sent him back to Newark. Back again with the Yankees in 1945, he was 6–3, and in 1946 he was 9–8, all as a starting pitcher.

Page was a playboy, which didn't endear him to Joe McCarthy. Bucky Harris couldn't care less as long as the results were good on the field. In early 1947, the first year for Harris with the Yankees, Page didn't figure too seriously among the starting pitchers: MacPhail had traded for Allie Reynolds, Frank Shea was the promising rookie who had to be given his chance, Spud Chandler was on hand, as was Bill Bevens. Randy Gumpert was a seasoned minor-league veteran. Don Johnson was another promising rookie, as was Karl Drews. Page got pushed to the bullpen as a place not only to work but also to sit down. There wasn't room for him on the bench.

Joe had done some sound relief work early in the season, but the exact date for Page as a relief star, the exact date the 1947 Yankees started going up and the Red Sox started down, and the exact date Bucky Harris got the inspiration for his toast, "Here's to Joe Page," was the night of May 26, at Yankee Stadium.

In 1946 the Yankees had finished third behind Boston and Detroit. Early in 1947 the Yankees had to take dead aim on both Boston and Detroit. The Red Sox came into the Stadium for 4 games, May 23–26. Detroit was in first place, leading New York by 3½ games.

The Yankees swept the Boston series. The big one that sent the Red Sox reeling and put the Yankees on their way was game four on Monday night, May 26. A record crowd for a single game—74,747—jammed the park while thousands outside tried to get in and were turned away. (The record attendance for Yankee Stadium was for the 1938 Memorial Day doubleheader with Boston—81,841 paid, and I don't know how they all got in.)

Bucky Harris used Allie Reynolds, Spud Chandler and Bill Bevens in the first 3 games, and had his star rookie, Frank Shea, ready for the finale. The Red Sox knocked Shea out in the third inning—the first time Shea had been unable to finish what he began. Wally Moses doubled and scored on a single by Johnny Pesky. Shea walked Dom DiMaggio, and Harris took Shea out. It wasn't his night. Joe Page walked in from the bullpen. Ted Williams waited at the plate. The place was alive in raucous sound.

Page got Williams to ground to McQuinn at first, who couldn't come up with the ball. His error loaded the bases with nobody out. The crowd roar went even higher. Rudy York, a most feared slugger, took his turn at the plate. Page threw York three wide ones. A 3–0 count. Page was left-handed, York batted right. Ball four and a run would be forced in. With one swing York could break the game wide open. He swung. He swung three times, and Page had one out.

Bobby Doerr was next. A dangerous man in the clutch. Page fanned him, and now the stands were really drowned in sound. Page disposed of Eddie Pellegrini on a fly to Tommy Henrich. Page had stopped the Red Sox, left three on, gotten past Williams, York, Doerr and Pellegrini and wasn't upset by an error, or by being behind 3–0 to York.

The other Joe, DiMaggio, came to bat in the last of the fifth. The score stood 3–3. Two Yankees were on, 2 were out. DiMaggio hit his fifth home run of the young season, and the Yankees went on to win 9–3 for the sweep. Page held the Red Sox to 2 scattered singles the last two thirds of the game.

The Yankees on this home stand won 8 out of 12 despite losing the 3-game set to Cleveland. They moved from sixth to second place, 3 games behind Detroit.

Perhaps that night—May 26—manager Harris, when he was finally where he could have a highball, lifted his glass, smiled and for the first time said, "Here's to Joe Page." It was a ritual toast for the rest of the season. Bucky Harris, who had recognized that Firpo Marberry in 1924 was more valuable in relief than in starting, certainly recognized in Joe Page a splendid relief pitcher when he saw him. Harris kept Page in the bullpen.

Two guys named Joe.

There is an expectant feeling, an alert, confident feeling that comes over a ball club when it realizes that it can win it all. Professional players aren't easily fooled. They know how good they are and how good the other fellows are. They can add it up for themselves, and they do. That is their business, their life. The Yankees knew after the two big 4-game series with Boston and then Detroit . . . in which they won 7 of the 8 . . . with DiMaggio having a great year . . . with Joe Page coming in as a fireman to hold the pitching staff together . . . they knew they could do it, barring serious injuries. Bucky Harris was experienced, held the reins of discipline loosely, and was a good man to play for. And he certainly knew a star relief pitcher when he saw him.

The team was almost put together. Two bad backs helped manager Harris answer some of his questions. Charlie Keller's back, which took the veteran out of it just when he was hitting well, gave Johnny Lindell his opportunity. Lindell made the most of it. Aaron Robinson's back flared up early in the season and allowed Harris to study his two rookie catchers, Ralph Houk and Yogi Berra. Houk was a good receiver but wasn't going to hit much, and certainly not for power. Berra was the greenest green pea behind the plate anyone ever saw, but he "swings that stick" at the plate. Berra hit, and hit for power.

Baseball men are not as a rule openly religious. Yet they speak of power—the power a player has to throw a ball hard, or to hit a ball hard—as God-given. Hard-bitten baseball men tell you there is no way to teach a boy how to throw hard or how to hit hard . . . that power is a gift that comes with the package and is truly a gift of the Creator.

Power in a young player means he is going to get every chance to develop and make the big leagues. There is no substitute for it. A young pitcher who is wild but can throw bullets—as was Johnny Vander Meer or Sandy Koufax—will be given chance after chance until he comes around or fails completely. Baseball is patient with power . . . power promises rich returns.

Just as Bucky Harris knew a relief pitcher when he saw him, he knew power at the plate when he saw it. He saw from the start that Lawrence Peter Berra—known far and wide as Yogi because his stocky build, thick neck and starkly rugged face made him look the way a Yogi was supposed to look—had raw power. Harris knew Berra could be taught—it would take time and patience and training—either to catch or play the outfield. And while Yogi was learning defensive skills, Harris wanted his bat in the lineup. Then too, crude as Berra was behind the plate, the pitchers, who are very selfish men, wanted him to catch them—they knew Berra would knock in more runs for them than any defensive lapses might cost. Also, everybody on the Yankees knew that the more games Berra caught, the better catcher he'd be.

Berra was the type hitter who doesn't come along often. He was a "bad-ball" hitter, meaning that he hit any pitch he wanted to no matter where it was delivered. He'd just make up his mind to hit the next pitch, and do it. Joe Medwick hit that way. Berra as a boy in St. Louis used to watch Medwick and copied him. Medwick (before Bobby Bowman beaned him) and Berra drove pitchers crazy. They didn't know how to pitch to them.

Very few batters can survive chasing bad balls. Branch Rickey spent much effort and time teaching Duke Snider the strike zone. Ted Williams hit only at strikes, as did Stan Musial. Williams never chased a pitch out of the strike zone. Musial, on occasion, would belt an outside pitch to left field, but not too often—just often enough to keep the pitcher honest or to break up a game. Joe DiMaggio waited for good pitches. Ty Cobb had a sharp eye and very happily would take four balls for a walk—it let him get on base to start running and sliding.

So it was that in early June the Yankees went into Detroit and won 3 out of 4. The team that would face the Dodgers in the World Series that fall was jelling—McQuinn at first, Stirnweiss at second, Rizzuto at short, Billy Johnson at third, Lindell in left, DiMaggio in center, Henrich in right, with Berra behind the plate more and more. The pitching staff had the fine rookie Frank Shea, Allie Reynolds, Spud Chandler, Bill Bevens as the regular starters, Randy Gumpert, Karl Drews, Don Johnson, Charley Wensloff for spots, and Joe Page.

The Yankees had good depth but didn't need to call on it too frequently. They had Lonnie Frey, Bobby Brown and Jack Phillips as infield reserves, with Allie Clark to fill in for an outfield assignment. However, the infield was very hardy: the season then was 154 games; Rizzuto played 153 games, Stirnweiss 148, McQuinn 144 and Johnson 134. DiMaggio's return to full health was of tremendous value—despite starting late because of the sore heel, DiMag played in 141 games, Keller was in 45 until his back flared up, and Lindell, who then took over in left was in 127. Henrich, who played at first when McQuinn was out, was in right field and played in 142 games after starting the season late with a sprained ankle. It was a pretty healthy ball club except for pitching aches and pains. When a manager can play his best men, day after day, he is in the tall cotton.

This summation of course was an appraisal after the season was over, after the hay was in the barn. However, MacPhail flew to Chicago on June 10, 1947, for a conference with Harris. They couldn't know then what lay ahead. They had to make their estimates and hold to them, hoping they were right, hoping serious injuries wouldn't occur to a DiMaggio or a Rizzuto.

The press speculated a trade was imminent. The trading deadline of June 15 was at hand. MacPhail was a man of action. He was not about to let June 15 catch him asleep at the switch. The writers had been saying MacPhail and Harris wanted a pitcher and a catcher.

However, when you trade for a front-line pitcher or an established catcher, what do you give up to get them?

MacPhail and Harris decided they'd stay with what they had, that it would be good enough. They allowed June 15 to come and go without a trade. MacPhail was never afraid to trade when he thought it was to his advantage. Now he refused to trade.

On June 15 the Yankees were home, beat the Browns a doubleheader, drew 55,691 and went into first place by .015 percentage points. Monday night June 16, the Yankees beat the White Sox 4–3 . . . Rizzuto squeezed DiMaggio home in the last of the ninth . . . 52,633 were on hand, and the Yankees had first place over Boston by a full game. However, the next day it rained, and then the White Sox won 6–4. There was an open day for the Mayor's Trophy Game. Boston sneaked into first place by five points.

This was it, however, for the defending champion Red Sox. Mark the dates: Friday June 20 through Sunday June 22, 1947. Detroit came in for 3 games at the Stadium. The Tigers had lost 6 in a row—they had charged early and now were falling back. The Yankees were primed to make their move. Cleveland was in Boston for 4 games.

The Yankees swept their set with Detroit, sending the Tigers to 9 straight losses. Boston split the 4 games with the Indians. When Sunday evening June 22 came, the Yankees owned first place by 2 games. Joe Page relieved effectively despite a sore back. "Mister" Berra hit a grand slam home run. Power. Raw power. No substitute. None.

The Cleveland Indians came down from Boston for 3 games. Mister Berra was getting in the groove. In the opener he had 2 singles and a triple. Joe Page again was worthy of manager Harris's highball toast. The Yankees won it 8–5. Rain postponed the second game, but in the final, Shea delivered a neat 3-hitter to win 3–0.

This recycled team had become exciting—rookies Frank Shea and Yogi Berra . . . Allie Reynolds new to the Stadium . . . George Stirnweiss at second base . . . the return of the authentic DiMaggio . . . the shining relief star, Joe Page. The paid for Frank Shea's shutout, and ninth victory, was 60,090, putting the Yankees for 28 dates at 1,018,082! During this home stand the Yankees won 10 of 12 from the invading western teams, and now sat on top of the pile by 2½ games.

To finish the month of June the Yankees won 2 of 3 at Philadelphia, drawing for a Friday night game the biggest crowd of the year at Shibe Park, 38,529. Spud Chandler won that one for his eighth. In a Sunday doubleheader at Washington the Yankees split; however, the Red Sox lost both ends of their double bill, and the Yankees rode high by 4½.

Two observations: one, the Yankees were gathering momentum. This word has been given new impetus in more current political shoutings. Vice-President Bush, in 1980 when he was a candidate for the top spot, went around for a while saying he had Big Mo going for him. In the world of sport, momentum was a workaday word—a football or a baseball team had it, or had just lost it, or never had it. Going into July 1947, make no mistake, the Yankees had Little Mo, Big Mo, or just plain momentum going. They knew it, and the rest of the league knew it. Two, in the second game in Washington young Don Johnson needed help. Page was healing his back. Harris called on Allie Reynolds, who strutted in from the bullpen, blew out that big chest of his, and promptly put the game to rest. Reynolds thus began his versatility as a Yankee pitcher—starting or relieving. When Casey Stengel took over in 1949 and won five straight world championships he used Reynolds both ways and proudly referred to the Chief as "My two-way man."

June 29 was when Reynolds came in from the bullpen to save a game for the Yankees for the first time. Having both Page and Reynolds to relieve was like having Jack Dempsey and Joe Louis as bodyguards. In their prime.

THE OLD MAN IN THE BROOKLYN
DUGOUT

It was a good thing Burt Shotton was already white-haired when he took over as manager of the 1947 Dodgers. Otherwise what he had to contend with would have turned his head the color of new-fallen snow. It was also fortunate Shotton had lived almost sixty-four years and had the patience that comes from long experience in the baseball wars. Shotton had learned the hard way to be a grass-roots philosopher. Further, he had left full retirement security when his old friend Branch Rickey called for help. And Shotton had the solid strength of Rickey's support behind his every move.

Shotton was steady as a rock. He didn't get excited. He didn't rave or rant or orate. He wore steel-rimmed glasses, and he looked steadily at you, looked calmly at the ball game, and watched keenly what was going on around him. Some writers and some fans said he wasn't colorful. He didn't have to be; he had enough dynamic ballplayers to take care of that department —Dixie Walker, Pee Wee Reese, Eddie Stanky, Jackie Robinson, Hugh Casey, etc.

Shotton was the only manager I ever knew or heard of who kept score during each game. He didn't keep score the way we did in the broadcast booth or the writers did in the press box. He would have a different total of hits than the professional scorers in the stands. Pee Wee told me that when he hit a line drive—hit it on the nose just as hard as he could drive a ball, but it went right at an opposing player for an out—Shotton would say when he came into the dugout, "That's a hit in my book, Pee Wee . . . that's a hit." I never saw Shotton's scorebook —he would stuff it in his hip pocket when the game ended. I never asked to see it because I knew he wouldn't want to show it to me, and as we were friends, he wouldn't want to have to refuse me. But he had his own record of every play. He knew what had happened. He never had to ask someone what so-and-so did in the first inning or in the eighth inning. He looked in his book. He knew the score. Shotton was alert to every play. Just as he was on to every one of his ballplayers.

Bucky Harris used to relax after a game with a highball, which went down better and better as Joe Page kept putting out more and more fires. Shotton would drink a Coca-Cola, sitting on a clubhouse trunk. He didn't have a set toast as he lifted the Coke, as Harris did with his highball glass.

After an afternoon game on the road, after dinner Shotton and I often walked, just the two of us. Somehow we were sympatico. I didn't say much in our walks. After all, I had talked for hours in the booth, and also I had learned long ago that the way to learn something, the way to gather information, is to listen. Usually we found a place that served ice cream. Shotton was a man who appreciated good ice cream. He'd sort of clear his mind talking as we walked. After the ice cream he'd be ready to go to his room to settle down for the night. He had very simple habits, which made it very hard for certain city-wise writers to understand him.

To repeat: Shotton was handed by Rickey and by the fates the most upset, torn-apart ball club in history. The coming of Jackie Robinson brought a seething turbulence that was waiting to explode. Shotton saw to it that serious internal trouble didn't break loose. He was handed a ball club that Rickey was trying to establish from veterans returning from the war and young players in various stages of development. Shotton soon saw he had enough infielders and outfielders, barring injuries. He felt he had enough catching if Edwards stayed well. He had sufficient bodies. But he had no set pitching staff. He had in the veteran Hugh Casey a star relief pitcher, but a star relief pitcher can't help you if the game is lost by the late innings when the bossman from the bullpen is due to take over. A star relief pitcher is

never wasted in a game that isn't close, one you haven't got a
good chance of winning. It's the same with your best pinch hitter—you hold your good pinch hitter back until he can help you
in the clutch.

I was always deeply interested in the formation of a winning
ball club. It required years of scouting for young players, selecting them, grading them, teaching them, waiting patiently for
them to develop, and then assembling the proper combination of
twenty-five men to fill the squad. Nine men don't win a pennant,
fifteen don't; it takes all twenty-five. Different players make their
contributions day by day. Games are won and lost by men who
are rarely mentioned in the newspaper accounts. Injuries happen, accidents occur, sore arms are professional hazards. A front-
line player gets hurt or sick or has a bad back. A good man must
be on hand if the winning machine is to keep functioning. Shotton had a sound bench except for pitching. He began 1947
knowing he had Casey. Branca came out of nowhere to have a
big year and be the bell cow. Shotton had to build a pitching
staff as the race ran its course.

To give you an idea of how scrambled the Dodgers' pitching
staff was in 1947, here are the pitchers eligible for the World
Series that fall, and their records:

Ralph Branca 21–12 . . . this was his only big year. His rec-
        ord coming into 1947 was 8–9.
        Shotton had to bring him along
        and hope.
Joe Hatten 17–8 . . . the best year he ever had. As a rookie
        the year before, he was 14–11.
Hugh Casey 10–4 . . . all games won and lost in relief. The
        only veteran of the staff.

The rest of the list and their 1947 records: Lombardi 12–11,
rookie Harry Taylor 10–5, rookie Clyde King 6–5, Hal Gregg
4–5, rookie Rex Barney 5–2, Hank Behrman 5–3. These men ac-
counted for 90 of the 94 games the team won to take the pennant from the Cardinals. Shotton was like a man walking a tight
wire. Because he didn't wear a uniform, Shotton couldn't go to

the mound either to confer with or to remove his pitchers. He sent coach Clyde Sukeforth. Sukey walked many a mile.

The Dodgers went into June in third place, tied with the Braves, 2 games back of the first-place Giants and a game behind the second-place Cubs. The defending champion Redbirds of St. Louis were in the second division; however, nobody doubted that the Cardinals would soon make their presence felt. The Giants had a veteran slow-footed team that could hit home runs but didn't figure to stay on top too long. The Braves under Billy Southworth were building behind pitchers Johnny Sain and Warren Spahn. The Cubs were playing above their abilities. However, any one of these teams could give you trouble anytime, and put a spoke in your wheel just when you got going.

June was typical of an agony-and-ecstasy month. The Cardinals came to Ebbets Field for 2 games. June began as young Harry Taylor beat Harry Brecheen and the Cardinals 6-1. That Sunday 34,109 Dodger fans jammed Ebbets Field. The next day 17,719 watched as the Cardinals nosed out a win in ten innings, 5-4. Pitcher Howard Pollet won his own game with a single. Shotton exposed the pitching staff he had to live with: Hatten started, then Eddie Chandler, Lombardi, Branca, who was charged with the loss, and finally Hugh Casey. Five pitchers.

The Pirates followed for 4 games, beginning with a double-header. The Dodgers won them both, and oddly enough Rex Barney, who won only 5 games all year, got credit for both of them. Casey had to relieve Barney in the first game for a save, then Barney was the fourth pitcher used in the nightcap, and got the credit.

The next night made the Dodgers laugh and cry. With 32,287 jammed into the small park, Branca pitched a 9-4 win. Pee Wee Reese unloaded a grand slam home run. But Pete Reiser took off in center field for a ball that was headed for extra bases. Pete caught it just as he crashed into the concrete wall. He held the ball but was knocked unconscious and carried from the field on a stretcher, then sent straight to a hospital. He was badly hurt. Young Duke Snider took his place. It was now a three-way tie for first with the Giants and Cubs.

Taylor pitched a beauty in game four, a 2-hit, 3–0 win over the Pirates. Robinson smacked his third home run, and as the Giants and Cubs split a pair at the Polo Grounds the Dodgers broke into first place by half a game. The Cubs were next.

Friday night 31,555 packed the place. Seats were hard to get at Brooklyn. Jackie Robinson was playing beautifully. He drew them. Hatten beat the Cubs for his sixth win, and the Dodgers' fifth straight. Saturday and Sunday were going to be big days, but it rained.

Stephen Foster wrote "The Sun Shines Bright in My Old Kentucky Home." While it rained in Brooklyn the sun was out in full force at Versailles, Kentucky, home town of Commissioner Happy Chandler. Branch and Mrs. Rickey were in that part of the country. The Dodgers were due in St. Louis in a week, the St. Paul farm team had a series at Louisville, and the Rickeys were "just drifting around in the area." Further, Rickey wanted another go at Chandler about Durocher.

So it was that the Rickeys and the Chandlers spent several hours together at what Chandler called the Promised Land. Chandler said the visit was "purely social"—they stayed for a couple of hours, had some Kentucky ham, and went on to Louisville. I'm certain it was not purely social when Mrs. Rickey and Mrs. Chandler talked while the two men were in Chandler's office. Rickey learned again that Chandler was adamant—Durocher was to stay suspended. Rickey was paying two managers for 1947, but only one was waiting for the rain to stop at Ebbets Field.

Cincinnati came in for 4 games, starting Monday night. If you hadn't gotten your seat well ahead of time you couldn't get in. The crowd was 32,864, which meant some people must have been pried in with crowbars. The Reds waded through four of Shotton's pitchers—Taylor, Gregg, Lombardi, and Casey—and hit Casey for a home run, won 9–6, ended the 5-game winning streak and dumped the Dodgers back into second place. This was the twenty-fourth date at Brooklyn, with a paid attendance of 510,357, amazing when you consider the size of the bandbox park.

The next day was even more of a jam. Owing to early season rain, Tuesday was a doubleheader, and the Reds were starting their young sensation Ewell Blackwell in the first game. Branca was to go against him. The paid was 33,045. The police kept telling people as they got off the subway, "If you haven't got a ticket, don't go any closer to the ball park."

Blackwell was a lanky 6'5", 190-pounder. He was long-armed, right-handed, and threw from byway of third base. He was a sidearmer. He was fast and had a most deceptive, wide-breaking curve; right-handed batters were not too enamored of hitting against him. He was rough as a corncob. He had won 7 games already.

Blackwell beat Branca and the Dodgers 3–1. The Dodgers pulled out the second game 6–5. Mrs. Jackie Robinson brought Jackie, Jr., to the games, and when the public address announcer said they were in a box seat by the Brooklyn dugout the crowd responded with a tremendous burst of applause. Jackie, Sr., did his part with his fourth home run. Shotton committed three pitchers: Barney, Gregg and Branca. Ralph had pitched the first game, but relieved and got the win for the second, thus was 1–1 for the long afternoon.

Dixie Walker hurt his hand in the opener and Duke Snider took his place for the second game. Snider struck out five times. Duke was a wild swinger as a young player. He swung at anything and everything. He had power when he connected, but he was a lamb for the selfish big-league pitchers who made a living preying on young wild-swinging batters. (The Dodgers really struggled with Snider on learning "the strike zone." Even Rickey himself tried to help. In spring training, strings were strung to form a "strike zone," and Snider had to stand there and judge what went through the strings. That was just one of the devices used to try to teach him to hit at strikes and lay off bad pitches. Snider couldn't do what Joe Medwick and Yogi Berra could and did do, hit bad balls.)

Wednesday was the getaway game of the series, which ended the home stand. The Reds won 5–4 despite Robinson's 4 hits— triple, double and 2 singles. The paid for the 3 dates was 76,480. The Reds put the Dodgers in second place, 1 game behind the Giants.

The Dodgers headed by train for St. Louis and serious business. (Aside from the Yankees, travel in 1947 was by train. MacPhail flew the Yankees increasingly, but the rest of the teams stayed on the rails.) The Reds had been raw reality. St. Louis was now beginning to move. Mr. Musial was quite healthy again. First place in the National League was getting to be as slippery as boiled and buttered okra.

Four games were on the books at Sportsman's Park: June 13, a Friday night, Saturday afternoon and a Saturday night booking because of an earlier rain-out, and a single game on Sunday. There was a transit strike in St. Louis, but the arrival of the Dodgers with Jackie Robinson had the turnstiles spinning. The 4 games drew 90,487. The Sunday crowd of 29,686 was the largest of the year at St. Louis. Robinson was the big reason.

It was a grand weekend for St. Louis. The Cardinals swept all 4 games and sent the Dodgers to Chicago aboard what seemed to be a funeral train. The Redbirds chewed up the pitching staff—they beat Taylor, they beat Branca, they beat Barney and they beat Hatten. They didn't beat Casey for the simple reason all 4 games were lost from the start—there was never a time for Shotton to send in his ace relief man. Casey would have been wasted.

Pete Reiser was traveling with the team but unable to play. He was still woozy from his collision with the concrete wall at Brooklyn. Hank Behrman, included in the package when Rickey dealt Higbe to Pittsburgh, had been returned to the Dodgers— the Pirates didn't think he was worth keeping. At least Shotton had in Behrman an extra arm to use from time to time when he needed to conserve his first-line pitchers. He used Behrman in the third game when the Cards were winning 12–2. There are times somebody has to be expendable. That's another reason you must have a squad of some twenty-five men.

So, St. Louis served notice in no uncertain terms that it was back in the race. Sunday night June 15, 1947, was the trading deadline. Rickey had to reduce his squad. Rube Melton was released, Eddie Chandler was sent to Fort Worth and outfielder Marvin Rackley was sent to Montreal. No trades. From now on, unless you had somebody in the farm system to bring up or you could get a man by waivers, you played with what you had.

The train rolled on toward Chicago. The Dodgers stormed the diner. The loss of the 4-game series in St. Louis was shattering, yes indeed, but not enough to dull the appetite of healthy young men who had done a day's work at Sportsman's Park. Ballplayers eat well, especially when the road secretary is picking up all the checks. Further, this train ride had been scheduled months in advance, and the dining car people had been alerted to have the steaks on board. This was 1947 when it was a joy to go first class on the railroad—our American civilization today has nothing to compare with the trains of that era: the Twentieth Century, the Broadway Limited, the Chief, the Super Chief, the Florida Special, the California Zephyr, the Spirit of St. Louis.

The players ate well, then settled down quietly for the rest of the ride to Chicago. Shotton didn't do anything unusual. He sat alone for a while, looked out at the flatland, then had his dinner when he got ready. Shotton wasn't an easy man to talk with casually. Players didn't stop by his seat and pass the time of day. But as he sat he preserved an air of strength, of calmness, of being in control of it all. What he had to say and do, he would do at the ball park the next day. Experienced managers learn not to blow up and pop off after a tough game, but to wait until the next day when everyone is cooler and events are in clearer perspective. Shotton knew how to wait.

The Old Man went over in his mind not only his problems with the job he had been given unexpectedly, but also what his players would be thinking. He added it up: just when his team appeared to be balanced and pushing for first place, just when there had been a very successful home stand before jam-packed crowds, after his men had so far played the Cardinals even, all hell broke loose in St. Louis. Shotton knew that to lose 4 games out of 4 is a disaster. To lose all 4 to the team you know you must finally defeat before the season ends is a double disaster. If you had only won 1 of the 4 it wouldn't be too tough—winning 1 of 4 means only a net loss of 2 games in the standings, but losing 4 means just that, a loss of 4 full games. You put 4 more defeats in your lost column while the Cardinals chalked up 4 more wins in their won column. You can't beat the Cardinals for the pennant if you can't beat them yourself.

The Old Man had warned the Dodgers they'd have to battle St. Louis for it sooner or later. He knew now that he wouldn't have to warn them again. In fact, he must restore the confidence of his players. He couldn't let this 4-game loss, just at the start of their second western swing, so upset his team that it would stumble around and fall out of contention. Chicago was at hand, then Cincinnati with Ewell Blackwell, and then Pittsburgh with Ole Higbe waiting to try to pay back the hurt he felt at being traded away.

But more than anything else, Shotton had to get the St. Louis fear complex out of his players' heads.

Durocher had always had an inflated respect for the Cardinals. When the Dodgers won the 1941 pennant they had to beat St. Louis 2 of the last 3 games in St. Louis. The next year was when the Cardinals put the fear of God, the fear of Mammon, the fear of Satan, the fear of Jupiter, the fear of the Golden Calf, the fear of the Furies, the fear of Buddha—call it what you may—into the Dodgers.

Larry MacPhail had built the 1942 Dodgers. Branch Rickey had assembled the Cardinals. The Dodgers were mostly veterans, the Cardinals were very young. Leo Durocher had the Dodgers under a full head of steam, and in mid-August the team led St. Louis by 10½ games. Billy Southworth kept telling his young Redbirds to keep playing, keep playing, keep playing.

Late in 1942 the Dodgers were due to head West beginning with 4 games at St. Louis. MacPhail was concerned about the attitude on the ball club—many of the players seemed to think they had the pennant as good as won and in the bank. MacPhail did something he rarely did—he went to the clubhouse and told the Dodgers if they didn't start bearing down, change their way of thinking, they were not going to win it, even with a 10-plus game lead. Dixie Walker answered MacPhail by offering to bet him $200 right then and there that they would. MacPhail didn't take the bet. He left, but repeated it all to the writers in the pressroom.

MacPhail was genuinely concerned. The Dodgers, from Durocher down, were not. They got on the train for St. Louis with a 7½-game lead, and that night as the train roared through

the hours they staged a wild party, as though they were celebrating a victory. I wasn't there, but I've heard, and it has been
written, that that night was some ride—singing, drinking, gambling. That was the last party the 1942 Dodgers had.

The Cardinals beat them 3 of 4 games. From then on the
Dodgers played good ball but the Cardinals played better. The
lead was whittled down to 2 games just as St. Louis came to
Ebbets Field for the last meeting of the two teams for the season. The Cardinals won them both for a tie. The Dodgers then
lost 2 to Cincinnati, the Cardinals won 2. St. Louis now had a
2-game lead, and that was that. The Dodgers won their last 8.
So did the Cardinals. The Dodgers won 104 games. The Cardinals won 106. And beat the Yankees 4 of 5 in the Series.

Shotton knew all this as he stared out the train window,
watching the night come across the cornfields. Rickey had built
his Cardinals so well they remained strong during the war years,
and handled the Dodgers with ease. St. Louis had been beating
on Brooklyn since 1942. However, the year before, 1946, the two
teams tied for first place. Then the Cardinals beat the Dodgers 2
straight in the first pennant play-off in the big leagues. St. Louis
went into the World Series and beat Boston. The Dodgers went
home.

Rickey was no longer at St. Louis. He had taken over at
Brooklyn in 1943. The Cardinals were now, in mid-June 1947,
defending world champions, and they had just belted Rickey's
Dodgers 4 straight.

Shotton knew it all. He knew his pitching staff was shaky and
scrambled. I would say this was the low point of 1947 for Shotton and for the Dodgers. This was the point of no return.

I don't know exactly what the Old Man said the next day. I
know that by his calmness and his personal strength he lifted his
ball club. This is about what he said: "Let's get out and play
this game today . . . we'll win some, St. Louis will lose some
. . . play this one today . . . that's all you have to do. That
series in St. Louis is gone. We'll see them again . . . in the
meantime we play today. Sukey will put up the batting order
. . . Taylor, you're the pitcher . . . Hodges, you'll catch. Now,
let's go."

Harry Taylor, a rookie pitcher, Gil Hodges, a rookie catcher. Taylor beat the Cubs 2–1. It rained the next day, but on Wednesday June 18 Gil Hodges came to bat with the score 3–3 and hit his first big-league home run . . . also, Jackie Robinson electrified the fans at Wrigley Field when he scored from first base on a bunt. Jackie's running got the Cubs to throwing the ball around, including two wild throws, and Jackie just kept going.

That same day at Cincinnati, Blackwell pitched a no-hitter against the Boston Braves. As soon as the Dodgers knew Blackwell had no-hit the Braves, they also knew they would have to face him when they got to Cincinnati. The fans knew, too. Sunday the 22nd was to be a big day. I mean big. It was a doubleheader, with Blackwell going after a second straight no-hitter in the first game. Johnny Vander Meer, who'd put 2 no-hitters back to back in 1938, was still with the Reds to add to the drama.

The Dodgers finished their business in Chicago with another win for a 3-game sweep. The total attendance for the series was 63,352, all weekday afternoon games. (Wrigley Field is the only major-league park without lights.) Robinson packed them in. It was a mob scene after the games as people tried to get autographs, touch Robinson, anything to be near him. It was difficult for the players to get to their bus.

Taylor, Hatten and Branca had won at Chicago, with Casey saving Hatten. Taylor opened in Cincinnati and, again with a save from Casey, pitched the Dodgers to their fourth straight win, a solid rebound from the disastrous series at St. Louis. Shotton had his players back in business, but Blackwell was the next day.

The Braves and Giants were winning. So was St. Louis. Boston was in first, half a game ahead of New York. Then came Brooklyn, half behind New York and in fourth place, St. Louis, now only 3½ behind the lead. It was getting interesting. The Cardinals had zoomed into it with a 9-game winning streak, including the 4 big ones from the Dodgers.

Little old Crosley Field in Cincinnati was jammed for the Sunday doubleheader. What else would you want? Blackwell after his second straight no-hitter . . . the Reds versus the

Dodgers . . . Jackie Robinson . . . beautiful weather. What else?

The paid was 31,204. Spillover capacity. Blackwell had it in the first game. He came into the ninth inning without giving up a hit. He was one inning from matching Vander Meer and Vandy was in the Redleg dugout cheering him on—or was he cheering for appearances' sake? The Reds led 4–0, but nobody now was thinking about the score. Could . . . would . . . Blackwell with that fearsome, buggy-whip, sidearm delivery do it? Match Vander Meer?

About broadcasting no-hitters: After I got to Cincinnati in 1934 I heard there was a superstition that once a pitcher went five innings without giving up a hit, no one was to mention it out loud for fear of putting a jinx on the pitcher. This superstition began in the dugouts, which made grass-roots sense; certainly if your pitcher didn't know he was working on a no-hit game, you didn't want to put unnecessary mental strain on him —just let him, blissfully ignorant, keep on pitching. In effect, in the dugouts it wasn't really a superstition—it was practical psychology.

However, it spread to the press boxes. Nobody in the press boxes would mention that a pitcher had gone into the sixth inning without allowing a hit. It then spread to the radio booths. To some booths.

I broke the radio-booth superstition the first big-league game I announced. I didn't even know there was such a hoodoo when I did Opening Day in Cincinnati, 1934. Lon Warneke pitched for the Chicago Cubs and went into the ninth inning without permitting a hit. Adam Comorosky sent a broken bat single between Warneke's feet with one out in the last of the ninth, the only hit Warneke allowed. I had him going for his no-hitter all during the game.

Before the World Series of 1935, Commissioner Landis told the radio people (all networks then covered the Series; exclusive coverage by one network didn't come until 1939) that we were to report everything we could see. We were to report but not to voice our opinions of what the managers, players and the umpires did. Just report what they did.

That became my philosophy and my working technique. I tried to report. I never withheld from the audience that a pitcher was working for a no-hitter any more than I withheld the total of runs or errors or the number of innings. I didn't feel that I or anyone else had the right to suppress any factual data because of some so-called superstition. Then too, what effect could what I said into a mike have on a pitcher down on the playing field?

I had the mike in 1938 when Vander Meer pitched his first no-hitter, an afternoon game against the Braves. I was the only announcer for that game. The Boston broadcast, with Fred Hoey at the mike, was home-and-home. Hoey did whatever team was in Boston. The Red Sox were home that day, so Boston never heard Vandy's first no-hitter. The only broadcast was in the Cincinnati area. Nobody heard his second, as he did it at Brooklyn in 1938, the fifth year of the five-year ban on radio by the two New York teams and Brooklyn. MacPhail broke that ban the next season.

I had done 3 more before Blackwell tried for 2 straight; Tex Carleton in 1940, Jim Tobin in 1944 (against Brooklyn), and Ed Head in 1946. Apparently nothing I said or didn't say had any bearing of how those games turned out. Later in that year of 1947, in the fourth game of the World Series, the Yankees at Ebbets Field, I was to run into another dramatic no-hit effort. That was a good year for me to decide whether I was a reporter or a dealer in superstition.

Anyhow, I was broadcasting this game Blackwell was pitching, from a studio on Broadway between Forty-fifth and Forty-sixth streets, in New York City. In those days out-of-town games were re-created from Western Union dot-dash reports. (All road games were re-created in the big leagues until Larry MacPhail put Mel Allen on the road in 1946. Brooklyn began to travel its broadcasts in mid-1948. Shortly thereafter there were no more re-creations.)

The interest in Blackwell's effort for the second straight no-hitter was tremendous. That's why thousands jammed the ball park, and why millions tuned in on radio. People wanted to know, batter by batter, inning by inning, what Blackwell was doing about a record-tying second straight no-hitter. I'd have been deservedly run from town had I tried to play the cute game of not mentioning after the fifth inning that Blackwell hadn't been touched for a hit.

Blackwell came close. He went eight innings without allowing a hit. He got the first Dodger out to start the ninth inning. Eddie Stanky came to bat. Blackwell was tall. He was 6'5" and long-legged as well as long-armed. If it had started to rain he'd have been the first to feel a drop. Standing atop the pitching mound he was even taller.

Stanky hit a ground ball right back at Blackwell. The ball didn't bounce. It hugged the ground. Blackwell with his long length of physical construction just didn't quite stoop low enough—the ball went under his glove, over second base, and into center field for a hit. The crowd moaned. So close, 2 outs away. Al Gionfriddo lifted a fly ball for out number 2. Robinson singled, and Blackwell got the next batter. Had Stanky's ball been fielded, Gionfriddo's out would have been a second straight no-hitter. Vander Meer still had his record.

There were hits and runs in the second game. Carl Furillo went wild, batted in 7 runs with 2 singles and a grand slam. The Dodgers won 9–8, and went on to Pittsburgh. Since the nightmare in St. Louis the team had won 5 and lost 1. Boston led by 1½. Johnny Sain was holding up the Braves with his good right arm and his curve ball. Warren Spahn was coming on strong too. Sain and Spahn.

Shotton had the Dodgers straightened out. It was as though the series at St. Louis hadn't happened. Like a bad dream. The 2 games at Pittsburgh were won 4–2 and 6–2, giving the club a trip mark of 7–5, but most important, 7 games to 1 since St. Louis. That is motion, momentum or whatever you wish to call it.

The crowds continued to pack the parks to see Robinson and the Dodgers. In the first game at Forbes Field Jackie sent 35,331 into a mighty uproar. It was in the fifth inning, score tied 2–2, the veteran Fritz Ostermueller pitching for the Pirates. Earlier in the year he had shut out the Dodgers. Ostermueller forgot for a second that Jackie was leading down off third base, and went into a windup. Robinson stole home for the first time in his big-league career. He was an exciting player on base. Any base.

In the getaway game, before heading for Ebbets Field and the first-place Braves, the Dodgers beat their old pal Kirby Higbe for the second time. The Braves now led the Dodgers by half a game, and it was face-to-face the next night at Brooklyn.

Shotton's worries were not completely over. Pete Reiser, still shaken from his crash into the wall three weeks before, was ordered to Johns Hopkins Hospital for an examination by Dr. George Bennett. Reiser was a key man. That terrible series in St. Louis might well have been different with Reiser in center field and taking his cuts at the plate.

All Brooklyn was waiting for this one—Thursday night, a makeup game, 33,102 managed to crush themselves into Ebbets Field. The Braves led the Dodgers by half a game, and Johnny Sain (with 8 wins) was held back a day to start for the Braves. The Dodgers knocked Sain out and won it 8–6. Shotton used four pitchers. Branca, brought on in the eighth, held the Braves and got credit for his tenth win. First place.

The two teams switched to Boston, where 35,801 poured into the small Braves field. Again the Dodgers won, this time 8–5, and moved ahead of the Braves by 1½. But Boston bounced back the next day for a ninth-inning win, cut the lead to half a game and snapped a 5-game Brooklyn winning string.

Sunday June 29 was a doubleheader at the Polo Grounds. The crowd was 52,147 paid. Not an empty seat. Taylor won the first one, 4–3. The Giants Johnny Mize, Willard Marshall and Sid Gordon hit homers to take the second 9–5. Jackie Robinson drew the crowd and he put on a show—in the first game he sparked the winning 2-run rally in the ninth inning when he singled and then stole second. In the second game he had 4 singles, to extend his hitting streak through 16 games.

Pete Reiser returned from Baltimore with the word that he was not to play for at least two more weeks. July was just around the corner. The Braves won both games with Philadelphia and sneaked back into first place by half a game over the Dodgers, 3½ over the Giants and 4½ over the Cardinals.

Shotton by now knew his ball club, knew what he had, knew

what he didn't have and knew for certain it would be St. Louis he would have to beat. He and the Dodgers had been through the league twice. He relished the competition, the challenge, the crowds, the travel, the making of decisions and the authority of command. This sure beat retirement in Bartow, Florida, in mid-summer.

THE LOWERING OF THE BOOM

The Yankees had started the season rated third, behind both Boston and Detroit. By early July both 1946 defending champion Boston and runner-up Detroit were falling well behind the streaking Yankees, and as far as a race in the American League in 1947 was concerned it was between the Red Sox and Tigers for second place. Starting with the second game of a doubleheader at Washington June 29, the Yankees won 19 straight games, which tied the American League mark set by Chicago in 1906. (The major-league record was set by John McGraw's Giants in 1916 with 26, which still wasn't enough to beat Brooklyn for the pennant. The 1935 Cubs reeled off 21 in a row, which was enough for them to overhaul and pass the Gas House Gang of St. Louis.)

Make no mistake, the Yankees were rolling in high gear. Manager Harris was directing his squad with sure decisions, and while he maintained correct discipline he did it lightly and with thoughtful grace. Bucky ran a happy ball club. He had an almost perfect relationship with the press. Harris managed quietly, he stayed relaxed yet alert, had a smile most of the time and didn't raise his voice. He had a group of grown men and he treated them as such. He knew his business. He had the respect of his players and of the press. And most important, he and MacPhail got along together, liked each other and their relationship worked smoothly.

The 19-game streak broke the back of the league. That was the added evidence, the ultimate convincer that the Yankees were on their way. June 20 was the day the Yankees took over first place, never to give it up again all season. The Red Sox, the team that had won the year before and was favored to win again, had slept the night of June 19 in first place, but only by .005 percentage points. Maybe that was the last time all season that manager/shortstop Joe Cronin of Boston thoroughly enjoyed his steak with trimmings. Cronin didn't know then that he wouldn't win back-to-back pennants, and he also didn't know then that this was his last year as manager of the Red Sox.

It was as though the Yankees had been tuning up for the serious business of taking over their league. In fact, that was exactly the situation, and this shaping of a pennant-winning ball club had begun in the fall of 1946. Larry MacPhail was not satisfied with the club that had finished third, 17 games behind Boston. MacPhail had an amazing ability to judge players, and he was clear-eyed and unemotional about appraising his own ball club.

He knew he needed at least another first-line pitcher. Allie Reynolds at Cleveland was available at the right price. Reynolds had been with the Indians four full seasons, but only in 1945 when he won 18 was he very impressive. In 1946 he had dropped to an 11–15 record. Too, there was a whisper here and there that Reynolds did not win the "big" game. MacPhail always trusted his scouts. He took their word. I don't know who had researched Reynolds for him, but he got back the word that Reynolds could be a fine pitcher, and that the tag of not winning the "big one" was unfounded baloney.

Joe Gordon had returned in 1946 from military service, had had an indifferent season, hit .210 and played in only 112 games. Gordon had a breezy manner as though he didn't much care whether school kept or not, which irritated MacPhail. Joe was irreverent. Larry wanted a more businesslike player. Joe was all ballplayer, but he didn't always appear to be. Gordon had had fine years under Joe McCarthy for the Yankees: he was voted Most Valuable Player in the league in 1942, when he batted .322, and had been a star in five World Series. Gordon was a prime favorite with both the players and the writers.

When MacPhail formed the group of Dan Topping, Del Webb and himself to purchase the Yankees from the Ruppert estate after World War II, among the players they bought was Snuffy Stirnweiss, a stocky yet agile infielder. His best position was second base, which he played very well the two years Gordon was in the armed forces. Stirnweiss those two seasons hit .319 and .309. In 1944 he led the league in stolen bases with 55. When Gordon returned in 1946 Stirnweiss became a utility man, filling in wherever he was needed. He had no regular spot.

MacPhail wanted Reynolds. He felt Gordon was expendable, valuable in a trade, and he believed Stirnweiss would do better for him at second than Gordon—or as well. MacPhail was a man who made up his mind and then acted. Sometimes he acted before thinking about it. However, he told me later, he very carefully got an appraisal on Reynolds. The deal was made, shortly after the World Series, on October 19, 1946. Gordon to Cleveland, Reynolds to New York. Reynolds not only helped win the pennant in 1947, but without him Casey Stengel couldn't have won those five straight when he came to the Stadium in 1949.

MacPhail also needed a first baseman. One of the strong points of both MacPhail and Branch Rickey—an ability that little has been said or written about—was their constant attention to the smallest details of their operations. Both men are known for their big deals and major innovations. But both of them always knew who was minding the store, insisted their staff personnel stay on the ball, and they themselves put in the required hours on matters so small the public never knew of it. Neither man trusted his associates completely to daily check the waiver lists—they also checked them themselves.

MacPhail more than Rickey was always sorting through what was in the baseball boneyard. Rickey at St. Louis and at Brooklyn (except for the war years) didn't have to search for a veteran who might be a bargain—he developed young players. MacPhail never stayed long enough at Cincinnati, Brooklyn or New York to harvest riches from his farm systems. At Brooklyn, for example, he had gotten Whitlow Wyatt and Dixie Walker for almost nothing after all the other clubs had lost interest in them. Wyatt in the pennant year of 1941 was the bell cow, winning 22 games, and was 1–1 against the Yankees in the Series. Walker, obtained on waivers in 1939, quickly became the most popular player ever at Brooklyn. He was batting champion in 1944, and in 1947 was a splendid player for Burt Shotton and a mighty help in the pennant drive.

Connie Mack decided on December 10, 1946, that he no longer needed first baseman George McQuinn. McQuinn was thirty-five years old, had been kicking around in pro ball since 1930, failed a chance in 1936 at Cincinnati when MacPhail was there, made it with the St. Louis Browns for eight seasons, but in 1946 for the Athletics his batting average dropped down to .225, with only 35 runs batted in. Such statistics were not good enough for a first baseman, especially with Ferris Fain waiting at San Francisco for his turn at Philadelphia.

The Athletics released McQuinn outright. No strings. He cost MacPhail nothing, aside from what he paid McQuinn to play. MacPhail's judgment was again sound. McQuinn was always a fine fielder. He anchored the infield of Stirnweiss at second, Rizzuto at short and Johnson at third. McQuinn had a great year: he hit .304, knocked in 80 runs, and hit 13 most acceptable home runs. McQuinn made the Yankee infield an excellent inner defense which stood up all season. There were troubles with the pitching staff, troubles in the outfield, troubles behind the plate, but the infield held together. It was hard to hit a ball through it. MacPhail reset the right half with Stirnweiss and McQuinn. Rizzuto and Stirnweiss were like a pair of hungry cats around second base.

Harris had to bring his catching along. Aaron Robinson had had a very good year in 1946. He caught 100 games, hit .297, drove in 64 runs and was named as catcher on *The Sporting News* All Star team. The raw rookie Yogi Berra was most impressive "swinging that stick." Harris at the start played Yogi both in the outfield and behind the plate. The third catcher was a case-hardened rookie, Ralph Houk, who'd spent eight years in the minor leagues and four in the armed forces. Houk was a Ranger, went in a private and came out a highly decorated major after receiving a battlefield commission.

Early in the season Harris had his hand forced—Aaron Robinson developed a bad back, which gave Berra more work behind the plate than had been planned. All told, Houk and Berra held down the catching when Robinson was out, but more and more it was Berra. He went to school behind the plate during 1947, which was possible because he could hit the ball out of the park . . . and hit any pitcher. Yogi caught 4 of the 7 games in the World Series and was in right field in 2 others. Houk was sent to Kansas City the next year. When the Yankees brought him back he was mainly the bullpen catcher, then coach, managed at Denver, coach again, then manager, then general manager and back to managing again. Aaron Robinson was traded to Chicago in a pivotal deal made by George Weiss early in 1948 for pitcher Eddie Lopat, who became a Yankee star.

It was another early season bad back that first threatened to upset the outfield but instead settled it. It was a serious disk ailment—requiring surgery—that took the veteran Charlie Keller out of the lineup for the year on June 23, just when the Yankees were in a tight three-cornered struggle with Boston and Detroit. This gave Johnny Lindell his chance, and he made good on it, which rounded out the outfield of Lindell in left, DiMaggio in center and Henrich in right.

Lindell had been sort of a spare part. He had been a pitcher some seven years in the Yankees' farm system. When he came up to the Yankees in 1942, even as the war was taking players, Lindell didn't show manager Joe McCarthy much on the mound. McCarthy turned him into an outfielder and pinch hitter. In 1946 he was used at times at first base. Lindell in the spring of 1947 was bench strength, and was on hand when the mighty King Kong Keller was laid low.

DiMaggio and Henrich were established Yankee stars; both had returned in 1946 from military service and both were counted on. Both delivered. DiMaggio was the leader of the team in his quiet way. Joe made the difficult catches look easy, he came through with the key hits, and with Joe healthy and playing regularly the rest of the Yankees felt little pressure. They knew DiMag would do the necessary.

Henrich was an early, and celebrated, free agent. He was buried in the Cleveland farm system, and appealed to Commissioner K. M. Landis for help. Henrich claimed he was being "covered up" in the minor leagues longer than the rules allowed. Judge Landis granted Henrich's appeal and declared him a free agent in April 1937. Tommy was a splendid prospect, and many clubs bid for his services. Henrich waited until all bids except the one from the Yankees were in. The high bid was $25,000. Henrich told the Yankees to match it, they did, and he signed with them forthwith. He wanted to play for the big team, in the big ball park, for the big money.

Pitching: Connie Mack always said pitching was 75 to 90 percent of a winning ball club. Hank Bauer, when he was managing at Baltimore, right after his staff had beaten the Dodgers 4 straight in the 1966 World Series—limiting the Dodgers to 2 runs total for the 4 games, 3 of them shutouts—said to me, "You never have enough good pitching . . . never."

MacPhail in early 1947 knew more about the Yankees' pitching than Harris did. MacPhail had been running the club two years. Harris had left the American League to manage the Phillies in 1943, and this job had blown up in his face that July. Young Bill Cox, who had just bought the Phillies from Gerry Nugent, hired Harris, and then fired him abruptly, upsetting the players. Cox was soon forced to sell the Phillies by Judge Landis, who had learned that Cox was betting on his team to win certain games.

Harris in 1944 became manager at Buffalo, in the International League, for two years, and in 1946 moved upstairs at Buffalo as general manager. MacPhail brought him to the Stadium to be an executive assistant. Just as the manager's job opened with the Yankees, Detroit offered Harris the post of general manager. MacPhail offered him the field managership. Harris preferred the uniform, the bench, the clubhouse and the action of the games, to say nothing of being with the Yankees.

So it was that Harris knew little of his ball club until he took over at St. Petersburg for spring training. I point this out to explain that MacPhail had made the key decisions until Harris was in command and gradually in position to have opinions. But at least Harris had his team for spring training—Shotton took the Brooklyn job just before the third game of the regular season.

It was MacPhail who realized he needed more pitching, and he made the deal on his own for Reynolds. Another amazing ability of both MacPhail and Rickey was not letting a good ballplayer get away from them. Many teams have been wrecked by tragic trades, by dealing away men who became stars later on, and by failure of judgment on young players. A book could be written—*The Bad Trades of Baseball*. But if such a book is written neither MacPhail nor Rickey will be in it. They'll be in it, all right, but for their successes.

Col. Jake Ruppert in late 1920 knew what he knew and what he didn't know. He knew he needed a baseball man to run his ball club, and he got Ed Barrow from the Boston Red Sox. Barrow was an experienced baseball man, both as a manager and a front office executive. He had discovered Honus Wagner, and Barrow went to his grave saying Wagner was the greatest player ever, better than either Babe Ruth or Ty Cobb. Ruth was a star left-handed pitcher with the Red Sox when Barrow was the manager. It was Barrow who began converting Ruth into an outfielder . . . a pitcher plays every fourth day, while an outfielder, especially one who can hit, as Ruth did, played every day.

Barrow built the Yankees into immediate pennant winners. Barrow had the judgment, Ruppert had the money plus the desire to build the best team in baseball. Under Barrow the Yankees became the scourge of their league and of their World Series opponents. Barrow directed the Yankees for a quarter of a century, and his teams won fourteen pennants and ten World Series—five of them without losing a game.

Barrow in 1932 brought George Weiss to the Yankees to develop a farm system. Rickey's creation of the farm system at St. Louis made the rest of baseball change. The Yankees got the right man in Weiss. He built solidly and surely. He stockpiled the farm teams. Once Weiss took over development of young players, it was a joint operation of Barrow and Weiss. Their successes were well-nigh incredible. After MacPhail bowed out and Weiss had full control from 1948 through 1960, in those thirteen seasons the Yankees won ten pennants and seven world titles. It was Weiss who brought in Casey Stengel, who won five flags and five championships in his first five years, and those ten pennants for Weiss.

Weiss had the farm well stocked when World War II began. Those players came back when the war ended.

MacPhail inherited all of it in 1945. He forced Barrow, then seventy-seven, into an "honorary" position and finally into retirement. Weiss was relegated to a lesser status. When MacPhail had it, he ran it. I don't know how much Weiss told MacPhail about the players in the farm system, or how much MacPhail listened. As I knew MacPhail, he would listen and remember. As I knew Weiss, he was never a man to volunteer anything, especially when he was drastically reduced in authority and freedom to make decisions. Weiss resented MacPhail deeply and brooded bitterly over the reduction of his authority with the Yankees. Weiss was now pushing papers. MacPhail was calling the shots.

The Yankees had two very promising young pitchers Weiss had brought into the system, Frank Shea and Vic Raschi. Both had been in military service. Shea in 1946, his first year back, was 15–5 at Oakland after being out of baseball three years. MacPhail had him in spring training, and he and Harris decided he was ready for the Yankees. Vic Raschi was a prime prospect but had less high minor-league experience than Shea. Raschi was sent to Portland in the Pacific Coast League to get more work. He bloomed at Portland, winning 8 against 2 in just 12 games. Raschi was in the bank.

Spud Chandler was figured to be the ace of the staff. He'd won 20 against 4 defeats in 1943 before going into military service. When he returned for 1946 he won 20 again while losing 8. That made Chandler a big man—40 victories and 12 losses his last two years with the team.

Bill Bevens had spent nine years in the farm system. He seemed to be ready, having been 13–9 in 1945, MacPhail's first year, and he improved that to 16–13 the following season.

Finding Joe Page was like striking oil in your backyard—the Yankees had had him four years in the farm system, and at the Stadium three years. He was a starting pitcher who had had indifferent success—with the Yankees he was 20–18 coming into 1947 when Harris bullpenned him because there wasn't a place for him as a starter.

Other pitchers in the spring were Tommy Byrne, who was farmed out, Mel Queen, who was sold to Pittsburgh, and Karl Drews, Randy Gumpert, Don Johnson and Charley Wensloff.

Reynolds and Shea started winning right away, as did

Chandler. Page applied the glue whenever a game needed saving. Bevens pitched well at the start. The Yankees got off better than expected largely on the strength of pitching. When arm troubles plagued Bevens, Shea and Chandler, MacPhail brought up Raschi, and he picked Bobo Newsom off the bonepile.

Newsom was a genuine character. His name was Louis Norman Newsom and at first he was called Buck. Then he began referring to himself as Bobo, and soon it became Bobo. When you read the record of teams he was with in his twenty years of big-league wanderings he should have been called Yoyo instead of Bobo.

Newsom was with some eighteen teams in organized ball. He was with Washington five times, the St. Louis Browns three times, and twice with the Athletics and the Dodgers. He could pitch. He won 211 big-time games. In 1940 he won 21 for the Detroit Tigers plus 2 more in the World Series against Cincinnati. In the seventh and last game of that classic he lost to Paul Derringer 2–1.

When Clark Griffith at Washington released Newsom on waivers July 11, 1947, and MacPhail got him for the Yankees (Shea, Chandler and Bevens all were out with bad arms) this was the second time MacPhail had reached for Bobo when he needed an extra arm. Late in 1942 when the Dodgers began fading before the onrushing St. Louis Cardinals, MacPhail got Newsom from Washington. Newsom helped the Dodgers somewhat, winning 2 and losing 2, but the Cardinals in 1942 were not to be denied.

But Newsom in 1947 gave the Yankees a powerful lift. He joined them in time to win games thirteen and eighteen of that 19-game streak that buried the rest of the league. He also won his next 2 starts, and by then most of the staff was sound again, the emergency was over, as was the pennant race.

I have gone into this length about the assembling of the team, and especially the pitching staff, to point out the successful meshings of MacPhail in the front office, taking full advantage of what material he had inherited and of what else became available, and his field manager Bucky Harris, who all season knew his men and how to use them. They worked together smoothly. The day the Yankees clinched the pennant the first thing MacPhail said was that he was most happy for Harris, who had turned down a marvelous offer to run the Detroit team and stayed with the Yankees. Harris had no trouble with MacPhail—his trouble came the next year with George Weiss, which was inevitable.

The 19-game string was dramatic, authoritative and left no doubts in anyone's mind. But the Yankees did more than just that surge—counting it, the team won 31 games out of 34.

After Freddie Hutchinson put on the brakes at Detroit, Friday July 18, pitching a 2-hit, 8–0 masterpiece, the Yankees were 10½ games in front. The train had pulled out of the station. It was merely a matter of riding the rails into the promised land called the World Series . . .

The streak was exciting. Each day of it the interest grew. Everywhere the Yankees went crowds assembled to see them. The Yankees were showing how baseball should be played, and can be played, and was being played. Attendance boomed.

COUP DE GRACE—YANKEE STYLE

June 29, is when the avalanche began. The Yankees were play-ing a doubleheader in Washington. The Senators won the first game 5–1. Then it started. Nobody had predicted it. Nobody thought much about it when the Yankees won the second game 3–1. The talk on the train to Boston for a makeup single game was that Boston that same afternoon had lost both games at Philadelphia and left the Yankees sitting on a 4½-game lead. It was a good lead—4½ games is always a sound margin—but on June 29 you couldn't take it to the bank and get anything for it. That lead could drop to 3½ the very next day if the Red Sox showed enough muscle. Don Johnson had pitched well to get the win, and Allie Reynolds had walked in from the bullpen to save the young man and the game.

Whenever the Yankees and the Red Sox played, New York or Boston, it was big business. Red Sox rooters are loyal, vocal and rabid. They packed Fenway Park with 34,705 paid, they yelled and they rooted, but young Frank Shea from nearby Connect-icut held the Red Sox to 1 run and walked off with the tenth win of his rookie year. That 4½-game lead went to 5½. The most important win in baseball is when you beat your nearest rival. Such a victory means picking up a full game plus whatever psy-chological benefits accrue. From another view, it means 2 games —the difference between 3½ had Boston won, and 5½ when New York won.

July began with an open day. The Yankees had a night game the second, another open date, and a Fourth of July double-header, all 3 games with Washington. The Yankees swept the series at the Stadium and ran their winning string to 5. Boston fell back, Detroit went into second place. The night of the Fourth the Yankees led by 7½ games, but the lead was now over the Tigers.

The Athletics came in and promptly ran afoul of Frank Shea. The rookie beat Philadelphia 5–1 for his eleventh win. The A's were in next day for a Sunday doubleheader at the big ball park. The crowd was 51,957 and the Yankees ran their string to 8, taking both games, 8–2 and 9–2. Randy Gumpert, with a save from Page, won the opener, and Reynolds took charge in the nightcap. DiMaggio and Berra hit balls into the stands. The Tigers also won 2 but remained 8 games behind.

The Yankees were ready for the road. They won, in fact, 13 of their 19 straight games away from home. It made no difference where or when they played. Open the gates, take infield, turn in the batting order, and play ball.

The only force that slowed the Yankees was the three-day break for the All Star game July 8 at Wrigley Field, Chicago. Shea went three innings for the American League and was the winning pitcher. Page, in his new specialty, came in last and protected a 2–1 American League victory. But Shea's win was costly. The first rookie pitcher to win an All Star game, Shea hurt his arm. It showed up his next time out in the very first inning.

To repeat—Spud Chandler beat Washington 7–3 in the first game of the Fourth of July doubleheader, and he iced his cake by hitting a home run. That was his last victory, not only for the season, but for his career. His arm went bad. He remained with the team through the World Series, in fact pitched two indifferent innings in the Series, but 1947 was his final year in the big leagues. Bone chips in his elbow.

Chandler started in St. Louis following the All Star break, and Joe Page took over for him in the seventh inning. Page not only held the Browns but hit a home run in the ninth for his seventh win. That made it 9 straight for the Yankees, but MacPhail was not decoyed, nor was Harris—Vic Raschi was recalled from Portland.

Reynolds pitched the Yankees to a 3–1 win over the Browns for game ten. It was Reynolds's ninth win. The trade of Joe Gordon for the Chief was looking better and better. A Saturday doubleheader closed the series, and while the Yankees won both to run the string to 12, the pitching problems became more obvious: Shea made his first start since the All Star game, his arm stiffened in the opening inning and Charley Wensloff took over and won it. Bill Bevens made his first start since June 23 in the second game, had to leave early, and Karl Drews and Joe Page pitched the rest of it.

MacPhail kept working in New York. He got Bobo Newsom on waivers from Washington. When a ball club has doubleheaders back to back and three front-line pitchers—Chandler, Shea, Bevens—with ailing arms, help must come from somewhere, and fast.

In Chicago for the Sunday doubleheader, the Yankees got help. Newsom took the mound for his Yankee debut and threw a 3-hitter at the White Sox and won, 10–3. Vic Raschi then made his first start for the big team and, although both Page and Reynolds had to nail it down for him, won the second game for the fourteenth straight.

It rained Monday July 14, which gave the Yankees a day of rest. The decision to postpone the game was entirely in the hands of the Chicago club as the game was in its park. But it couldn't have pleased Bucky Harris more. A troubled pitching staff needs rest more than any other therapy. Page needed rest, Reynolds was to start at Cleveland Tuesday in a doubleheader (the third doubleheader for the Yankees in four days) and he had been used in relief Sunday to help Raschi. Everybody got a day off, which figured in sustaining the winning streak. The day of rain didn't show in the statistics but it was important.

Reynolds won the first game at Cleveland 9–4 for his tenth win. Bill Bevens gave the team a big lift when he beat Bob Feller 2–1 in the second game. It was Bevens's first win since May 25. The winning run came in the ninth when DiMaggio singled and Billy Johnson tripled to make it 16 straight, and over Mr. Feller. The Yankee lead jumped to 11 over Detroit. The interest now was in how long the winning streak would go.

Because of early season rain, the Yankees had a single game and then another doubleheader remaining at Cleveland. Charley Wensloff gave the staff a needed lift when Harris started him

Wednesday in the single game. He made it 17 straight. Page nailed it down but Wensloff had given the other pitchers an extra day to rest and to heal, especially with another double-header the next day. The two new pitchers, the veteran Newsom and the rookie Raschi, who had done so well Sunday at Chicago were fully rested, and they did it again at Cleveland. Newsom won the opener—his two-hundredth major-league victory, by the way—3–1, and Raschi went all the way too in the nightcap and brought it home 7–2 to make it 19 straight.

The Yankees, with a pitching staff that got into serious trouble, won the last 9 of their string in six days, including the day off in Chicago because of rain. That was 4 doubleheaders in six days, which is a killing pace. MacPhail did not let his players down. He knew Raschi was in Portland, and he brought him up. He searched the highways and the byways and got old Bobo on waivers. Those two stepped in and won 4 out of 4 starts. They won other games later, but the 4 they won at the time of their arrivals kept the team moving straight ahead and silenced any hope of either Detroit or Boston. If the Yankee players needed any further convincing that they would go all the way, this was it.

The players remembered. They knew. Before the game Friday, September 26, at Yankee Stadium, just before the season ended on Sunday, with the Yankees long since the pennant winners, MacPhail was summoned to home plate. He was totally surprised. An elaborate seven-piece silver service was presented to him from the players, with all their names inscribed and with this statement:

"To Larry MacPhail, greatest executive in baseball, whose zealous efforts were a major factor in our 19-game streak, and the winning of the American League pennant. From his Yankees, 1947."

MacPhail was unable to respond. He cried.

All winning streaks end. Freddie Hutchinson beat the Yankees the next day at Detroit with a 2-hit shutout, 8–0. When it ended there was no doubt about its being over. Hutchinson was in complete command. But so were the Yankees with a 10½-game lead, and with Newsom and Raschi aboard for the rest of the ride.

To wrap it up: the club was steady—only twice all season the Yankees lost 3 games in a row, never more than that. Detroit after breaking the 19-game string got within 9½, but then fell back. Boston was unable to mount a sustained challenge. The lead stayed between 9½ and 13½ games. DiMaggio had a sore ankle. Berra was in the hospital with a strep throat and was out three weeks. Chandler's arm trouble was bone chips in the elbow, and Harris knew he couldn't count on him. Reynolds had a strained arm and was out two weeks. Newsom was in 17 games, won 7 and lost 5 . . . Raschi was in 15 games, won 7 and lost 2 . . . they took up the slack along with Joe Page. Manager Harris late in the year confessed, "My conscience is beginning to hurt, calling on Page so often." Nevertheless, the toast rang out repeatedly, "Here's to Joe Page."

Any lingering doubts were dispelled September 3 at Boston before a full house at Fenway Park of 32,723. The Yankees unloaded on the Red Sox a barrage of 34 hits and won both games of a doubleheader, 11–2 and 9–6. The lead jumped to 12½, and the magic number of Yankee wins and Boston losses was 12. Jimmy Dawson wrote in his story to the New York *Times*, "The actual clinching is a mere formality . . . to all actual purposes the Bronx Bombers wrapped up the pennant."

Newsom won the opener, and this broke the Red Sox winning streak of 7, their last gasp. Frank Shea started the second game, his first sound work since hurting his arm in the All Star game. Page relieved and saved the win for Shea, but most important, it meant that Shea would be ready for the World Series. With the exception of Chandler, whose career was over, the Yankees were at full strength.

The Yankees that night announced they would accept mail orders for World Series tickets.

LANDMARKS

The 19-game winning streak by the Yankees was a major event in 1947, but it was only one of many dramatic and pivotal events that occurred during the period of June 29 to July 18.

Walter O. Briggs, president of the Detroit Tigers, announced June 3 that lights for night games were being ordered, to be installed for the 1948 season. This meant that only Wrigley Field, home of the Cubs in Chicago, would be without lights. Larry MacPhail had lived to see his idea of night baseball in the big leagues a complete success and he had seen it happen in a dozen years.

I was broadcasting in Cincinnati when MacPhail, then general manager of the Reds, played the first game under lights in the major leagues, May 24, 1935. MacPhail missed no tricks in his promotion. He had pre-game fireworks and when it was time for the lights, President Franklin D. Roosevelt in the White House touched a special key and the lights came on. The game was broadcast over the fledgling Mutual Broadcasting System composed then of four stations—WLW, Cincinnati; WOR, New York; WGN, Chicago and a station in Detroit, WXYZ, I think. That was the first sports event Mutual did, and as the resident announcer at Crosley Field, I had the assignment.

It wasn't easy for MacPhail to get permission to play games at night. Most of the club owners didn't like the idea, said baseball had always been played in the sun and it was "against tradition." Perhaps that was as good a way as any to define MacPhail— "against tradition." Anyhow, he got Commissioner Landis to approve, and then he got the National League to agree to 7 night games in 1935 at Cincinnati. Each competing team would get a night (each league in 1935 had eight teams) with extra attendance money. MacPhail kept saying that 7 night games was the same as adding seven Sundays to the schedule. Sundays had always been the big days.

I remember clearly that before that first night game many club owners and executives from baseball came to see what this thing was going to be. Most of them were openly critical. Bob Newhall had a sports show on WLW at 6:30, Monday through Friday evenings, and before the game he had a bunch of the big shots on it. They berated MacPhail and night baseball. One of the most critical was Clark Griffith of the Washington Senators. However, Griffith saw the crowd, saw how effective the lights were and before you knew it he was leading the fight, not for 7 night games a year, but for "unlimited" night ball. And that's what it became at Washington.

Wrigley Field has held out as the only ball park in the majors without lights. Phil Wrigley, who headed the Cubs from 1934 until his death in 1977, simply liked his ball park the way it was —brick walls with ivy on them—and he thought his park looked better in daylight than it ever would at night. Once he weakened. Just as World War II started, he ordered lights, then canceled the order so that the materials could be used in the war effort. Thereafter he said "No" to light towers and to playing after dark. The Chicago Tribune Company bought the Cubs in the summer of 1981, despite the ballplayers' strike, and it remains to be seen what the new owners will do about artificial lights.

Knowing MacPhail, I doubt that when he read the announcement from Detroit he spent much time thinking back to when he pioneered night ball. MacPhail and Rickey were always too occupied with the present, planning for the future, to be looking over their shoulders. When Satchel Paige said, "Don't never look back, 'cause somethin' might be gaining on you," he didn't have either MacPhail or Rickey in mind.

But three days later an announcement was made in Cleveland that stirred both MacPhail and Rickey. It was another of the 1947 turning points in baseball history. Bill Veeck was running the Cleveland Indians, and on July 3 Veeck jumped into the bit-

ter controversy that Rickey had stirred up with Jackie Robinson
—and jumped into it alongside Rickey and Robinson. Veeck
bought Larry Doby, a black player, from the Newark Eagles of
the Negro National League and promptly put Doby on the
Cleveland roster. This was the first Negro player in the American League. Now both leagues were integrated.

Veeck said, "Robinson has proved to be a real big-leaguer—so
I wanted to get the best of the Negro boys while the grabbing
was good. Why wait? Within ten years Negro players will be in
regular service with all big-league teams, for there are many
colored players with sufficient capabilities to make the majors."

MacPhail, usually ready to hold forth at length upon almost
any subject, had a terse "No comment." Eloquent statement.

Rickey spoke carefully, knowing far more about it than he was
going to reveal. He said, "If Doby is a good player, and I understand he is, the Cleveland club is showing signs it wants to win."
Masterful understatement.

The UP story summed it up. "With Robinson proving a success both as a Brooklyn first baseman and as a gate attraction,
Bill Veeck indicated that a wide-open scramble for Negro players was under way."

Two weeks later the St. Louis Browns announced they had
signed two Negro players, Henry Thompson and Willard Brown.
The flow of black players was beginning to gather strength and
soon would become a flood of talented athletes.

Veeck bought Larry Doby from the Newark Eagles for
$20,000—$10,000 immediately and $10,000 more if Doby made
good. He did. After stumbling around the rest of 1947, when he
was shuttled between the infield and the outfield, he was put in
center field in 1948 and helped the Indians win both the pennant
and the World Series. He hit .301 for the season and .318 in the
World Series, with 7 hits, including a monstrous home run off
Johnny Sain.

MacPhail with his "No comment" on Doby being signed by
Veeck at Cleveland was being consistent. He was still angry
with Rickey about jumping the gun on signing a Negro. The
more successes Robinson had, the madder MacPhail got. Doby
added fuel to his inner fires. But in this situation he held his
tongue. He must have known he could not now blast both

Rickey and Veeck without publicly blasting the Negro movement in baseball. It was too late. A blast would have had serious
and lasting repercussions.

It makes me smile, however, to read that Rickey said, "If
Doby is a good player, and I understand he is . . ." Rickey at
that time knew more about all the good Negro players than anybody else. He had had his scouts grading them. He had made
his choice from all of them. He believed Robinson was the man,
both as player and as the individual with the spiritual strength
and depth to break the color line. He certainly had carefully
considered Doby as a possibility. Also, by now Rickey had
signed Roy Campanella and Don Newcombe and had them playing on his Nashua farm team. However, Rickey at this time used
to tell me privately he had to be certain he didn't overdo, that
he must not bring in too many black players at first and risk upsetting the directors of the ball club as well as the fans. The director he was concerned most about was Walter O'Malley, who
would sooner than not have skipped the whole integration problem.

Rickey terribly wanted another club to bring in a Negro. This
would take some of the pressure off him. Once another club, especially in the other league, accepted a black player, then
Rickey's shattering of the unwritten law in baseball wouldn't be
viewed so harshly. In other words, Rickey not only wanted, he
needed somebody else to support him, to give him a vote of
confidence.

Young Bill Veeck was his man. Veeck's dad was president of
the Chicago Cubs when Bill was growing up. Bill broke into
baseball on his own when he ran the Milwaukee club in the
American Association. At Milwaukee he showed his flair for promotion. He was always interested in trying anything to make it
fun for the fans in the ball park. He got control of the Indians in
1946 when he was just thirty-two years old.

Veeck had served with the Marines in World War II, and had
lost a foot. This was to plague him continually as more and more
of his injured leg had to be removed. But he never complained.
He had enormous energy and slept little. He was a born maver-
ick. He relished new ideas and new promotions (in 1951 when
he was running the St. Louis Browns he used a midget, Eddie

Gaedel, as a batter). It gave Veeck much pleasure to ruffle the tail feathers of the conservative baseball establishment. He found most owners and general managers stuffy and as flexible as a post set in six feet of concrete.

Mr. Rickey was a most persuasive man, once he zeroed in on you. He sold Veeck, not so much on being the innovator in the American League, although that aspect of it wasn't missed by Veeck, but on having first choice (after Robinson, Campanella and Newcombe) of such rich material. Rickey had his eye on Doby for the Dodgers, and it was my understanding that Rickey had first refusal. In other words, Rickey hadn't actually bought Doby, but was in position to buy him if he chose to do so. He had Doby if he pulled the string.

What Rickey also planted in Veeck's receptive mind were Doby's ability as a player to improve the Cleveland team and, make no mistake about it, Doby's extra gate appeal. Veeck was always after attendance. Rickey, I'm certain, simply purred on the phone as he told Veeck how Robinson and the Dodgers had overflow crowds on the field at Pittsburgh, turned away thousands of fans at Cincinnati and Chicago, filled the park at St. Louis despite a transit strike, jammed the Polo Grounds, and that tickets for Ebbets Field were worth their weight in gold. Rickey would pause, puff his cigar, and then tell Veeck the fans were coming to games in Boston as they hadn't in years, and records were being set in Philadelphia. Yes, Robinson was a tremendous attraction. Yes indeed.

Veeck was never "an afraid man." Once he got an idea he thought had merit, he tried it. The more he talked with Rickey, and the more Robinson played and drew people with ready money in their eager hands, the more Veeck's eyes brightened. After all, it was his money he had in the Cleveland club, his finances weren't deep, and he was willing to shoot for the moon. He needed to.

Veeck signed Doby. Rickey was delighted for Veeck to have Doby instead of having him for himself—the American League now had broken the ice. Instead of being 1 club against 15 others, it was now 2 against 14. Two weeks later, when the Browns broke the line, it became 3 against 13, and before long the opposition melted down more and more.

Veeck the next year signed the venerable Satchel Paige, the black pitcher of fabulous reputation. Veeck's Indians won the pennant in 1948, plus the World Series, and drew an almost incredible home attendance of 2,620,627. Both Doby and Paige were strong assets.

Branch Rickey, on his own, against unified opposition, brought in Jackie Robinson. Quite properly Rickey and Robinson have received full credit. They were first. But Bill Veeck and Larry Doby have not been given the due they deserve for their roles in 1947–48 in furthering and speeding up the pioneering of integration in big-league baseball.

Because of Rickey—whatever his motives—in 1947 a black athlete played in what had been an all-white major sport. This was a watershed year for all sports in the United States. We do not today appreciate what a pivotal year it was. Actually, few people even wish to think about it. There are many whites who wished it hadn't happened, and there are many blacks who want to take their present-day athletic acceptance for granted, and do not want to be beholden to Jackie Robinson or to Branch Rickey or to Bill Veeck. It is human nature not to want to be reminded that other men paid a heavy price for what is currently and easily available.

Commissioner Bowie Kuhn before the 1972 World Series, Oakland and Cincinnati, realized this would make twenty-five years since Jackie Robinson first played for the Dodgers. There was a special tribute at home plate before the second game, at Cincinnati—Robinson was there, nearly blind, white-haired and forcing himself to stand erect. The Commissioner spoke, a representative of the Rickey family was on hand, and as the announcer at Brooklyn in 1947, I was asked to be master of ceremonies.

I didn't know it then but I heard later that Jackie was taken—led, so to speak—into the Oakland dressing room. It was thought the black players on the Oakland team would want to meet him, want to shake his hand, want to say some sort of thanks to the man who had a major role in their being in baseball in 1972 and in the World Series. I heard that the Oakland black players paid him no attention, were not interested in coming over to greet him, and Jackie was quietly led away. It is terrible when human beings forget their blessings and fail to say thank you. There is the bitter story in the seventeenth chapter of Luke, of the ten lepers who desperately begged Jesus to cleanse them. Jesus had pity on them, healed them, and told them to show themselves to the priest in order that, being again clean, they would now be permitted to resume their lives in their home town. The ten started away. One of them stopped, turned and came back to say thanks. Jesus said, "But weren't there ten healed? Where are the other nine?"

I don't know what Jackie thought about his lack of reception in the Oakland dressing room. But speaking of the nine lepers who didn't return to say thanks, Robinson died nine days after his last afternoon in the ball park. The public appreciation he got at Cincinnati was carried by national television. I've always been glad Commissioner Kuhn, and whoever else had a part in it, said thanks to Jackie while he could still know it, hear it, see it. Done in time by nine days.

Let's take stock. *Time* magazine in 1970 had a special issue, Black America. *Time,* after considerable research, stated that twenty-five years before (1945) "there were no blacks on any pro (baseball, football, basketball) team roster. The percentage of blacks in the pro leagues today (1970):

"Baseball—25% (150 out of 600)
Football—32% (330 out of 1040)
Basketball—55% (153 out of 280)"

Today, 1982, the percentage of blacks relative to whites in professional and college sports has gone even higher. Statistics can get boring and lose their meaning. Quickly then, let me note that today in pro basketball there are more than 70 percent black players, in pro football blacks are 55 percent, and in pro baseball there are nearly as many black as white players.

Aside from numbers, in baseball black players have dominated in star quality: Willie Mays, Hank Aaron, Bob Gibson, Maury Wills, Elston Howard, Billy Williams, Ernie Banks, Larry Doby, Monte Irvin, Willie McCovey, Lou Brock, Cecil Cooper, Willie Stargell, Juan Marichal, Roberto Clemente, Frank Robinson, Rod Carew, George Foster, Reggie Jackson, David

Winfield, Tony Oliva, Jim Rice, Vida Blue, Dave Parker, Roy Campanella, Don Newcombe and Jackie himself, to name only a few. Where would baseball be today without the black players?

Baseball had sixteen teams when Rickey put Robinson on the 1947 Dodgers. Today there are twenty-six. Baseball added ten new clubs in the face of the decreasing number of minor-league teams. This expansion could not have been possible without the black players.

In passing—and this is not meant to be in any sense a play on words about football—in passing, every college coach knows he must win, and he knows that in order to win he must have some black players. It took a while, especially in the Deep South, for this to strike home, but strike home it did in Alabama, Georgia, Florida, Mississippi, Louisiana, both Carolinas. Everywhere. The word became, "If you want to win, you better get some of them." There is an old saying, "All cats are gray at night." All athletes today are gray, day or night. Rickey and Robinson, Veeck and Doby in 1947 began painting out all contrasts of color.

First, Abraham Lincoln. Then, Branch Rickey. Between them they certainly changed sports on the North American continent.

Larry MacPhail

Larry MacPhail was a hard man to describe. I could say he was a Dr. Jekyll and Mr. Hyde, and this would be quite accurate. It would depend upon when you encountered him. He was a smoldering volcano with smoke signals indicating fires were burning inside. The explosion was coming, but when? He was a juggler keeping several projects moving and spinning at the same time. He was a chameleon. Just as a chameleon changes colors in response to varying stimuli, so did MacPhail blow hot, then cold, as different factors came and went. He could focus his attention for hours upon a single subject, or he could cut you off in the middle of a sentence and go to something entirely foreign.

There were innocent-seeming smoke signals the last two months of 1947. They weren't taken too seriously at the time or given much play in the papers. They didn't warn the press that an explosion was imminent. Of course, hindsight is perfect vision. We know now what happened. We know now that with MacPhail one had better take note of any signal. He was volatile, resourceful, determined, restless—and he knew what he wanted.

MacPhail had stayed at Cincinnati three years. What happened between him and Powell Crosley is not known: one story is that Crosley didn't like the public troubles MacPhail got into when he was drinking, another said MacPhail wanted to buy stock in the Reds and Crosley turned him down, a third said Crosley, a careful man with money, didn't like MacPhail's expensive operation. MacPhail stayed at Brooklyn five years—the longest he stayed at one place in baseball—before he left to enter the Army as a lieutenant colonel. Some sources said the directors of the Dodgers were displeased at the costly operation of the club under MacPhail.

While he was at Brooklyn, MacPhail bought a run-down farm at Bel Air, Maryland. He named it Glen Angus Farms and he began building a herd of high-quality Black Angus cattle. He modernized the old house on the property. He built new barns. He restored the fertility of the land. His manager told me, "Colonel MacPhail bought the most run-down place in this area, and turned it into the best farm in the state of Maryland." He made Glen Angus Farms a showplace. His attention to detail was complete. He loved to hear music and he asked me to put him in touch with the engineers at CBS to have them install a music room that would have as perfect sound conditions as possible. He soon went from breeding Black Angus cattle to breeding thoroughbred horses. He did well with both projects, especially with horses. He had one horse, as I remember, General Staff, that won some races for him.

As the years went by he shut down his breeding farm, sold the land for a housing development, and finally sold the house. By then he had moved to Key Biscayne. Sometime in his comings and goings he bought a yacht and spent much time on it. He got tired of that. He beat cancer twice with surgery. He was always restless, resilient and, at times, ruthless.

Before he left Brooklyn he began developing and restoring Glen Angus Farms. While he was in the Army his wife, Jean, ran the farm and kept it all together. All the time he was with the Yankees he had Glen Angus Farms and each year it was coming into fuller maturity.

Late in 1944 as the war was winding down, MacPhail started looking around. He thought he might get the New York Giants, but that didn't hold water or his interest. The Yankees were waiting for a buyer. Colonel Ruppert had died and left the ball club to his estate—to two nieces. Ed Barrow, now an old man, was running the club. MacPhail didn't have much money. He had to get financing for his share. He had know-how, and he found in Dan Topping and Del Webb two men with money who were content for MacPhail to be the boss. The Yankees were bought, lock, stock, and barrel, in January 1945 for $2,850,000. MacPhail, Topping and Webb each had a third of the club. MacPhail was president and general manager. He ran it.

For the first time MacPhail had part ownership of a ball club. He had complete ownership of Glen Angus Farms. There was his record of losing interest in a struggling project once he had it on its feet: department store in Nashville, automobile agency in Columbus, ball clubs in Cincinnati and Brooklyn. MacPhail had his hatred of Rickey. His relationship with Commissioner Chandler was becoming more and more strained. He and his partners, particularly Del Webb, were pulling apart. And, MacPhail had never had real money, net money, for himself.

Now it seems very clear. Then it didn't appear to be anything more than what MacPhail intended it to be. He was making his moves, sending out signals. Topping and Webb certainly knew the pressure was being put on them, but they said nothing, and apparently no writer asked them anything. MacPhail's statements were accepted at face value.

On August 16, 1947, MacPhail called the writers together and said that despite rumors, he had a contract to head the Yankees through 1955. What rumors? The only rumors were vague hints that some Wall Street fellows might like to buy MacPhail's share of the Yankees. Who do you think started those rumors? The Yankees were leading by 13½ games that day, so the writers enjoyed the hospitality of the pressroom, and wrote about such a splendid first-place lead. However, the seed was planted.

The last day of August was Sunday, and a doubleheader at

the Stadium with Washington. Before the first game MacPhail told the writers that he would not sell his stock and quit the Yankees. He went on to state that he and his partners "will control the Yankees through 1955, barring death, illness, or other matters which cannot be anticipated." That was the MacPhail touch, the qualifying phrase, "other matters which cannot be anticipated." The Yankees won both games, held a 12½-game lead, and a young catcher just brought up from Newark, Sherman Lollar, made his Stadium debut and hit a bases-loaded triple. The writers wrote about the 2 games and about young Lollar. MacPhail's statement was just a note in the story.

The volcano almost blew out in Washington on Friday September 5. The Yankees were to open their final series of the year at Griffith Stadium. The Senators were now addicted to night games. The players were at the park when MacPhail sat down at a table in the hotel dining room with three New York writers: Will Wedge of the *Sun*, Hugh Bradley of the *Journal-American*, and Al Buck of the *Post*. All three writers were pros, and very experienced reporters.

Here is what Bradley wrote that MacPhail said:

"It's a hundred to one that he [meaning Durocher] won't be back in Brooklyn. Do you think Leo would have been suspended for a year if Rickey hadn't wanted him suspended?

"I'll buy anybody a suit of clothes if he can show me anything presented in Leo's hearing before the Commissioner which warranted such a suspension. I've got all the testimony in the case, two hundred and fifty pages of it, in my office and you all can come in and read it if you wish to.

"Months ago Chandler promised to write me a letter erasing that suspension from Dressen's record. So far, he has not done it. Meanwhile I continue to maintain that Charlie was suspended for no known or just reason."

Just like that, without any prompting, MacPhail exploded. He thus reopened the Durocher case which for months had been fairly quiet, accused Rickey and Chandler of collusion in Durocher's suspension, accused Chandler of breaking his word on Dressen, and above all else, MacPhail violated the silencing Chandler had imposed on all parties to the Durocher case, especially on MacPhail.

Throughout the long summer Rickey and his staff had scrupulously refrained from comments. They had obeyed the Commissioner to the letter and in the spirit of his instructions. Rickey had tried to get Chandler to soften his sentence on Durocher, but always directly and in private with Chandler. Arthur Mann wrote in *Baseball Confidential* that Rickey was so angered by MacPhail's outburst in Washington, he thought of suing MacPhail for a million dollars. He didn't. MacPhail quickly denied that he had "authorized" publication of his remarks.

Here it went again. MacPhail said he had been talking in an off-the-record session, and the sportswriters who quoted him had no right to do so. Al Buck had written the same story Bradley had. When MacPhail denied "authorization" Bradley and Buck went to bat promptly. In the next editions of their papers they not only repeated what they had written but made it more emphatic. They both stated MacPhail had volunteered his remarks and had been completely sober. In other words, they didn't leave MacPhail the excuse of popping off when he was drinking.

This put Commissioner Chandler's back in a high arc. He got copies of the stories by Bradley and Buck and wired Buck an invitation to come to Cincinnati. In his wire there was no offer of travel expenses. Buck wired back that he was too busy for such a visit, but that he stood upon every word he had written. Chandler then ordered MacPhail to appear at his Cincinnati office September 11.

MacPhail was in Kansas City September 10, and said he was going to Cincinnati on World Series matters, and, "anytime Chandler or anyone else labors under the impression I cannot express my opinion on baseball matters he is entirely wrong."

Chandler was watching a game at Crosley Field, and when asked for a comment on MacPhail's remarks said, "I am not going to say anything about anything."

Later that evening, September 10, after the Yankees beat Cleveland at the Stadium (Joe Page had relieved Vic Raschi in the sixth inning and won the game for his fourteenth victory of the year) Bucky Harris and his coaches, Charlie Dressen and Red Corriden, gathered for a drink. Bucky was not under any edict of silence. Harris raised his glass, said, "Here's to Joe

Page," and Dressen and Corriden replied, "Amen . . . to Joe Page."

The meeting with Chandler and MacPhail at Cincinnati on the eleventh was behind closed doors. There was no statement issued to the press afterward. MacPhail, as he left, did say this, "The statement attributed to me that Leo would not have been suspended for a year if Rickey had not wanted him suspended is not true."

Al Buck in the next day's *Post* restated what MacPhail had said at Washington on September 5. Buck had the last word. MacPhail said nothing more on the matter. He let it drop as though it had never happened, which was one of the ways MacPhail disposed of certain matters he didn't wish to bother with anymore. Change the subject, go to something else. Like the ending of the second Chandler hearing at St. Petersburg in the spring: the Commissioner ended the session, and MacPhail promptly sought out Rickey, maneuvered him into the bathroom where they could talk alone, and said, "I can let you have Etten." Etten being a first baseman MacPhail didn't plan to use, now that he was going to go with George McQuinn. Needless to say, Rickey's only answer was to push past MacPhail and depart.

The meeting MacPhail had with Chandler on September 11 must have been deadly serious. The silence that followed it was eloquent. However, on the seventeenth, MacPhail made one additional mention of the Commissioner. He stated that he was not "out to get Chandler." Everything a person says has a meaning. Why would MacPhail have said that? Was he smoldering about Chandler? Was he making a threat to Chandler?

Next, MacPhail divulged that he had received an offer of $3 million for half interest in the Yankees from three brokerage firms on behalf of various clients. But, he said, "My contract has three more years to run. As a matter of fact, I would have quit after we clinched the pennant if it weren't for my responsibilities to my partners."

The price was being set. The pressure was being applied. MacPhail next stated that two separate offers of $2 million had been made to him for his third of the Yankees. The offers were from two syndicates. Apparently, MacPhail had attractive offers at the $2 million figure—over twice what he had paid three years before.

This was by and large put aside in the excitement of the World Series, of the meeting of the Dodgers and the Yankees, and of another MacPhail-Rickey encounter—this time through their ball clubs. New York was steamed up for this Series. So was the country. It had been some spring. It had been some summer. It would be some World Series.

Branch Rickey

> No two men could have been more unlike than Larry MacPhail and Branch Rickey. Unlike MacPhail, who put a team together by patchwork, Rickey built his teams from the bottom up, and built them to last.
> Leo Durocher, *Nice Guys Finish Last.*

Leo knew. He had played for both of them and managed for both of them. When he wrote that "No two men could have been more unlike" he was thinking only of building ball clubs. His appraisal could have applied to almost everything else.

Rickey in the early 1920s started his farm system: sending scouts around the country searching for young players, placing the youngsters on various minor-league teams; training, developing and grading them; moving them upward until they made the Cardinals. Or fell by the way; or were sold for cash as surplus; or used in trades for a certain needed player.

Rickey's farm system, which revolutionized baseball, produced its first championship in 1926 when his Cardinals upset and defeated in 7 games the mighty Yankees of Ruth, Gehrig, Hoyt, Pennock, Lazzeri, Combs and other stars. From then on Rickey's Cardinals were always a formidable force.

Rickey's last year at St. Louis was 1942, when his young Redbirds under manager Billy Southworth jelled in midseason, and came rushing on to win 106 games and defeat MacPhail's last Brooklyn team, managed by Durocher, which won 104 games. The Cardinals lost the first game of the World Series to Joe McCarthy's Yankees, then swept the next 4.

Sam Breadon owned the Cardinals. Rickey's contract expired after that World Series. The two had been moving farther and farther apart. After directing the Cardinals for twenty-six years, Rickey was out at St. Louis. MacPhail left Brooklyn for the Army, Rickey was available, and the pieces fell together. Often a man is free and able, but there is no job opening. Again, a job may be there but the right man isn't in position to accept it. In the fall of 1942, the job and the man met. Rickey came to Brooklyn.

World War II was going full force. Rickey's first task was to preside over the disintegration of MacPhail's last team at Brooklyn, which had won 104 games. This was a ball club mostly of veterans—as Durocher said, a patchwork team. Between the military services and Father Time there wasn't much left at Ebbets Field: the 1943 team fell to third place, the 1944 club dropped to seventh. The 1944 team won 63 games, 43 fewer than MacPhail's 1942 runner-up club.

Pee Wee Reese was gone, Pete Reiser was gone, Hugh Casey was gone. Dolph Camilli, Whit Wyatt were finishing. So was Joe Medwick. It was a scramble to keep a semblance of a team on the field. Durocher became a juggler, getting an inning here and a game there out of men who would never have been in a big-league uniform if there hadn't been a war.

MacPhail had been tremendously popular with the fans. They read gleefully about his explosions, they loved to hear him roar, and they rejoiced in the scrappy, colorful teams he built for them—to third place in 1939, to second in 1940, then in 1941 the pennant—the first in Brooklyn since 1920. His 1942 team still won 104 games and was in the race with St. Louis until the end of the season. MacPhail and Durocher suited Brooklyn. Now with the war taking its toll on players, with MacPhail safely tucked away in the happy memories of the fans as well as being in uniform in Washington, Rickey got the blame. Rickey reaped the whirlwind.

Rickey was a very orderly man. He didn't get into scrapes and he didn't rave and rant. He talked freely to the writers but they had trouble piecing together what he had said. When he was setting up a deal he kept his thoughts to himself. There would be no story until the deal was made. Rickey did not want leaks, and he had people around him who did not leak to the press.

When Rickey took over he had no good news to give out. Everything was going downhill. This player was called into military service, this player was sold because he wasn't useful, or this player was simply released. This was not the sort of material the writers wanted, and it certainly wasn't what the rabid Dodger fans relished reading. All Rickey could tell the writers, and the fans, was that the Brooklyn club was signing every young prospect who looked as if he had a chance to be a ballplayer, that the war would end, and that when it did he, Rickey, and the Dodgers would have a great crop of promising players. The other clubs had pulled in their scouts—they had stopped signing kids for fear they'd get wounded or killed . . . and anyhow, with the war raging why bother with raw rookies you wouldn't see for heaven knew when?

Rickey's promises of kids that you couldn't see, made against an uncertain future, didn't make good stories in the papers. Example: Gil Hodges was signed in Indiana, brought to Ebbets Field, played in one game at third base, and was gone the next day into the armed forces. That couldn't be a story, but that was the way it was. Most of the young men Rickey's scouts were signing never even saw Brooklyn until after the war.

Rickey came to Brooklyn with the reputation of being a sharp trader . . . of building his farm system into what some writers called a chain gang, meaning, sign a boy for almost nothing, work him for years in the system, and if he didn't make the big ball club in St. Louis, then toss him out. Rickey knew the value of money. He certainly didn't throw it away. His salary disputes with Dizzy Dean had been widely publicized. He believed in having hungry players who fought to get into the World Series in order to get more money. Further, in St. Louis, with smaller attendances than larger cities, with no income then from radio and with television not even in the picture, Rickey had to sell players from time to time. Make no mistake, he sold them well. No bargains from Branch Rickey. MacPhail for one had been a buyer, spending other people's money.

Stop a moment. Read over the above paragraph. It must sound strange to us, accustomed to the fortunes in baseball today—the million-dollar contracts free agents receive, as when George Steinbrenner of the Yankees gave David Winfield a contract of some $20 million. It must sound strange to think of a time when a few thousand dollars was a lot of money. Ballplayers in 1947 used to bargain desperately for a thousand-dollar raise, even $500. There was no income from television then. Today television has surfeited the owners with wealth. In 1947 the owners of ball clubs built and maintained their ball parks. Today parks are built by taxpayers. In 1947 the players' pension plan was just beginning. In 1947 ball clubs lived basically on what fans paid at the gate. Ballplayers had to get into the World Series in order to make extra money. Today there are no hungry ballplayers. In 1947 Rickey had to run a tight ship. MacPhail had much more leeway—Yankee Stadium could hold twice what Ebbets Field could, and MacPhail had two rich men as partners. Rickey, without money, conceived the farm system, and it not only provided him with fine players but also with money. Rickey was a shrewd trader, a keen businessman, a sound operator, the best judge of player talent, and a man who could look into the future. He had had to be brainy, patient, resourceful, and possessed of tremendous faith. Call it courage. Rickey started with nothing but his inner self when he left Saranac Lake, New York, after a year in a tuberculosis sanitarium. He had come all the way. He helped many others. I don't know who helped him, except Jane, his wife. She was always there. His rock.

On May 3 Rickey sent Kirby Higbe to Pittsburgh. Frank McKinney, an Indianapolis banker new to baseball, had the Pirates. He had Hank Greenberg and Ralph Kiner, two sluggers who could hit the ball, and for a short time McKinney thought he might even win the pennant, if he got another starting pitcher. Rickey estimated he could spare Higbe, a veteran. Further, in 1947 the Dodgers had trained in Havana, Cuba—as did the farm team, Montreal. The Cuban fans weren't interested in exhibition games. Hotel costs were high in Havana, especially for the Dodgers at the Nacional. Meals were expensive and ballplayers on the cuff are good, steady eaters. The Dodgers paid resort rates. It was probably the most costly spring training tour on record. Rickey had to pay for it. Frank McKinney at Pittsburgh had money and wanted to spend it. The way baseball was operated in 1947 and the tightness of Rickey's finances made the trade necessary. In addition to the players involved, Pittsburgh paid Rickey $100,000. . . . That's the way it was in those days. That's the way the spring training bills were finally paid and the books balanced.

I don't know why it is, but it is: let a man be absolutely faithful to his wife and his family, let him not take a drink, let him not curse, let him go to church regularly—even at times get up in the pulpit and preach, and preach effectively—let him pay his debts, let him keep the peace, let him stay out of ball parks on Sunday because of a promise to his mother, let him sing hymns, let him be interested in civic good works, and writers delight in taking pot shots at him.

Once Rickey arrived at Brooklyn the New York press began doing a job on him, and they kept it up. It was a disgrace. Jimmy Powers, who wrote a column in the *Daily News* called "The Power House," led the pack. Powers hadn't met Rickey, didn't want to meet him, and refused to meet him—yet Powers began calling Rickey El Cheapo. He made a vicious campaign of it. It got so bad Rickey called in Walter O'Malley, who was the lawyer for the ball club as well as Rickey's partner, and told O'Malley he was going to sue Powers for slander. O'Malley talked Rickey out of it by claiming that if Rickey sued one of the sportswriting brethren then all the rest of the lodge brothers would turn on him even more fiercely. I don't know how they could have been more destructive in the picture of Rickey they gave the public.

One night Lylah and I had dinner at a small, distinguished restaurant, La Crémaillère, on New York's East Side. It was run by Antoine Gilly, a great chef and by then a personal friend. Jimmy Powers was there having dinner alone. We stopped to say hello, and he volunteered, "I don't know your man Rickey . . . never met him . . . don't intend to meet him. I have heard he is a fine man. I know you like him and think the world of him. The two of you get along very well. If I met him, from what I've heard, he might make me change my campaign, and I'm not going to do it. The El Cheapo campaign is the best campaign I've ever had for the column. I've never had the response

from readers I'm getting from El Cheapo. Rickey is El Cheapo."
And he remained so in the *Daily News.*

It wasn't just Jimmy Powers who painted Rickey as either
cheap and grasping or else a religious fanatic, or both. About
the only New York sportswriter who didn't get on the band-
wagon was Dan Parker of the *Mirror,* and for two reasons: Dan
was a fair man, and further, anything Jimmy Powers was for,
Dan Parker knew there was something phony about.

Joe Williams in the *World-Telegram* wrote, among his charges
of Rickey's chain-gang tactics, that Rickey cost the Dodgers the
1946 pennant (tied with St. Louis, lost in play-off) because he
kept Jackie Robinson at Montreal instead of bringing him up to
the big club!

This was a period of many papers in New York, and sports
cartoonists flourished. Rickey was ideal for them. He was drawn
as Scrooge, as Simon Legree, as a skinflint wearing a stovepipe
hat, smoking a big cigar, raking in money while refusing poor,
ragged ballplayers bread for their hungry children. Rickey and
his wife were aghast. They couldn't understand it. With the war
taking players, Rickey's hands were tied. He couldn't move until
the war was over, and then when his young men, plus such valuable veterans as Pee Wee Reese, returned, a new dynasty was
put together in Brooklyn.

The fans were taught by the press to blame Rickey. They
began to chant outside Ebbets Field, "Rickey ruint the
Dodgers." One day they burned him in effigy at Borough Hall,
across the street from his office, in plain sight.

If Spiro Agnew had done some research when he attacked the
press, had he known to cite what happened to Rickey, he'd have
made a stronger and more unanswerable point. Harold Parrott,
in his book *The Lords of Baseball,* devotes a half-dozen pages to
the persecution of Rickey by the press—and Harold, remember,
was a former sportswriter before joining the Dodgers as road
secretary.

Rickey finally had a big story for the writers. When he announced, late in 1945, that he was signing Jackie Robinson to a
Montreal contract, that was a story. But you could tell—why did
it have to be Rickey? Why not some of the good guys? Why
hadn't MacPhail done it over at the Yankees?

Once Rickey broke the color line, my guess is that down inside—he never would admit it—MacPhail bitterly resented Rickey's doing it before he, MacPhail, had had time and made plans to do it. MacPhail was chairman of a committee on black players for baseball, and when Rickey announced Robinson, MacPhail accused Rickey of "jumping the gun." Was MacPhail beginning to make his own plans? That surely would have given him another genuine "first" to go with his other achievements.

As if Rickey hadn't had enough trouble his first two years at Brooklyn, MacPhail bounced back into New York as part owner and president of the Yankees. There had to be blood on the moon. The fireworks, the rhubarbs, the bitterness and the final never-to-be forgotten anger of 1947 were inevitable.

THERE WERE DAYS AND THERE WERE
NIGHTS

"Rickey built his teams from the bottom up, and built them to last." That's what Durocher said.

The last teams he built at St. Louis challenged the Dodgers in 1941, caught and beat them for the pennant in 1942. Then Rickey went to Brooklyn but his handiwork at St. Louis held fast: the Cardinals won the pennant in 1943 and again in 1944. The team lost the pennant to the Cubs in '45—the last time the Cubs won it—and in 1946 the Cardinals tied the Dodgers and beat them in a 3-game play-off, then beat Boston in the World Series. Rickey had built well at St. Louis.

In 1946, at Brooklyn, Rickey was able to assemble for the first time a team that, as he put it, would be "more respectable." Reese, Reiser, Lavagetto and Casey were back. There were youngsters like Furillo, Hermanski, Branca, Edwards, Lombardi and Barney. The men were coming back from the war. Some of the new faces had been planted in the Dodgers' farm system by MacPhail. Some were Rickey's. The veterans were MacPhail's. Rickey had a mixed bag. During the war he traded for Bobby Bragan and Eddie Stanky. Rickey himself admitted that this 1946 club came along faster than he had anticipated. Durocher was delighted to have decent material again, and he drove the team furiously.

The 1947 Dodgers would be more Rickey's team than any he had had yet at Ebbets Field. He disposed of veterans he didn't need, especially several who went back to the debacle of 1942 when the team got overconfident and too much interested in fun and games (gambling games) in the clubhouse and on trains.

Rickey had to evaluate and develop the youngsters already in the farm system plus those he had scouted and waited for during the war. He had to decide which veterans to retain. There is an old adage in baseball—Joe McCarthy, when he was managing the Yankees, first told me of it—concerning a winning ball club: "Who to keep and who to get rid of." Rickey had a lot of both to do.

The 1947 Dodgers had speed, led by Robinson. The team fielded, made double-plays and hit. There was depth for the infield, outfield and catching. The problem was pitching, and it was a problem through the season and through the World Series.

The best way to appraise the 1947 pitching staff of the Dodgers was a conversation between Branch and Mrs. Rickey. The conversation was short and it was so acutely to the point that it hurt Rickey. It was as though he been stabbed with a knife in a most sensitive area. Keep in mind, it was the custom all their married years that Branch talked over with Jane his problems, hopes and fears. She was his sounding board. She was a smart person. She knew baseball and she knew people. He valued her advice, and I doubt he made a big decision before he talked it out with her. She, in her way, was as smart as he was. Her influence on him was impressive, but the public never knew this. The Rickeys kept their private life private. It was precious to them.

The Dodgers went into first place by 1 game July 6 when Branca shut out the Braves. This was just before the All Star game break. Coming out of that the Dodgers won 6 straight, including a 5-game sweep of the Cubs. The team was never out of first again, although the Cardinals kept the heat on.

Things looked good. Things always look good in a winning streak, better than they are, just as things are not as bad as they might seem in a losing string. Winning streaks start and end. It's like monkeys on a string . . . up and down. Baseball is a long season.

Rickey, after the sixth straight win, said to his wife, "Jane . . . I don't have a World Series pitching staff."

"Branch," Mrs. Rickey replied, "are you sure you have a pennant-winning staff?"

Mrs. Rickey put her finger on the sore spot. Mr. Rickey didn't have a pennant-winning staff. Manager Shotton was a magician. He had one of his coaches, Clyde Sukeforth, go to the mound for him, and by the end of the season Sukey must have worn out an extra pair of walking shoes. It seemed that about every time I looked over the microphone, there was Sukey walking slowly to the mound, either to give advice or to bring the pitcher back with him. The infielders, outfielders and catchers carried the pitchers.

Just as the 1947 Brooklyn club was not entirely Rickey's, neither was the New York team all MacPhail's. In fact, the Yankees were mainly George Weiss's team with some help from Ed Barrow. Barrow had bought Joe DiMaggio from San Francisco despite Joe's requiring surgery on a bad knee. Barrow had paid the price for free agent Tommy Henrich.

Weiss had the Yankees well stocked. The Yankees came out of the war years with more good players than any other team in the American League. For 1947 Frank Shea was ready (Weiss), Vic Raschi was ready by midseason (Weiss), Yogi Berra was too good a batter to be sent to the minors (Weiss). It was Weiss or Barrow—mainly Weiss—all over the roster except for George McQuinn at first, Allie Reynolds on the mound, and another pitcher, Bobo Newsom. Weiss became general manager when MacPhail left, and in thirteen years his teams won ten pennants and seven World Series. Weiss hired Casey Stengel.

MacPhail inherited riches, but he knew how to take advantage of his wealth, knew what positions needed help and when. He got McQuinn for first, traded Joe Gordon for the big pitcher he needed, Allie Reynolds, and brought in Raschi at the same time he bought Newsom on waivers.

It was destiny that Rickey and MacPhail would collide in the 1947 World Series. The Yankee club improved while the Red Sox and Tigers fell back. The Red Sox lost 21 more games than the year before when they won the pennant. The Dodgers played at the same pace in 1947 as the year before, but the Cardinals got off to a terrible start and lost all told 9 more games than in 1946. The Dodgers increased their tempo of beating St. Louis themselves. Rickey said the Dodgers won the pennant when they went into St. Louis for the final meeting with the Cardinals, a 3-game series, and won 2 of them.

The Yankees started their drive for the pennant when June gave way to July. So did the Dodgers, although not as dramatically as the Yankees with their 19-game winning streak. The Dodgers had to grind it out with threats from the Cardinals all the way into late September. Their uncertain, scrambled pitching gave Shotton no peace.

The Yankees were in first place for the All Star game break (July 7–9) and stayed there the rest of the way. The Dodgers on Sunday July 6 sneaked into first place by 1 game when Branca blanked the Braves with 3 hits for his twelfth win and third shutout. And the Dodgers were never out of the top spot again all season, but it was like trying to pick up fresh watermelon seeds: it was slippery.

That first week in July, for example, Barney got his fifth win and that was his last one for the year. Hatten for the sixth straight time failed to finish a start. The Giants slugged Gregg, Behrman, Hatten and King for 5 home runs and a 19–2 win. The Dodgers returned the favor the next day, beating the Giants 16–7 but Shotton had to use five pitchers . . . Casey got the win in relief. Robinson had a 21-game hitting streak stopped July 4. Strong games by Taylor and Branca got the club into first and the All Star game gave the team a needed respite. The Dodgers were packing Ebbets Field. By now 752,231 had paid to get into the small park.

The Dodgers had to go to work after the three-day break. The Braves were 1 game back, then came the Giants, with the Cardinals in fourth merely 4½ out of the top spot. The Cubs came into Brooklyn for 5 games, and the Dodgers won them all to push their first-place margin to 3½. The series opened with a doubleheader. To emphasize the condition of the pitching staff, Branca won both—he pitched the entire first game, and then relieved in the second. Reiser put on a uniform but said the doctors at Johns Hopkins wanted him to wait another four or five days before playing. It was now six weeks since Reiser hit the concrete wall.

The Reds were next at Ebbets Field. The crowds continued to jam the place. Sunday, the thirteenth, rookie Clyde King made his first start and was the winning pitcher. Casey saved it. Reiser pinch-hit. But the Braves won a doubleheader and the lead was down to 3.

Billy Southworth took over as manager of the Boston Braves in 1946. He had won three pennants and twice was second, his last five years at St. Louis. He got the Braves into fourth in '46 and this year he had Johnny Sain and Warren Spahn to build around. Sain in 1947 won 21 as did Spahn—42 victories between them. This was the team that was to win the next year. The Braves gave Shotton no time to catch his breath. Sain and Spahn were capable anytime of throwing a monkey wrench into the works.

The Giants could, and would upon occasion, knock your brains out. Johnny Mize that year hit 51 home runs, the most ever in the National League by a left-handed batter. Willard Marshall, Walker Cooper, Sid Gordon and Bobby Thomson also belted the ball. All told, the Giants that year blasted 221 home runs, a new record. (Cincinnati tied it in 1956 and Mickey Mantle, Roger Maris and fellow Yankees broke it with 240 in 1961 when Maris hit 61.)

There wasn't a soft spot in the league for the Dodgers. However, the balance of the league worked for Brooklyn as much as it threatened. When the Braves or the Giants or Ewell Blackwell weren't pitted against the Dodgers, they gave the Cardinals fits. A working simile could be: as merciless as a hot baseball pennant race.

The Dodgers won 7 straight, but when they thought they might shake loose, Bud Lively of the Reds, who had won just 4 games all year, on July 14 stopped them 9–1. Reality rolled right on when the Pirates beat the Dodgers twice the next day, knocking out Hatten and Taylor. The lead went down to 2½. The Dodgers outscrambled the Pirates 10–6, only to have Mel Queen (sold by MacPhail) get his first National League win, 7–1. King and three more did the pitching. The Pirates took the series 3–1.

The Cardinals, 4½ behind, were next at Ebbets Field for 3 games—Friday night July 18, Saturday and Sunday. Tickets were not available. I took my phone off the hook. Branca had been carefully rotated in order to open. He was superb. He had a perfect game through seven innings and only a single by Slaughter prevented a no-hitter. The score was 7–0, and all Brooklyn slept well. People in the borough took their Dodgers seriously.

Ebbets Field was a rhubarb patch. Things happened in Brooklyn. They just happened. The players knew it, the managers knew it, the umpires knew it, and fans took it for granted. I don't know why: a combination of colorful players over the years—but the same man would be a routine player on another team and be transformed once he got to Ebbets Field—with a small park which put the fans almost in the game with the players. Brooklyn made a ball game into warfare against everybody else, particularly the Giants from across the river. I began saying on the air from time to time, "Anything can and probably will happen in Brooklyn." It was a phrase that after a certain amount of time became factual reporting.

The Cardinals evened the series with a so-what 7–5 win the next day. That cut the distance between them back to 4½ games. Sunday, the rubber game, had to be a double-jointed doozy. It was. Ebbets Field rocked; 33,420 wild fans were crammed into every crack and crevice. Stevens's vendors could barely make it between the aisles. The Dodgers won it 3–2. But they didn't. It took them another month to win it.

What follows was genuine Ebbets Field stuff. Lightning struck fire in Brooklyn. The Cardinals came to bat in the top of the ninth with a 2–0 lead. Ron Northey was the batter, and he hit one high into deep left center field. There was a row of box seats on the top of the wall, and the boxes were packed with fans like a can of sardines—waving hands, handkerchiefs, faces and bodies jumping up and down. Ebbets Field on Sunday with the Cardinals in town!

Pete Reiser was back in center field. He ran close to the wall and jumped. The ball went over his hands. Dixie Walker came rushing over from right. The ball came back onto the field. Walker grabbed it and threw to second baseman Eddie Stanky, who relayed it to catcher Bruce Edwards at the plate. The question was: did the ball clear the box seat rail, then bounce back from contact with a fan and become a home run, or did the ball, without fan interference, hit the top of the wall, bounce back and remain in play?

Northey was built top-heavy, with a large torso like a barrel on two legs. He wasted no time in running full stride. He wheeled around first, wheeled around second, and as he went around third he visibly slowed down and trotted home. He was out by a country mile at home plate. When Edwards put the tag on him Northey acted very surprised. Manager Eddie Dyer ran out, spoke to Northey, and then Dyer started jumping around between the umpires as if he were on the business end of a cattle prod. The umpires—there were three of them in those days—had a huddle. Coach Sukeforth, Shotton's on-the-field representative, was straining his ears for all that was being yelled. Nobody was speaking in a calm, orderly, well-modulated voice.

Larry Goetz was the umpire in chief, calling balls and strikes behind the plate. Jocko Conlon was at first, and Beans Reardon was at third. All three were veteran umpires, all of them good at their work. When Northey's drive went sailing out to deep left center all three umpires watched the ball, not each other. That was proper. Conlon ran at top speed toward short center to get a closer look. Reardon remained at his station at third. He stood there.

Reardon's hand went up signaling a home run. Goetz and Conlon gave the sign that the ball was still in play, and that the runner was entitled only to what he could make. Northey never saw Conlon, and when he came charging into third Reardon barked in that raspy voice of his, "What are you running so hard for—it's a home run." Northey slowed down.

The Dodgers claimed the ball was in play, that Northey was out, and two of the three umpires supported them. Manager Dyer went from umpire to umpire saying Reardon had ruled it a home run, and further, had slowed down the runner. The two-on-one decision stood. Northey was out. Dyer didn't smoke, but had he been a smoker he could have lighted his cigarettes without matches. Just by breathing on them.

The Cardinals took the field with a 2–0—not a 3–0—lead. However, the afternoon wasn't over. Reardon could have been off the hook had St. Louis held on and won it. But no, the Dodgers scored 3 in the home half of the ninth to win it 3–2.

You should have heard the crowd when the winning run came home. You should have heard Eddie Dyer. He protested the game to the league office—should I say, vigorously?

The next two months—the rest of the race—was like a roller coaster. The Dodgers would get on a winning streak, then start losing, and here would come the Cardinals, always chasing, always falling short as Shotton rallied his forces just in time to widen the gap again.

Snatching back the Reardon-rhubarb game from the Cardinals seemed to be the spark the Dodgers needed. The Reds were in next for a doubleheader—July 21. A record crowd jammed Ebbets Field—35,092. The Dodgers won them both. Hatten won one and Lombardi got credit for the other—but it required four pitchers. St. Louis was idle and the lead went to 4½ over Boston and 6½ over the Cardinals. However, Pete Reiser, who always played every play as though it were the grand finale of his career, made a diving catch and hurt his shoulder.

The next night the Dodgers beat the Reds in Cincinnati 12–1. It was easy for Branca to pitch his sixteenth victory. Little old Crosley Field fitted in 31,808. I'm noting some attendance figures on this western swing to give an idea of how excited the fans were to see this Brooklyn team that ran, slashed, fielded, hit and often won despite a shaky pitching staff—and had Jackie Robinson playing first base, knocking the cover off the ball and running the bases as nobody had ever seen them run. Jackie's dancing off first base, dancing off, dashing back, dancing off, breaking for second kept the stands in an uproar, and upset many an opposing veteran player.

The Dodgers won the next 2 games at Cincinnati to make it 6 straight, and took the train for Pittsburgh. Friday, July 25, a season's record crowd of 42,017 overflowed onto the outfield grass to see Harry Taylor beat the Pirates 4–1 and run the string to 7. Correction, 6, not 7. Ford Frick, president of the league, after reviewing the circumstances of umpire Reardon ruling a home run and causing Northey to slow down and be out, ordered the game replayed in full. Branch Rickey announced it would be played on the night of August 18, when the Cardinals were again in Brooklyn. There was already an afternoon game scheduled for that date. Before certain writers could point out that skinflint Rickey was going to gain another paid crowd of plus 30,000 to enrich his coffers, Rickey announced that all receipts for the replay game would go to the Brooklyn War Memorial Fund. Frick's upholding of managing Dyer's appeal also cut a game off the Brooklyn lead, reducing it to 5½ over St. Louis.

The Dodgers just kept playing. They knocked off the Pirates in a single game Saturday, with a crowd of 24,937 on hand. The next day, Sunday, was wild. An even bigger crowd—42,716—overflowed onto the outfield grass to see a doubleheader. The Dodgers won both to make it 9 in a row. The Braves beat the Cardinals. The Dodgers were plus 7 over the Redbirds. The 3 dates at Pittsburgh drew 102,336 . . . you had to be with the Dodgers in 1947 to know what an attraction Jackie Robinson was.

St. Louis was watching . . . 3 games, big crowds, and the Cardinals knew they had to pull down the Dodgers. Old man Shotton was unimpressed by it all. He didn't need to say something like, "Just play your regular game." His calmness spoke all that was necessary. The Dodgers went into St. Louis and swept the series. They came out of there July 31 with their winning streak upped to 13, their margin over St. Louis a resounding 10. One night game drew 31,709, and the other night game drew the season's record of 32,419. There was an afternoon game record crowd of 21,873—and remember, it is hot in St. Louis on an afternoon—July 31. Hot? Before MacPhail introduced night ball, if you could play a season at St. Louis, or Cincinnati, then forevermore you need have no fear of hellfire.

The crowd figures—the crowds Robinson and the Dodgers drew—seem small today. Today we have new parks with vastly more seating space. All Jackie and the Dodgers did in 1947 was overflow all the ball parks then in the league. There is no way to know how many fans were unable to get into those old parks to see him.

Burt Shotton was a hard man for many of the writers to cover. Shotton didn't spout long sentences. He didn't talk and talk until he had practically given the story to the writers. Shotton believed it was up to the writers to write their own material. As the winning streak went along he would say something like this, "We'll win some—we'll lose some—so will St. Louis—we'll have to see how it comes out." That, in essence, is a pennant race. Shotton was the same when the team was winning as when it was losing. Play one game at a time. Play your regular game. Don't get excited. Go out there and play. Don't look at the scoreboard. Play your own game.

Shotton's statement, "We'll lose some," came true as soon as the Dodgers got to Chicago. The Cubs rudely notified the Dodgers that the dog days of August were here. The Little Bears swept the 3-game series and chewed up the pitching staff. Shotton used four in the first game, seven in the second, and had his ace, Ralph Branca, beaten in the third—and beaten by Johnny Schmitz with a shutout. The 3 afternoon games in Chicago drew 99,547 paid, plus thousands of women on a Ladies' Day. St. Louis made hay, winning every time the Dodgers lost. The Cardinals trailed now by 7, picking up 3 games in three days.

August 2 was Army Air Forces Celebration Day, and Leo Durocher was invited to appear at San Antonio, Texas. The papers the next day quoted Durocher at length . . . that he hoped to be back at Brooklyn as manager next year . . . that "Burt Shotton is a great guy, and he knows baseball—but he doesn't want to manage the club. He doesn't even want to wear a Dodger uniform."

Shotton merely said in response, "I think I can do a better job managing the Dodgers in civilian clothes. I've never planned to go on the coaching lines. I feel I can do a better job of managing by remaining on the bench at all times." That's all he said. Nothing else. No mention of Durocher or of next year.

Add it up: Durocher, out of baseball for the first time in his adult life, not a manager of a big-league team for the first time in nine years, and smarting under Chandler's suspension—the Dodgers leading the Cardinals, and he wasn't part of it. Playing golf every day in Los Angeles wasn't nearly as exciting as leading a big-league team to a pennant . . . Shotton, back in baseball again, and in his old age in charge of a big-league team that might very well win the pennant—and that was just what Shotton had every intention of doing. Shotton had some bad ball clubs to manage at Philadelphia; now, for the first time, he had

a fine team with some stars. Shotton had had a taste of retirement in Bartow, Florida, a small inland town in flat country,
where it got as hot in summer as it did in St. Louis. Bartow
wasn't Brooklyn, New York, Chicago, Cincinnati, Boston, Philadelphia, St. Louis, Pittsburgh—trains—hotels—taxies—crowds—
excitement—writers—radio. Bartow could wait. No hurry. . . .
Rickey, torn between Durocher whom he'd nurtured since 1933,
whose suspension he was trying to get Chandler to lift, to whom
he was paying full salary, and Shotton, who had dropped everything when Rickey called and taken the managing job of the
Dodgers without warning, when the team needed a manager
worse than any big-league team ever needed a commanding
hand, and now had the team in first place. . . . Walter O'Malley, in the silence of the background, wishing, no doubt, that
Durocher would never come back, and not enamored of Shotton
—Shotton was Rickey's man. (O'Malley had to wait until after
the 1950 season—then he retired Shotton to Bartow perma-
nently.)

After Chicago, the Dodgers had to grab a train for Boston and
Johnny Sain and Warren Spahn. The schedule had to be played
out. The first game went ten innings before the Dodgers won it
4-2. Dixie Walker had 4 hits, one being his one hundredth career home run. Hugh Casey saved it in relief and got his eighth
win. Pete Reiser was back in center. Jackie Robinson broke the
back of the Boston rally in the last of the tenth. The Braves had
the tying runs at first and second with nobody out. A bunt was
pushed toward first. Robinson charged, scooped, and in the same
rapid motion fired the ball to third, just forcing the lead runner.
That killed the rally. The conservative and scrupulously accurate
Roscoe McGowen of the New York *Times*, which doesn't permit
flowery language, wrote, "It was a fine play."

It was a 4-game series at Boston, and for the Dodgers the picnic was over. Mr. John Sain won the second game for his fifth
straight and fifteenth of the year. St. Louis won at Chicago, their
fifth straight. Mr. Warren Spahn in the third game walked away
with it, Pete Reiser had to leave in the middle of it—he was ill.
The Cardinals won again at Chicago. Red Barrett beat Harry
Taylor in the fourth game, the Cardinals won their seventh
straight, and were now trailing the Dodgers by 4, and it was

only August 7. St. Louis had gained 6 games while the Dodgers were losing 6 of 7. The only fairly happy man on the train ride down to New York was road secretary Harold Parrott. He had a check worth taking home—attendance for the 4 games at Boston, in that little old ball park, totaled 103,038 paid.

Ebbets Field looked most welcome. The last western trip, which had begun in such fine fettle, had ended sourly—6 losses out of 7 while the Cards were winning 7 of 7. The Phillies were the visitors, and 32,170 of the faithful paid to see their Dodgers. Ralph Branca sent everybody but the Phillies home happy with a 5–0 beauty—his seventeenth win and fifth shutout. Inasmuch as St. Louis won its eighth in a row, the win at Brooklyn was useful.

Another cat came back. Early in the year Rickey had sold Howard Schultz to Philadelphia. In the second game of the series Schultz hit a grand slam home run which beat Vic Lombardi. The borough didn't mourn unduly—the Cardinals finally lost.

Joe Hatten pitched a gem in the Sunday single, 2–0. However, the Cardinals won 2 games at Pittsburgh, to get closer—3½ back with plenty of time left. The Cardinals had another trip to Brooklyn, and the Dodgers had to beard the lion again at St. Louis. St. Louis was back in the race, winning 10 out of 11. Monday was an off-day at Brooklyn, but not at Pittsburgh. St. Louis won again—11 of 12. Only 3 games back . . . plenty of time. And the Cardinals would be at Brooklyn in a week. Seven more days. The fans at Brooklyn knew it—the park was already sold out.

The Braves came in and beat Branca and the Dodgers while 33,794 suffered in the tightly packed stands. The rest of the week ran along. The St. Louis series was coming up, starting with an afternoon game, then with the appeal replay that night. When the series began the margin was 4½ in Brooklyn's favor.

August 18. Monday afternoon, probably the worst time to play a game and hope for a crowd. Monday afternoon, and with another game that night—yet 32,781 paid to be there. Several hours later 33,723 jammed into Ebbets Field for the night game —66,504 paid for the 2 games. The Dodgers won them both. This made it 5 straight Dodger wins over the Cardinals. That is the ideal way of nailing down a pennant: beat your rival for yourself; you can't trust other people to do that job for you. And especially since St. Louis had been such a nemesis for Brooklyn the preceding few years. A little more breathing room between first and second place—6½ games. If I had wanted Cardinal manager Dyer's autograph, I wouldn't have asked him for it that Monday night.

St. Louis wasn't through. The Cards whacked the Dodgers Tuesday 11–3, cutting the differential to 5½, with 33,465 crowded into Ebbets Field. Game four went twelve innings before St. Louis won it 3–2 to even the series and cut the margin back to a reachable 4½ games. Whitey Kurowski hit a home run off relief pitcher Hugh Casey to decide it. The paid attendance for the 4 games was 125,751. Had there been unlimited seats the total might have topped a million for the 4 games.

In the seventh inning of that fourth game, the career of Jackie Robinson came within an inch of being ended.

I saw it happen, and of all the incidents in this book, this is the one I wish to be most careful with. My memory is of Country Slaughter running as hard as he could to first base, trying to beat out an infield ground ball . . . of Jackie Robinson with his foot on the inside of the bag, reaching out into the infield to take the throw, which he got just before Slaughter reached first . . . of Robinson suddenly hopping around with his right foot in the air . . . of trainer Doc Wendler running to Robinson, getting him to sit down, take off his shoe and stocking . . . working on his foot . . . of Robinson pulling his stocking back on, then his shoe, and testing his foot . . . then continuing to play. Slaughter returned to his dugout without pausing to see if Robinson was hurt or not. I remember clearly the Dodgers were thoroughly aroused and very angry.

There was no love lost between the two clubs. Early in the season Stanley Woodward, sports editor of the New York *Herald Tribune,* exposed a plot by some of the Cardinals to strike, to refuse to take the field of St. Louis, if Robinson played. Many of the Cardinals, including Slaughter, were from the South. It was not to my knowledge ever written that Slaughter was the ringleader in that threatened strike, but the writers and the players said he was. Apparently Slaughter had made it no secret he wanted no part of playing in a game with a black man. Slaughter was a hard-nosed player—rough, ready for trouble, and he would step on his mother to win a ball game. Pete Rose today is a direct descendant of Slaughter.

Here is what Roscoe McGowen, a dispassionate veteran writer, said in the New York *Times*, the next morning:

". . . Robinson ran to the bag. Slaughter's foot landed on Robinson's right foot, which was not on the bag but against it. Jackie hopped around a minute or two and Doc Wendler came out, but Robbie stayed in the game, apparently not seriously hurt."

Harold Parrott, then road secretary, wrote in his book *The Lords of Baseball*:

". . . Enos Slaughter, the Cardinal outfielder, came down hard with his spikes on the back of Robinson's leg as Jackie stretched out to take a throw at first base. Slaughter had crossed first base perhaps two thousand times before that and had never cut a defenseless first baseman. But hate was running high in that first Robinson year, and his career was close to ending at the moment Slaughter narrowly missed the Achilles tendon."

Robinson was closer to the play than anyone else. It was his right foot that got stepped on. This is what he wrote in his book *I Never Had It Made*:

"The 1947 season was memorable in many ways. Some of the incidents that occurred resulted in far-reaching changes for the club. In late August we played the St. Louis Cardinals. In one of our last games, Enos Slaughter, a Cardinal outfielder, hit a ground ball. As I took the throw at first from the infielder, Slaughter deliberately went for my leg instead of the base and spiked me rather severely.

"It was an act that unified the Dodger team. Teammates such as Hugh Casey came charging out on the field to protest. The team had always been close to first place in the pennant race, but the spirit shown after the Slaughter incident strengthened our resolve and made us go on to win the pennant. The next time we played the Cardinals we won two of the three games."

I have no way of knowing what was in Slaughter's mind. I never asked him his intentions, and we were associates as player/broadcaster many years thereafter. My guess is that if he had been asked if he cut Robinson deliberately, he would have spit tobacco juice and answered two words in that harsh voice of his that rasped and grated, "Hell no."

Tradition is powerful and lives on long after actual events. When Lylah and I were in Jerusalem in 1959, after we had finished a USO tour of the Mediterranean, I was struck that our guide constantly repeated, "Tradition says this was this place," and, "Tradition says that this was that place."

Tradition had it then, and still has it, that Enos Slaughter led the St. Louis Cardinals in their threatened revolt against Robinson, and that Slaughter intended to spike Robinson on that play at first base. That's the tradition. Baseball writers are human beings, swayed by emotions and memories. Slaughter has never been voted into the Hall of Fame. In my opinion his playing ability, his spirit on the field, and his value to championship teams should have merited his election. I suspect Slaughter's failure of Cooperstown selection stems from the tradition of those two key events in 1947. Certain writers have told me so. Jackie Robinson has more friends and admirers today than he had in 1947.

The Dodgers were tremendously relieved that Robinson would be able to stay in the lineup. It was a tough game to lose to St. Louis in those twelve grueling innings. Also, it was announced that Harry Taylor, who'd been nursing a sore arm, was to go to Johns Hopkins Hospital. Shotton said one grim sentence, "We'll get another pitcher somewhere." The club dressed and went home. Ewell Blackwell and Cincinnati would be at Ebbets Field the next day.

The train got back on the track. The Dodgers won their next 5. They began the streak with a decisive win over Blackwell, who was gunning for his twentieth of the season. However, in that game Pete Reiser slid home when Blackwell was covering the plate and sent the tall pitcher sprawling. The Reds protested that Reiser had been unnecessarily rough. . . . In the getaway game of the series Bert Haas of the Reds slid very hard into Pee Wee Reese on a play at second base, spiking Reese, putting the shortstop and key man of the Dodgers out of action for an indefinite time. Eddie Stanky also got spiked by a Redleg and had to leave the game. That removed the second-base combination. Bench strength saved the emergency—Stan Rojek went to short, Eddie Miksis to second, and they held the fort efficiently until Reese and Stanky got back.

The Pirates were next at Brooklyn, on Sunday August 24. This is a date to be kept in mind—more baseball history was being written. There were 33,207 in the ball park, but that wasn't history—the Dodgers were packing all the parks, especially their own. Branca won his eighteenth, with a save from Casey—but that wasn't news. These were the two big pitchers for Brooklyn. St. Louis was rumbling along too, with Stan Musial swinging a red-hot bat, but that wasn't news.

Shotton had said, "We'll get another pitcher somewhere." Branch Rickey made two moves. He brought up right-hander Phil Haugstad from St. Paul, and after flying to Memphis for a personal inspection, Rickey bought pitcher Dan Bankhead, to report immediately.

This was history. August 24, 1947. Bankhead was the first black pitcher in the big leagues. Rickey purchased Bankhead from the Memphis Red Sox of the Negro American League. Bankhead was twenty-six years old, 6'1", 185. He had served in the Marines during the war. He was a quiet, pleasant man. Both Bankhead and Haugstad were at Ebbets Field the next day.

Life can move mighty fast sometimes. Bankhead pitched a full game at Memphis Saturday night, which Rickey saw. Bankhead traveled to Brooklyn Sunday. He was in a Dodger uniform Monday. He was in the ball game against Pittsburgh Tuesday despite short rest. Hal Gregg had started for the Dodgers, and the Pirates greeted him like a long-lost cousin. Shotton, seeing this was going to be another one of those things (the Pirates won it 16-3) and needing bodies, figured this was as good a spot as any for Bankhead's baptism of big-league fire. Bankhead was in the game three and a third innings and was hit hard. But it meant nothing except that it got him started. His first pitching assignment was now behind him. However, he added material for the trivia department . . . not only was he the first black pitcher in the major leagues, but on his first at bat he hit a home run. Up at Boston, Musial hit one for the Cardinals.

Big excitement was brewing at Ebbets Field, which again wasn't news. There wasn't a time in all of 1947 that something wasn't cooking on the front burners, and often boiling over. Now the Giants were coming in for Friday night and Saturday and Sunday afternoons. No seats available. Phones off the hooks. The high-water mark in all baseball history was a game between the Dodgers and the Giants, especially at Ebbets Field. When Walter O'Malley took the Dodgers to Los Angeles and set it up for Horace Stoneham to move the Giants at the same time to San Francisco, something vital, precious and never replaceable went out of baseball.

The Dodgers sent Flatbush Fever higher than any thermometer could register. They beat the Giants all 3 games. Brooklyn was boiling. Branca won his nineteenth. Stanky returned to second, and teamed well with Rojek; Reese was still out of it. The Friday night crowd was 34,568, and Saturday afternoon it was 37,512. How did they get in? How many were turned away? Sunday was a mere 33,837. The total was 105,917! The Giants hit enough home runs in the series to tie the major-league mark of the 1936 Yankees, with 182, but that was scant consolation for manager Mel Ott and his noble athletes. The Cardinals lost ground as the Dodgers now surged to win 9 out of 11. The margin was 7½ games.

HEY RED!

The Monday following the tremendous series with the Giants was Labor Day. Anybody who was at Ebbets Field that morning won't forget it. I won't. I learned a lesson. I took a beating which I had asked for.

Ebbets Field held about 32,000. Rickey, instead of playing a Labor Day doubleheader with the Phillies, scheduled a morning game and an afternoon game—2 separate games, two separate admissions. Sunday noon I talked with Jack Collins, the business manager in charge of ticket sales, and Jack was emphatic that the morning game the next day would not draw well. There had been little advance sale. Jack recalled previous morning games at Brooklyn and said none of them drew well—wrong time for a game, wrong time for fans to get up, have breakfast, and get to the park. There was tremendous interest in the afternoon game, big advance, but the morning game was a nothing. "Plenty of seats" for it.

Baseball excitement in Brooklyn that weekend was as high as an angry cat's back. There were jam-packed thousands in the park, but as the Dodgers and the Giants fought it out Sunday afternoon, there were millions listening on radio. You couldn't go anywhere in the borough without hearing the game.

On the broadcast, I talked about the morning game the next day. There was nothing much to say about the afternoon game except that only bleacher seats and standing room would be available. I told the audience Jack Collins had said there had been no real advance sale for the morning game, that there would be "plenty of seats." I didn't use numbers, I kept saying there would be "plenty of seats," just come to the park and come in. Then I got inspired and said something like this, and said it over and over . . . "Why don't you fathers give the little woman the morning off . . . why don't you bring the kids out to Ebbets Field . . . 'plenty of seats' . . . easy way to take care of the youngsters . . . see a ball game for yourself . . . Mom will sure appreciate getting a few hours to catch her breath . . . 'plenty of seats.'" That was when I put my foot in my mouth—I kept saying there would be "plenty of seats" for the morning game. I sold two things: "plenty of seats" and "bring the kids with you and give your wife a break."

Monday morning I drove from home in Westchester County as I would for any game. I allowed sufficient time to get to the park, check the two managers, get the batting orders, and find out the pitchers for the afternoon game. I had a reserved parking place in an open lot across the street from Ebbets Field.

About two or three blocks from the park there were people all over the streets. They started yelling at me. "Hey Red, where are those plenty of seats?" I was stalled by the crowd. The police got me through and to the parking place. Then they forced a path for me to the players' entrance to the park. I was abused and cursed. Some people shoved me. Without the police I'd have been in serious trouble. Angry people were milling around. Children were crying. I couldn't understand what was going on, and why the people weren't going into the ball park. I had been a very popular figure in Brooklyn since the broadcasts began in 1939. Now I was a bum. I had done these people in. They were shouting at me, blaming me.

Once I got inside I found the trouble. Jack Collins lived out on Long Island. He hadn't expected many people for the morning game; he had hired only a few ticket sellers and had left orders that only a few gates were to be opened at nine o'clock. He had not arrived, nobody was in charge and nobody was going to change Collins's orders. Thousands were milling around outside with the gates closed.

It was a dangerous situation. Men were getting mad, getting frightened that their children, caught in the crowd, would get stepped on, trampled, or badly upset by the pushing, shoving bodies.

Riot squads were ordered to Ebbets Field. It was learned later that fans had started arriving at five o'clock that morning. The police reported that by eight-fifteen there were thousands pressed against the closed gates unable to get back out because of thousands more pressing in from the outside. Finally the gates were opened at nine o'clock. People swarmed in. Some 27,000 tickets were sold between nine and ten. For an hour or so after the game got underway fans continued filling the park, coming in and coming in. Many men in the upper stands who could see into the radio booth, yelled and shook their fists at me throughout the game. Their angry cry was, "Hey Red . . . plenty of seats, huh? . . . You said plenty of seats."

The paid attendance for the morning game was 28,153. Thousands—nobody knows how many thousands—were turned away, unable to get in. The police kept turning back people once it became a mob scene at Ebbets Field. It got too dangerous. The riot police wanted no more people descending upon the place.

As expected, there were 35,468 for the afternoon game . . . 63,621 for the day for the 2 games. The Dodgers beat the Phillies 5–0 in the morning; Joe Hatten got the win. The Phillies reversed it in the afternoon; Ralph Branca lost it. The Cardinals won 2 games from the Pirates and cut the lead to 6½ with a month to go.

The next day the New York *Times* gave more space to the mob than to both ball games. The sports page carried a picture, not of an athlete in action, but of thousands jammed together outside Ebbets Field. The story of the mob scene was almost as lengthy as the accounting of both games.

In those days radio fellows didn't get much space in the newspapers. But I was in the *Times* account:

". . . sales talk broadcast by Red Barber during the Sunday game with the Giants . . . repeatedly Barber had assured his listeners . . . 'a small crowd is expected tomorrow morning, business manager Jack Collins tells me. So come right on out and see the morning game. There will be plenty of seats.'"

Roscoe McGowen wrote the story for the *Times*. He could have quoted what I broadcast much more in detail, except he was working in the press box all Sunday afternoon and didn't hear what I said. He was told by somebody.

I was sick. I had been frightened coming through that crowd even with police clearing the way. I knew I had told them to come, that it would be a great morning. "Plenty of seats . . . bring the kids." I felt deeply responsible. Also, I was as angry as I have ever been—why the hell wasn't the ball park opened? Why didn't somebody see what was building up and take immediate steps to get all the gates opened and let those people, those men with small children, into the ball park even if they had to let them come in free of charge? Jack Collins wasn't there and his few people who were there didn't act. Nobody, from all I could discover, was strong enough to risk disturbing Collins at his home with a phone call. Branch Rickey was in Maryland for the weekend.

As soon as I got on the air for the morning game I reported the mob scene, I said that Collins had not been on hand, that the gates were not opened until nine, and I said I was sorry. Precious good that did. I promised the audience that morning, and I never broke that promise in the nearly twenty years I continued to broadcast baseball, that never again, under any circumstances, would I ever announce there would be "plenty of seats."

From then on I always said that the business office stated there were so many such-and-such seats available. I gave the precise numbers. That and nothing more.

Rickey hurried back to Brooklyn and made elaborate apologies to the public for the staff breakdown, and promised it would never happen again. It was a nightmare. It should not have happened. I still don't believe it did. But it did. I don't think any child was badly hurt. Hey Red!

The next ten days did it. The Dodgers had to play the dangerous Giants 4 games in four days at the Polo Grounds, then 2 games at Chicago, then the series of the year, 3 games in three days at St. Louis. The Dodgers were going to have to do it on the road, far from the rabid support of the fans in Brooklyn.

Vic Lombardi, who had a hex on the Giants, beat them 2–0 to open the series. This made the small left-hander 10–1 lifetime over New York. Pee Wee Reese returned to short, and hit a home run. Game two, Friday, was played in mud, and the Dodgers slogged through it 7–6. Shotton had to commit Behrman, Hatten, Haugstad and Casey. Branca started the third game on Saturday, trying for the second time for his twentieth victory. The Giants beat him. Walker Cooper hit 2 home runs. Ray Poat, just purchased, pitched for the Giants. The Cardinals defeated the Reds in thirteen innings to be minus 6. The 3 games coming up in St. Louis would be decisive.

The Giants won the last game 7–6. Johnny Mize hit his forty-seventh home run for the winning edge. St. Louis split a double-header with Cincinnati, and cut the margin to 5½. To make matters more serious, Jackie Robinson missed his first game of the season. He came up with a bad back. Harry Lavagetto, who'd never been at first base, played it. The old pro did well. Shotton used five pitchers. The 4 games drew 166,404 paid.

The Dodgers took the train for Chicago, St. Louis, Cincinnati, and Pittsburgh. The 3 games at St. Louis . . . that would be it. A sweep for St. Louis and they might very well go all the way . . . 2 out of 3 would be a boost. The Dodgers had to go into St. Louis and win at least 2 to beat back the Cardinals. The writers asked Shotton for a statement as the team headed for the western half of the league. Shotton responded with his type of statement, which drove some writers up the wall.

"If we win," Shotton said, "we win. If not, what of it?"

Shotton didn't get excited, and he didn't want his ball club to get in a tizzy.

There were 2 games in Chicago. The first one shook the Dodgers badly. The crowd was waiting at Wrigley Field—25,983 for a Tuesday afternoon single. Lombardi had the Cubs shut out into the eighth inning with just 1 hit. The Dodgers led 3–0. Jackie was still hurt, Lavagetto was again at first, but all seemed well.

Bob Scheffing and Bill Nicholson singled. The next batter hit a perfect double-play grounder to Reese. But Pee Wee booted it, and with nobody out the bases were loaded. The Cubs had a rookie, Cliff Aberson, whom they had just recalled from their Class A Des Moines farm team. Aberson had played halfback the year before for the Green Bay Packers. The Cubs put Aberson up to pinch-hit. He hit a grand slam home run. That was the game, 4–3. St. Louis won from Philadelphia. The lead was down to 4½, with those 3 games coming up at Sportsman's Park.

After the dramatic denouement the writers came into the clubhouse. Shotton as usual was sitting on a trunk, sipping a Coca-Cola. What did he think?

"Vic's pitch to Aberson," said the Old Man, "was exactly what I told him to throw—a curve, low and inside." He took another sip of his Coke. That was all.

Shotton was not a second-guesser, not an alibi man. Further, he was the manager and he took the weight from his players' shoulders. No moaning in the clubhouse. The game was gone. Another one tomorrow. We'll get to St. Louis when we get to St. Louis.

In the second game at Chicago, Joe Hatten won with a save from Casey. Robinson was back at first. Shotton made one significant change. For the first time he placed Jackie in the batting order hitting fourth.

The Cardinals won too, the teams remained separated by 4½ games, and the Dodgers rode through the gathering night to St. Louis. Now it would be head-to-head: Thursday and Friday nights, and Saturday afternoon. It was sizzling hot in St. Louis. Tickets were scarce. This series needed no ballyhoo. Just turn the two teams loose. One team had to get hurt.

Edward VIII said it when he began his radio abdication speech. "At long last. . . ." At long last the Dodgers and the Cardinals were face-to-face. This was the final meeting of the year of the two bitter rivals. All of St. Louis was primed for a sweep. On Thursday night September 11, 29,452 crowded in. Shotton had Ralph Branca ready. Eddie Dyer had the Little Cat, Harry Brecheen, hero of the last World Series, as his starting pitcher.

Trouble threatened in the second inning. Trouble was expected. The teams were playing for the entire year's work. The Dodgers were still smarting from losing the 3-game play-off series the year before to the Cardinals; in fact, Brecheen ended that series when he struck out Howard Schultz with the bases loaded. The Cardinals were defending world champions and they wanted to muscle back into the World Series again. The World Series meant glamour, and more than that, it meant extra money. In those days of basic baseball, before bonus players and free agents and rich ego-mad owners, the only extra money a player got at the season's end was from the World Series. That's what you trained for, worked for, sweated for, waited for—the World Series. Now it was on the line in St. Louis in the Missouri heat and humidity of mid-September.

In the second inning the trouble started. It wasn't Slaughter this time, but catcher Joe Garagiola. Garagiola ran to first base trying to beat a double-play throw. He didn't beat the throw but he stepped on Robinson's foot, which again, as in the Slaughter incident at Brooklyn the month before, was against the bag, not on the bag.

The next inning Jackie came to bat. He was seething, remembering the close call he had suffered when Slaughter's spikes just missed his Achilles tendon. Robinson forgot his pledge to Rickey of turning the other cheek for three years. The two spoke angrily and menaced each other. Robinson and Garagiola. Plate umpire Beans Reardon wasted no time. He knew it wouldn't take much to have a brawl on the field, which might well lead to a riot in the ball park. Reardon stepped between the two men, pushed them apart, and warned them that another word, or another threatening move, and both would be thrown out of the game. The stands were in an uproar. Reardon acted in the nick of time.

Robinson batted again in the fifth inning. He let his bat speak for him. A home run with one man on. Those were the first 2 Dodger runs. In the eighth, with the bases full, Lavagetto pinch-hit a single for 2 more. The Dodgers won it 4–3. Branca got his twentieth with a save from Hank Behrman in the eighth. Brecheen was beaten. The lead went to 5½ with 15 games remaining. There would be no disaster in St. Louis for the Dodgers.

It still wasn't over. Friday night 31,957 jammed in to see a wild game with an even wilder ninth inning. The Dodgers got 4 in the top of the ninth, but the Cardinals bounced back with 2 to win it 8–7 and reduce the lead to 4½. Shotton committed six pitchers, including Ralph Branca who had started the night before. Branca faced only one man, Enos Slaughter, who singled and drove in the tying and winning runs. All St. Louis was hot again. The last game was mortal.

Saturday morning Andy High, a veteran scout for the Dodgers, came to the hotel to see Shotton. Shotton was in no mood to cut up old touches.

"Brooklyn must have the worst scouts in the world," Shotton began. "All I hear in reports on pitchers is 'They can't help you.' You guys don't seem to know how much I need help."

The final encounter was Saturday afternoon. The record crowd for the season at St. Louis overflowed the creaking old stands. The paid was 33,510—the total for the 3 games was 94,919. The Dodgers, with Jackie Robinson, had drawn on the road 1,735,356, which was some 35,000 more than the paid total at Ebbets Field. This was still the era of small, old ball parks. It was an exciting team to watch—I never saw one more exciting. They battled on the field while Shotton sat calmly in the dugout keeping score.

It was another wild-and-woolly 8–7 struggle, but the Dodgers this time had the 8. However, the Cardinals scored 3 in the last of the ninth, and had 2 men on base when Dixie Walker caught the last out in right field. I don't believe a single fan in any of the 3 games left before the final out was made. Lombardi got the win with help from Gregg and Behrman—only three pitchers this time.

The Cardinals didn't get their needed sweep. They didn't get a 2–1 edge. The Dodgers came to town with a 4½-game lead and left with the margin 5½, and with 13 games remaining. Time and the Giants were now with Brooklyn.

The meat ax fell the next day. The Giants came to St. Louis, and Larry Jansen beat the Cardinals 9–1 for his nineteenth win. On hand were 29,950 still hopeful Cardinal fans, and most of them left early. The Giants crushed the Cardinals with a barrage of 2 home runs, 3 triples and 8 singles. There wasn't a big crowd again at St. Louis the rest of the season.

James P. Dawson, traveling with the Giants for the New York *Times,* began his story:

"Take it away Brooklyn! And when the pennant is flying in

Flatbush, don't forget the Giants were in there swinging for you all the time."

The Dodgers attended strictly to their own business in a Sunday doubleheader at Cincinnati. Here is how Roscoe McGowen of the *Times,* covering the Dodgers, began his story:

"The Dodgers virtually completed wrapping up the National League pennant today when they swept a doubleheader with the Reds, 13–2 and 6–3, before 34,622 cash clients and moved seven full games ahead of the Cardinals."

The Dodgers had been in first place since July 6. Finally they had a lock on it. Any combination of 7 Brooklyn wins and/or St. Louis defeats would do it. The Brooklyn office at 215 Montague Street made the joyful announcement that the Dodgers were ready to receive mail orders for World Series tickets.

It was downhill. The thoughtful Giants on Monday beat the Cardinals again with only 5,914 in the stands. The Dodgers relished an open day. The magic number was 6. The Giants won Tuesday to make it a sweep at St. Louis. Branca won his twenty-first over the Reds, and the number was 4. The Cardinals were crushed—they had had their final chance against the Dodgers. Now the Cardinals had had it.

The Pirates were down in the second division—in fact were in eighth place—but the people in Pittsburgh still wanted to see this Brooklyn team. Wednesday 33,916 filled Forbes Field. The Dodgers won 4–2. Behrman saved it with strikeouts in the ninth inning of both Ralph Kiner and Hank Greenberg. The Boston Braves added indigo to the St. Louis blues with a 10–8 win. The Cardinals were finished. The number was 2. Back at 215 Montague Street the Dodgers announced they would accept no additional mail orders for Series seats.

The Dodgers had a game left at Pittsburgh before taking the overnight train to Penn Station. If they won and St. Louis lost, it would be a train ride home to tell the neighbors about all winter. Road secretary Harold Parrott would have the champagne available, and on ice. Private Pullmans for the night, after a long tough pennant race, with a right honorable spender in the traveling secretary, with a guaranteed sober engineer on the head end, was a prospect devoutly to be desired. St. Louis did its part—it lost. The Pirates, however—nothing personal, just business—were spoilers. Shotton kept feeding in a half-dozen pitchers, and with Clyde King on the mound the Pirates came to bat in the last of the ninth behind 7–6. A man got on, and Wally Westlake hit a home run. That made it a dry run through the night. A tie was clinched, but not the pennant.

Ralph Kiner got into the record books. He hit his fiftieth home run, joining Babe Ruth, Jimmy Foxx, Hank Greenberg and Hack Wilson as the only men until then to hit half a hundred round-trippers in a season. Johnny Mize of the Giants joined the club two days later. Kiner and Mize each hit 51 for the year.

It was tantalizing. The number was 1 but it came hard. The Dodgers got off the train at Penn Station well rested and clear-eyed. It was Friday and no game was scheduled. St. Louis was sadistic, winning at Chicago to keep the Dodgers in suspended animation. Still the magic number held at 1.

Saturday September 20, began sadly with the news that Fiorello H. La Guardia, former three-time mayor of New York City and a genuine baseball fan, died before morning with cancer. La Guardia had gone to Cincinnati in 1939 to see the conclusion of the World Series. The Yankees wrapped it up in 4 straight. Lou Gehrig had received his sentence of impending death at the Mayo Clinic in early May. He played his last game in that awesome endurance streak of 2,130 straight games April 30. The next morning Lou asked manager Joe McCarthy to take him out of the lineup. Gehrig was the captain of the Yankees, and he stayed with the team the rest of the season, putting on his uniform, taking the batting orders to home plate before each game, running out his string as best he could. He asked no sympathy, accepted none. He went knowingly to his fate.

Gehrig and Bill Dickey were roommates on the road. They were fast friends. On the Yankee Special train after the 1939 Series was over, and Gehrig had worn his Yankee uniform for the last time as field captain, Dickey and I happened to be seated at the same table in the diner. Gehrig had his dinner brought to his room—walking a fast-moving train would have been too much for him. Dickey and I finished our meal at the same time and he said, "Let's go see Lou." We walked to his room, pushed the buzzer, and entered. Mayor La Guardia was sitting with Gehrig. After a few quick, routine pleasantries the mayor said, and he was beaming:

"Bill, Lou has accepted my offer to be a member of the parole commission. He is going to help decide what men should be let out of prison on parole, and which men should stay behind bars."

The mayor had not come to Gehrig to spread sadness about his fatal affliction. La Guardia had said, in effect, "Lou, what days you have left . . . what strength you have left . . . give them to your less fortunate fellow men." This Gehrig did. I've always remembered that moment: Gehrig sat, looked out the window into the darkness of night, into the darkness of death, and after having agreed to give back what he had left to give back, had the sweetest smile I ever saw on a strong man's face.

Gehrig and La Guardia sitting together on a train. Gehrig died June 2, 1941. He didn't have much time left. La Guardia had six more years before the sand ran through his hourglass.

This Saturday was the first chance for the Brooklyn fans to see for themselves their Dodgers who were 1 game shy of clinching the pennant. Just 1 game—a loss by the Cardinals, a win by the Dodgers. The Boston Braves were at Ebbets Field with their two splendid selfish men Johnny Sain and Warren Spahn (selfish men—that's what Casey Stengel called all pitchers), and 29,762 paid to be on hand when the Dodgers won. They wanted to be in on the celebration. They paid to jump and yell and pound on backs, be pounded, and storm the bars when the Dodgers won it by beating the Braves. But Brother Sain was his usual selfish self. He won his twentieth game, 8–1. St. Louis kept it going with another win in Chicago.

Branch Rickey uttered one word late that day. The word was "pitiful." He wasn't referring to the delay in the mathematical clinching—he knew that would have to come as day follows night. He wasn't referring to the fact that his Dodgers, before the home folks, instead of conducting their affairs as befitting the new champions of the league, had made four errors in the very first inning, plus another boot in the second inning, all of which put Mr. Sain in the catbird seat. He knew all ball clubs have off-days. No, what Mr. Rickey was referring to when he said with abiding sincerity, "pitiful," was the return of over $3 million in money for World Series seats at Brooklyn that could not be accepted. The small park was sold out as quick as a streak of lightning.

Sunday, this would be the day. Ralph Branca, the ace, was going to pitch against Warren Spahn. The pennant was surely going to be nailed down, and in Brooklyn, this very day. This had to be it, and 34,123 fought to get in. Shortly after Branca and Spahn matched arms, the scoreboard showed St. Louis was rained out in Chicago. Good. Just as it should be. Win it right here, right now. This was the day.

Casey Stengel spoke from long and bitter experience when he said all pitchers were selfish men. Warren Spahn sat on the Boston bench the day before and watched Sain win his twentieth. A pitcher wants to win 20 games a season above all else. Sain got his yesterday. Spahn wanted his today, and he got it. He not only whipped the Dodgers, he shut them out, 4–0. The magic number was still the smallest number possible, still 1. The Cardinals had nothing else to do but laugh, which I am certain they did on the train ride to St. Louis.

The Dodgers didn't have a game on Monday. The Cardinals in St. Louis had 2—one in the afternoon and a separate game at night with Chicago. The Cardinals won in the afternoon. The clincher had to come, but when? Hugh Casey had a bar and grill in Brooklyn, and many of the Dodgers with their wives assembled there that evening. An amazing thing happened—all the Dodgers became Cub fans. Johnny Schmitz was pitching for Chicago, and they were pulling for good old Johnny. The Cubs and Schmitz finally did it—they finished off St. Louis 6–3, and Brooklyn had a midnight celebration on its hands, all over the borough. Hugh Casey's bar and grill closed later than usual. Much later.

Rickey was telephoned at home. He said, "The flag was won when the team took two of three at St. Louis." I expect, knowing how he and Mrs. Rickey talked to each other, he repeated to her what he had said in July. "Jane . . . I don't have a World Series pitching staff." Now she agreed. It had required all that Robinson, Reese, Walker, Reiser, Edwards, Stanky, Jorgensen, Furillo, Hermanski, Lavagetto, Gionfriddo, Snider, Hodges, Rojek, Miksis, Bragan and the others could do to carry such shaky pitching, and carry it all season.

For the Dodgers it was tying up loose ends, resting the regulars, tuning the pitchers, and enjoying the satisfactions that come with a job well done over a long period of time. The Giants were at Ebbets Field Tuesday and Wednesday for the last 2 home games. It was Jackie Robinson Day Tuesday. Jackie was given speeches, gifts and an automobile—it was a different Tuesday from Tuesday April 15, five months before, when he played his first major-league game at Ebbets Field as the first black man in the big leagues, before 26,623 paid, got no hits, and the Dodgers had no manager.

Thursday the Dodgers were in Philadelphia, a lull before the storm hit downtown Brooklyn Friday. To add to the gathering tumult, Leo Durocher and Laraine arrived Thursday in New York. This was great stuff for the photographers. The Durochers had come for the World Series, and Leo stated openly that he wanted his job back in 1948 as manager of the Dodgers. Shotton had bailed out Rickey, brought order to a deeply disturbed team, and won the pennant. Now Durocher was back in town, his one-year suspension apparently nearing its end, and wanting what he regarded as his. Which man? Rickey would have to decide.

Durocher stayed out of Brooklyn Friday. It wasn't his day. It was Shotton's, and the Dodgers'. Some half a million people assembled to salute the ball club. The players rode in cars through blocks of waving, applauding fans. Shotton beamed and waved his hat—this was a long way from Bartow, Florida. The papers next day carried one picture after another of the crowds, of the motorcade, of the players, of Shotton. The New York *Times* said it was a "paper snowstorm."

When the motorcade reached Borough Hall, borough president John Cashmore gave watches to twenty-seven "heroes." The crowd was estimated at 500,000 . . . the number of police assigned to handle the crowd was 1,524. It was Brooklyn's day!

That day J. G. Taylor Spink, publisher and editor of *The Sporting News*, announced that Jackie Robinson was the paper's selection of "Rookie of the Year."

The Dodgers set all-time attendance records in the National League for fans on the road and at home. In the bandbox of Ebbets Field the total was 1,807,586.

As an idea of the drawing power of this Brooklyn club at home versus that of the Yankees at the Stadium—Yankee Stadium held over 2⅐ times the number of people that Ebbets Field could contain. For example: the first game of the World Series at the Stadium drew 73,365. The third game of the Series, which was the first at Brooklyn, drew 33,098 . . . no more room. For the season the Yankees had, all told, 2,200,369 or just 392,783 more than the Dodgers had at Ebbets Field. What if Yankee Stadium had been in Flatbush?

There was a New York *Times* story, in a box to itself, almost lost in the accounts of the victory celebration in Brooklyn, that marked the beginnings of what would shortly become the dominant element in all sports in the United States. I doubt that very many people read the small story, and of those who did read it, few understood what it meant.

The heading was, "Series to be Televised—2 Sponsors pay $65,000." The story said briefly that Gillette and Ford would televise the games and put them on all the video outlets along the eastern seaboard . . . that Chandler had asked $100,000 . . . that the Liebmann Brewery agreed to pay it, but Chandler then rejected the Liebmann offer and took the lesser figure because it would "not be good public relations for baseball to have the Series sponsored by the producer of an alcoholic beverage."

In the World Series of 1981, $65,000 wouldn't have been enough to buy even a half-minute commercial. The asking price for thirty-second commercials was $150,000 and twice that amount for a full minute. Miller Beer had not only two commercials but enough clout to freeze out all other beers, which made Miller a dominant sponsor.

Baseball is now paid such fortunes by the networks that it happily schedules the World Series to be played in television prime time and on Sunday afternoon. Television today routinely tells the colleges when to play football, moving games as it suits the TV schedules. In 1947 television wasn't even the tip of the tail of the dog—today television is the whole dog.

THE MOST EXCITING WORLD SERIES—
1947

Friday September 26, John Drebinger in the New York *Times* began his appraisal of the Series that would begin Tuesday at Yankee Stadium. Drebbie was not only a polished writer, he was also a veteran baseball observer with an acute sense of balance and value. In my years of reading baseball data, if I had to select one writer to cover an important game for me, it would be Drebbie.

The heading on his story:

"Greater Experience of Pitchers
Gives Yankees Edge on Defense"

The story began, "Pitching is easily the most vital single factor in World Series competition. Seldom have two hurling staffs been saddled with so many ifs and buts as those which Harris and Shotton will command in this struggle.

"The Dodgers have perhaps the youngest and most inexperienced group of starting hurlers ever to go to the mark."

Game One

Tuesday September 30, 1947, was clear with a light wind. The great triple-decked Stadium was gaily dressed in red, white and blue bunting, fourteen league pennants and ten world championship flags. A record crowd for a World Series surged in: 73,365, of which 7,000 were standees. Not only the Stadium but all the hotels in New York were jammed.

Dignitaries were a dime a dozen. Former President Herbert Hoover, New York Governor Thomas E. Dewey, Secretary of State George C. Marshall and former Secretary of War Robert Patterson (MacPhail's wartime boss) were down front. New York Mayor William O'Dwyer threw out the ceremonial first ball. Governors from Connecticut, Rhode Island, New Jersey and Pennsylvania were there.

Commissioner Chandler headed the baseball list: after all, he was in charge of the Series, and before the game he and MacPhail posed for the photographers hugging each other. Ford Frick and Will Harridge, presidents of the National and American Leagues respectively, had their box seats. Babe Ruth, Tris Speaker and Ty Cobb were surrounded by fans asking for autographs. Bill Terry, Rogers Hornsby and Ralph Kiner were seated snugly in the press box—they had special writing assignments. Cy Young was there, a spry eighty-year-old man, unknown to the crowd. Young won more games—511—than any pitcher. The first World Series was 1903 when the Boston Red Sox beat the Pittsburgh Pirates. Young pitched in 4 games for Boston and won 2 of them.

That first Opening Day World Series crowd in 1903 was 16,242. It would be twenty more years—1923—before Graham McNamee broadcast "live," from this same Yankee Stadium, the first World Series game on radio. Today, surrounded by over 73,000 strangers, Old Cy Young wouldn't have known or cared if someone had tried to tell him that today was the first time a World Series game would be aired on a new thing called television.

Radio . . . television . . . baseball . . . Yankee Stadium. Our civilization moves so rapidly, consuming carelessly as it goes. The human race waited all its time on earth until the late 1880s for a means of long-distance communication that did not require connecting wires. Shortly before the twentieth century Guglielmo Marconi, in Italy, began sending dots and dashes. He was the first to send the Morse Code through the air. His own government wasn't interested, but the British Admiralty was. The British Navy had long wanted a system of communication between ships, and between ships and the shore, that didn't need physical connections and that worked in fog, at night and in rain. . . . Touch a key and instantly the sound was heard at great distances. Wireless.

The first sporting event on "wireless" was in 1899, forty-eight years before radio and television would cover the 1947 Yankee-Dodger World Series. There was a great yacht race, the Kingstown Regatta, and the Dublin, Ireland, *Daily Express* decided to have bulletins sent to its newspaper offices *from the scene, by wireless*. The results were printed and the papers were being sold on the streets long before the yachts and the reporters returned to port. That did it. That fall the New York *Herald* brought Marconi and his equipment to this country to repeat his wireless coverage for the America's Cup Race. When 1900 dawned two months later it marked the century of the age of wireless.

Radio was the natural development. August 31, 1920, a weak station, 8MK in Detroit, operated by the Detroit *News,* broadcast returns of a local election. Then on November 2 came the landmark: KDKA in Pittsburgh broadcast the returns of the Harding-Cox presidential election. KDKA continued with daily programs. The first sporting event on radio was the Dempsey-Carpentier fight for RCA, July 2, 1921. On August 5, 1921, Harold Arlin, a foreman at Westinghouse, on KDKA broadcast the first baseball game—Philadelphia at Pittsburgh. That fall the World Series was on radio for the first time, but was not broadcast as we know it.

WJZ had studios then in Newark, New Jersey. The announcer was Tommy Cowan, strictly a studio announcer. Arrangements were made for a Newark newspaper reporter to talk into a telephone . . . Cowan in the studio in Newark repeated into the microphone what he heard, or thought he heard, the reporter say. Cowan had no idea of balls or strikes or runs or errors. He was a reporter of the actual reporter. The next fall, 1922, there wasn't enough interest shown by anyone to broadcast the World Series in any fashion.

Radio . . . the World Series . . . baseball . . . listeners were never the same after the World Series of 1923. WJZ had a rookie announcer, Graham McNamee, who had started in studio radio earlier that year. WJZ decided to broadcast the World Series live—broadcast what an announcer said who was watching the game, who was on the scene.

A well-known newspaperman was to do the play-by-play, and McNamee was assigned to do color. McNamee was a trained singer who wandered into the WJZ studios one afternoon during a break when he was on jury duty. He had no knowledge of sports, but he had a magnetic voice that suited the microphones of his day. There is a debate as to who that newspaperman was —I know Grantland Rice said it was he. What is certain is that the newspaperman, in the middle of game three, walked away and left the entire broadcast to McNamee. Rice told me, "It just got too much—it wasn't for me."

The response to McNamee's broadcast was electric . . . fan mail poured in, more than WJZ had ever known. Each year as radio stations multiplied, as the networks went coast to coast, as receiving sets increased, the broadcasts of the World Series became more important. McNamee's voice was vibrant, dominant through the World Series of 1934, his last one doing play-by-play. Then NBC demoted him. In 1935, my first World Series broadcast—on Mutual—I remember seeing Graham McNamee being thrown two bones a game; he was allowed to say a few words about the weather and the crowd before the first pitch, and then, after the action was over, he was brought back to do a summary. He wasn't heard on another World Series.

Radio rapidly became vitally important. It changed the mores of the country. Suddenly we became news-conscious because we could hear immediately what the news was. Our homes became places of wonderful entertainment. When Pearl Harbor was attacked, all of us felt the immediate impact that dreadful Sunday afternoon because radio brought it to us. Roosevelt used radio as though it had been invented for him, and from F.D.R.'s use of radio our presidency has become increasingly intertwined first with microphones, and then with microphones plus cameras. Kennedy . . . Johnson . . . Nixon . . . Ford . . . Carter . . . Reagan.

Yankee Stadium was opened for the season of 1923. That fall was McNamee and the first live World Series broadcast. An exact duplicate lifespan, the great Stadium and the impact of instant communication.

Twenty-four years later—1947—radio was so big it was frightening if you thought about it. Mel Allen and I were to broadcast the 1947 World Series—broadcast it to almost a thousand radio stations in the United States and over Armed Forces Radio around the world. I had no idea how extensive the coverage was. I knew that if I started being impressed by the numbers of stations, and the millions of listeners, I'd be sick in my stomach. The dread butterflies. What I did, as I'm sure Mel did, was to think in terms of one microphone only—the one I spoke into, the one I was responsible to—and the rest of the enterprise would have to do the best it could for itself. I nestled before my microphone, became one with it, and from it I drew strength, warmth and support. There was the game, here was the mike, and the rest of it was shut out. Broadcasting a complex game with its intricate details and uncertain events requires absolute concentration. Every mistake I ever made was because I broke my concentration.

The radio broadcast of the 1947 World Series was the big assignment in all sports. This was the first time television would cover, but there were only a few stations along the eastern seaboard. Television was new, just starting. True, I had announced the first telecast of a big-league game in August 1939, but World War II had put TV in the deep freeze, put it on hold. Now the war was over and television was gathering momentum.

In terms of World Series broadcasting, radio reached its peak in 1947. It would never be as dominant again. Television was small, but it was like a little touch of pregnancy. It grew rapidly.

Two dozen years—1923–1947—that's all radio had to itself. Television had such a voracious appetite. It was the hungriest fetus in the broadcasting family. Each year television would become increasingly dominant, pushing radio into a secondary role. Radio remained important for homes and places without a TV set, for open spaces, sparsely populated, that television didn't cover, and for a vast audience of automobile listeners. But television soon had numerous viewers and where the viewers were, the big money and the sponsors were. This was my last World Series radio assignment—I was to do play-by-play on TV the next fall.

Commissioner Chandler and the president and co-owner of the Yankees, MacPhail, hugged each other as the flashbulbs popped. . . . Branch Rickey, head of the Dodgers, had his box . . . Leo Durocher and Laraine sat in their box not far from that of Chandler (the Chandlers and the Durochers did not meet). George Weiss who, more than MacPhail, had built this Yankee team, merged unnoticed with the crowd. Bucky Harris and Burt Shotton were in their dugouts . . . the field was cleared of all but the players . . . the six umpires marched together to home plate . . . it was time to start. It was a long way in every dimension from spring in Havana, Cuba, to Yankee Stadium in early fall.

This was a Series of many "firsts." When I wrote that six umpires came onto the field, that was the first time more than four umpires were on the field actively making decisions in a World Series. The credit goes to Commissioner Chandler, to Uncle Charley Moran (a longtime friend of Chandler's, by the way), and to Joe Gordon, the same Joe Gordon who was traded by MacPhail for Allie Reynolds.

In game three of the 1938 World Series, Yankees and Chicago Cubs, Saturday afternoon at Yankee Stadium, umpire Charley Moran was working at second base. The other three umpires were Ziggy Sears, also of the National League, and Lou Kolls and Cal Hubbard of the American. Early in the game shortstop Frank Crosetti of the Yankees flipped a ground ball to his second baseman, Joe Gordon, to start a double-play. Gordon's relay throw hit umpire Moran squarely in the mouth . . . Uncle Charley had gotten too close to the line of fire. I remember vividly the old man standing there, his cap knocked off, his thin white hair exposed, and his mouth broken. There wasn't too much blood to be seen—we learned later Uncle Charley kept swallowing it to keep it from looking too bad. He was a tough old fellow, bowlegged, hamlike gnarled hands, and thick chest. He'd played and coached football—coached the Praying Colonels of Centre College of Kentucky when they upset a highly favored Harvard team.

Moran's fellow umpires tried to get him to leave the game, but he wouldn't desert his post at second base. He picked up his cap, put it on, and as far as he was concerned, that was that. His boss, National League president, Ford Frick, had Moran come to his rail box, and Frick tried to get him to leave. Moran wouldn't go. Finally, Commissioner K. M. Landis called him over and tried to get Moran to retire and have medical attention. The mouth was badly cut. No sir, Uncle Charley had started the game and he was going to finish it. He walked away from Landis and Frick and went back to his position. He finished the game, got his mouth stitched afterward, and umpired the Series next day, which mercifully for him was soon over—the Yankees swept the Cubs in 4 straight.

Moran's injury alerted the Commissioner and the two league presidents to the risk of having only four umpires on the field, and on hand. It was decided to have, beginning the next Series in 1939, an alternate umpire from each league, seated in uniform, in reserve, alongside each dugout. There they sat quietly in their neat blue serge suits through the next eight World Series. Chandler did nothing about them his first two Series. However, he said before the 1947 Series that as long as they were sitting there, in uniform, and getting paid (not as much as the four field umpires) why not put them in the foul corners and get some use out of them . . . Today six umpires rotate all six positions on an equal status.

Joe DiMaggio has told me 1947 was the most exciting World Series he played in or saw. Tommy Henrich agreed. So did Harry Lavagetto and Al Gionfriddo, who would, of course. It was a testing of raw strength, of mass numbers—thirty-eight players were involved in it, a record. It had two dramatic explosions not equaled since. It marked the coming of big money—it was the first World Series to gross more than $2 million: $2,021,348.92. The first television fee, $65,000, sent the gross over the mark. It wouldn't be many years before television would pour in such a golden stream that it would dictate when World Series games would be played and at what time.

John Drebinger of the *Times* wrote before the Series began of the importance of pitching and of the young, inexperienced staff Shotton had at his command. The 7 games displayed the shallow status of the Brooklyn pitchers, except for Hugh Casey, who relieved in 6 of the 7, and was a hero, which balanced his books for the 1941 Series—with the Mickey Owen-Tommy Henrich third strike. The Dodgers didn't have a starting pitcher last five innings, much less pitch a complete game, and yet it went to the ninth inning of the seventh game. It was sheer struggle. It was an excellent Series for radio to reach its crest, and for television to make its entrance.

The television pictures for that Series were in black-and-white. For the first time—and forever after—the players were also black-and-white. Jackie Robinson captured all attention when he got on base. People who hadn't seen Jackie dance off first, draw a throw, dart back . . . dance off again, worry the pitcher, draw a throw, dart back . . . dance off, and GO . . . and make it safely at second! . . . could hardly believe the testimony of their startled eyes.

There are always pre-game statements and casual remarks picked up by the pack of hungry writers. Writers are everywhere, and since the development of tape recorders, so are broadcasters. TV with its small, portable equipment now muscles in. There is no privacy for a World Series manager, coach or player except in the clubhouse or on the playing field.

Bucky Harris, always at ease with the writers, and an easy man for the fourth estate, said "If I have to do it I'll use Page to finish every game." Shotton made no quotable pre-game remark. The pre-game quote that backfired was made by young Yogi Berra. Berra had been at Newark the year before, in the same league as Robinson at Montreal. When asked by a writer about Robinson on the bases, Yogi said that Jackie had not stolen a base on him last summer, and that he didn't expect him to steal on him during the Series. The writers promptly apprised Jackie of Yogi's remarks. Jackie walked, his first at bat against Shea, and immediately stole second—Berra's throw was late, and into the dirt. After the game Robinson said, "I wish Berra was catching in the National League . . . I'd steal sixty bases."

Before the first game, Arthur Daley, columnist of the *Times*, asked Jackie was there much pressure on him . . . World Series . . . first Negro player in a World Series . . . record crowd of over 73,000 . . . Yankee Stadium. "Gosh," Jackie said, with a smile, "it can't be any more nerve wracking than that St. Louis series. After that, nothing can seem too important."

Bucky Harris in this Series paid little attention to The Book. The Book is not a book of bound pages filled with statistics and salty sayings. Yet people in baseball go around referring to The Book—The Book says bunt in this situation, The Book says have a right-handed batter face a left-handed pitcher, The Book says use experience in a big situation, etc. The Book, The Book, The Book—but nobody has ever seen it.

Harris named Frank Shea as his starting pitcher. Shea had won 14 against 5 his rookie year, and had his arm not troubled him, he might well have had a more impressive record. This was the first time an American League rookie pitcher had opened a World Series. The Book said to open with an old hand, a battle-tested pitcher. But Shea was twenty-five with the maturity of three years in military service.

Shotton didn't have to worry about The Book. He opened with Ralph Branca, twenty one years old, almost a rookie, but a 21-game winner and the ace of his uncertain mound staff.

The Action

Shea and the Yankees found out about Robinson in the first inning. Jackie walked and promptly stole second base well ahead of Berra's throw into the dirt. Dixie Walker singled Jackie home, putting the Dodgers ahead 1–0. Shea settled down until he walked Robinson again in the third inning. Again Jackie went into his dance off first base—darting off, ducking back, faking a run, until he caught Shea in a balk—the only balk Shea committed all year. This was a Robinson special, making pitchers balk.

However, the threat with Jackie on second was erased as he was trapped between second and third on a ground ball.

Shea was pitching soundly but Branca was pitching perfectly through the fourth inning. The 1–0 lead looked good. Joe DiMaggio led off the Yankee last of the fifth. He hit one savagely into the hole between third and short—Reese made a fine stop of the ball but had no play on DiMaggio. Branca wilted. Did the sound of DiMaggio's bat seem like impending doom? Did inexperience suddenly set in? Did the majestic presence of the packed triple-deck Stadium with over 73,000 show-me fans make its impression? As rapidly as the rules permitted, the Yankees took away the game.

Branca then walked McQuinn without throwing him a strike. On the first pitch he hit Billy Johnson on the left wrist, loading the bases with no one out. Johnny Lindell laced a double, scoring 2 and putting the Yankees ahead 2–1. Branca refilled the bases with a walk to Rizzuto.

Shea was due to bat, but manager Harris threw away The Book. He sent up Bobby Brown to pinch-hit. Harris wanted all the runs he could get, and right now. The biscuits were on the table and he was helping himself. A bases-loaded opportunity with nobody out might not happen again today, and even The Book says you must win today's game today if you can. Perhaps Harris felt Shea as a rookie had a sufficient baptism of fire. Further, Harris knew something The Book didn't—he had Joe Page in the bullpen.

Branca threw two wide pitches to the medical student— Brown used his baseball income to pay for his doctor's degree. On the road he and Yogi roomed together, and it was a study in contrasts: Brown's medical volumes, and Berra's comic books. Neither roommate borrowed literature from the other.

When Branca delivered ball two to Brown, Shotton spoke to coach Clyde Sukeforth in the Dodger dugout, "Go get him, Sukey," he barked. "He's aiming the ball. Bring him back with you."

Hank Behrman was brought in. Behrman, remember, wasn't deemed good enough to keep early in the season by the Pittsburgh Pirates, and was returned to the Dodgers. Shotton could and did use him in 40 games, including all 3 in that final series at St. Louis. It was in St. Louis that Shotton said to scout Andy High, "You scouts don't know how bad I need (pitching) help."

Behrman finished the walk to Brown. That pushed another run home, 3–1. Tommy Henrich singled, and sent 2 more runs in, making it 5–1. Joe Page came on and it was as good as over. Page wasn't as sharp as usual, giving up 2 runs, but he brought it safely in, 5–3. "Here's to Joe Page," was the familiar toast of the evening. The Yankees bagged Game One.

The pattern was emerging, although it couldn't be seen after one game. Joe Page was Harris's anchor man . . . Shotton used three pitchers, with Hugh Casey as his ace fireman. Casey finished the game, wasn't scored on, but by then it was too late . . . Joe DiMaggio hit a drive some 415 feet in the eighth inning which Carl Furillo caught.

Bucky Harris in his clubhouse said, "You have to win one before you can win four." Burt Shotton said, "We lost. What is there to say?" Branch Rickey on his way to the Dodger clubhouse said, "You ask me about Branca? I told you this spring at training camp, and several times during the season . . . there is no substitute for experience."

Larry MacPhail, Dan Topping and Del Webb, the owners, were the first to enter the Yankee clubhouse to offer congratulations. Commissioner Chandler and Leo Durocher did not meet.

Yankee Stadium empties quickly. Game One was over. The Stadium cleanup crew was hard at work. 73,000 people deposit a great deal of debris. The busiest place now was in the offices of the concessionaire, Harry M. Stevens. The money counting machines sang steadily while supplies were brought in for the next day.

Game Two

How far down can a ball club get, and still bounce back? Game Two was an embarrassment for the Dodgers. Some writers put it even stronger, wrote that the Dodgers played like schoolboys, like amateurs, like beginners. After this game there were observers who began speaking of a 4-game sweep by the Yankees. Not manager Harris, not any of his players, not MacPhail—but the Yankees moved into the catbird seat, as heavy gloom moved into every corner of the Brooklyn clubhouse.

Ball games are played by two groups of human beings. One day all goes well. Another day, as Joe Jacobs had said at Baker Field, just up the Harlem River from Yankee Stadium, "I shoulda stood in bed." Game Two belongs in this World Series because it shows plainly how much humanness was involved, how low a group of men can fall, how desperate their plight, and then how strongly they can rebound.

This is the way Drebinger's story of Game Two began on page one of the New York *Times*, "The Dodgers did not get lost in the Yankee Stadium yesterday. Instead, the entire arena crashed right down on their heads.

"Victims of an horrendous afternoon of misadventures, which included a bruising attack by the Bronx Bombers and an assortment of ghastly misplays on their own part, Burt Shotton's Flatbush Flock took a terrible drubbing from Bucky Harris's Yankees in the second game of the current world series.

"The score was 10–3, with Allie Reynolds hurling the entire nine innings for the victors. It was that easy, they didn't even have to call on Joe Page . . .

"What it did to the followers of Brooklyn's battered Bums almost beggars description . . . In vain Shotton, starting with his diminutive left-hander, Vic Lombardi, hurled four pitchers into the fray . . ."

It was a ball game until the last of the fourth inning. Dixie Walker had just homered to tie it all 2–2. Everything was quite in order and most respectable. The crowd of 69,865—3,500 less than Game One—had settled down. The sun was shining. Indian summer, a beautiful afternoon if you didn't have to play either left or center field at Yankee Stadium. The autumn haze was thickened by tobacco smoke and the body heat rising from the large crowd. Most ball parks are laid out so that right is the sun field. At the Stadium, however, the sun was in the eyes of both the left and center fielders. Playing out there you faced the sinking sun as it threw shadows across the infield, and you hoped you'd locate the batted ball as it rose out of a confusing background of triple-decked shirts and faces. The haze was an added hazard as the ball must first rise above it . . . Babe Ruth was not a sun worshiper: he played right field at the Stadium, and left field on the road.

The Stadium itself was in many ways a strong force in the success of the Yankees. Visiting players had to be impressed by the towering strength and threatening size of the place. I've heard visiting players call it a monster, relentless and waiting. Fill Yankee Stadium, as it often was filled, then dress it with the flags and pennants already won, and it becomes a menacing maelstrom. Right-handed batters knew they were overmatched by the depths of left, left center and certainly, straightaway center field. It was known to the trade as The Big Ball Park— that's what I called it the years I broadcast there. When the World Series came, in early fall, the Stadium worked another handicap on the visiting players: the sun and the shadows, plus the flickering, dancing haze. Added to it all was the devilish wind factor. The Yankees knew their own ball park, they knew that the winds blew one direction up above, then the reverse down on the playing area because the wind bounced back from the high construction of the stands. For an outfielder to look at the way the flags blew and think that was the wind the ball would be riding in, or going against, might be a fatal mistake.

Drebinger wrote far more acutely in his opening sentence of his story of Game Two than he knew. Drebbie was writing a sentence that would stop the eye of the reader, which it did. What he wrote was also in deep truth exactly what happened. He wrote, "The Dodgers did not get lost in the Yankee Stadium yesterday. Instead, the entire arena crashed right down on their heads."

Dixie Walker tied the game—as I said—in the top of the fourth with his home run. Billy Johnson led it off for the Yankees in the bottom of the frame. Here is where the arena started crashing down, with assists from the elements.

Pete Reiser, in center field, was a star ballplayer, with a ferocity for chasing fly balls that cost him many serious crashes against concrete walls. Leo Durocher and others have said that Reiser, had he not been hurt so frequently and so seriously, would have been one of the all-time great players.

Casey Stengel, in his years of command at the Stadium, used to tell his men they'd go for broke if they kept hitting balls straightaway into that yawning space in center. Casey would say, "Pull the ball . . . don't make those center fielders look good at your expense."

Billy Johnson hit a high fly to straightaway center. He hit it some 400 feet. Center fielders catch such shots. But Reiser went back uncertainly. He didn't know where the ball was. Then he turned, turned the wrong way, and fell. I still remember seeing Pete Reiser twisting and falling under the fly ball that went for a triple. Phil Rizzuto lifted a high fly to short left, which Gene Hermanski lost in the sun, and it fell for a double.

The collapse continued. Jackie Robinson overran a bunt and never did pick it up. Johnson singled sharply to center, Reiser let the ball go through him and Johnson made it to third. Robinson fielded a ground ball and nobody covered first—Jackie had to hold the ball. Henrich hit a home run. Behrman and Barney, two of the four pitchers Shotton used, wild-pitched. Stanky mistimed a low line drive by jumping too soon. Yes, the Stadium came crashing down. 10–3.

Shotton, after the game, said, "I don't feel good about this. Who would feel good about losing the first two games of a World Series? The boys got some bad baseball out of their systems. Tomorrow will be different. We'll be at home. You certainly can quote me that we'll be on the field, and that we'll have a pitcher."

Bucky Harris, all smiles, said, "They just simply can't be as bad as they looked. They really had a tough day, didn't they? . . . We're certainly in the driver's seat now but we're taking this Series one game at a time. I'll pitch Bobo Newsom tomorrow."

Mel Allen and I were the broadcasters on radio. I had done the first half of Game One, and the second half of Game Two. The job of reporting the plays of a World Series to millions who couldn't see those plays for themselves was a most severe challenge that left an announcer no space for personal feelings. I was surprised that Reiser had such trouble. But that was all. My work did not hinge on who won or who lost. That was the province of the teams and the fans.

Further, I had my own problem. I was having throat worries.

Not as serious as the severe laryngitis I developed during the World Series of 1942 when I cracked my vocal chords. But serious enough, when your profession hangs on your voice, and you are one of the two announcers doing the biggest coverage radio ever had for a World Series.

Dr. Stuart Craig was a noted throat specialist and a warm friend. His waiting room would be populated by famous singers, actors and people. He sat with Lylah. When the game ended and Mel and I signed off the broadcast, I went down through the stands, joined Dr. Craig and Lylah, and we went straight to his office.

I was ready for Game Three. Good man, Stuart Craig.

Game Three

Brooklyn is a different place. Ebbets Field is a different ball park (to use the present tense for what is now a group of apartment buildings). The Brooklyn fan was different, to use the past tense. The Brooklyn ballplayer was another combatant when he felt the smallness of Ebbets Field, when he walked the sod of Brooklyn, and when he heard the never-ceasing encouragement of his fans. The Dodgers at Ebbets Field were much like Antaeus, whom Hercules couldn't kill as long as Antaeus was standing on his native soil. Hercules finally picked him up, took him to a foreign land and despatched him forthwith.

Dixie Walker put it somewhat into focus before the third game when he said, "Now we cannot only see the ball but also who's hitting." 33,098 packed the small park. There were great distances at Yankee Stadium. In Ebbets Field the fans and players blended almost into a oneness.

Joe Hatten started for Brooklyn; Shotton had little choice. Bucky Harris started Bobo Newsom, a familiar figure in Brooklyn. Newsom had begun his big-league career in this bandbox way back in 1929. His journeys had taken him to eight minor-league towns and thirteen big-league cities, some of them twice. Larry MacPhail had brought him back to Brooklyn to try to save the 1942 pennant, which the Cardinals saw to it was beyond redemption. Branch Rickey sent him packing in 1943. MacPhail had reached for him again this year when the Yankees needed pitching, and Old Bobo had served well. He had won 200 games lifetime in the American League. At Detroit in the 1940 World Series he started 3 games against the Reds, won the first 2 and lost the final game to Paul Derringer 2–1. Old Bobo, as he called himself, could be formidable. He was certainly battle scarred and tournament tough. He knew all about Ebbets Field.

Frank Shea, the rookie star of the Yankees who'd started the first game, got his picture taken several times. It was his twenty-fifth birthday. Charlie Dressen, who'd jumped Durocher, Rickey and the Dodgers for MacPhail and the Yankees, snorted and said, "Too bad he won't get to celebrate his birthday by starting another game." What Dressen meant was that the Yankees would take 2 more, sweep it, and Shea who was due to start Game Five, wouldn't because there wouldn't be Game Five.

This wasn't to be Pete Reiser's Series. He walked in the first inning and promptly tried to steal second base. Sherman Lollar, catching today in place of Berra, threw Pete out. As he slid into the bag he hurt his right ankle, limped off the field, and was out of the Series as a regular. It was called a bad sprain. Later it proved to be all of that plus a broken bone.

Hatten kept the Yankees away from the plate the first two innings. In the last of the second Ebbets Field exploded like Mount St. Helens. The Dodgers fell on Newsom, and on his replacement Vic Raschi like hungry wolves upon a crippled deer. Hermanski walked and Edwards doubled, driving in the first run. John Drebinger wrote in his story, "Then the crowd, though less than half the size of either of the two great Stadium gatherings, appeared on the spot to make twice as much noise as ever had been heard in the Bronx."

The noise didn't let up for another fifteen minutes. Pee Wee Reese singled, sending Edwards home. With 2 men out, pitcher Hatten singled. Catcher Lollar had a passed ball. Eddie Stanky doubled and scored both runners. That made it 4–0. Newsom was taken out. Raschi came in. Jackie Robinson singled. Carl Furillo, who had replaced Reiser, doubled, and the Dodgers had 6 fat runs. The din was beyond belief. Bedlam in Brooklyn.

From here on it was hitting, pitching, running, arguments, scoring. It became a slam-bang battle that went on over three hours, the longest World Series game until then. The Yankees fought back, step by step. The Dodgers added 3 more to make it a total of 9, and they needed every one of them. The Yankees scored 2 in the third, 2 in the fourth, 2 again in the fifth. The last 2 came when DiMaggio whacked a home run into the upper left center-field stands. That finished Hatten, and brought in Branca. In the sixth Bobby Brown, the pinch hitter who was never retired in the Series, doubled, and Tommy Henrich scored him with a single. In the seventh Yogi Berra hit for Lollar, got his first Series hit, the first pinch-hit home run in a World Series. That was enough for Branca. The score was now 9–8. Shotton called in Hugh Casey.

Joe Page had taken over in the sixth inning for New York. Now it was a contest by the two relief men, the two top relief pitchers of the year. Page held the Dodgers scoreless, but so did Casey the Yankees. It was Casey who saved it, and was credited with the win. He said in the clubhouse afterward, "My arm hurts all over—but it'll be all right tomorrow."

Bobby Brown's pinch-hit double had the Yankees grumbling. The foul screen in right, a three-foot-wide screen that extended above the top of the wall, was then under the ground rules "in play"—meaning that a ball that hit it, even though it hit above the top of the wall, was in play. The runner could get only as much as he could make. Brown's hit was well above the wall but only good for two bases. The rule was later changed to make it a home run. For Game Three, however, it was a break for Brooklyn. Instead of a tie, the game stayed 9–8.

Johnny Lindell was tagged out in the eighth inning by second baseman Stanky. Umpire Bill McGowan of the American League ruled that Stanky tagged him as the first out of a double-play. Stanky, of course, said he tagged him. Lindell said Stanky missed him. Manager Harris backed his player. All the Yankees said Lindell should have been safe. Had he been, maybe another ball game.

Shotton walked into his clubhouse, grinning like a Cheshire cat. "I feel a lot better today than I did yesterday," he said.

Harris gave the writers this statement:

". . . we couldn't quite catch up to them. They got one run more than we did. I'll throw Bill Bevens at them tomorrow . . . Berra will catch."

Several million more dinners were enjoyed in Brooklyn that night than were the night before.

Game Four

This is the date and the place: Friday afternoon, October 3, 1947, Ebbets Field, Brooklyn. This was the game with the impossible finish. Some writers said it was more dramatic than anything a Hollywood script artist could have created. The reporters in the press box desperately needed a book of synonyms. One writer, in fact, yelled to his colleagues, "Don't bother writing it . . . nobody will believe it."

This, of course, was the last half of the ninth inning encounter of Harry Lavagetto and Bill Bevens, with 2 Dodgers on base, 2 men out, and the Yankees leading 2–1. 33,443 people were jammed into the park. As Lavagetto came to the plate, all of them were on their feet. Nobody sat down again.

Bevens had already placed his name twice in the record books when Lavagetto faced him. The big right-hander had pitched eight and two thirds innings without allowing a hit. He had, by a full inning, passed Red Ruffing's World Series mark in 1942. His second record was walking ten batters. Now, Bevens wanted not only to win the game in which he held a 2–1 lead, but also he wanted to be the first pitcher in a World Series to deliver a no-hit game. He couldn't be any closer than he was at the moment. One more out to go. That was all.

Lavagetto was sent up to bat for Eddie Stanky. Bevens pitched and Lavagetto swung and missed. Strike one. Bevens was closing in . . .

The impact of this game was not just in its explosive climax. From the very start this was the material of high human drama. Looking back, you wonder how it was the Yankees didn't score more runs than the 2 they did. You wonder how the Dodgers stayed in the game. Whenever people gather and begin talking of baseball games, they speak and think and second-guess this one, from start to finish.

Bevens had been carefully slotted and rested for this starting assignment for the Yankees. He had had an up-and-down season. When his arm permitted he was a strong pitcher. Today he was strong.

Harry Taylor—a rookie—started for Brooklyn. Harry had won 10, lost 5, including a big win over Harry Brecheen and the Cardinals. But in that victory over St. Louis he had torn a tendon in his elbow, been examined at Johns Hopkins Hospital, and had been resting his arm. Shotton had no one else. Taylor was his hope.

Stirnweiss hit Taylor's first pitch for a single. Henrich followed with another single. Robinson scooped up a hot grounder hit by Berra and threw to Reese covering at second for a force, and maybe a double-play, but Pee Wee dropped the ball. Nobody out and the bases full. Hal Gregg was warming up rapidly in the Brooklyn bullpen. The error was damaging. Taylor was in immediate deep trouble. It looked like the Yankees were on their way again.

DiMaggio waited at the plate. Taylor walked him, forcing in a run. Shotton recalled Taylor, and Harry was finished for the Series. Gregg took over. Bases loaded, 1 run in, and still nobody out. George McQuinn popped up to short—an automatic out under provisions of the infield fly rule. Billy Johnson banged into a sparkling double-play, Reese to Stanky to Robinson. It was a miraculous escape for the Dodgers to get out of it with only 1 run for the Yankees.

Bevens walked 2 Dodgers in the first inning, walked another 1 in the second, but avoided any hits or runs. Gregg got into trouble in the third with 2 out. He walked DiMaggio. McQuinn got an infield single on a ball in front of the plate. Catcher Edwards fired the ball wide of first, and it bounced off the stands. DiMaggio was waved around third base by coach Dressen. Right fielder Walker alertly charged the play, recovered the ball and threw out DiMaggio at the plate by a wide margin. Another Houdini escape by the Dodgers, and the Yankee second-guessers went to work on Dressen, and cried "He shoulda held him."

Now it was the Yankees' turn for heroics. In the last of the third Stanky was on second base, courtesy of pitcher Bevens—a walk, and a wild pitch. But Robinson slapped a foul along the left-field line and Lindell made a diving, tumbling catch.

The Yankees threatened to tear it apart in the fourth inning. Had they done so and won the game they would have led the Series 3 games to 1. Billy Johnson shook the center-field gates with a shot that went for a triple, which is a wicked base hit to begin an inning with. Then Lindell almost hit it out of the park in right. It was a double and Johnson scored—2–0 New York. But Gregg pitched out of it, stranding Lindell.

Gene Hermanski was first up in the last of the fourth and belted a drive to deep center field. DiMaggio made one of his patented catches—his specialty was to make the hard ones look easy. A big save for Bevens and his no-hitter.

In the last of the fifth the Dodgers eked out a run to make it a 2–1 game. Bevens's wildness hurt him. He walked the first 2, and the run followed from a sacrifice and an infield out.

On it went. Gregg held the Yankees until he left for a pinch hitter, and Hank Behrman took over in the eighth. Hank got by that frame. Big Bevens continued strong with good stuff. He walked a man in the sixth and in the seventh but nothing happened. Tommy Henrich saved his no-hitter in the eighth with a jumping catch against the right-field scoreboard against Hermanski—who was twice robbed.

The eight previous innings set the stage for the ninth. A lot of people think only the last half of the ninth was where the fireworks were. There was a story in itself in the top half.

Let me go back to the middle of the fifth inning. Mel Allen and I alternated announcing halves of the games. He had done the first four and a half innings. I took over and described the walks to Jorgensen and Gregg, the sacrifice by Stanky, and the run that scored as shortstop Rizzuto threw to third baseman Johnson to retire Gregg, the runner from second. Reese had gotten on by a fielder's choice, and he promptly stole second. Berra threw wildly for an error and Pee Wee took third. Jackie Robinson struck out, and there it was, the end of the fifth inning.

The totals at end of five were: New York 2 runs, 6 hits, 1

error—Brooklyn 1 run, no hits, 2 errors. The superstition came alive in the press box and in the Yankee dugout. No mention of Bevens pitching a no-hitter after five innings. This was exactly five innings. Had Mel had the microphone for the last half of the game there would not have been any radio mention. Mel was a devout practitioner of the fifth inning no-hit hoodoo. He'd have said things like, "Don't go away—something big is happening" and when he gave the inning totals, he'd have just taken a big long pause when he should have said how many Dodger hits there were. He'd have ducked and dodged but he wouldn't have said Bevens had given no hits.

Mel didn't have the last half. I had it, and I was quickly confronted with my decision. This was a tremendous radio broadcast—all over the world. I never had respected the superstition, and I didn't intend to respect it now, whatever the scope of the broadcast. In fact, as I sat there I thought quickly of several things . . . people by the millions will be tuning in and will want to know all the details of the game . . . what right did I have to withhold any statistic of the game because of a superstition? Why not withhold how many runs, or errors, or walks? . . . And in my "third ear" I heard a dead man's voice say "report . . . report everything you can see . . . that is your job . . . report . . . but leave your opinions in your hotel." For a split second I heard Judge Landis remind me who I was and what my work was. I heard him say the key word, "Report."

What maturity as a broadcaster I achieved came in 1947. It came over the long season when I was the announcer for the first black man in the big leagues. It was completed in the last half of the fourth game of the World Series. I remained a reporter, not a dealer in superstition.

I gave the five inning totals: the Yankees 2 runs, 6 hits and 1 error—the Dodgers 1 run, no hits, and 2 errors. Mel, sitting by me, started making choking sounds like he was trying to swallow chinaberry seeds. I continued broadcasting that Bevens was giving up no hits. That became the story of the game, a story that finally overrode the winning and losing of the game itself. Bevens, years later, thanked me for reporting what he was doing, otherwise he said he would not have gotten the full credit for his performance.

That near no-hitter became the story. However, my broadcast of it, my reporting of it, set off strong repercussions that night. Several announcers on various sports programs said I had done the most unsportsmanlike broadcast in radio history. Yankee fans telephoned the papers and radio stations complaining that I had jinxed Bevens. It was a real rhubarb around my red head.

The next day I knew what I had to do. I went straight to manager Harris. Bucky was sitting in his dugout. I told him that he couldn't have heard what I broadcast but that he must have heard stories and complaints about it. He said he had heard some complaints. I told him what and how I announced the last half of the game. He smiled, and said, "Red, if you can control what the ball does by what you say about it, I'll pay you a lot more money than radio does to sit by me on the bench."

Bevens was tossing a ball back and forth with a teammate. He was behind first base. I went to him, and repeated what I had broadcast. He was the man who had gotten hurt. Lavagetto with one swing had brought him down, ruined his no-hitter, and cost him the game. He also smiled, but much more sadly than had Harris.

"Red," he said quietly, "you didn't have a thing to do with it . . . it was those bases on balls that did it." He had walked 10. Walks 9 and 10 scored in the ninth inning.

Throughout the tense battle the Yankees had their chances. In the top of the ninth the Yankees appeared poised to again blow the game apart. Against Behrman, Lindell singled but was forced at second by Rizzuto. One out. Pitcher Bevens bunted in front of the plate, and catcher Edwards threw to second too late to force the flying feet of Little Phil. Stirnweiss singled to center but Rizzuto could only make third as it seemed Furillo might catch the drive. Three on. One out.

That was enough for Shotton. He sent Sukeforth for Behrman. In lumbered Hugh Casey, the pitching hero of the day before. Waiting to bat against him was Tommy Henrich, and anyone who followed baseball remembered when Casey faced Henrich in game four of the 1941 World Series, with two men out, and the Dodgers leading the Yankees 4–3. Casey threw a wicked curve, Henrich swung, and missed for the third strike. The game should have been over, and the Series tied at 2 games per team.

That might have been the best curve Casey ever threw. It certainly was the worst as far as results went. Catcher Mickey Owen couldn't hold the ball which rolled back to the stands. Henrich raced to first. The Yankees went on to score 4 runs and win 7–4. All Brooklyn was stunned. Manager Leo Durocher afterward admitted freely that his wheels stopped and that he didn't go out to the mound to calm Casey down. MacPhail cried openly.

Here, in 1947, they were again—Casey and Henrich—and again in the ninth inning. Again in Game Four, again in Ebbets Field, and the Yankees again leading in games 2–1. I had time to recall this for the listeners as Casey leisurely threw his warm-up pitches. (Bob Elson and I had announced that 1941 World Series, and Elson had done the last half of that fourth game. But I saw it, had to comment upon it, and then sign off the broadcast.)

Both Casey and Henrich showed no emotion. Both were professionals. The runners—Rizzuto at third, Bevens at second, Stirnweiss at first—took their careful leads. One out. The Dodger infield was pulled in a step to double-play depth. The defense was swung a step around toward right. Henrich pulled the ball.

Casey had apple cheeks. He was a big man with a sizable stomach. He looked like a roly-poly boy in his short baseball pants. From a distance he seemed playful in facial appearance. But no matter how he looked or seemed to look, Casey was a killer. When you saw his flinty, light blue eyes, then you saw Hugh Casey. Arthur Daley wrote in the *Times* that when he asked Frankie Frisch what made Casey such a great relief pitcher, Frisch said one word, "Stomach," and Frisch didn't mean the one so clearly visible. He meant intestinal fortitude. Guts.

Henrich was a cold-blooded batter. He was a clutch hitter. He had earned the nickname, Old Reliable. Russ Hodges had given it to him when Russ was announcing in New York. (Henrich was the leading Yankee batter in the '47 Series with a mark of .323, 10 hits and 5 R.B.I.s.)

Casey took his sign from Edwards. Everybody knew what the pitch would be. It would be a low sharp curve, Casey's best pitch . . . the big right-hander checked the three runners . . . checked the alignment of the defense: Robinson at first, Stanky at second, Reese at short, Jorgensen at third . . . Walker in right was straightaway. Furillo in center and Hermanski in left were slightly toward right. Henrich, a left-handed hitter, waited, balanced, his eyes ready to pick up the white ball as soon as it left Casey's hand. A batter has pitifully little time to decide whether to swing or take the pitch. The distance from Casey to Henrich was sixty feet, six inches. That's the measurement from the pitching slab to the plate. When a ball is released the distance is even less.

One pitch. Henrich swung and bounced it back to Casey. Casey threw at once to catcher Edwards, already standing on the plate, and the catcher's throw to first to Robinson was well in time to double Henrich. If Casey had prayed before he threw the ball, his prayer couldn't have been better answered. A come-backer. A thank you, ma'am.

Ebbets Field went up in sound. Casey walked calmly from the mound, and Bevens, who'd been the runner at second base, took his place in the center of the diamond. The score remained 2–1, favor the Yankees. Another hair-raising escape for the Dodgers. Now Bevens was to have his final chance.

Bevens threw a few tosses to Berra. McQuinn at first warmed up the rest of the infield, Stirnweiss at second, Rizzuto at short, Johnson at third. DiMaggio stood impassively in center field, flanked by Lindell in left and Henrich in right. Henrich knew the angles of the right-field wall behind him—he'd had fungoes hit against that tricky wall in pre-game practice in order that he might study their bounces. Already he had gone against the scoreboard to rob Hermanski and save the no-hitter.

Larry Goetz of the National League was the ball-and-strike umpire. Bill McGowan of the American League was at first, Babe Pinelli of the National was at second, with Ed Rommel of the American at third. Big George Magerkurth of the National was on the right-field line. Jim Boyer of the American was in left field. To repeat: this was the first World Series to have six umpires on the field.

For the Dodgers in the bottom of the ninth it would be Bruce
Edwards, Carl Furillo and Spider Jorgensen. Bevens stood on
the mound, a towering figure, 6'3", 215 pounds. His uniform
shirt was sweat stained. It had been a long, tiring afternoon. He
had walked 8, and Shotton had had his hitters taking, taking,
taking—making Bevens pitch, pitch, pitch.

The Dodgers belonged to the people of Brooklyn just as children do to their parents. Dodger fans were free to criticize the
players—often they did—but nobody else had better lift their
voices negatively. Veteran police officers know that the surest
way to get into more trouble than bargained for is to interfere in
family fights, especially between wife and husband—often the
police become the attacked. Dodger fans always had a fanatical
desire to see their Dodgers win the game, any game, any way,
any time.

As Bevens stood in the center of the diamond an almost
breathless hush fell upon Ebbets Field. It was a tension silence.
It didn't last long, but it was a tribute by the wild-eyed Dodger
fans to the big Yankee pitcher and his record-breaking opportunity. How often do you see a man trying to set a major World
Series record? Within 3 outs of pitching a no-hitter? Already
he had gone further with his no-hitter than any pitcher. The old
scoreboard didn't show hits or lack of hits, but the electrified,
super-charged news spread throughout the packed stands. Everybody in the ball park knew, not only the score of the game but,
even bigger than the outcome of the game, they knew they were
seeing living history . . . something they might never see again.
It hadn't happened since World Series began in 1903. It was
going to happen now. The Dodger fans put Bevens above
winning . . . for a few moments.

Bruce Edwards stepped in the batter's box. The noise level
now lifted. Jake Pitler, coaching at first was a cheer leader, clap-
ping his hands together and shouting mouthfuls of nothingness.
Ray Blades was the third-base coach, and for now he had no
signs to flash. Edwards was on his own. Shotton and the
Dodgers needed Edwards to get on base, get on with a hit, get
on with a walk. Get on.

Bevens knew his dual destiny as he faced Edwards—he said
afterward that he knew he had a no-hitter going. He was after

the game, yes indeed, and also he was hungrily after the no-hitter. He had had an undistinguished career. He'd been in George Weiss's farm system seven years, and with the Yankees three seasons. His record was 40 games won against 36 lost. He had been plagued with a sore arm. Now after ten years of labor, travel, travail, small salary and an uncertain arm he stood suddenly at the very pinnacle of his profession. The last of the ninth inning. Three more outs. So close. Closer than any pitcher before him.

Bruce Edwards was a dangerous batter . . . strong, he could hit it into the seats . . . he had batted .295 for the season and in 130 games had knocked in 80 runs. Bevens knew all about him—Bill Skiff and Johnny Neun had scouted the Dodgers, and coaches Dressen and Corriden had been with the Dodgers until this year.

Edwards hit it, high toward left field and the waiting stands. He hit it a shade too high. His round bat had not met the round ball exactly . . . when you think of it, it is quite an achievement in timing for a man to make his round bat meet a moving round ball so dead center the ball is driven sharply. The ball doesn't move in golf. It is always in motion in baseball.

Edwards hit it, and the crowd, already standing, let out a roar. Fans watch the flight of the ball. I had learned long ago to watch the outfielder. I described Lindell, who backed against the stands in left and waited for the ball. An announcer should always describe what the fielder does, not what the ball is doing. The fielder will take the ball, or else watch it go into the stands. Many an announcer has exclaimed "Home run!" when a ball takes off, only to have to eat his words when a catch is made. You can't take back, can't erase what you say into an open microphone. There is no editing in a radio box.

One man out.

Carl Furillo was next, another right-handed batter. Bevens was coming very close. Two outs more. The thousands were torn between rooting for Furillo or for Bevens. Furillo had played two years for Brooklyn, had played mostly when Reiser was hurt. Carl had gone in yesterday when Reiser sprained his ankle. For the year Furillo had also like Edwards batted .295. Bevens knew he couldn't hope to throw a fast pitch past Furillo, who was noted for being an "anxious" hitter—he hit at anything close to the strike zone. Furillo was a swinger, a hitter of strength. Bevens worked on him carefully, too carefully, and walked him. This was the ninth walk Bevens had allowed, which tied him with Jack Coombs in the 1910 World Series—but this record wasn't in Bevens's mind. He and millions and millions of listeners were thinking of an entirely different record.

One out, one on.

Spider Jorgensen came to bat, a slender left-handed batter. Spider had had a fine rookie year, had teamed with another rookie, Robinson, and with the second base combination of Reese and Stanky gave the Dodgers an excellent infield. Jorgensen was small—5'9" and 155 pounds. Furillo was at first, the potential tying run. I didn't second-guess managers at microphones, but I wondered then, and I still think now, why didn't Shotton send in a pinch runner for Furillo as soon as he got ball four? Furillo wasn't fast or an accomplished base runner.

Perhaps Sukeforth, Shotton's right-hand man on the bench failed him . . . or someone else failed. Before each game the list of players on both teams is stuck on the dugout wall by adhesive tape. It is the duty of whomever the manager appoints to run a pencil line through each player's name as he enters the game. Thus there is the clear listing of those players remaining. It is vital for the manager to know what players the other manager has at his disposal, as well as those remaining at his command. The coach who does this name-keeping, is also to suggest to the manager such matters as pinch runners, pinch hitters, pitchers in the bullpen. The manager has his mind full as he directs his squad. He is supposed to get all the help possible. No one man can keep it all in his head.

Jorgensen came to bat. Furillo took a short lead at first. Carl was no threat to steal. Bevens pitched and Jorgensen fouled it into the air alongside first base. McQuinn gratefully gloved it. That was the second out. The twenty-sixth out by the Dodgers. There was only one out left. This was the point of no return, as they say in aviation, the moment of truth, in the bloody arena of the bull fight.

Did Sukeforth—with two out—speak to Shotton? or Did the Old Man make the move by himself? I don't know and I was careful never to ask either. Al Gionfriddo was sent to first to run for Furillo. Now with one out left, Gionfriddo was the tying run, and little Al could run. He was a threat to steal. He was a polished player. He just couldn't hit enough, but he played a beautiful outfield. He'd been valuable as utility all season since the trade with Pittsburgh. He would accept an order and execute it. Shotton desperately wanted Gionfriddo to score, but, before he could score he had to get to second base. Shotton wasn't thinking for one second that Bevens was after a record. Shotton wanted to win this ball game. He was still alive. He had one out left.

Hugh Casey, who had thrown one pitch to Henrich and gotten a double-play in return, was scheduled to bat. Nobody anywhere in the world thought he would. Shotton looked down his dugout. He looked at Pete Reiser.

Shotton didn't have much choice. Reiser was the only remaining left-handed batter. Pete had the swollen right ankle, and couldn't run. He could barely walk. But as a left-handed batter he hit from his rear foot, his left one, which was perfectly sound. Reiser couldn't run but he could swing. Reiser had batted .309 for the season, and back in 1941 he was the National League batting champion with a mark of .343. What Shotton didn't know, and I didn't know in the radio booth, was that had Reiser listened to the trainer, Doc Wendler, he wouldn't have been in the dugout and available to pinch-hit. Pete was unable to take pregame practice because of the bad ankle, and was in the clubhouse soaking it. During the first three innings of the game he was back in the clubhouse soaking the ankle again. Doc Wendler, an expert trainer and a thoughtful man, told Pete he might as well put on his street clothes, that he couldn't play. However, Pete put his uniform back on and returned to the dugout, available to pinch-hit. Was it just the basic need to be where the action was that made Reiser reject the trainer's advice and be where Shotton could use him? Whatever it was that returned Reiser to the bench probably cost Bevens his no-hitter.

W. C. Heinz in his book *Once They Heard the Cheers*, written in 1979, over thirty years later, quoted Reiser as saying that Shotton barked, "Aren't you going to volunteer to hit?"

I had never heard that, but it sounded like genuine Burt Shotton. Except Shotton would have said "Ain't" instead of "Aren't."

Reiser told Heinz that he and Shotton had never gotten along well. I don't know about that, either, except I knew Shotton never worried about getting along well with any ballplayer. Further, Reiser was a devoted Leo Durocher man—they were suited for each other.

Consider: Here was Shotton standing in his dugout. He had one out left. Bevens hadn't allowed the Dodgers a hit. Gionfriddo was on first base and if somehow Gionfriddo could score, it would be a brand new ball game. Shotton had to pinch-hit for relief pitcher Casey. He looked down his bench, he had certainly kept track of the list of his remaining players, and there was Reiser, the only left-handed batter left. But Reiser had a badly swollen ankle. Shotton had neither the time nor the disposition to hover over Reiser and murmur, "How do you feel, Pete, old boy? Do you think, Pete, old man, you could possibly pick up a bat and somehow get up to the plate and maybe get a base hit? You know, Pete, old fellow, the whole season hangs on this . . . it's been a hell of a tough season, Pete, my man . . . Pete, you might just get a fat pitch right down the middle, right to your liking, and you might save us all and be a hero."

Shotton either ordered in a blunt phrase, or he stuck in a needle that made you mad. He didn't order a man with a badly sprained ankle (which proved later to be also a broken ankle) to pinch-hit. He wanted Reiser. But he wanted Reiser to respond to a personal challenge. Reiser always responded when challenged.

"Aren't (ain't) you going to volunteer to hit?"

Motivation: Knowing Reiser, when Shotton asked him if he wasn't going to volunteer to hit, that did it. Reiser's neck probably turned red, and he grabbed a bat and went to the plate so mad at Shotton he would have batted now if it killed him. Shotton wanted Reiser at the plate, and if he was mad enough to have his painful ankle misdirected, that was all right too.

The crowd was standing and yelling. It was almost impossible to hear the announcement on the public address system, "batting for Hugh Casey—Pete Reiser!" The sound reached an even higher level.

Bevens went to work on Reiser. The count reached two balls and one strike. Bevens set himself for the 2–1 pitch, peered over his left shoulder at Gionfriddo . . . and threw to first base.

Gionfriddo was back. First baseman McQuinn stayed glued to the inside corner of the bag, trying to hold the runner on. Bevens came down into his set, pitching position with a man on first . . . looked at the runner . . . and threw for him again. Gionfriddo was back, then led off again, led off as far as he could without getting picked off. To steal second base the runner must get all the lead off first that he can . . . he must get such a lead that he can just get back to the bag should the pitcher throw for him . . . then he must study the pitcher carefully, and know when the pitcher is going to throw for him again, or is going to pitch . . . the runner must get the lead, then get the jump, then run at top speed, and finally slide.

Reiser waited at the plate. Bevens checked the runner, then pitched. Gionfriddo went. Reiser took the pitch—he didn't swing at it. Berra grabbed the ball and threw to Rizzuto, the shortstop covering the bag at second. The throw was high, and by the time Rizzuto brought the ball down and tagged Gionfriddo, umpire Pinelli was giving the safe sign. Rizzuto jumped around like he had electric shock in both feet. Rizzuto claimed Gionfriddo was out. In the years we broadcast together Rizzuto consistently said Gionfriddo was out. He will say today Gionfriddo was out. However, Pinelli said he was safe, and Gionfriddo, the tying run, was at second base. The pitch on which he stole was wide for ball three . . . the count on Reiser was now 3–1.

Shotton ordered Gionfriddo to steal. Shotton wanted the tying run at second where a single could score it. It would have taken an extra base hit to score it from first. Suppose, however, Berra's throw to Rizzuto had been a shade sooner and lower? Suppose Gionfriddo had been out, and Bevens thus had his no-hitter, what would the second-guessers have done to Shotton? Ending the game with an order to try to steal second base! And with Reiser at the plate, who with one swing could have depositied the ball into Bedford Avenue behind right field!

Shotton never gave a thought to anything except, "I wanted him on second base." And, Shotton might have added a four-letter, Anglo-Saxon word for excrement. Tough old man.

Time was called by the Yankees. Bucky Harris again took The Book and threw it into the trash can. He ordered Bevens to throw ball four to Reiser. The Book, and don't think the writers weren't referring to it right now, says never to put the winning run on base. Harris put Reiser on first, bad ankle and all. It wasn't anything to do with the ankle. Harris knew Shotton would send in a pinch runner as soon as Reiser hobbled to first base and touched the bag to make it legally his.

Harris knew Shotton had no more left-handed batters. He knew Bevens had been a wild man all afternoon. He knew Reiser was hitting off his left foot, which was healthy and strong . . . he was afraid Bevens in his effort not to throw ball four would groove the pitch, and that Reiser might very well hit it against or even over the nearby right-field wall. Harris never hesitated. He didn't want Reiser hitting a fat pitch. Instead, he wanted him on first base. Harris made his move. Ball four, and you know what you can do with The Book. Harris was paid handsomely to make the first guess. He made it. Tough man.

Nobody had to be alert in the Dodger dugout about a pinch runner for Reiser. Eddie Miksis, a young infielder, who could fly, replaced Reiser. Pete limped out of sight.

On the broadcast of a ball game the engineer will have a microphone suspended outside the booth to pick up the sounds of the crowd. He feeds crowd-level in, balancing it against the level of the announcer's voice. For the last half of this ninth inning the engineer had turned the crowd mike off, and had kept motioning me to talk as close to the mike as possible. It was bedlam.

Eddie Stanky was due to bat, and started for the plate. He had been on deck while Reiser was facing Bevens.

Shotton made another move. He recalled Stanky, only the second time in all of 1947 that he pinch-hit for him. Up came Harry Lavagetto, better known as Cookie. Lavagetto was a veteran. He'd come up to the Pirates in 1934, been traded to Brooklyn in 1937, and after the pennant season of 1941, was the first Dodger to go into military service. He was gone four years. His career was closing out.

Lavagetto walked toward the plate swinging two bats to make the one he would use feel slightly lighter. He was a right-handed hitter. The Book says to put a left-handed batter against a right-handed pitcher, but Shotton had no left-handed batter. Reiser was his last one.

In a hospital in Oakland, California, Mrs. Lavagetto woke up. She had earlier given birth to their first child, had been listening to the game, had dropped off to sleep, but the second I began announcing that Lavagetto was coming in to hit for Stanky she woke up. She didn't doze off again.

Bevens had a 2–1 lead. He had two men out. He almost had had his no-hitter on the play on Gionfriddo at second base. Had Berra been a more experienced catcher the no-hitter might now be history—keep in mind, the Dodgers in 3 games had stolen five bases on the rookie. After the game Larry MacPhail second-guessed, "Bevens should have held Gionfriddo closer to first base."

Pee Wee Reese waited on deck as the next batter. Jackie Robinson was batting after Reese.

Lavagetto set himself at the plate. Bevens checked Gionfriddo at second. There was no reason to worry about Miksis at first. The infield was back, the outfield slightly into right. Lavagetto didn't pull.

Bevens delivered. Lavagetto swung and missed on a high, slightly outside pitch. Strike one. Two out. Runners at second and at first. Yankees 2, Dodgers 1.

The big right-hander was ready. He pitched, again slightly high and outside. Lavagetto swung and connected solidly. The ball took off toward the right-field wall. Tommy Henrich, who'd robbed Hermanski earlier with a leaping catch, judged the ball, positioned himself, and jumped. The ball was too high for him, and struck the concrete wall for a clean hit.

It's a great advantage to be a base runner with two out—you just go full speed. Gionfriddo went around third and into home with the tying run. No possible play on him. Miksis, starting from first, swooped around second, was given the green light at third by coach Blades, and streaked for the plate. Henrich retrieved the ball and started his throw in. First baseman McQuinn relayed it to Berra. Miksis slid home ahead of the tag, well ahead of it.

This was then, and still is to this day, the biggest explosion of noise in the history of Brooklyn. The Dodgers started pounding Lavagetto, then picked him up and carried him off. I recall I said, "The Dodgers are beating Lavagetto to death." They almost did.

Bevens walked off the mound. His no-hitter was gone, his game was gone, all on one pitch. Hugh Casey was the winning pitcher, all on one pitch.

Reese as the on-deck batter, was the closest Dodger to home plate as Gionfriddo ran across it and then Miksis slid across it. In the clubhouse afterward Pee Wee told Roscoe McGowen of the *Times*, with a straight face, "You know, I was sorry for that guy—Bevens. It just broke my heart right square in two when I saw those two runs crossing the plate. I just couldn't stand it."

And then Reese started yelling and laughing.

I turned the microphone over to Mel Allen for his summation and sign off. I remember the final sentence I said as Mel came on. Edward R. Murrow, my boss then at Columbia Broadcasting System where I was director of sports, told me later I had ended my account perfectly. Murrow was a stickler for straight reporting, for precise grammar, and for due care with adjectives. What I said was:

"I'll be a suck-egg mule!"

Game Five

Lavagetto's pinch-hit double the day before let all the steam out of the pressure pot. For a while, it was a wild night in Brooklyn. You could have heard a pin drop in the Bronx. However, one day later, Saturday afternoon, October 4, Ebbets Field, it started all over again: pressure, tenseness, men on base, and another dramatic game coming down to the last of the ninth. Again two men out, the Yankees again leading 2–1, the Dodgers again having the tying run at second base, and again Harry Lavagetto as the pinch hitter.

The day before Al Gionfriddo stole second base in the last of the ninth with two out. His manager, Burt Shotton, said that Gionfriddo's steal was the key play of the Brooklyn victory. Today Gionfriddo pinch-hit in the sixth inning, walked, and raced home on a single by Jackie Robinson. That was the only

Brooklyn run of the day. In the ninth inning today Gionfriddo was in the clubhouse, listening to Mel Allen, who had the second half of the broadcast. Several writers were there, keeping score as they listened to the play-by-play. With two out, with pinch runner Vic Lombardi at second, Lavagetto was sent to bat. Gionfriddo said to the writers, "Put down a home run . . . he's gonna hit one."

The writers, trained to wait until the play actually took place, waited. What they wrote was the letter K—the universal scoring symbol for a strikeout.

This was the pinnacle game in Frank Shea's career. He would never reach such a height again. This had been his rookie season and he'd led the American League in winning percentage with 14 victories against 5 defeats. His record would have been more impressive but for a sore arm that began at the All Star game. Shea had been credited with winning Game One but had given way in the fifth inning for a pinch hitter when the Yankees made 5 runs. Today was his second start in the World Series. He was rested and ready. Further, he had watched and suffered for Bevens the day before, and he made no secret he was going to try to avenge Bevens today. Where Bevens failed in the ninth with a 2–1 lead and 2 out because of Lavagetto, Shea today took a 2–1 lead into the ninth and with 2 out, fanned Lavagetto. I don't know how much Bevens felt he was avenged, but Shea rejoiced mightily, as did the Yankees in the clubhouse.

Shotton started Rex Barney, who hadn't started a game for the Dodgers since July 4. Rex was a tall, slender right-hander—6'3", 185 pounds. He could throw the ball hard, so hard it resembled an aspirin tablet to the batters, but most of the time was so wild he couldn't hit the side of a barn. Rex had been in military service and returned the year before, winning 2 and losing 5. This year he had reversed the figures, made them 5 and 2. His record for two seasons balanced at 7–7. Shotton had to start him. Who else?

Bucky Harris was going to get a complete game today from Frank Shea. He had gotten one from Allie Reynolds in Game Two, and another complete job from the ill-fated Bill Bevens in Game Four—3 complete games in 5. Shotton hadn't and wouldn't get one of his starting pitchers to go longer than five innings.

Barney started, was wild, at times was effective and lasted four and two thirds innings. He had three encounters with Joe DiMaggio which riveted attention in the crowded ball park.

Barney walked 9 Yankees. Had Shotton been able to leave him in, or better still, had the Dodgers gotten Rex some runs so that he would have been left in, Bevens's World Series record of walking 10 the day before surely would have been bettered.

The pattern was set at the start. Barney walked his first batter, George Stirnweiss. Tommy Henrich promptly doubled and Stirnweiss had to hold at third. Barney walked Johnny Lindell, and here it was: 3 men on, nobody out, and Joe DiMaggio at bat. What was Shotton to do? Barney could throw it if he could get it over. He did to DiMaggio, and struck him out. George McQuinn bounced weakly back to Barney, forcing Stirnweiss at the plate, Barney to Edwards. Billy Johnson came up, and Barney struck him out. Three on with nobody out . . . then 3 left on and no runs. This promised to be another one of those days.

Frank Shea took the mound, a stocky right-hander, 6', 200 pounds. Shea had it. He brought it to the ball park with him. He set the Dodgers down in order the first inning. One, two, three.

This was Shea's day. He set the Dodgers down in order again in the second inning, although he got a lift from his second baseman, George Stirnweiss, who leaped at the precise split-second to grab Dixie Walker's line drive—he caught it in the webbing of his glove. Then Shea mowed down the next three batters, which gave him nine straight.

Meantime Barney wasn't as efficient in the number of Yankees he faced, but allowed no scoring the first three rounds. In the second inning he walked Rizzuto, then wild pitched, which got Rizzuto to second. Phil was out a minute later trying to steal third.

In the top of the third Barney got in the pickle vat again. He walked both Henrich and Lindell—that made 5 walks so far by the Brooklyn fireballer—and Joe DiMaggio waited at the plate. Barney had fanned DiMaggio in the first inning. DiMag didn't suffer such indignities often . . . Henrich led off second, Lindell off first. Barney pitched, DiMaggio swung, and it was a ground ball to shortstop Pee Wee Reese, who scooped, flipped to Stanky, who threw to Robinson. DiMaggio hit into a double-play. DiMaggio, voted by the baseball writers as the American League's Most Valuable Player for 1947, had struck out his first at bat with the bases loaded, and then with two on, had banged into a twin killing. DiMaggio had batted with five Yankees on base and hadn't scored one of them.

Joe took his position in center field. His face was impassive. He steeled himself to show no emotion in public, but inside DiMaggio was seething. Joe was always his own severest critic.

No score after three innings—Shea hadn't permitted a runner, and Barney had been living a charmed life. Rex had had six runners, and had twice gotten out of trouble at the expense of DiMaggio.

Shea made it more his game and his day in the fourth inning. Barney got the first two Yankees and seemed on the way to a less hair-raising session. However, ball four again. (They say in the trade that many a manager has ordered to be chiseled on his tombstone, "Put here by bases on balls.") Barney walked Aaron Robinson, and then walked Rizzuto. That made it 7 walks by Barney. Sooner or later, if you keep putting them on with walks somebody is going to hit one.

Frank Shea hit one, a clean, line drive single to left, and in came Aaron Robinson with the game's first run. Barney walked Stirnweiss, but with the bases full, got Henrich on a ground ball to Stanky. One run in four innings from ten runners. Bucky Harris didn't like it—he certainly wanted more than this slender margin. Burt Shotton wore his poker face, kept writing down the doings in his scorebook, but must have been wondering how long this could last, and if the game could be kept low score until it was time to bring in Hugh Casey.

Shea started defending his run—he'd knocked it in. He got Stanky in the bottom of the fourth, then walked Reese, the first Dodger he'd allowed on base. Pee Wee stayed on first as Jackie Robinson and Dixie Walker were easy outs.

Inning five. Lindell bounced out, and DiMaggio and Barney

faced each other for the third time. Barney got behind two balls and no strikes. DiMaggio went for the 2–0 pitch and fouled it back. Barney pitched again, and somebody in the upper left-field stands got a most interesting souvenir. That made it 2–0, New York. It's in the record books: you get DiMaggio out just so often. Barney said later the first two times he pitched to DiMaggio he kept the ball low. The ball Joe hit for the home run, and the decisive run of the game, was higher than he, Rex, had meant it to be. Wildness by a pitcher is not just walking batters.

Barney got George McQuinn but walked Billy Johnson, his ninth base on balls. Manager Shotton told his coach, Clyde Sukeforth, "Go get him, Sukey," and Clyde went to the mound. That was all for Barney, who in four and two thirds innings had thrown about as many pitches as Shea would in nine. Joe Hatten came in.

The Dodgers finally got a hit. Gene Hermanski opened the last of the fifth with a single to right, but Shea left Gene stranded at first as he took care of the next three hitters. Five innings, and Shea had allowed 1 walk, 1 single, not a man to second base, and had batted in a run with a single.

The sixth inning was routine one, two, three and back to the field for the Yankees. The Dodgers now finally broke through against Shea, and threatened to take command. It became very much a ball game.

Al Gionfriddo pinch-hit for relief pitcher Hatten. The Book, in its section Advice to All Pitchers, says, "Do Not Walk the First Batter in an Inning." Shea broke the rule. He walked Gionfriddo. However, Stanky fanned, but Pee Wee Reese, an excellent judge of a pitched ball, worked Shea for another walk, and the tying runs were on. Jackie Robinson whistled a single over the button on Shea's cap, and in came Gionfriddo, who knew where home plate was after the ninth inning yesterday. Reese, an excellent base runner, took third even though DiMaggio was the center fielder. Joe's throw was late at third and Jackie Robinson, who took advantage of everything in sight, took second. Now Shea was in trouble. Nobody in Ebbets Field had to inquire who was the left-hander warming up hurriedly for the Yankees.

Manager Harris had to decide—was Shea suddenly losing his stuff? Dixie Walker was the batter. Reese was on third, Jackie Robinson on second. The Yankees were ahead, but just: 2–1. Harris went by The Book this time. In such a situation The Book recommends allowing the starting pitcher to work on one more batter, to see what happens. Shea pitched to Dixie who fouled up and out to third baseman Johnson. Then Harris let Shea pitch to one more hitter, Gene Hermanski. Gene lined out to DiMaggio. The storm had hit, passed, and the damage was minimal: 1 run.

The excitement of a baseball game is a man on base. A man on base can bluff a steal, can try to steal, can steal, can run on outs, and after fly balls are caught can run home and score. When there is a man on base the defense has to be aware of him. The infielders have to vary their positions. The pitcher has to conform to stringent rules of procedure. The pitcher is free with the bases open, but in reality he is a prisoner of the runner, especially if the runner is a Phil Rizzuto, a George Stirnweiss, a Pee Wee Reese, or especially a Jackie Robinson. A pitcher who gets careless with Robinson on third finds that Robinson has stolen home. A pitcher has leeway in working to the batter when the bases are open. Once a runner or runners are on base, the pitcher can't be as cavalier.

The fan gets very interested when there are men on base. The runners take their leads, the pitcher has to check them carefully. It is tense. Any slip or error and it is costly. A hit means something on the scoreboard.

In this fifth game there were men on base every time you looked up. Three on and DiMaggio at bat . . . two on and DiMaggio at bat . . . and a kid pitcher, wild as a hungry chicken hawk on the mound. There were base runners every inning of this game.

Bill Bevens came within one out of pitching a no-hit game the day before. Yet he walked 10. There were Dodgers constantly on base. There was always a threat by the Dodgers. Something was going on.

When Don Larsen at Yankee Stadium in the fifth game of the 1956 World Series pitched a no-hit game against the Dodgers, he also pitched a perfect game. He got all twenty-seven batters. He didn't allow a man on base. This was the first no-hit game in the history of the World Series, and the first perfect game in the big leagues since 1922 when Charles Robertson of the White Sox retired all the Tigers at Detroit. This span of thirty-four years between perfect games, games with no runner at all by one side, was just about right, in my opinion. Think about it. Nothing happened for the Dodgers against Larsen. They went to the plate, back to the dugout, out to the field and, with nothing to show for the afternoon, went home. Baseball can't afford many perfect games. The game is played by human beings. It is watched by human beings. Human beings are not perfect, and can stand only a small touch of perfection, and that only at long intervals of time.

Hank Behrman came out of the Brooklyn bullpen for the seventh inning, the fourth time in 5 games Behrman was in relief. He was in hot water at once. Henrich singled to right. Lindell was ordered to bunt—Harris was now playing for another run—and Lindell fouled off two pitches and then Behrman fanned him. DiMaggio, who had hit the home run in the fifth that was the difference in the game right now, got a walk. Behrman was very careful with DiMaggio. Two men on base, one out. McQuinn fanned, but catcher Edwards let the third strike get away from him for a passed ball. McQuinn was automatically out with a runner at first and less than 2 out. Henrich and DiMaggio advanced to third and second. Any kind of a hit would bring them in. Billy Johnson bounced back to pitcher Behrman who didn't bother to say thanks—he just threw to Robinson at first, and another threat went by the boards.

Shea began the seventh as though he would dig his own grave. Again he walked the first man up, Bruce Edwards. This put the tying run at first. Carl Furillo was the batter and he didn't have to look at third-base coach Ray Blades for a sign—of course Shotton wanted Furillo to bunt and get Edwards to second base. In addition to the obvious strategy of moving Edwards to second by a sacrifice, Furillo started slowly from the plate, then wasn't too fast a runner, hit a ball sharply, and therefore if allowed to hit away could be doubled-up if he drove the ball at an infielder. Furillo tried to bunt. He tried twice, and fouled off both attempts. Then he lifted an easy fly to DiMaggio.

Spider Jorgensen flied to Lindell. Arkie Vaughan batted for relief pitcher Behrman, Vaughan doubled and sent Edwards to third. Shotton sent up Pete Reiser, sore ankle and all, and again Bucky Harris wanted no part of Reiser hitting a fat pitch into Bedford Avenue. Harris ordered Reiser walked, which loaded the bases. Eddie Miksis, as he did the day before, ran for Reiser.

Pee Wee Reese got the count to two and two, then Shea fired a third strike that Reese took. The threat was over. Three men left on, the Yankees still leading, 2–1. The red-hot question was, "Suppose Furillo had bunted successfully, and gotten Edwards over to second, wouldn't Edwards have scored on Vaughan's double, and tied the score?"

In fact, Eddie Stanky growled in the clubhouse that had Furillo bunted, and advanced Edwards to second, "we'd still be playing, tied at two all." Shotton had ordered Furillo to bunt. How did Shotton feel about it? He ended the probing by the writers by saying, "Had Furillo bunted Edwards over . . . how do you know Vaughan would have gotten the same pitch from Shea that he got when he doubled?" The Old Man was not one to second-guess his players or his coaches. He defended them. So did Bucky Harris.

To start the eighth inning, who else but Hugh Casey? The big fellow lumbered to the mound for his fourth relief assignment in 5 games. He hadn't been scored on, and he was credited with 2 victories and no defeats. He was now the pitcher the Dodgers wanted. The Yankees led 2–1. It was up to Casey to keep it that close.

Casey got his first two batters, then had Shea double to left center. Frank really hit it—he was having a day for himself. However, Casey struck out Stirnweiss.

Shea set the Dodgers down in order the last of the eighth. He was strong. Joe Page in the bullpen didn't get up to throw. Shea was moving again at full speed.

It appeared the ninth inning would be almost a duplicate of the one the day before. Henrich got on for the Yankees on an error by Eddie Miksis at second. Lindell tried to bunt and got nicked by the pitch. Two on, and now it was Casey against

DiMaggio. DiMag hit into a fast double-play for the second time in the game—Reese to Miksis to Robinson. McQuinn came up with Henrich leading off third. Casey pitched and the ball got away from catcher Edwards. Henrich came running in, Casey tore off the mound, Edwards recovered the ball, Casey blocked the plate and on Edwards's throw, Casey tagged Henrich out. Into the last of the ninth with the Yankees again leading 2–1.

Shea was on the mound for the last of the ninth, ready to make his 1-run lead hold up. Joe Page was throwing, and ready in the bullpen. Things can happen lightning-fast in such a tight situation—particularly at Ebbets Field.

Bruce Edwards promptly put the tying run on first with a line single. Shotton sent in Vic Lombardi to run for Edwards. Bucky Harris was halfway up the steps of the Yankee dugout. Furillo, who failed to move Edwards to second in the seventh inning, now bunted fair, and got Lombardi over to second. Two rookies faced each other: Shea pitching, Spider Jorgensen batting. Jorgensen brought the crowd to its feet with a drive to deep right, but not quite deep enough. Henrich caught it.

How much should you ask of a hero? Casey was scheduled to bat next, but it would be a pinch hitter. Lombardi at second had to be brought home or the game would be history. Harry Lavagetto came out of the dugout, swinging two bats, and the crowd went wild. Yesterday's hero was on the march again.

Shea had vowed to avenge Bevens. Here was his specific opportunity. Here was the man who had undone Bevens, and at the exact same stage of the game—2 out, tying run at second, Yankees ahead 2–1.

Against Bevens, Lavagetto went after the first two pitches—missing for strike one, and then connecting for the doomsday double. Bevens made his first two pitches so good Lavagetto went after them. Today Shea was very careful. He had witnessed the finale yesterday. He knew exactly what Lavagetto had hit, what the pitch was and where it was. Pitchers study such things. They do, if they want to continue pitching.

Lavagetto was a veteran. He wasn't going to chase a bad ball. The duel between the central characters jockeyed until the count was three balls and one strike. Lavagetto hadn't offered.

Now the count was in his favor. Shea had to come into the strike zone or else walk the winning run to first base. The Book warns against doing that.

I have heard Ty Cobb say, I have heard Ted Williams say, I have heard Stan Musial say that if you wait long enough you are going to get your pitch. I have also heard all three of them say that the terrible thing is finally to get your pitch and then pop it up, foul it off or miss it.

Shea had to come in. Lavagetto knew it and was waiting, his bat cocked behind his right ear. Shea pitched, Lavagetto swung, and fouled it off. Now the count was three to two. Lavagetto said in the clubhouse, "I got my pitch."

Shea let loose a fast ball, Lavagetto swung again, and struck out. There was no mob scene waiting for Lavagetto this day. The mob scene was for Frank Shea. He had pitched, and batted, the Yankees into a 3–2 edge in the Series, and sent the Series back to Yankee Stadium. He had stopped the Dodgers after they had won 2 straight.

Bucky Harris said a lot of things in the clubhouse. One of his remarks was, "Going down to the last pitch is too much wear and tear on the nerves."

Game Six

The action returned to vast, menacing, flag-draped, triple-decked Yankee Stadium. After the 3 wild games in Brooklyn, the last 2 ending with pinch hitter Harry Lavagetto at bat, two out, last of the ninth, the general expectation was that the Yankees, back in their own ball park, leading in the Series 3–2 would routinely end matters. Lavagetto had made history in Game Four. He had failed the next day. Just so much can be asked of a hero.

Allie Reynolds, the ace of the Yankees, who'd won 19 games in the season and had breezed to an easy win in Game Two of the Series, was rested and ready. Manager Shotton had to start somebody from his scrambled staff. It was Vic Lombardi. The weather was perfect. Sunday afternoon in the South Bronx.

Here is how John Drebinger began his story of Game Six in the New York *Times* the next morning:

"Incredible as it may seem to the bewildered world at large, the 1947 World Series is still with us, and so are the Dodgers.

"For in one of the most extraordinary games ever played, one that left a record Series crowd limp and exhausted, Burt Shotton's unpredictable Flock fought the Yankees in a last ditch stand at the Stadium yesterday and defeated them 8 to 6."

This was a game for strong men only. It raged over a record time of three hours and nineteen minutes. It consumed a record total of thirty-eight players—twenty-one Yankees and seventeen Dodgers. The two great bullpen bullies, Joe Page and Hugh Casey were pivotal. Manager Harris used six pitchers, Shotton four. The record crowd—74,065—paid a record sum, $393,210. And, it featured a remarkable catch by Al Gionfriddo that shattered the public aplomb of DiMaggio. Johnny Lindell played with a cracked rib, got 2 hits, and got a dressing-down afterward from MacPhail. Commissioner Chandler had ordered the lights to be turned on had the game gone another inning, but Hugh Casey was a practical energy conservationist—he saved both the game and the extra light bill.

It was a picture book setting when it started. Sunshine, green grass, gaily dressed stadium, and a capacity crowd in Sunday-best. The Chief, Allie Reynolds, stood strong and confident on the mound.

Eddie Stanky led off for Brooklyn. Reynolds wound up, pitched, and Stanky lined a single to left field. Just like that. Pee Wee Reese looked quietly at ball one, then at ball two. Reese stared at third-base coach Ray Blades to see if Shotton wanted him to hit, if he so pleased, or take the pitch no matter where it was. Reese was a manager's dream; intelligent, balanced disposition, a team man first, alert to orders and instant in response . . . he would steal a base but not unless it was needed . . . he never played for his own records. Reese always backed out of batter's box and looked at the third-base coach, whether there was an order on or not. It was hard for the other team to steal signs from the actions of Reese—he always gave the impression something was going on. If a batter only looked at the third-base coach when there was a signal to be flashed, that was a clue—

with Reese at the plate it seemed there was action on every pitch. As a rule, when a batter goes to the plate he is on his own —he has "the privilege" of taking pitches or hitting when he wishes. However, the manager can "remove the privilege," can order a pitch to be taken, can order a hit-and-run play, a bunt, etc. It is up to the third-base coach to get the sign from the dugout, then flash it by secret code to the batter, and also to the runner or runners. So it was, Pee Wee stepped out, stared at Blades, stepped back in.

Reynolds pitched and Reese singled to center. Stanky was not running on the pitch and stopped at second. Shotton had not removed the privilege from Reese. Now the first two Dodgers were on. This wasn't starting like a quiet Sunday afternoon in the Bronx with the Yankees routinely wrapping up another World Series.

The infield tightened into position to defend against a sacrifice. Jackie Robinson was the batter, and a beautiful bunter. Jackie took a long look at Blades before he stepped in against Reynolds. Reynolds pitched but it was no bunt. Jackie swung and sent a high fly to left field. Lindell was uncertain. He lost it. Left field at the Stadium is the sun field, and it is doubly hard to play it in the slants and shadows of an October afternoon. The ball fell for a single, but Stanky could only take third—he had had to wait between second and third to see what happened.

Dixie Walker batted next. Three on. Nobody out. This was in Yankee Stadium, yes, but it was starting as if it were back in Ebbets Field. Walker hit it hard, but at shortstop Rizzuto, who stepped on second and threw to first for a double-play. Stanky raced home for the first run of the game, and Robinson slid full force into Rizzuto, sending the small shortstop into a high spin. Phil lay stunned, but after a few minutes got up, and continued. Robinson didn't vary from his straight-in slide. Rizzuto in the follow-through of his throw to first was squarely in the path of the runner. It's rough out there around second—the lead runner is supposed to "break up the double-play." Robinson had been a star football player at UCLA. Rizzuto told me many times he well remembered that takeout play. However, little Phil got his out at second and made his throw to first for another out. Nobody was asking favors.

Reynolds faced Gene Hermanski. Allie needed Hermanski to get out of the inning with no more than 1 run, which wouldn't be too expensive, not when you have DiMaggio, Henrich, Lindell, etc., on your side and coming to bat through nine innings. Allie pitched and the ball got loose from catcher Lollar—the official scorers charged a passed ball. Reese, leading off third, didn't wait for the scorers' decision—he streaked home for run two. Hermanski got a base on balls, but Reynolds got Bruce Edwards to ground to third to end the first half inning. Despite the double-play, the Dodgers scored twice. The team that had successfully played the Cardinals 22—no, 23 times, counting the Northey-Reardon play-off game—had played the Giants who hit home runs—had played the Braves with Sain and Spahn, was still full of fight in Game Six.

The little left-hander, Vic Lombardi, set the Yankees down in order. Reynolds, almost before he knew it, was back on the mound. He took rapid care of the last third of the Dodger batting order. Lombardi got the Yankees in a one-two-three sequence again, and things appeared calm in the South Bronx: routine outs since Reese scored run two.

Reynolds began the third inning getting Stanky to lift a fly to center. It would be news if DiMaggio dropped it. There wasn't any news. Joe caught them; easy, high, low, soft, deep, short or even behind the monuments—once he did go behind the distant markers to rob Hank Greenberg. Reynolds seemed to have found his usual efficient stride—seven straight put-outs for the Chief.

Reese stepped in. This was the end of one out following another. There would be no more peace all afternoon. Reese doubled over third. Robinson bounced a ground rule double into left field, scoring Reese, 3–0. Walker hit a low line drive to right that Henrich dove for but missed. It went for a double, scoring Robinson, 4–0. Reynolds was taken out, Karl Drews was brought in. Drews got the needed two outs, and the Dodgers took the field leading 4–0. The Yankees had not had a base runner.

Sherm Lollar first up in the last of the third, broke the spell with a line-drive double in the left-field corner. Hermanski dove for it too late. Lombardi wild pitched as he was striking out Drews, permitting Lollar to reach third. The fates were impartial—Lindell had lost a fly ball in the first inning—now third baseman Jorgensen fumbled a sharp ground ball hit by Stirnweiss, and Lollar scored for the Yankees, 4–1. Henrich, the batting star of the Series for both sides, singled to center and Stirnweiss, a fast man, sped toward third. He, and many others in the years to come, learned about the strength and accuracy of Carl Furillo's right arm. Furillo threw Stirnweiss out at third. Henrich took second on the play. Two out, but the Yankees had batted around once on Lombardi, and were now taking dead aim in their second encounter with him. Lindell, playing with a broken rib which he knew about, his manager knew about, but no one else did, singled and Henrich scored, 4–2. The team that won 19 straight in the season by taking advantage of every opportunity, kept beating a tattoo on Lombardi. Now came DiMaggio, a highly respected player who was generally liked except by the pitchers he hammered, and by all third basemen. DiMaggio was a pull hitter, with drastic power. At times he drove baseballs at third basemen that were murderous. Lombardi pitched to DiMaggio, and Spider Johnson at third almost got his head knocked off—Jorgensen defended himself with his glove but the ball tore away and into left field. This put the tying runs aboard. Manager Shotton said one word, "Sukey!", and coach Sukeforth started walking to the mound. Sukey returned to the dugout with Lombardi, after waving in Ralph Branca, who had begun the Series brilliantly by retiring the first twelve Yankees, and then retiring only himself. This must have seemed like old home week to Shotton; changing pitchers with the regularity of changing the guards at Buckingham Palace. It was much too early in the struggle to commit Casey.

Branca finished his warm-up tosses, patted the mound with his spikes, and stood face-to-face with Billy Johnson, the veteran third baseman. It was Branca's assignment to put on the brakes and hold this 4–2 lead. The Dodgers couldn't lose this game and play tomorrow. The Yankees had them down, 3 games to 2. It would be the height of redundancy to say, "This was it." Catcher Edwards held up two fingers and waved them for his teammates to see—"two men out"—"play for one," "play for the sure out." Then Edwards sank onto his haunches. Johnson stepped in, looked at Branca, and Edwards gave his wiggle-finger sign for the pitch he wanted Branca to deliver.

Johnson slashed a single to right. In came Lindell to make it 4–3, and DiMaggio—the tying run—easily went to third. Di-Maggio had the advantage of running with two out. He didn't hesitate. His long loping strides simply ate up ground: few people fully appreciated how fast he was, the ground he covered, because he made it look so effortless. He glided. Baseball men would tell you to mark where DiMaggio started, then mark where he was when he pulled down a difficult fly ball, and then mark the ground he covered. Rizzuto was small and ran with quick, short, almost mincing steps and appeared to be flying—also Phil had a gimmick: he kept his cap loose so that as he ran it would fly off, adding to the illusion. Fans talked about Rizzuto's speed and not DiMaggio's.

Manager Harris now had to play the type game Shotton had lived with all summer. Bucky needed the tying run, and he put up Bobby Brown to hit for rookie Jack Phillips, who had started at first base. Brown, who wasn't retired all through the Series, singled to left. Hermanski tried hard for it but missed. DiMaggio trotted home with the tying run, 4–4. Johnson made it to third. The Yankees were roaring back. They had changed a 4–0 deficit into an even battle, and they thirsted for more. Branca was the young ace of the Dodgers—he'd won 21 in the season. Shotton left it to him as Rizzuto came to bat. Phil hit a line drive, but at Eddie Stanky, and the third inning ended with it all even. The Yankees had wiped out the early Dodger advantage. The weight of their 3–2 game edge got heavy again.

Bucky Harris had to reset his team. Lindell's broken rib began hurting still more, and Big John had to leave. Henrich was shifted from right to left, and Yogi Berra was sent to right. McQuinn took over at first base, and Aaron Robinson went behind the plate. A baseball squad is twenty-five men—what good are reserves if you don't use them?

Drews got the Dodgers out without fireworks in the top of the fourth. The Yankees, needing 1 game to win it all, came in and broke the tie against Branca: singles by Aaron Robinson,

Henrich, and Berra made it 5–4. Berra's line drive was down the right-field foul line—it was ruled fair by a hair. The Dodgers raged and stormed that it was foul. An angry rhubarb was added to the afternoon.

Pee Wee Reese led off the fifth, and worked Drews for a base on balls, which placed the tying run at first. Robinson swung and rolled to third—Reese was forced at second on Johnson's throw to Stirnweiss. Dixie Walker stepped in, pumped his bat, moved his feet as he always did, and hit a high drive into the upper right-field stands—just foul. Drews was shaken, and missed the plate with his next two pitches. Manager Harris decided this was the moment for Joe Page, and in came the big left-hander. This was the spot. Page was the man. Joe hadn't been needed too much; this was the third time in the Series he was called to the rescue. Without any trouble Page ended the mild threat by fanning Walker and getting pinch hitter Miksis, batting for Hermanski, on an infield roller. Page was now the man the Yankees wanted to lock up the Series and send everybody home for the winter.

Branca was now pitching full strength. He put the Yankees down without incident in the last of the fifth, and Joe Page walked to the mound to start the sixth inning. The Yankees led 5–4 behind the top relief pitcher in the American League, the relief man who had held the pitching staff together, won 14 for himself in addition to saving 17 games in the season. Harris now had his star relief pitcher in the ideal spot.

But the Dodgers fell on Page like hungry bears on a row of beehives. Edwards singled and Furillo hit the next pitch for a double. Boom. Boom. Just like that Page had runners on second and third, and here came Harry Lavagetto from the dugout to hit for Jorgensen. Page didn't need to hear the public address announcer say who was going to bat. He'd seen Lavagetto against Bevens and against Shea. This was dramatic stuff for the big crowd.

Page threw, Lavagetto swung and missed. Strike one. Page pitched again and again Lavagetto missed. Two strikes. Page had Lavagetto in a hole—the batter couldn't afford to risk taking a pitch that was even close to the strike zone. This situation has created a widely used phrase in our language that accurately describes when a fellow is between a rock and a hard place— "had two strikes on him." Lavagetto backed out of the box, rubbed some dirt on his hands, then got back in. He had no place to go but back against the plate and against Joe Page. The strong left-hander turned it loose, Lavagetto swung, and fouled it off. He stayed alive. Page didn't waste time on the mound. He got a new ball, took the sign from his catcher, and fired. Lavagetto hit this one, high into right field, and deep enough for Edwards to tag at third and score after the catch. That got the Dodgers the precious tying run. They were back even, and gladly had spent an out to get it 5–5. Lavagetto had delivered again—not as dramatically as against Bevens, but efficiently. You must tie when you are behind before you can win. Also, this run took away Page's advantage and, made him the pitcher of record.

It didn't stay even any longer than it took a new man in the Series to get to the plate and swing. Branca was due. Shotton looked down his bench and called for Bobby Bragan, a right-handed batter, who had backed up Edwards in the catching department. Bragan doubled, scored Furillo and for the second time in the struggle the Dodgers broke in front, now 6–5. Shotton, like Harris, was sending in the troops—no reason at this stage to hold back anybody. Dan Bankhead went to second to run for Bragan. Page was kicking dirt around the mound as though he would level it. Eddie Stanky singled sharply to right, and third-base coach Blades held Bankhead at third. Berra's throw got away from Aaron Robinson at the plate long enough for Stanky to scoot to second, but not long enough for Blades to send in Bankhead. Men at second and third and the Dodgers were teeing off on Page. Harris brought in Bobo Newsom, who'd been bombed in the third game.

Page walked away. After his great year he'd been roughed up as though the Dodgers had never heard who he was. Pitching is a hard way to earn a living. Relief pitching is doubly hard. The top relief pitcher is called on when things are tough. All Page could think as he headed for the shower was, "There'll be another day." To add to his anger, that other fellow, that other relief pitcher, Hugh Casey, had gotten 2 wins and hadn't been scored on. It was not exactly the right moment to ask Joe Page for an autograph.

Newsom fussed around on the mound getting ready. As he threw the allowed warm-up tosses, I remember I was talking about him—I had the broadcast of the second half of the game —all the clubs he'd been with, that this year he'd been a saving help to the Yankees, had won 2 that kept the 19-game string alive . . . and of the day in the 1940 World Series he learned his father had died, and he went to the ball park and, pitching for Detroit, beat Cincinnati, crying as he pitched.

Newsom had twice been a Dodger. Right now he was going to pay back, with interest, the two times the Dodgers let him go . . . he was going to return the favor for the Dodgers whacking him in Game Three at Ebbets Field.

Old Bobo was ready, a big man. Pee Wee Reese, a slight figure, was ready at the plate. You stay ready in a World Series. Newsom checked the runners at second and third, pumped, and pitched. Reese broke it open with a line single to left center, scoring Bankhead and Stanky, and putting the Dodgers ahead 8–5 in the sixth inning. Newsom got Jackie Robinson and Dixie Walker, walked off the mound, and as was his lifelong superstition, was careful to step across the foul line and not on it on his way to the dugout.

Shotton was rich with this 3-run lead. He didn't have to bring in Casey just yet. He sent in left-hander Joe Hatten. And he made another move—he put Al Gionfriddo in left field. Hermanski had started there, then Eddie Miksis had hit for Hermanski, and had gone to left for an inning. Miksis was an infielder and had had troubles in the outfield. Left field at Yankee Stadium was no place for an amateur, certainly not in a World Series game you had to win or else go back to the farm to start plowing behind the family mule.

Serendipity is not the precise word for Gionfriddo. Back on May 3, Branch Rickey sent pitcher Kirby Higbe to the Pittsburgh Pirates, along with three other players, for some $100,000 cash and a throw-in player named Al Gionfriddo. The Pirates then had ambitions of going places if they had another starting pitcher. The new owner of the Pirates also had ready money. Rickey had had a most expensive spring training, and never at any time was allergic to the green of our currency. Rickey in a trade, just before it was closed, always wanted a player to be thrown in. George Weiss of the Yankees always did the same. Both of them seemed to be able to cash in later with the player who sweetened the deal.

The Pirates had Hank Greenberg and they had Ralph Kiner. Big, booming base hits were all the Pirates dreamed about, thought about. A little fellow, 5'9", 160 pounds who sliced singles and didn't hit close to .300 wasn't what the big, bold Buccaneers wanted. It made no difference that the little man could run and could field. "Mr. Rickey, here's the check for a hundred grand, and as you go out put Gionfriddo in your coat pocket." Rickey had uses for the money, and manager Shotton all season had uses for Gionfriddo, especially with Pete Reiser losing one contest after another to outfield fences. Serendipity is finding something of value that you were not looking for—Rickey didn't know how much value he had in Gionfriddo, but he knew there was some value. Shotton discovered how much.

Lavagetto got the dramatic hit against Bevens in the fourth game at Brooklyn; yet, after that hair-raiser, manager Shotton told the writers that the key play was Gionfriddo's steal of second base.

His name was lost in the noise of the capacity crowd as four player changes were announced: Joe Hatten now pitching for the Dodgers, Harry Lavagetto now playing third base, Al Gionfriddo now playing left field, and for the Yankees, Allie Clark now batting for Bobo Newsom. There he was, a small man, almost lost against the vastness of left field. He wore his glove on his right hand.

Hatten was wobbly. He got Allie Clark on a line drive at Reese. Then he walked Stirnweiss. Henrich hit a shot that just missed being a home run—like Walker the inning before— just foul. Tommy then fouled to Edwards. Berra slapped a single to left, and Gionfriddo retrieved it. Two on, two out, and it was Joe and Joe—Hatten pitching, DiMaggio batting.

DiMaggio hit it, a rifle shot to left center. It was going into the bullpen, 415 feet away. It was going to be a home run and tie the game at 8–8. The great crowd was instantly jumping and roaring. The little man in left field was running as DiMaggio swung. He never looked back. He raced to the low fence in front of the bullpen, reached in with his right hand, and pulled back the ball. I'll never forget the sight of Gionfriddo turning to face the field, holding his dark glove for all to see the precious white spot in the center of it.

DiMaggio prided himself on showing no emotion in public. As he came trotting into second base, rejoicing over his home run, then seeing that he had nothing but an out, he kicked dirt viciously. When he got to his position in center field he walked around in short circles, still unbelieving.

The crack of DiMaggio's bat was the sound of doom for the Dodgers. Gionfriddo's remarkable catch—and it is rated as one of the all-time great ones in baseball history—turned that dismal destiny squarely around. Had the ball landed in the bullpen the game would have been leveled again, and I doubt the Dodgers could have digested that savage a stroke. Had it landed, the Yankees would have been stimulated into surging on for the final kill. Their man, DiMaggio, would have done it again. No, it wasn't serendipity, it was Gionfriddo.

There is an old prayer that includes the phrase, "Amid the changes and chances of this mortal life . . ." Mel Allen and I had the radio play-by-play assignment. Just before the Series began, Ed Wilhelm of Maxon, the agency for Gillette, flipped a coin to see which one of us would do the first half of the game. It would be strict alternation thereafter. I went first, which meant I did the second halves of the even-numbered games. I had the mike when Bevens made his run into history and Lavagetto joined him—that was Game Four. I was announcing when DiMaggio connected and Gionfriddo caught it.

The Lavagetto hit and the Gionfriddo catch have been re-broadcast over the years countless times. A flip of a coin and I had them both.

Anything after Gionfriddo's catch would have been more than the crowd could stand. Yet there was a kick left in the Yankee last half of the ninth inning. Everything until then was almost routine: Vic Raschi pitched the seventh, Charley Wensloff the eighth and ninth, but the Dodgers were docile. Hatten struggled through the seventh and eighth innings, holding the score at 8–5.

The Yankees came in with 3 outs left and 3 runs behind. Billy Johnson kindled their hopes with a single. George McQuinn got a base on balls, placing the tying run at the plate. The crowd was roaring again. No one was surprised to see the slender figure of coach Clyde Sukeforth walking slowly to the mound. The public address man could have saved his breath— there was no need to identify the large, heavy-bodied right-hander walking slowly across the outfield, Hugh Casey. He walked deliberately, with a sureness of purpose that said he was not coming to his execution, but to execute others, and with his own right hand. All season long Casey had steadied the ball club. He had saved games. He had stopped trouble. He had put out fires. Leo Durocher said immediately after the Dodgers clinched the 1941 pennant, "We couldn't have won it without Casey!" Shotton wasn't glib of speech, or he would have echoed those words of the man whose place this hectic year he had taken because of the Chandler suspension. The bat boy ran out to meet the big, apple-cheeked pitcher and took his jacket—it would be kept for Casey in the dugout. Sukeforth waited at the mound with the ball. He handed it to Casey, and left. There was nothing Sukeforth could tell Casey. You don't tell a supreme artist how to paint a canvas or sing an aria.

Casey had become a star in the Series. This was the fifth game he had been in, and the Yankees had been completely baffled. They had not scored on him. It was almost overlooked in the Bevens-Lavagetto explosion that Casey relieved in the top of the ninth inning, when the Yankees had three runners on, one out, Henrich at bat, and, that with one pitch Casey had settled it— Henrich bounced back to him, for a double-play.

Casey in a tight situation in a ball game was a cold-blooded butcher. His private life was something else—he had hot inner fires that finally led to self-destruction when he blew his brains out. Now he was at a peak few pitchers ever reach. He had defended completely in the Series everything his manager had entrusted to him.

Billy Johnson, who had started this last-ditch counterattack, was on second. George McQuinn, who had added in, was at first. Phil Rizzuto was at bat. Casey went to work, and got Rizzuto on a fly to Furillo in center. One out, but the tying run was still at the plate. Now it was Aaron Robinson, a dangerous man. Aaron singled to left, Gionfriddo recovered, and threw the ball in quickly. Third-base coach Charlie Dressen stopped Johnson at third, filling the bases. You don't risk an out by sending in a runner when you need three runs to tie. You play it safe, you wait. Now Casey had the tying run on, with the winning run at the plate, 8–5. One out. Lonnie Frey batted for Wensloff, the sixth Yankee pitcher. Frey and Casey were no strangers to each other—Frey had been in the National League many years before the Yankees picked him up. There was no movement by the crowd toward the exits. A base hit or two and the World Series would be over. Frey grounded a ball wide of first base—Jackie Robinson speared it and threw to Reese at second. This forced Aaron Robinson for out number two, but also it kept the tying run at first base, not at second. Now it was 8–6. The Yankees were reduced to their last out. George Stirnweiss was next. It didn't take long. Stirnweiss bounced right back to Casey, who threw to Jackie Robinson. The Series would have to be settled the next day. That's what Bucky Harris said afterward.

There was little else to be said in the Yankee clubhouse. Gionfriddo had caught the ball. Casey had stopped them again. The most that was said was by Larry MacPhail. Jimmy Dawson assigned to the New York clubhouse wrote in the *Times:*

"The explosion which sent the Yankees down to defeat and tossed the World Series into the seventh and rubber game, had its echoes in the Yankee clubhouse.

"President Larry MacPhail went into an explosion of his own when he discovered that Johnny Lindell . . . started yesterday's game with a fractured seventh rib on the right side."

Dawson's story about MacPhail's outburst and Lindell's defense went on for eleven more paragraphs, and ended with, "But for this verbal explosion the clubhouse was as quiet as a morgue."

It was a field day for the writers and photographers in the Dodger clubhouse. Gionfriddo was the center of it all. Roscoe

McGowen, covering for the *Times,* wrote that ". . . photographers got Pee Wee Reese to kiss Gionfriddo on the cheek. They kept getting Pee Wee to repeat this performance so often that he finally said, 'Let somebody else kiss this guy . . . I'm tired of it.'"

Game Seven

Monday afternoon, October 6, 1947, Yankee Stadium. The team that won this game would win it all.

There was another big crowd, 71,548 paid, 2,517 less than the day before. Some of the Sunday standees must have had to go to work. I don't know how many spectators arrived hoping for a continuation of baseball miracles, but for those who did, there was disappointment. The miracles had run out. It was a business-like ball game without such explosive moments as Lavagetto-Bevens and Gionfriddo-DiMaggio.

True, the two top bullpen men, Joe Page and Hugh Casey, were finally pitted head to head, but from the time they both appeared, the die was cast. Page took over after the Yankees had gotten on top, and he most efficiently kept them there. Page pitched the final five innings and faced but fifteen men—Miksis singled with one out in the ninth, but was doubled up as the curtain slammed down. Casey worked the last two innings and was finally scored on, a meaningless run, which would not have scored had a professional left fielder been in service.

A young man named Bobby Brown wanted this Series over. He needed to leave for Tulane University to resume his medical studies, and he pinch-hit a fourth inning double which drove in the tying run. Brown set a mark—3 for 3 as a pinch hitter—and he also got a walk. Tommy Henrich, top batter for the Yankees, immediately followed Brown's double with a single, and drove in the run that put the Yankees ahead. They were never headed. Page came out of the bullpen, silenced the Dodgers completely, and put a blanket of silence over the mammoth Stadium.

The Yankees won the game 5–2. Page got his revenge. The Yankees functioned like a well-oiled machine. The Dodgers, as

Arthur Daley wrote in the *Times*, ". . . from the first inning it was obvious Burt Shotton didn't have his Ouija board . . . his communication system with the spirit world broke down . . . Dodger luck ran down like an unwound clock." The Yankees won the World Series, something to which they had grown accustomed. This was their eleventh championship in twenty-five years. What happened after the game, and into the night, was cut out of new cloth. And has never been repeated.

The Dodgers all season—paced by Jackie Robinson—had been a running ball club. They had taken full advantage of their fleetness of foot. As Rickey often said, "there is no substitute for running speed." On a trip into St. Louis during the season, manager Eddie Dyer took catcher Joe Garagiola out and put Del Wilber back of the plate because Dyer said he was tired of the Dodgers running on Garagiola. In Game Seven manager Harris of the Yankees had Aaron Robinson catching, and Berra in right field. Berra, a rookie, and green behind the plate, had allowed the Dodgers to steal five bases, including Gionfriddo's in the Bevens game. Lindell was out with his broken rib, but had Lindell been healthy, I suspect Harris would have started Aaron Robinson anyhow—he had not had Yogi catch since the Bevens game.

As he did the day before against Reynolds, Stanky led it off with a single against Frank Shea. Harris had announced after the Sunday game that Bevens would start, but on second thought, Shea was his choice—he had had such a splendid rookie season, had won 2 games in the Series, and in winning Saturday had delivered a 2–1 beauty—and had fanned Lavagetto for the final out.

On the next pitch it became a different game than the day before. On Sunday, Reese followed Stanky's single with one of his own. Today, Stanky started from first on Shea's delivery. The hit-and-run was on—some writers reported that Stanky was out stealing . . . Stanky couldn't steal, slow-footed as he was, if his life and that of his entire family depended on it. Reese was an excellent man to play hit-and-run with—he'd get the sign the play was on and he'd hit the ball behind the runner, or at least get a piece of the ball, foul it off, and so protect the runner. Stanky going to second from first needed all the protection he could get. This time, however, the reliable, talented Reese got the sign all right, swung, but missed the pitch. Stanky was out so far the umpire's call wasn't needed. Aaron Robinson threw the ball to second baseman Stirnweiss with time to spare. Aaron was a professional catcher. Berra became one, but it takes time to learn that position.

Pee Wee, left on his own with no base runner, waggled a walk from Shea, and this brought up Jackie Robinson, who lined to Henrich in left field. Two out, and now came another clue as to the way the Fates were watching this encounter. In the *Iliad* and the *Odyssey* the gods and goddesses were always getting involved with the heroes—either for or against them, protecting them, helping them, or seeing to it they got dispatched from further earthly activity. I doubt too many of the ballplayers this afternoon at Yankee Stadium knew about the interferences from Olympus, but they knew when things seemed to be going their way or not.

Dixie Walker got hold of a Shea pitch, and hit it into the lower right-field stands. Foul! Just barely foul, and instead of 2 runs in the Brooklyn bank, the score remained zero, and Reese remained at first. Not too long. Pee Wee tried to steal—he was an excellent base runner and a constant threat to steal. Aaron Robinson was expecting the maneuver, and again had the ball at second waiting for the runner.

Branch Rickey knew about the *Iliad* and the *Odyssey*. He probably could have named all the characters. But I'm sure what he said to Jane as they sat quietly watching two of three batters get on base, both of them get thrown out at second, and only three men bat officially was, "I don't like what I see." If Rickey made any reference to Homer it was in sadness about how close Walker's drive came to being one.

Hal Gregg started pitching for the Dodgers, and retired the Yankees in order the last of the first inning.

The Dodgers didn't know, nobody could know, but in the top of the second inning the tide came in, then went out for them. With one away Hermanski hit a ball into the right-field corner that bounced away from Berra for a triple. Edwards singled and the Dodgers drew first blood, 1–0. Furillo whacked a single, and Harris knew this wasn't Shea's afternoon. Bevens took over.

Jorgensen hit a double that scored Edwards and put Furillo on third. This made it 2–0 and it seemed the Dodgers were ready to roll. Runners at second and third, one out. Gregg hit a roller to shortstop Rizzuto, Furillo tried to score, and Rizzuto threw him out easily. Did coach Blades send him, or did Furillo run on his own? What is definitely known is that when Furillo slid into Aaron Robinson's mitt, with the baseball inside it, that was the closest a Dodger would come to home plate the rest of the day. Edwards got a single off Bevens in the fourth, and Miksis singled against Page in the ninth. The rest of the game belonged to the Yankees.

Gregg said after the game he couldn't get the ball where he wanted it. In the last of the second he walked both McQuinn and Aaron Robinson. Rizzuto slashed a hit off third base itself, to cut the deficit in half. McQuinn scored and it was 2–1.

The Yankees took over in the last of the fourth. Billy Johnson walked, and with two out, the tide turned. Rizzuto singled, and Harris sent in Bobby Brown who hadn't failed as a pinch hitter. Brown didn't fail now. He doubled to left, scoring Johnson and tying the game. Shotton sent Sukeforth to bring back Gregg. Hank Behrman took over, and walked Stirnweiss to fill the bases. Tommy Henrich singled to score Rizzuto, and the Yankees went ahead to stay. Now it was 3–2. They finally won 5–2, but with Joe Page pitching the rest of the way, 3–2 was plenty good.

In the sixth inning the Yankees got their fourth run as Shotton used three pitchers. Rizzuto singled and stole second. Stirnweiss walked and Joe Hatten replaced Behrman. Allie Clark batted for Berra and singled, scoring Rizzuto. Rex Barney was sent in, and got DiMaggio. Now it was 4–2.

Hugh Casey took over in the seventh and pitched the last two times the Yankees batted. This was his sixth appearance in the 7 games. He had won 2 and had not been scored on. Casey's personal god, or goddess, must have gone to the ambrosia parlor or something. Anyhow, Eddie Miksis was now in left field. Miksis was by trade an infielder, but he batted right-handed. Joe Page was a left-handed pitcher. The Dodgers needed hits and runs. Shotton wasn't worrying about defense as he had been the day before when he took Miksis out of left field in favor of Gionfriddo. You play defense only when you are ahead.

Billy Johnson hit a high, long fly to left field. Miksis, playing in too much, got a hesitant start on the ball, and then couldn't catch it. It fell for a triple. Many of the writers pointed out that Gionfriddo would have caught the ball in his hip pocket. Aaron Robinson hit another fly to left. This one Miksis caught, and after the ball touched the pocket of his glove, Johnson tagged at third, and ran home for run five. This was the only run against Casey, otherwise he would have had an unblemished record of runless relief pitching. But it made no difference in the outcome of the game or the Series.

After four innings the Yankees were ahead 3–2. Harris had just had Bobby Brown hit for the pitcher, Bill Bevens. He had to bring in somebody from the bullpen. There were several throwing there under the watchful eye of the bullpen coach, John Schulte. Page had been roughed-up the day before, and charged with the loss of the game.

In the early days communication between the dugout and the bullpen was by hand signals and pantomime. The telephone ended that. Harris rang the phone and Schulte got on. Harris asked about Page. Schulte said, "He ain't got nothing." Harris said, "I don't care what he ain't got . . . send in Joe Page." Page had saved game after game all year, and made it pleasantly possible for Harris to often lift his glass and say, "Here's to Joe Page." Now Harris was going all the way with his man. In fact, Harris said that if he hadn't used Page the day before he might just have started him in the showdown seventh game. As the girl said, "I'm going home with the guy that brung me."

Page told the writers amid the joyous hubbub of the Yankee clubhouse, ". . . this makes up for everything, particularly that cuffing they gave me yesterday. They had their fun then. I had mine today. I had it and they didn't. I really poured it on. I threw one slider. That went to Walker. I threw one curve. Hodges hit that one foul into the stands. All the rest were fast balls."

As he said, he really poured it on. Once Page took command it was no contest. One, two, three—fifth inning, sixth inning, seventh inning, eighth inning, and then with one out in the ninth, after Page had retired thirteen straight men, Miksis singled. Edwards grounded to Rizzuto—over to Stirnweiss, on to McQuinn—double-play. Page had gotten fifteen outs from fifteen batters, and the World Champion Yankees raced for their clubhouse. The doors were open for the first time immediately after a game in the Series. Photographers poured in, writers swarmed in, well-known people pressed in.

It was a joyous celebration. It had been a hard Series. The Yankees had earned this moment, and they knew how to appreciate it, enjoy it, relish it, taste it, give the interviews, pose for the pictures, bear hug each other, drink the iced champagne, splash it, squirt it, waste it, jump, yell. A world championship is a precious achievement. Many a fine player never gets to know how it feels.

Bucky Harris stood in his Yankee clubhouse. His players were celebrating. Questions were coming from the writers. The answers were happy. Flashbulbs were popping. The noises of victory bounced back and forth off the concrete walls. He stood—he'd been out of the big leagues a long time, had turned down a desk job at Detroit, took on the managership under MacPhail after Joe McCarthy, Bill Dickey and Johnny Neun wanted no part of it. He hadn't had such a moment in twenty-three years during which his life and career seemed slipping down. He'd been the manager of a world championship team in 1924, when he was the second baseman and also the Boy Manager of the Washington Senators, who beat John McGraw and the Giants. That was an exciting 7-game Series too.

Bucky Harris stood, smiled, began answering questions, began turning in this direction or in that as the photographers yelled. This was his hour, far richer than the similar one twenty-three years ago. A great success tastes better when a man is fifty-one and beginning to think it may be getting late, perhaps too late. This was October of 1947—and it was also October in the life cycle of Bucky Harris. He stood, and let it wash over him.

It was my custom after a World Series ended to leave the booth, go the winning clubhouse, work my way to the manager, shake hands, say "Congratulations," and leave. As I left I'd say best wishes to whatever players I encountered. They were usually too intent on their horseplay and merriment to pay me or anyone else much mind. The managers noted the courtesy call, and remembered it, especially Casey Stengel. A strong reason I always made my exit as quickly as possible was that if I stayed around very long some player would turn a fizzing bottle of champagne on me and on my custom-made clothes. This would inspire another to do likewise. These were my expensive clothes and this wasn't my celebration.

Then I would walk to the loser's clubhouse, which would be drastically different. It would be quiet, no champagne, maybe here and there a tired man would be having a can of beer, which he would have to pay the clubhouse attendant for. The manager would be quite free, almost alone. He'd look up; surprised that I had bothered to come in. There are two worlds in baseball. You see them in stark contrast after a seventh game: the winning clubhouse, crowded, noisy, ribald, riotous—and the losing clubhouse, almost empty, sweat-smelling, with silent, downcast men, drained, moving slowly in and out of the shower. You can't know the hurt of losing an entire year's work in just one afternoon until you stand in the clubhouse of the 1947 Dodgers as I did.

I shook hands with Shotton. We just looked at each other. There was nothing to say. I shook hands with Pee Wee Reese, Jackie Robinson, Dixie Walker, Hugh Casey—I wished these men I'd been with all year a "good winter" . . . "see you next spring." What else? They'd come so close, fought so hard. They'd lost the World Series but they'd won their biggest assignment—they'd accepted Jackie Robinson. I heard many of them tell him what a fine man he was, as well as one hell of a ballplayer. I suspect Dixie Walker in that hour wished devoutly he hadn't written his letter to Rickey demanding to be traded. He was, next year, to Pittsburgh. Eddie Stanky, to his bitter surprise next spring, went to the Boston Braves.

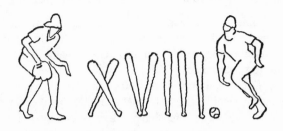

AFTERSHOCK

They were all inside the Stadium for the seventh game, Monday, October 6, 1947: Larry MacPhail, Branch Rickey, Commissioner Chandler, Leo Durocher, Burt Shotton, Jackie Robinson, Bucky Harris, Dan Topping, Del Webb, Charlie Dressen, George Weiss, Walter O'Malley, John Smith. These were the principals —all alive, alert, aggressive. Only Chandler—eighty-three—and Durocher—seventy-six—are alive today.

Mel Allen and I were in the broadcasting booth in the upper stands behind home plate. I had done the first half of the game, and Mel detailed the almost machine-like efficiency of Joe Page the last half. Jimmy Dawson was covering the Yankee dressing room, and its immediate area, for the New York *Times*. Roscoe McGowen had the same assignment for the Dodgers. Jimmy and Roscoe had done the postgame stories throughout the 7 games. Both gathered first-hand information I couldn't.

Leo and Laraine Durocher saw all the games. Their box seats were not too separated from those of Commissioner Chandler, but Leo and Happy, to my knowledge, never spoke to each other, or had any contact with each other. When the Series ended the Durochers left as quietly as possible and went downtown to Leo's apartment—the same one that had figured in the George Raft dice-game rhubarb.

O'Malley and Smith, each one-fourth owners of the Dodgers, left the Stadium without hanging around. Smith would soon die, and O'Malley, as the lawyer for Mrs. Smith, used the leverage of 50 percent control to oust Rickey three years later, and take over the ball club.

Jackie Robinson had a busy future ahead of him. It was announced earlier in the day he would star in a motion picture. He had a barnstorming tour to make. There were banquets and other public appearances waiting.

Charlie Dressen, Larry MacPhail's man from 1934 at Cincinnati, started to enjoy the celebration in the Yankee clubhouse, but in a few minutes, his sharp mind attuned to the sudden events around him, he began wondering about his future.

The Dodgers walked into their clubhouse, and manager Shotton ordered the door shut to everyone—everyone but the one person who could override that command, Branch Rickey. Rickey left his wife in her seat and said to wait for him. He had not had to say again, "Jane, I don't have a World Series pitching staff." It had been plain to see. Not a starting pitcher for the Dodgers got past the fifth inning.

During the Series Rickey had sat in his box almost unnoticed. He was not a man who yelled, jumped, moved around and did the things that attract public notice. He went to the clubhouse after the first game, said a few encouraging words to Shotton, and left without interviews or pictures. Now that the Series was over he went to the clubhouse for the second time. He went in, and came out fifteen minutes later. Shotton told McGowen that Rickey had called the team together, and with no media around, in the privacy of the clubhouse, had told them what a fine season they had had, what a triumph it was to win the pennant, how wonderfully well they had played the Yankees, how far they had gone with a young pitching staff that was developing, and what a bright future the team had in the years to come . . . to go to their homes as proud men.

Once Rickey departed, the clubhouse was open to the press. Commissioner Chandler arrived—he had already congratulated Bucky Harris—and when asked would he pose with Jackie Robinson and Dan Bankhead, the two black players, said, "Of course." Chandler and MacPhail had posed at length before the first game of the Series, picture after picture, arms around each other. This World Series was the Commissioner's Series—he had complete charge of it.

This was the third World Series conducted by Chandler. No question—it had been exciting, dramatic, the first to be on television, the first to go over the $2,000,000 mark in total revenue and to be heard all over the world on radio. It was the first World Series to have a black player. Chandler had been blessed with good weather for the Series and with record crowds. I doubt that on this afternoon he understood he couldn't win as Commissioner of Baseball. He thought he was supposed to follow the pattern of Judge Landis, and be a strong Commissioner for the best interests of baseball, the players, the umpires, the public and then the owners. He had it backward. The owners had had enough of the iron rule of Landis. They were determined to get their business back in their own hands, and, keep it that way. They did.

Every time Chandler ruled against an owner, that owner marked it well and waited. Del Webb was the architect of the revolt that dumped Chandler late in 1950. Webb boasted of unseating Chandler. Chandler, in addition to other differences with Webb and Topping (both of them nurtured by MacPhail's anger), had investigated Webb after he built a hotel gambling resort—the Flamingo—in Las Vegas. Chandler wanted to be certain Webb had no connection with the gambling that went on once the hotel was opened. Webb was furious and swore to get even. He did. One of the owners who supported Webb in unseating Chandler was Fred Saigh, of the Cardinals, who soon thereafter went to the federal penitentiary for income tax evasion.

Chandler would preside over only three more World Series. The owners were taking back baseball. There has not been a strong Commissioner since.

There is another world under the stands of Yankee Stadium. The public doesn't see it or know it exists. The clubhouses are there, offices are there, storage spaces are there and the pressroom is there. This room is reserved for the writers, photographers, broadcasters, club officials—the working press. There are tables, chairs, toilet facilities and a well-stocked bar . . . free food and drink. Leave a tip, if you wish, but otherwise it is on the house. The bartenders don't get rich on the tips.

As a rule the pressroom is empty in the ninth inning of a game. The writers are upstairs in the press box, the photographers are at their stations, and the broadcasters are in their booths. Today, however, it was a crowded place. This was the deciding game of the Series. There were hundreds of extra writers from all over the country. Writers Dawson and McGowen kept a constant watch down below in the catacombs of the Stadium. There was a radio in the pressroom, behind the bar. To add to the drawing power in that room at this time, Mac-Phail was there. He had been all over the Stadium, and Ebbets Field, throughout the Series. He had made headlines. He was always unpredictable, always talking, always a story. This was his Yankee ball club. And his Yankees were on the verge of winning the Series.

The Dodgers came to bat in the ninth inning, behind 5–2. Joe Page had not allowed a runner in the four innings he had pitched. He was in superb form. But the Dodgers had bounced back so often, with such resiliency, that nobody took them for granted, not as long as they had one out left, and now they had three remaining. Everybody wanted to hear what Mel Allen was saying—everybody but MacPhail. MacPhail was drinking a beer from the bottle, and he was talking, almost drowned out by the radio and the other noises. Dawson heard him say, "If they win it, I'm through." Dawson paid it no mind. It sank in later.

Bruce Edwards banged into the game-ending double-play.

"That's it!" MacPhail screamed, "That does it. That's my retirement!"

"Larry MacPhail," Dawson reported in the *Times*, "was shouting at the top of his lungs in an emotional outburst, tears streaming down his face, as the curtain descended on the 1947 World Series yesterday.

"He was announcing his retirement as president of the Yankees, the club he took over three years ago from the estate of Jacob Ruppert with Del Webb and Dan Topping as co-owners."

The writers who had planned to rush into the winning clubhouse were stunned. MacPhail held them. He was more of a story right then than the Yankees themselves. They crowded around him as he said he was through, couldn't stand any more such pressure, that his health couldn't stand it, didn't know who'd run the club—maybe Topping, and said, "I've got what I wanted . . . I'm through."

He stood and talked, waving the half-finished bottle of beer, crying, and mopping his tears with a handkerchief. He started to go to the Yankee clubhouse and bumped into George Weiss, the quiet man MacPhail had made even quieter and less noticeable the past three years.

"Here you," MacPhail shouted to the writers, throwing his arm around Weiss's shoulder, "I want you to say this in your story. I built the losing team out there, but he's the guy who built the winners."

Dan Topping and Del Webb, co-owners and partners with MacPhail, came in after the sudden announcement, and both professed they knew nothing about it in advance. Topping, however, said that MacPhail was an emotional type, and not to believe it until tomorrow, when he had had a chance to think it over.

I got down from the broadcast booth as MacPhail broke up Bucky Harris's biggest moment in baseball. I saw MacPhail take the show away from Harris and the players. He repeated in the clubhouse that he was quitting, and he called the Yankees into a group and thanked them for being such a fine ball club. He praised them as a team, and said the victory was a team effort. It was an extraordinarily emotional performance—a one-man show amid an all-star cast of many players.

I left as MacPhail stopped the celebration for his farewell address. I went to the other dressing room, then went home. Branch and Jane Rickey went home but not before a chance encounter with MacPhail.

Arthur Mann sat with the Rickeys in their box. He remained with Mrs. Rickey when Branch went to the clubhouse to thank Shotton and the Dodgers for their efforts and achievements. Arthur was a party to the final meeting between the two men.

Rickey left the Brooklyn clubhouse, MacPhail the New York one. By chance they came together. There were still people in the stands, people who waited rather than get jammed in the rush, people who sat for a while and watched the ground crew

smoothing out an infield that wouldn't be used again for baseball until next spring.

Here is what Mann, the sole witness, aside from Mrs. Rickey,
wrote in his book:

". . . even more unforgettable was the meeting of Branch
Rickey and Larry MacPhail . . . in the emptying stadium . . .
Walking alone and taking galling defeat as hard as ever, Rickey
encountered the jubilant redhead. MacPhail draped his arm over
Rickey's tired shoulder, grabbed his hand and began murmuring
felicitations.

"It was too much—not just the baseball defeat—but the over-
powering recollection of bitter words and lies and year-long chi-
canery. Rickey interrupted the congratulatory mouthings and
abruptly terminated a somewhat fantastic relationship that had
survived nearly seventeen turbulent years.

"'I am taking your hand,' he said, 'only because people are
watching us.'

"Rickey then gave full expression to his bitter disappointment
in MacPhail the man. He detailed his deep feeling of remorse
and shame, and closed with the stern warning, 'Don't you ever
speak to me again.'"

To my personal knowledge that was that. The break was final,
they never spoke to each other after that. I never heard Rickey
mention MacPhail again—it was as though he hadn't existed.
Rickey had other things on his mind. MacPhail fed on anger.
Nearly twenty years later both MacPhail and I moved to Key
Biscayne in Miami. We saw each other frequently and I soon
learned not to mention Rickey. However, MacPhail would bring
up Rickey and belittle him. He got to saying that Landis said to
him, "The only thing I regret is that I didn't run Rickey out of
baseball." When MacPhail would start downgrading Rickey,
Lylah would touch me and whisper, "Be careful, Red . . . he's
an old man . . . and a good friend of yours."

For a while Larry and I were quite close. We played a few
rounds of golf together. When I returned from South Vietnam,
after a USO tour in early 1967, I brought him something for his
seventy-seventh birthday—February 3—which seemed to please

him. I got involved in raising money to build a small Episcopal Church—St. Christopher's by-the-Sea. We needed publicity. I asked MacPhail if he would preach a sermon on Sunday morning. He did, and did it well. That was news, with a picture of MacPhail in the pulpit. Then I asked if he would throw a cocktail party for the opening of our fund raising. He said he would. He did—a beautiful, expensive party, and during the party he got several fat cats, twisted their arms until they wrote hefty checks, and we were on our way. He was a powerful help in getting St. Christopher's off the drafting table and into reality.

It is the custom—an obligation—for the winning team to throw a victory party after the last game. The Yankees threw one at the Biltmore Hotel. Lavish. Everything first class and plenty of it. All sorts of people got in. John McDonald was there. John had worked for MacPhail at Cincinnati, then when MacPhail took over at Brooklyn, John was brought East. John's health went bad. Shortly after he retired from the Dodgers, he did an article for the *Saturday Evening Post* on MacPhail. It was ghost-written, of course, and MacPhail didn't like the article. He resented it. He felt McDonald had betrayed him, and he sent McDonald a telegram calling him a Judas, and accusing him of selling out for thirty pieces of silver.

MacPhail came to his party roaring. He encountered McDonald at the bar, and after berating him again for being a Judas, he hit John in the eye, a genuine shiner, a fat, black one.

Next, MacPhail pounced upon George Weiss, and in the presence of George's wife and other women, MacPhail after giving Weiss a livid lecture fired him. Weiss withdrew in tears.

MacPhail then got into a heated argument with Dan Topping, and they went into a nearby room to settle matters. Some say blows were exchanged, others say they just yelled at each other. Both came back to the shocked party, and soon MacPhail left. Shortly after he was gone Del Webb came in—he'd been upstairs on other business, and had missed MacPhail.

According to Webb, in an article in *Sports Illustrated*, when he came to the party and Topping told him what had happened, he and Dan rehired Weiss, then got their lawyers, worked into

the small hours, and gave MacPhail until six o'clock that afternoon to sign the papers—for $2,000,000. MacPhail signed them,
and went out of baseball.

There were three major questions to be answered after the
Series: (1) In the New York *Times* both John Drebinger and
Arthur Daley wondered "had Commissioner Chandler, when he
called MacPhail on the carpet, given him the rest of the
season . . . and no more?" (2) How would Chandler settle
the status of Leo Durocher? (3) And what about Burt Shotton?

Durocher? This was now a big story for the writers, and they
could get nothing from Rickey. Rickey kept saying he couldn't
make a move until he knew the exact position of Chandler. Did
Durocher's suspension end when the World Series did? Chandler
had no immediate public comment. Leo was in California.

Rickey went to work rebuilding the Dodgers the very day
after the Series ended. He kept Shotton and the coaches in town,
and they went over player personnel. He sent out word to the
writers he had nothing to say about Durocher.

Rickey had two managers. He had paid Durocher in full for
the season. Shotton had come to his rescue, had won the pennant, and carried the Yankees to Game Seven. Shotton had settled a badly torn ball club. He had handled the Jackie Robinson
situation. Maybe Shotton was a better manager for the 1947
Dodgers with Robinson than Durocher would have been—
maybe Leo with his tongue, his abrasiveness and his quick
temper might have stirred up additional trouble and reaction.
Who knows? We know Shotton handled it. Now what was
Rickey to do with his longtime friend who had bailed him out?

Rickey went to see Chandler in late November. The meeting
was at Versailles, Kentucky, at Chandler's home. The two men
thrashed it out. Rickey was adamant that Chandler say what
was the status of Durocher. Finally, with much heat, the Commissioner said that Rickey could do what he damn well pleased,
and that he—Chandler—didn't care.

A press conference was called for 215 Montague Street, Brooklyn, the morning of December 5. Chandler had been notified
what was coming. Rickey was out of town at the baseball winter

meetings. Branch, Jr., presided, and at his side stood Burt Shotton. The press announcement was:

> The 1947 contract of Leo Durocher has been renewed for 1948 by the Brooklyn Baseball Club.
> Branch Rickey.

Shotton told the writers, "I'm giving Durocher his job back." Shotton then thanked the writers for their treatment of him, hoped they'd give the same to Leo, and wished Leo and the Dodgers good luck.

Thanks to Shotton, the year ended quietly. There would be trouble enough, problems enough the next year. The Dodgers under Durocher would falter . . . Rickey would convince Horace Stoneham that Leo should replace Mel Ott as manager of the Giants . . . and then Shotton returned to the Dodgers, to remain until Walter O'Malley got the ball club, forced Rickey out, and immediately dismissed Rickey's old friend and manager.

Rickey and MacPhail both died quietly. Rickey was giving a speech at the University of Missouri, and fell. He remained unconscious in a hospital for weeks. He was eighty-four. MacPhail was eighty-five when he died in a nursing home in Miami. Lylah said it was not right . . . that both should have died in the heat of battle.

Other DACAPO titles of interest

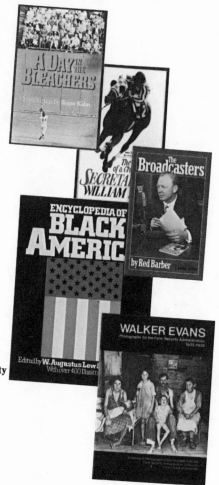